D0723937

PORTUGUESE
LEARNER'S DICTIONARY

PORTUGUESE-ENGLISH / ENGLISH-PORTUGUESE
Revised and updated

LIVING LANGUAGE®

PORTUGUESE
LEARNER'S
DICTIONARY

PORTUGUESE-ENGLISH / ENGLISH-PORTUGUESE
Revised and updated

Revised by Jura D. Oliveira, PH.D.

Senior Lecturer in Portuguese

Cornell University

Based on the original by Oscar Fernández

This work was previously published under the title *Living Language™ Common Usage Dictionary—Portuguese* by Oscar Fernández, based on the dictionary developed by Ralph Weiman.

Copyright © 1965, 1986, 1993 by Living Language, A Random House Company

All rights reserved.

Published by Living Language®, A Random House Company, New York, New York.

Living Language is a member of the Random House Information Group

www.livinglanguage.com

Living Language and colophon are registered trademarks of Random House, Inc.

If you are traveling, we recommend **Fodor's guides**

This book is available for special discounts for bulk purchases for sales promotions or premiums. Special editions, including personalized covers, excerpts of existing books, and corporate imprints, can be created in large quantities for special needs. For more information, write to Special Markets/ Premium Sales, 1745 Broadway, MD 6-2, New York, NY, 10019 or e-mail specialmarkets@randomhouse.com.

Printed in the United States of America

ISBN 978-1-4000-2449-0

10

CONTENTS

CONTENTS

INTRODUCTION

The *Living Language® Portuguese Dictionary* lists more than 18,000 of the most frequently used Portuguese words, gives their most important meanings, and illustrates their uses. This revised edition contains updated phrases and expressions as well as many new entries related to business, technology, and the media.

1. More than 1,000 of the most essential words are capitalized to make them easy to find.

2. Numerous meanings are illustrated with everyday phrases, sentences, and idiomatic expressions. If there is no close English equivalent for a Portuguese word, or if the English equivalent has several meanings, the context of the illustrative sentences helps to clarify the meanings.

3. Because of these useful phrases, the *Living Language® Portuguese Dictionary* also serves as a phrase book and conversation guide. The dictionary is helpful both to beginners who are building their vocabulary and to advanced students who want to perfect their command of colloquial Portuguese.

4. The Portuguese expressions (particularly the idiomatic and colloquial ones) have been translated into their English equivalents. However, literal translations have

been added to help the beginner. For example, under the entry "**ABRAÇO** embrace, hug," you will find: *Rebeca um abraço do seu amigo.* Cordially yours, ("Receive a hug from your friend"). This dual feature also makes the dictionary useful for translation work.

EXPLANATORY NOTES

1. Although the Portuguese spoken in Portugal and Brazil is the same language, there are certain differences, just as there are between British and American English. In this dictionary, the Brazilian Portuguese version of a word is given first. The Continental Portuguese variation follows in parentheses:

DIRETOR (DIRECTOR) *m. director.*

The spelling and accents in this dictionary have been revised in order to conform to the new orthography determined by the Brazilian Law of December 18, 1971 (Law number 5765), which reflects the Orthographic Agreement established between Brazil and Portugal on December 29, 1943.

2. If more than one form is commonly used, both are given:

toicinho

toucinho *m. bacon.*

3. Ⓑ will be used to indicate a term or meaning particular to Brazilian Portuguese, and Ⓟ for words particular to Continental Portuguese:

Suéter *m. sweater* Ⓑ.

garage Ⓑ, **garagem** *f. garage.*

ALMOÇO *m. lunch.*

Primeiro almoço. *Breakfast* Ⓟ.

Pequeno almoço. *Breakfast* Ⓟ.

4. The pronunciation of *x* between vowels is indicated: **abacaxi** *(x = sh);* **exame** *(x = z);* **próximo** *(x = s);* **táxi** *(x = ks).*

5. A few literal translations are given in quotation marks: **o Rio de Janeiro** ("the river of January").

6. Usually only the masculine singular form of an adjective is given.

7. The dictionary uses the following abbreviations:

adj.	adjective
adv.	adverb
conj.	conjunction
f.	feminine
fam.	familiar
fig.	figurative
ind.	indefinite
m.	masculine
n.	noun
pro.	pronoun
prep.	preposition

Portuguese-English

A

A *to, in, at, by, for, the, her, it, on, with.*
   Vou à cidade. *I'm going to the city.*
   A tempo. *In time.*
   A que horas? *At what time?*
   Um a um. *One by one.*
   A janela está aberta. *The window is open.*
   Não a vimos. *We did not see her.*
   Ele a comprou ontem. *He bought it (fem.)*
   yesterday.
   Vamos a pé. *We're going on foot.*
abacate *m. avocado.*
abacaxi *(x = sh)* **(ananás)** *m. pineapple;*
   difficult situation, mess Ⓑ.
abafado *adj. stuffy, close, sultry, hidden,*
   oppressed; annoyed, very busy,
   swamped Ⓑ.
abaixar *(x = sh) to lower, to bring down, to*
   humiliate.
abaixar-se *(x = sh) to stoop down, to humble*
   oneself.
ABAIXO *(x = sh) below, under.*
   Abaixo e acima. *Up and down.*
abalado *shaken, loose; moved, touched (fig.).*
abanar *to fan, to shake.*
   Ele abanou a cabeça. *He shook his head.*
abandonado *adj. abandoned, forsaken;*
   friendless.
abandonar *to abandon, to give up, to leave.*
   Ele abandonou a família. *He abandoned*
   his family.
abandono *m. abandonment, desertion;*
   neglect, destitution.
abanico *m. a small hand-held fan.*
abarcar *to comprise, to enclose, to contain, to*
   grasp.
   Quem muito abarca, pouco aperta. *Those*
   who try to have it all end up with only
   a little.
abastado *adj. wealthy, rich, well-off.*
abastar *to supply, to provide.*
abastecer *to provide, to supply.*
abastecimento *m. supplies, provisions.*
abatido *adj. depressed, discouraged.*
abatimento *m. decrease, reduction, discount;*
   low spirits, depression.
abdicar *to abdicate, to renounce, to resign.*
abdome, abdômen (abdómen) *m. abdomen.*
abecedário *m. the alphabet; primer.*
abelha *f. bee.*
abençoado *adj. blessed; happy.*
abençoar *to bless; to make happy.*
abertamente *openly, frankly, plainly.*
ABERTO *adj. open, opened; frank.*
   A loja está aberta? *Is the store open?*
   João não tinha aberto as janelas. *John had*
   not opened the windows.

abertura *f. opening.*
abismo *m. abyss, chasm.*
abjurar *to renounce, to repudiate.*
abolição *f. abolition.*
abolir *to abolish, to revoke, to cancel.*
abominável *adj. abominable.*
abonado *adj. trustworthy, creditable; wealthy,*
   well-off Ⓑ.
abonar *to guarantee, to vouch for; to advance*
   (money) to.
abono *m. loan; warranty, surety.*
abordar *to go aboard, to board; to accost, to*
   broach.
   Ela não quis abordar o assunto. *She did not*
   wish to broach the subject.
aborrecer *to hate, to detest; to annoy, to*
   bother.
   Tudo isto nos aborrece. *All this annoys us.*
aborrecido *adj. annoyed, bored; tiresome.*
aborrecimento *m. annoyance, nuisance, bore.*
aborto *m. abortion.*
abotoar *to button; to bud.*
abraçar *to embrace, to hug; to encompass.*
   Os dois amigos se abraçaram. *The two*
   friends embraced each other.
ABRAÇO *m. embrace, hug.*
   Receba um abraço do seu amigo. *Receive a*
   hug from your friend (in a letter, a
   complimentary close, "Cordially
   yours," or equivalent.)
abreviar *to shorten, to abbreviate, to*
   summarize.
abreviatura *f. abbreviation.*
abricó, abricote, albricote *m. apricot.*
abridor *m. opener.*
abrigar *to shelter, to protect.*
ABRIGO *m. shelter, protection, sanctuary.*
ABRIL *m. April.*
ABRIR *to open; to unlock; to begin; to*
   turn on.
   Faça o favor de abrir a porta. *Please open*
   the door.
   Não abra a torneira. *Don't turn on the*
   faucet.
abrupto *adj. abrupt, sudden.*
abscesso *m. abscess.*
absoluto *adj. absolute, complete,*
   independent.
absolver *to absolve, to acquit, to pardon.*
absolvido *adj. absolved, acquitted,*
   pardoned.
absorto *adj. absorbed, enraptured.*
abster *to abstain, to refrain, to repress.*
abstinência *f. abstinence; fasting.*
absurdo *adj. absurd, foolish; n. m. absurdity,*
   nonsense.
abundância *f. abundance, plenty.*
abundante *adj. abundant, plentiful.*
abundar *to abound.*

abusar *to abuse, to take advantage of.*
O oficial abusou de sua autoridade. *The officer abused his authority.*

abuso *m. abuse, misuse.*

abutre *m. vulture.*

ACABADO *adj. finished, complete; exhausted.*

ACABAR *to finish, to complete, to end, to have just (with de).*
Você já acabou o trabalho? *Did you already finish the work?*
Acabamos de jantar. *We have just had dinner.*

acabrunhar *to oppress, to distress, to afflict.*

academia *f. academy, school; learned society.*

acalmar *to calm, to appease, to soothe.*
Eu vou acalmá-lo. *I'm going to calm him down.*

acampar *to camp, to pitch camp.*

acanhado *adj. shy, bashful, timid; miserly; close, narrow.*

AÇÃO (ACÇÃO) *f. action, act, deed; share of stock.*
Houve muito falar e pouca ação. *There was much talk and little action.*

acariciar *to caress, to pet, to cherish.*

ACASO *adj. by chance, perhaps, possibly; n. m. chance, accident.*
Por acaso. *By chance.*
Escolhemos ao acaso. *We picked at random.*
Foram os acasos da fortuna. *They were the hazards of fortune.*

aceder *to accede, to assent, to agree.*

ACEITAÇÃO *f. acceptance.*

ACEITAR *to accept, to take.*
Aceitam cheque de viagem? *Will you accept a traveler's check?*

ACEITÁVEL *adj. acceptable.*

ACEITE *m. acceptance; adj. accepted.*

ACEITO *adj. accepted.*

acelerador *adj. accelerating; m. accelerator.*

acelerar *to accelerate, to speed up.*

ACENDER *to light (up), to ignite, to turn on (a light); to animate.*
Deixe-me acender um fósforo. *Let me light a match.*

ACENTO *m. accent, accent mark.*
Escreva o acento circunflexo, e não o agudo. *Write a circumflex accent, not an acute one.*

acentuar *to accent, to stress.*

acepção *f. meaning, sense.*

acerca de *about, concerning.*
Escrevemos-lhe acerca de nossa viagem. *We wrote him about our trip.*

acercar *to approach, to enclose.*

acertado *adj. proper, right.*

ACERTAR *to hit the mark, to be right, to accomplish, to set right.*
Acertámos no alvo. *We hit the mark.*
Tenho que acertar o relógio. *I have to set my watch.*

acerto *m. hit; discretion.*
Com acerto. *Properly.*

acessório *adj. accessory, additional; n. m. accessory.*

ACHAR *to find, to discover; to think, to believe.*
Não achei o livro. *I did not find the book.*
Acho que ele não vem. *I don't think he's coming.*
Acho que sim. *I think so.*

acidental *adj. accidental, incidental.*

ACIDENTE *m. accident.*
Foi um acidente. *It was an accident.*

ácido *adj. acid, sour; n. m. acid.*

ACIMA *above, up.*
Eles foram pela rua acima. *They went up the street.*
Acima de tudo. *Above all.*

acionista (accionista) *m. and f. stockholder, shareholder.*

aclamar *to acclaim, to proclaim, to applaud.*

aclarar *to explain, to make clear, to clear up; to illuminate.*

aclimar *to acclimate.*

aço *m. steel.*

acolá *there, to that place.*
Cá e acolá. *Here and there.*

ACOLHER *to receive, to welcome; to heed.*

ACOLHIDA *f. welcome, reception.*
Todos tiveram boa acolhida. *They all received a good welcome.*

acomodar *to accommodate.*

ACOMPANHAR *to accompany, to escort, to attend.*
Queremos que ele nos acompanhe. *We want him to accompany us.*

ACONSELHAR *to advise, to recommend.*
Eles me aconselham a estudar mais. *They advise me to study more.*

ACONTECER *to happen, to take place.*
Não aconteceu nada. *Nothing happened.*

ACONTECIMENTO *m. event, happening.*

ACORDAR *to awake; to come to an agreement.*
Ele ainda não acordou. *He hasn't woken up yet.*

acordeão *m. accordion.*

ACORDO *m. agreement, accord.*
Chegamos a um acordo com eles. *We came to an agreement with them.*

ACOSTUMADO *adj. accustomed, used to; usual.*
Estamos acostumados a deitar-nos tarde. *We are used to going to bed late.*

ACOSTUMAR *to accustom, to be in the habit of.*

AÇOUGUE *butcher shop, meat market.*

AÇOUGUEIRO *m. butcher.*

acre *adj. sour, bitter; n. m. acre.*

ACREDITAR *to believe; to believe in.*
Não acredito nisso. *I don't believe in that.*
Você acredita? *Do you believe it?*

AÇÚCAR *m. sugar.*

açucena *f. Easter lily.*

açude *m. dam, reservoir.*

acudir *to assist, to help, to run to help.*

acumulador *m. storage battery, accumulator.*

acumular *to accumulate, to collect.*

acusação *f. accusation, charge, indictment.*

acusado *adj. accused, charged.*

acusar *to accuse, to charge; to acknowledge.*
Acusamos o recebimento de sua carta. *We acknowledge the receipt of your letter.*

adaptação *f. adaptation.*

adaptar *to adapt, to adjust.*

adequado *adj. adequate, proper.*

aderente *adj. adherent, attached.*

aderir *to adhere; to unite, to join.*

adestramento *m. training.*

adestrar *to train, to instruct.*

ADEUS *good-bye, farewell.*

adiantado *adj. advanced, ahead.*

ADIANTAR(-SE) *to advance, to get ahead; to be fast (clock).*
Meu relógio (se) adianta. *My watch is fast.*
Não adianta. *It doesn't do any good.*

ADIANTE *ahead, forward.*
Adiante! *Go on!*

adiar *to postpone, to defer.*

adição *f. addition, sum; bill, check (restaurant).*

adicional *adj. additional.*

adido *m. attaché.*

adivinha *f. puzzle, riddle; female fortune-teller.*

adivinhar *to guess, to find out; to predict.*
Acho que você nunca adivinha. *I think you'll never guess.*

adivinho *m. male fortune-teller.*

adjetivo (adjectivo) *m. adjective.*

adjunto *adj. joined; n. m. adjunct, assistant, deputy.*

administração *f. administration.*

administrador *m. administrator, manager.*

administrar *to administer, to manage.*

admiração *f. admiration, wonder, surprise.*

admirador *m. admirer.*

admirar *to admire; to be surprised.*
Não é de admirar. *It's not surprising.*

admirável *adj. admirable, wonderful.*

ADMISSÃO *f. admission, entrance.*
Exame de admissão. *Entrance examination.*

ADMITIR *to admit, to accept, to grant.*

adoção *f. adoption.*

adoecer *to become ill.*

adolescência *f. adolescence.*

adoração *f. adoration, worship.*

adorar *to adore, to worship, to like very much.*

adorável *adj. adorable.*

ADORMECER *to put to sleep; to fall asleep.*

adornar *to adorn, to dress, to ornament.*

adotar (adoptar) *to adopt.*

adquirir *to acquire, to get.*

aduaneiro *adj. customs, of customs (in an airport, etc.); n. m. customhouse officer.*

adulador *m. flatterer.*

adular *to flatter.*

adultério *m. adultery.*

adulto *adj. adult; n. m. adult.*

advérbio *m. adverb.*

adversário *adj. adverse; n. m. opponent, adversary.*

adversidade *f. adversity.*

advertência *f. warning, notice.*
Você recebeu a advertência? *Did you receive the warning?*

advertir *to warn, to advise.*

advogado *m. lawyer, attorney.*

aéreo *adj. aerial, air.*
Por via aérea. *By airmail.*

aeródromo *m. aerodrome, airport.*

aeronáutica *f. aeronautics.*

aeroplano *m. airplane.*

aeroporto *m. airport.*

afã *m. enthusiasm; effort; eagerness.*

afanar *to work hard; to steal* ®*.*

afastado *adj. apart, distant.*

afastar *to separate, to remove.*

afeição *f. affection, fondness.*

afetar (afectar) *to affect, to pretend.*

afeto (afecto) *adj. affectionate, friendly; n. m. affection, friendship.*

afetuoso (afectuoso) *adj. affectionate, kind.*

afiar *to sharpen; to make pointed.*

aficionado *adj. fond, enthusiastic; n. m. fan (sports), follower.*

afilhado *m. godchild, protégé.*

afiliado *adj. affiliated.*

afiliar *to affiliate.*

afinal *finally, at last.*
Afinal de contas. *After all.*

afirmação *f. affirmation.*

afirmar *to affirm, to state.*

afirmativamente *affirmatively.*

afixar *(x = ks) to fix, to fasten, to post (posters, etc.).*

aflição *f. affliction, distress, grief, agony.*

afligir-se *to grieve, to worry.*
Não se aflija. *Don't worry.*

aflito *adj. grieved, worried, distressed.*

afogar (-se) *to drown, to suffocate, to stifle.*
Ele se afoga em pouca água. *It doesn't take much to bother him.*

aforismo *m. maxim, aphorism.*

AFORTUNADAMENTE *fortunately, luckily.*

AFORTUNADO *adj. fortunate, lucky, happy.*

afrontar *to affront, to insult; to strike, to meet.*

afundamento *m. sinking.*

afundar *to sink.*

agarrar *to grasp, to hold, to seize.*

agasalhar *to receive, to welcome, to shelter.*

agência *f. agency, bureau, office.*

agenda *f. agenda, memorandum, diary notebook.*

agente *adj. acting; n. m. agent.*

ágil *adj. agile, quick.*

agir *to act, to do.*

agitação *f. agitation, commotion, trouble.*

agitar *to agitate, to disturb, to shake.*

agonia *f. agony, great grief, suffering.*

AGORA *now, at the present time.*
Vamos agora. *We are going now.*
Agora mesmo. *Right now.*
Agora não. *Not now.*

AGOSTO *m. August.*

AGRADAR *to please, to like.*
Isso não me agrada. *I don't like that.*

AGRADÁVEL *adj. pleasant, agreeable, nice.*
Ela é muito agradável. *She is very nice.*

AGRADECER *to be grateful (for), to thank.*
Agradeço muito a sua bondade. *I thank you for your kindness.*

AGRADECIDO *adj. grateful, thankful.*
Fico-lhe muito agradecido. *I am very grateful to you.*

agradecimento *m. gratitude, thanks.*

agrado *m. pleasure, liking, satisfaction.*

agravar *to aggravate, to make worse.*

agregar *to bring together, to accumulate.*

agressão *f. aggression, offense.*

agressivo *adj. aggressive.*

agressor *m. aggressor.*

agrícola *adj. agricultural.*

agricultor *m. farmer.*

agricultura *f. agriculture, farming.*

agrupamento *m. grouping, group.*

agrupar *to group, to gather.*

ÁGUA *f. water.*
Água corrente. *Running water.*
Água doce. *Fresh water.*
Água mineral. *Mineral water.*
Água potável. *Drinking water.*
Água gelada. *Ice water.*

aguaceiro *m. shower (rain).*

água-marinha *f. (pl. águas-marinhas) aquamarine.*

aguardar *to wait for, to expect, to observe (laws).*

Aguardo a sua resposta. *I'm waiting for your answer.*

aguardente *m. brandy; distilled liquor.*

agudo *adj. sharp; acute; witty.*

agüentar (aguentar) *to bear, to stand, to put up with.*
Não agüento mais. *I can't stand any more.*

águia *f. eagle; m. talented person; an untrustworthy person* Ⓑ.

AGULHA *f. needle.*
Isso é procurar agulha em palheiro. *That's like looking for a needle in a haystack.*

ah! *ah! oh!*

ai! *oh! (exclamation of surprise, pain, etc.)*
Ai de mim! *Poor me!*

AÍ *there, over there (near you).*
Aí mesmo. *Right there.*
Ponha-o aí. *Put it there.*
Por aí. *That way. Over there.*

AIDS *f. AIDS.*

AINDA *still, yet.*
Ele ainda nos escreve. *He still writes us.*
Ele chegou? Ainda não. *Did he arrive? Not yet.*

AINDA QUE *although.*

aipo *m. celery.*

ajoelhar (-se) *to kneel.*

AJUDA *f. help, assistance.*

ajudante *m. and f. assistant, helper.*

AJUDAR *to help, to assist, to aid.*
Você quer que ajude? *Do you want me to help?*

ajustar *to arrange, to fix, to settle.*
Vamos ajustar contas. *Let's settle accounts.*

ala *f. wing, row.*

alarde *m. show, display, parade.*

alargar *to enlarge, to widen.*

alarma *f. alarm.*

alarmar *to alarm.*

alarmar-se *to become frightened.*

alarme *m. alarm.*

alavanca *f. lever.*

albergue *m. inn, shelter.*

albricoque *m. apricot.*

álbum *m. album.*

alcachofra (alcachofa) *f. artichoke.*

alcançar *to reach, to attain, to catch up with, to be enough.*
Não o alcancei. *I did not catch up with him.*

alcance *m. extent, reach, scope.*
Está ao alcance de todos. *It is within everyone's reach.*

alçar *to raise, to lift.*

alcatrão *m. tar, pitch.*

álcool *m. alcohol.*

Alcorão *m. the Koran.*

alcunha *f. nickname.*

aldeia *f. village.*

aldraba, aldrava *f. latch, knocker (of door).*
alecrim *m. rosemary.*
alegação *f. allegation, claim.*
alegar *to allege, to claim.*
alegrar *to cheer, to make happy.*
alegre *adj. cheerful, happy.*
alegria *f. joy, gladness.*
aleijado *adj. lame, crippled.*
aleijar *to cripple, to maim.*
ALÉM *beyond, besides, farther.*
  Além disso. *Besides, furthermore.*
  Muito além. *Much farther.*
alemão *adj., n. m. German.*
alento *m. breath, courage.*
alerta *adj. alert, vigilant.*
alfabeto *m. alphabet.*
alface *f. lettuce.*
  Salada de alface. *Lettuce salad.*
alfaiataria *f. tailor shop.*
alfaiate *m. tailor.*
alfândega *f. customhouse; customs (in an airport, etc.).*
alfinete *m. pin.*
  Alfinete de gravata. *Tie pin.*
algarismo *m. number, figure.*
algibeira *f. pocket.*
algo *some, something; adv. somewhat.*
ALGODÃO *m. cotton.*
  Tecido de algodão. *Cotton fabric.*
ALGUÉM *somebody, someone*
  Alguém entrou. *Somebody came in.*
ALGUM *adj. some, any; pl. a few.*
  Alguma coisa. *Something.*
  Algum dia. *Some day.*
  Algumas vezes. *Sometimes.*
  Quero alguns. *I want a few.*
alheio *adj. belonging to somebody else; foreign; alienated.*
alho *m. garlic.*
ALI *there, over there (away from person spoken to).*
  Está ali. *It's over there.*
  Ali mesmo. *Right there.*
  Ele desapareceu por ali. *He disappeared that way.*
aliança *f. alliance, association, wedding ring.*
aliás *however, besides; otherwise.*
alicate *m. pliers.*
ALIMENTO *food, nourishment.*
alisar *to smooth (out).*
alistar *to enlist, to enroll.*
aliviar *to alleviate, to mitigate.*
ALMA *f. soul, heart, spirit, essence.*
  Não apareceu nenhuma alma. *Not a soul (person) appeared.*
  Ele tem boa alma. *He has a good heart (is kind).*
almanaque *m. almanac.*
almirante *m. admiral.*

ALMOÇAR *to have lunch.*
  Sempre almoçamos ao meio-dia. *We always have lunch at noon.*
ALMOÇO *m. lunch.*
  Primeiro almoço. *Breakfast* Ⓟ.
  Pequeno almoço. *Breakfast* Ⓟ.
almôndega *f. meatball.*
almotolia *f. oilcan.*
alô! *hello!*
alojamento *m. lodging.*
alojar *to lodge, to billet.*
alparca, alparcata, alpercata *f. sandal.*
alteração *f. alteration, change, disturbance.*
alterar *to alter, to change, to disturb.*
alternar *to alternate.*
alternativa *f. alternative, choice.*
altitude *f. altitude.*
altivo *adj. haughty, proud, lofty.*
ALTO *adj. high, tall; loud; n. m. top, height.*
  Ele é alto e magro. *He is tall and thin.*
  Aconteceu no alto mar. *It happened on the high seas.*
  Fale mais alto, por favor. *Speak louder, please.*
  A vida tem muitos altos e baixos. *Life has many ups and downs.*
alto! *halt! stop!*
alto-falante *m. loudspeaker.*
altura *f. height, point (of time).*
  Não sei a altura. *I don't know its height.*
  Nessa altura. *At that point.*
aludir *to allude to.*
ALUGAR *to rent, to hire.*
  Aluguei a casa para o verão. *I rented the house for the summer.*
  Alugam-se quartos. *Rooms for rent.*
ALUGUEL *m. rent, hiring.*
  Quanto é o aluguel? *How much is the rent?*
alumiado *adj. illuminated, light.*
alumiar *to illuminate, to light (up).*
alumínio *m. aluminum.*
ALUNO *m. pupil, student.*
  Você conhece esse aluno? *Do you know that student?*
alva *f. dawn.*
alvo *m. target, aim, white.*
  Ele deu no alvo. *He hit the target.*
ama *f. housekeeper, nursemaid, governess.*
AMABILIDADE *f. amiability, kindliness.*
amado *adj. loved, beloved.*
amador *adj. loving; n. m. amateur, fan.*
amadurecer *to ripen.*
amaldiçoado *adj. cursed, damned.*
amaldiçoar *to curse, to damn.*
AMANHÃ *m. tomorrow.*
  Eles chegam amanhã. *They are arriving tomorrow.*
  Vou depois de amanhã. *I'm going the day after tomorrow.*

Até amanhã. *See you tomorrow.*
amanhecer *to dawn.*
amante *m. and f. lover.*
AMAR *to love, to like.*
AMARELO *yellow.*
amargo *bitter.*
amarra *f. chain, cable.*
amarrar *to tie (up), to fasten, to moor.*
amassar *to knead, to mix, to beat.*
AMÁVEL *adj. kind, amiable.*
    O senhor é muito amável. *You are very kind.*
ambição *f. ambition.*
ambicioso *adj. ambitious.*
ambiente *m. atmosphere, milieu, environment.*
AMBOS *both.*
    Fico com ambos. *I'll take both.*
ambulância *f. ambulance.*
ameaça *f. threat.*
ameaçar *to threaten.*
ameixa *(x = sh) f. plum.*
ameixa *(x = sh)* **passada** *or* **preta** *f. prune.*
amêndoa *f. almond.*
amendoim *m. peanut.*
ameno *adj. pleasant, gentle, mild.*
AMERICANO *adj., n. m. American.*
amido *m. starch.*
AMIGO *m. friend.*
    Apresento(-lhe) o meu amigo, João. *This is my friend John. ("I am introducing my friend John [to you].")*
    Meu caro amigo: *My dear friend:*
    Você é amigo da onça! *You're a fine friend! (disapprovingly).*
amiúde *often.*
amizade *f. friendship.*
amo *m. master.*
amolação *f. sharpening; bother, annoyance* Ⓑ.
    Desculpe a amolação. *Please excuse the bother.*
amolar *to sharpen; to bother, to annoy* Ⓑ.
    Não me amole com isso! *Don't bother me with that!*
AMOR *m. love, affection, a lovely person or thing.*
    O amor é cego. *Love is blind.*
    Julieta é um amor. *Julie is a lovely person.*
amostra *f. sample.*
    Ele me deu (deu-me) uma amostra. *He gave me a sample.*
amparar *to protect, to shelter.*
ampliação *f. amplification, enlargement.*
ampliar *to amplify, to enlarge.*
amplo *adj. ample.*
ampola *f. blister.*
amputar *to amputate, to cut off.*
analfabeto *m. illiterate.*
analisar *to analyze.*
análise *f. analysis.*

ananás (abacaxi Ⓑ) *m. pineapple.*
anão *m.* (**anã** *f.*) *dwarf.*
anatomia *f. anatomy.*
âncora *f. anchor.*
ANDAR *to walk, to go, to be.*
    Andamos à casa de João. *We walked to John's house.*
    Anda! *Get going!*
    Não ando muito bem hoje. *I don't feel very well today.*
andorinha *f. swallow.*
anedota *f. anecdote.*
anel *m. ring, link.*
    Ele esqueceu o anel de casamento. *He forgot the wedding ring.*
ângulo *m. angle, corner.*
angústia *f. anguish, distress.*
animado *adj. lively, animated.*
    Desenho animado. *Animated cartoon.*
animal *m. animal.*
animar *to animate, to encourage.*
ânimo *m. courage, mind.*
aniversário *m. anniversary, birthday.*
    Quando é o seu aniversário? *When is your birthday?*
anjo *m. angel.*
ANO *m. year.*
    Quantos anos você tem? *How old are you?*
    Tenho vinte e dois anos. *I am twenty-two years old.*
    Quando você faz anos? *When is your birthday?*
    Ano bissexto. *Leap year.*
    Ano bom. *New Year.*
    Ano novo. *New Year.*
    Feliz ano novo! *Happy New Year!*
    Em que ano aconteceu? *In what year did it happen?*
    Vamos todos os anos. *We go every year.*
    Eles não vão no ano que vem. *They are not going next year.*
    Elas foram no ano passado. *They went last year.*
anoitecer *to become dark.*
    Ao anoitecer. *At nightfall.*
anônimo (anónimo) *adj. anonymous.*
anormal *adj. abnormal.*
anotar *to note, to record, to comment.*
ânsia *f. anxiety, anguish, sorrow.*
ansiedade *f. anxiety, care, concern, yearning.*
ansioso *adj. anxious, desirous.*
    Estamos muito ansiosos para fazer a viagem. *We are very anxious to take the trip.*
ante *before.*
antecedente *adj., n. m. antecedent.*
antecessor *m. predecessor.*
    Antecessores. *Ancestors.*
antecipação *f. anticipation.*

antecipado *adj. anticipated, expected.*
antecipar *to anticipate, to expect, to precipitate.*
antemão, de antemão *beforehand.*
antena *f. antenna.*
anteontem *the day before yesterday.*
antepassado *adj. past; n. pl. ancestors.*
anterior *adj. anterior; previous, former, preceding.*
ANTES *before, rather.*
   Quanto antes. *As soon as possible.*
   Telefone-me antes de partir. *Phone me before you leave.*
   Antes tarde do que nunca. *Better late than never.*
ANTIGO *adj. old, ancient; former.*
   Lisboa antiga. *Old Lisbon.*
antiguidade *f. antiquity, ancient times.*
antipatia *f. antipathy.*
antipático *adj. unpleasant.*
antiquado *adj. old, obsolete.*
anual *adj. yearly.*
anular *to cancel, to void.*
ANUNCIAR *to announce, to advertise.*
   Anunciaram-no ontem. *They announced it yesterday.*
ANÚNCIO *m. announcement, notice, sign, advertisement.*
   Sempre leio os anúncios nos jornais. *I always read the ads in the papers.*
AO *(contr. of* **a** + **o**) *to the, at the; on, when.*
   Vamos ao teatro. *We are going to the theatre.*
   Ao anoitecer. *At nightfall.*
   Ao contrário. *On the contrary.*
   Ao chegarem, disseram-nos tudo. *When they arrived, they told us everything.*
AONDE *where.*
   Aonde foram? *Where did you go?*
apagador *m. extinguisher, eraser.*
apagar *to extinguish, to erase.*
apaixonado *(x = sh) to fall in love.*
   Apaixonaram-se. *They fell in love.*
apanhar *to catch, to get, to take, to pick.*
   Apanhei um resfriado. *I caught a cold.*
   Eles foram apanhados dois dias mais tarde. *They were caught two days later.*
aparador *m. sideboard, buffet.*
APARECER *to appear, to show up, to turn up.*
   Ele não apareceu ontem. *He didn't show up yesterday.*
aparelho *m. apparatus, device; phone* Ⓑ.
   Não tenho aparelho de rádio. *I don't have a radio set.*
   Quem está no aparelho? Ⓑ *Who's on the phone?*
aparência *f. appearance.*
aparentar *to seem, to appear, to feign.*

aparente *adj. apparent, evident.*
apartado *adj. apart, remote.*
apartamento *m. apartment; separation.*
apartar *to separate, to set apart.*
apelar *to appeal.*
apelido *m. surname, nickname* Ⓑ.
apenas *only, hardly.*
   Ele apenas me falou. *He hardly spoke to me.*
aperitivo *m. apéritif.*
apertado *adj. tight, close.*
APESAR DE *in spite of.*
   Apesar de ser tarde, vamos. *In spite of the fact that it is late, we are going.*
apetecer *to long for, to have an appetite for.*
apetite *m. appetite, hunger.*
   Quando ouvi isso, perdi o apetite. *When I heard that, I lost my appetite.*
apinhar *to crowd.*
apitar *to whistle.*
apito *m. whistle.*
aplaudir *to applaud.*
aplauso *m. applause.*
aplicação *f. application, use.*
aplicado *adj. applied; industrious, studious.*
aplicar *to apply.*
aplicar-se *to apply oneself, to be diligent.*
apoderar-se de *to take possession of.*
apodo *m. nickname.*
apoiar *to support, to favor, to defend, to aid, to lean.*
apoio *m. support.*
apólice *f. policy, bond, share.*
   Apólice de seguro. *Insurance policy.*
apontar *to sharpen; to point out, to indicate.*
aportuguesar *to render in Portuguese.*
após *after, behind.*
aposentar *to lodge, to pension; to dwell.*
aposta *f. bet.*
apostar *to bet.*
   Quanto você apostou? *How much did you bet?*
apóstrofo *m. apostrophe.*
aprazer *to please.*
apreciar *to appreciate, to value.*
apreço *appreciation, esteem.*
APRENDER *to learn.*
   Paulo não aprendeu muito português. *Paul did not learn very much Portuguese.*
   Ela o aprenderá de cor. *She will learn it by heart.*
APRESENTAR *to present, to introduce.*
   Apresento(-lhe) os meus cumprimentos. *I send you my regards.*
   Vou apresentar(-lhe) o meu amigo Carlos Costa. *I'm going to introduce my friend Carlos Costa to you.*
apressar-se *to hurry.*
apropriar *to appropriate.*

aprovação *f. approval, praise; passing grade.*

aprovado *adj. approved; passed (in an examination).*
João não foi aprovado. *John did not pass (was not passed).*

aprovar *to approve; to pass (a student in an examination).*

aproveitar *to make good use of, to profit.*
Ele aproveita tudo. *He makes good use of everything.*

aproveitar-se de *to take advantage of, to make good use of.*
Ele se aproveitou da oportunidade para escapar. *He took advantage of the opportunity to escape.*

aprovisionar *to supply.*

aproximar *(x = s) to approach.*

aptidão *f. aptitude, ability.*

apto *adj. apt, able.*

apunhalar *to stab.*

apurar *to improve, to select, to settle.*

apuro *m. precision, elegance; plight.*
Ele se veste com apuro. *He dresses very well.*
Agora estamos em apuros. *We're in a mess now.*

aquarela *f. watercolor.*

aqueceder *m. heater.*

aquecer *to heat, to warm.*

aquecimento *m. heating.*

AQUELA *(f. of* **aquele**) *that, that one; the former.*
Aquela jovem dança muito bem. *That girl dances very well.*
Esta cadeira é mais nova que aquela. *This chair is newer than that one.*

AQUELE *that, that one; the former.*
Não quero aquele, prefiro este. *I don't want that one (over there); I prefer this one.*
José e Eduardo chegaram ontem. Este (Eduardo) me telefonou, mas aquele (José) ainda não comunicou comigo. *Joseph and Edward arrived yesterday. The latter telephoned me, but the former has not communicated with me yet.*

AQUI *here, in this place.*
Ficamos aqui? *Do we stay here?*
Aqui mesmo. *Right here.*
Daqui a nove dias. *In nine days.*
Venha por aqui. *Come this way.*

aquilo *that (neuter form).*

AR *m. air, wind; aspect, look.*
Vamos sair ao ar livre. *Let's go out into the open air.*
Quero quarto com ar condicionado. *I want an air-conditioned room.*
Ele tem ar de inteligente. *He has an intelligent look.*

arado *m. plow.*

arame *m. wire.*

aranha *f. spider.*

arar *to plow.*

arbitrar *to arbitrate.*

árbitro *m. arbiter, umpire, referee.*

arbusto *m. bush, shrub.*

arca *f. chest, ark.*

arcar *to arch, to bow.*

arcebispo *m. archbishop.*

arco *m. arc, arch.*

arco-íris *rainbow.*

arder *to burn, to glow.*

área *f. area, region.*

areia *f. sand.*

arengar *to harangue.*

argamassa *f. mortar.*

argola *f. ring; door knocker.*

argumento *m. argument, reason, topic, plot.*
Esse argumento não me convence. *That argument does not convince me.*

árido *adj. arid, dry.*

aritmética *f. arithmetic.*

arma *f. weapon, arm.*
Não temos armas de fogo. *We have no firearms.*

armada *f. fleet.*

armamento *m. armament.*

armar *to arm.*

armário *m. cupboard, closet.*

armazém *m. grocery store, warehouse.*

armistício *m. armistice.*

arquiteto (arquitecto) *m. architect.*

arquitetura (arquitectura) *f. architecture.*

arquivo *m. record, filing cabinet.*

arrancar *to pull out, to tear out, to start (as a motor).*
O motor não arrancava. *The motor wouldn't start.*

arranha-céu *m. (pl.* **arranha-céus**) *skyscraper.*
Há muitos arranha-céus em Nova Iorque. *There are many skyscrapers in New York.*

arranhar *to scratch.*

ARRANJAR *to arrange.*
Não se preocupe, nós arranjamos tudo. *Don't worry, we'll arrange everything.*

arranjo *m. arrangement.*

arrastar *to haul, to drag.*

arrebatar *to grab, to carry off.*

arrebentar *to burst, to explode.*

arredores *m. pl. outskirts, suburbs.*

arregalar *to open the eyes wide, to stare.*

arrendar *to rent, to hire.*

arrepender-se *to repent, to be sorry for.*

arrepiar *to frighten, to terrify.*

arriba *up, above.*

arribar *to put in to port.*

arriscar *to risk, to dare.*
   Quem não arrisca, não petisca. *Nothing ventured, nothing gained.*
arrogante *adj. arrogant.*
arroio *m. brook.*
arrojar *to throw, to hurl.*
arrolhar *to cork.*
arroz *m. rice.*
arruinar *to ruin, to destroy.*
arrumar *to arrange, to put in order.*
   Ainda não arrumaram as malas? *Haven't you packed your bags yet?*
   Ela arruma tudo. *She keeps everything in order.*
arte *f. art, skill; way.*
   E uma verdadeira obra de arte. *It is a true work of art.*
   Belas artes. *Fine arts.*
ártico (árctico) *adj. arctic.*
artigo *m. article.*
   Não gostei do artigo de fundo. *I did not like the main editorial (or main article).*
artista *m. and f. artist.*
árvore *f. tree; shaft.*
   Árvore de Natal. *Christmas tree.*
   O tronco da árvore. *The trunk of a tree.*
   A árvore não tem folhas. *The tree doesn't have any leaves.*
ás *m. ace.*
asa *f. wing.*
   Vamos cortar-lhe as asas. *We're going to clip his wings.*
ascender *to rise.*
ascensão *f. ascension, elevation.*
ascensor *m. elevator.*
asfalto *m. asphalt.*
asilo *m. asylum, shelter.*
asneira *f. foolish thing, nonsense.*
   Mas isso é asneira! *But that's nonsense!*
asno *m. ass, fool.*
aspas *f. pl. quotation marks.*
aspecto, aspeto (aspecto, aspeito) *m. aspect, appearance.*
aspirador de pó *m. vacuum cleaner.*
aspirante *m. and f. aspirant, candidate; m. cadet.*
   Aspirante de marinha. *Midshipman.*
aspirina *f. aspirin.*
assado *adj. roast, roasted, baked.*
   Frango assado. *Roast chicken.*
   Assado de carneiro. *Roast lamb.*
assaltar *to assault, to attack.*
assalto *m. assault, attack.*
assar *to roast, to broil, to burn.*
assassinar *to assassinate, to murder, to kill.*
assassinato *m. assassination, murder.*
assassínio *m. assassination, murder.*
assassino *m. assassin, murderer.*

asseado *adj. clean, neat.*
assear *to clean, to tidy up.*
assear-se *to be neat, to dress well.*
assegurar *to insure; to secure, to fasten; to assure; to affirm, to assert.*
assembléia (assembleia) *f. assembly, meeting.*
   Assembléia legislativa. *Legislative assembly.*
assemelhar-se *to be similar, to resemble.*
assentar *to set, to place, to seat, to adjust.*
assento *m. seat, chair; place; record, entry.*
ASSIM *so, thus, in this manner, therefore, so that.*
   Assim espero. *I hope so.*
   Você deve fazê-lo assim. *You should do it this way.*
   Não é assim, asseguro-lhe. *I assure you that's not so.*
   Assim, assim. *So-so.*
   Assim que ele chegar, falaremos. *We'll talk as soon as he arrives.*
assinado *adj. signed.*
assinar *to sign, to assign, to subscribe.*
   Faça o favor de assinar o cheque. *Please sign the check.*
assinatura *f. subscription, signature.*
   Quero uma assinatura anual. *I would like a year's subscription.*
assistir *to attend, to be present; to help, to assist.*
   Ele não asistiu à aula. *He did not attend (the) class.*
assoar *to blow the nose.*
assobiar *to whistle.*
assobio *m. whistle, whistling.*
associação *f. association, company, society, club.*
assomar *to arise, to appear.*
assomar-se *to become angry.*
assombrado *adj. astonished, frightened.*
assombrar *to astonish, to frighten.*
assombro *m. astonishment, fright.*
ASSUNTO *m. subject, matter, business.*
   Preciso de mais detalhes sobre este assunto. *I need more information on this matter.*
   Conheço a fundo o assunto. *I am thoroughly acquainted with the matter.*
   Qual é o assunto dessa peça? *What is that play about?*
assustar *to startle, to frighten.*
asterisco *m. asterisk.*
astro *m. star (astronomy).*
astucioso *adj. cunning, astute.*
atacado *adj. attacked.*
   Por atacado. *Wholesale.*
atacar *to attack, to assail.*
ataque *m. attack.*
atar *to tie, to tighten.*

atarefado *adj. busy, occupied, "tied up."*

atas *f. pl. proceedings, minutes (of a meeting).*

ataúde *m. coffin, tomb.*

ATÉ *until; as far as; up to; also, even.*

Até logo. *So long. See you later.*

Até a vista. *See you soon. See you later.*

Até amanhã. *See you tomorrow.*

Até breve. *See you soon.*

Até segunda. *See you Monday.*

Fomos até o parque. *We went as far as the park.*

O elevador sobe até o quinto andar. *The elevator goes up to the fifth floor.*

Até onde vai este caminho? *How far does this road go?*

ATENÇÃO *f. attention.*

Quero chamar a sua atenção para isto. *I want to call your attention to this.*

Em atenção a sua carta. *With regard to your letter.*

Atenção! *Watch out!*

atencioso *adj. attentive, thoughtful, polite.*

atender *to attend (to), to take care of; to answer (the telephone).*

Maria, atenda o telefone, por favor. *Mary, please answer the telephone.*

atentar *to attempt.*

atento *adj. attentive, courteous.*

Ele é muito atento. *He is very attentive.*

Atento e obrigado. *Very truly yours.*

aterragem *f. landing (aircraft).*

aterrar *to cover with earth; to frighten.*

aterrissagem *f. landing (aircraft).*

aterrissar *to land (aircraft).*

aterrorizar *to terrify, to frighten.*

atestar *to attest.*

atinar *to hit on (discover), to find out.*

atingir *to attain, to reach.*

atitude *f. attitude, position.*

atividade (actividade) *f. activity.*

Em plena atividade. *In full swing (activity).*

ativo (activo) *adj. active.*

atlântico *adj. Atlantic.*

atleta *m. and f. athlete.*

atlético *adj. athletic.*

atmosfera *f. atmosphere.*

ATO (ACTO) *m. act, action, deed; meeting.*

No primeiro ato não acontece nada. *Nothing happens in the first act.*

átomo *m. atom.*

átono *adj. atonic, unaccented.*

ator (actor) *m. actor.*

atormentar *to torment.*

atração (atracção) *f. attraction.*

atracar *to come alongside, to tie up (a ship), to dock.*

atraente *adj. attractive.*

atrair *to attract.*

ATRÁS *behind, backward; past; ago.*

Eu fiquei atrás. *I stayed behind.*

Eles tiveram que voltar para atrás. *They had to turn back.*

Que há atrás da caixa? *(x = sh) What's behind the box?*

atrasado *adj. behind, backward, late.*

Os meninos vão chegar atrasados. *The children are going to be late.*

Parece que meu relógio está atrasado. *It seems my watch is slow.*

atrasar(-se) *to hold back, to delay, to run slow (watch).*

atraso *m. delay.*

atrativo (atractivo) *adj. attractive.*

através *through.*

atravessar *to cross, to pass over; to hinder.*

atrever-se *to dare.*

Alfredo não se atreveu a fazê-lo. *Alfred did not dare to do it.*

atrevido *adj. daring, bold.*

atribuir *to attribute.*

atriz (actriz) *f. actress.*

atroar *to thunder, to roar.*

atrocidade *f. atrocity.*

atropelar *to step on, to trample, to run over.*

Ele foi atropelado por um automóvel. *He was run over by an automobile.*

atropelo *m. trampling, running over.*

atroz *adj. atrocious, cruel.*

atuação (actuação) *f. performance, acting.*

ATUAL (ACTUAL) *adj. actual, present.*

atualidade (actualidade) *f. the present, today.*

ATUALMENTE (ACTUALMENTE) *today, nowadays, at the present time.*

Atualmente eles estão em São Paulo. *At the present time they are in São Paulo.*

atuar (actuar) *to act, to put into action.*

atum *m. tuna.*

aturdido *adj. bewildered.*

audácia *f. audacity, boldness, presumption.*

audacioso *adj. bold, audacious.*

audição *f. audition.*

auditório *m. auditorium, audience.*

auge *m. height, summit.*

augusto *adj. august, venerable.*

aula *f. class, recitation.*

Hoje não tenho aulas. *I don't have any classes today.*

aumentar *to increase, to augment, to enlarge.*

aumento *m. increase.*

Aumento de preços sem aumento de ordenado, não adianta. *An increase in prices without an increase in salary doesn't help.*

áureo *adj. golden, brilliant.*

aurora *f. dawn, daybreak.*

ausência *f. absence.*

ausentar-se *to be absent, to be away.*

AUSENTE *adj. absent.*

autêntico *adj. authentic, true.*
auto *m. automobile, auto; document; public act; short dramatic work.*
autocarro *m. bus* Ⓟ.
automático *adj. automatic.*
automóvel *m. automobile.*
autor *m. author.*
autoridade *f. authority.*
autorização *f. authorization.*
autorizar *to authorize.*
auxiliar *(x = s) to aid, to help; adj. auxiliary.*
auxílio *(x = s) m. help, aid, assistance.*
avaliar *to evaluate, to judge.*
avançado *adj. advanced.*
avançar *to advance, to go ahead, to progress.*
avante *forward.*
    Avante! *Forward!*
avaria *f. damage, loss.*
avariado *adj. damaged.*
avariar *to damage.*
avaro *adj. miserly, greedy.*
ave *f. bird, fowl; hail!*
    Ave, Maria, cheia de graça. *Hail, Mary, full of grace.*
aveia *f. oat, oats.*
avenida *f. avenue.*
avental *m. apron.*
aventura *f. adventure.*
averiguar *to inquire, to find out, to investigate.*
    Averigue a que horas sai o trem. *Find out (at) what time the train leaves.*
avesso *adj. opposite, contrary.*
avestruz *m. and f. ostrich.*
aviação *f. aviation.*
aviador *m. aviator.*
avião *m. airplane.*
aviar *to get ready, to prescribe (medicine), to supply.*
    Numa farmácia aviam receitas. *In a pharmacy they fill prescriptions.*
avisado *adj. notified, advised.*
avisar *to inform, to notify, to let know; to warn.*
    Eu o avisarei assim que souber. *I'll notify you as soon as I know.*
aviso *m. notice, warning.*
avistar *to sight, to see.*
avô *m. grandfather.*
avó *f. grandmother.*
azar *m. misfortune, bad luck, mishap.*
azeite *m. oil.*
    Ele sempre deita azeite no fogo. *He's always adding fuel to the fire.*
azeiteira (almotolia) *f. oilcan.*
azeitona *f. olive.*
AZUL *blue.*
    Gosto mais do vestido azul. *I like the blue dress better.*

Tudo azul! *Everything's fine!*
azulejo *m. glazed tile.*

babá *f. nursemaid* Ⓑ.
bacalhau *m. codfish.*
bacharel *m. bachelor (graduate).*
bacia *f. basin.*
báculo *m. staff, rod.*
badalada *f. sound, stroke (of a bell).*
badalar *to ring, to toll; to hype up* Ⓑ.
bagagem *f. baggage, luggage.*
    Onde posso deixar *(x = sh)* a bagagem? *Where can I leave my luggage?*
bagatela *f. bagatelle, trifle.*
bagunça *f. confusion, mess* Ⓑ.
baía *f. bay.*
bailar *to dance.*
baile *m. dance.*
bairro *m. district, neighborhood, suburb.*
    Moro no bairro residencial. *I live in the residential district (suburb).*
baixa *(x = sh) f. fall, depreciation (price); casualty.*
BAIXAR *(x = sh) to go (come down); to get (bring) down; to get off; to lower, let down; to drop (fever, temperature, etc.).*
    Quando voces vão baixar os preços? *When are you going to lower prices?*
BAIXO *(x = sh) adj. low; under, below; short.*
    Ele é baixo e gordo. *He is short and fat.*
    Fale mais baixo. *Speak more softly.*
bala *f. bullet.*
balança *f. balance, scale; justice.*
    Balança de plataforma. *Platform scale.*
balanço *m. swinging, balancing, balance.*
    Diga-me o balanço para este mês. *Give me the balance for this month.*
balar *to bleat.*
balbuciar *to stutter, to stammer, to blubber, to babble.*
balbúrdia *f. disorder, confusion.*
balcão *m. balcony; counter (in store, etc.).*
balde *m. pail, bucket.*
baldear *to bail (water); to tranship; to transfer; to change trains.*
    Temos que baldear antes de chegar ao Rio? *Do we have to change trains before we arrive in Rio?*
baleia *f. whale.*
balneário *m. boathouse, health resort.*
baluarte *m. bulwark, stronghold; shelter.*
bambu *m. bamboo.*
banal *adj. banal, trite, commonplace.*
banana *f. banana.*

banca *f. table, desk, stand; board (examining).*
Comprei na banca (no quiosque) de jornais. *I bought it at the newsstand.*
banco *m. bank (commercial); bank, bar, reef; bench; seat (car).*
Hoje o banco está fechado. *Today the bank is closed.*
Elas se sentaram no banco. *They sat down on the bench.*
banda *f. band; strip, stripe.*
Aqui vem uma banda de música. *Here comes a brass band.*
bandeira *f. flag, pennant, banner; colonial exploratory expedition* Ⓑ.
bandeirante *m. member of a* bandeira Ⓑ.
bandeja *f. tray, platter.*
bandido *m. bandit, robber.*
bando *m. band, gang; flock.*
banhar(-se) *to bathe, to wash.*
banheira *f. bathtub.*
BANHEIRO *m. bathroom* Ⓑ.
BANHO *m. bath, bathing.*
Gostaria de tomar banho de chuveiro. *I'd like to take a shower.*
Casa de banho Ⓟ. *Bathroom.*
banir *to banish, to forbid.*
banqueiro *m. banker.*
bar *m. bar, tavern.*
baralhar *to shuffle (cards); to mix up.*
barata *f. cockroach.*
BARATO *adj. cheap, inexpensive.*
barba *f. chin; beard.*
Eu ainda não fiz a barba. *I haven't shaved yet.*
Pincel de barba. *Shaving brush.*
bárbaro *adj. barbaric, coarse, brutal.*
barbear *to shave* (**barbeio,** *etc.*).
barbearia *f. barbershop.*
barbear-se *to shave (oneself)* (**barbeio-me,** *etc.*).
Primeiro vou barbear-me. *First I'm going to shave.*
Sempre me barbeio antes de sair de casa. *I always shave before leaving home.*
barbeiro *m. barber.*
barbudo *adj. heavily bearded.*
barca *f. boat, barge.*
barco *m. boat, ship, vessel.*
Barco a motor. *Motorboat.*
Barco a vapor. *Steamship.*
Barco a vela. *Sailboat.*
barômetro (barómetro) *m. barometer.*
barquinha *f. small boat; ship's log.*
barra *f. bar, ingot; strip, band; sandbar.*
barraca *f. hut, tent, shelter.*
barragem *f. dam, barrier.*
barranco *m. ravine, gully; precipice.*
barrar *to make metal bars; to bar, to obstruct.*
barreira *f. barrier, bar, obstruction.*

barriga *f. belly, stomach.*
barril *m. barrel, cask.*
barro *m. mud, clay.*
barulho *m. noise.*
Meninos, isso é muito barulho. *Children, that's too much noise.*
base *f. base, basis.*
basear *to base.*
básico *adj. basic.*
basquetbol *m. basketball.*
BASTANTE *enough, sufficient; quite.*
Ele não tem bastante dinheiro. *He does not have enough money.*
Acho bastante caro. *I think it's pretty expensive.*
bastão *m. cane, walking stick.*
BASTAR *to suffice, to be enough.*
Isso basta. *That's enough.*
Basta! *Enough! Stop!*
bata *f. dressing gown; smock.*
batalha *f. battle, combat, fight.*
batalhão *m. battalion.*
batalhar *to battle, to fight, to struggle.*
batata *f. potato.*
Batatas fritas. *Fried potatoes.*
Purê de batatas. *Mashed potatoes.*
Batata-doce. *Sweet potato.*
BATER *to beat, to strike; to knock.*
Quem bate à porta? *Who's knocking at the door?*
bateria *f. battery, drums (music).*
Bateria de cozinha. *Kitchen utensils.*
batida *f. blow, knock; collision; a mixed drink with a brandy base* Ⓑ.
batismo (baptismo) *m. baptism, christening.*
batizar (baptizar) *to baptize, to christen.*
batuque *m. Afro-Brazilian dance* Ⓑ.
baú *m. trunk, chest.*
baunilha *f. vanilla.*
bazar *m. bazaar, store.*
bêbado *adj. drunk, intoxicated; m. drunkard.*
bebê (bebé) *m. baby.*
BEBER *to drink.*
bebida *f. drink, beverage.*
Ele se deu à bebida. *He took to drink.*
beco *m. alley, lane, side street.*
Beco sem saída. *Blind alley.*
beijar *to kiss.*
beijo *m. kiss.*
beira *f. brink, edge, bank.*
beira-mar *f. seashore, coast.*
beleza *f. beauty.*
bélico *adj. bellicose, warlike.*
belicoso *adj. bellicose, warlike; hostile.*
BELO *adj. beautiful.*
Ela é bela! *She is beautiful!*
O belo sexo ($x = ks$). *The fair sex.*
As belas artes. *The fine arts.*
BEM *well, right; m. loved one, darling.*

Você está bem? *Are you all right?*
Muito bem, obrigado. *Very well, thank you.*
Não muito bem. *Not very well.*
Passe bem. *Good luck. Good-bye.*
Está bem. *All right. O.K.*
Bem educado. *Well brought up.*
É bem longe. *It's quite far.*
É bem pouco. *It's not very much.*
Por que chora, meu bem? *Why are you crying, my darling?*
bem-estar *m. well-being, welfare.*
bênção *f. blessing, benediction.*
bendito *adj. blessed.*
bendizer *to praise; to bless.*
beneficiar *to benefit, to profit.*
beneficiário *adj. beneficiary.*
benefício *m. benefit, profit, advantage.*
benfeitor *m. benefactor.*
bengala *f. cane, walking stick.*
benigno *adj. kind.*
bens *m. pl. property, possessions.*
bento *adj. blessed, holy.*
benzer *to bless.*
benzer-se *to make the sign of the cross.*
Ela se benzeu ao entrar na igreja. *She made the sign of the cross on entering the church.*
berço *m. cradle, crib; birthplace, birth.*
Desde o berço até a morte, o estado entra na nossa vida. *The state enters our life from birth to death.*
berinjela *f. eggplant.*
berrar *to roar, to shout.*
berro *m. roar, shout.*
besta *f. beast; fool.*
besteira *f. foolish thing, nonsense.*
Eles só dizem besteiras. *They speak nothing but nonsense.*
beterraba *f. beet.*
bexiga *(x = sh) f. bladder; smallpox.*
bezerro *m. calf.*
Bíblia *f. Bible.*
bibliografia *f. bibliography.*
biblioteca *f. library.*
bicarbonato *m. bicarbonate.*
bicho *m. animal, insect, worm; unpleasant person; crafty person.*
Ele é um bicho. *He's a nasty guy.*
Jogo do bicho. *A type of lottery in Brazil.*
bicicleta *f. bicycle.*
bico *m. beak, bill, point.*
bife *m. steak, beefsteak.*
bigode *m. moustache.*
bilhar *m. billiards.*
BILHETE *m. ticket, note.*
Quero bilhete de ida e volta. *I want a round-trip ticket.*
Ontem Carlos recebeu o bilhete azul. *Charles was fired yesterday.*

Bilhete postal. *Postcard Ⓑ.*
bilheteria (bilheteira) *f. ticket office.*
binóculo *m. binoculars, opera glasses.*
biombo *m. screen.*
bip *m. beeper, pager.*
Mandar chamar por bip. *To page someone.*
bis *again; encore!*
bisavô *m. great-grandfather.*
bisavó *f. great-grandmother.*
biscoito *m. biscuit, cookie, cracker.*
bisneto *m. great-grandson.*
bispo *m. bishop.*
bissexto *adj. bissextile.*
Ano bissexto. *Leap year.*
bitola *f. gauge (railroad); measure.*
blindado *adj. armored.*
blindar *to armor, to cover.*
bloco *m. block; writing pad.*
Compre-me um bloco de papel. *Buy me a writing pad.*
BOA *adj. f. of* **bom.**
boas-vindas *f. pl. welcome.*
bobagem *f. nonsense, foolishness.*
bobo *adj. foolish, silly; m. fool, clown.*
BOCA *f. mouth.*
bocadinho *m. bit.*
Espere um bocadinho. *Wait a bit.*
bocado *m. bite, piece; short while.*
bocejar *to yawn.*
bochecha *f. cheek.*
boda *f. wedding.*
bofetada *f. slap in the face, blow.*
boi *m. ox, bull.*
BOLA *f. ball, globe; wits.*
Bola de tênis (ténis). *Tennis ball.*
Ora bolas! *Baloney! Nuts!*
boletim *m. bulletin, report.*
bolo *m. cake; stake, kitty.*
BOLSA *f. purse, bag, scholarship.*
Bolsa de estudos. *Scholarship.*
Bolsa de valores. *Stock exchange.*
BOLSO *m. pocket.*
Esta é uma edição de bolso. *This is a pocket edition.*
BOM *adj. good; kind; satisfactory; suited, fit; well.*
Bom dia. *Good morning.*
Boa tarde. *Good afternoon. Good evening.*
Boa noite. *Good night.*
É uma boa idéia (ideia). *That's a good idea.*
Eu acho muito bom. *I think it's great.*
Ele está bom. *He's well.*
Nós lhe fizemos uma boa! *We played a fine trick on him!*
bomba *f. pump; fire engine; bomb.*
bombeiro *m. fireman; plumber.*
bombom *m. bonbon, candy.*
BONDADE *f. goodness, kindness.*

Tenha a bondade de sentar-se. *Please sit down.*

bonde *m. streetcar* Ⓑ.

bondoso *adj. kind.*

boné *m. cap.*

bonitão *m.* (**bonitona** *f.*) *adj. good-looking.*

bonito *adj. pretty, good.*

borboleta *f. butterfly; wing nut.*

bordar *to embroider; to edge.*

bordo *m. board (ship); border; course, tack (boat).*

Peço licença para ir a bordo. *I ask permission to go aboard.*

borracha *f. rubber; eraser.*

borrasca *f. storm.*

bosque *m. forest, woods.*

bosquejo *m. sketch, draft.*

bossa nova *f. type of Brazilian popular music.*

bota *f. boot.*

botão *m. button; bud.*

BOTAR *to cast, to throw; to put, to place* Ⓑ.

Bote fora! *Throw it out!*

Botou cinco dólares no balcão. *He put five dollars on the counter.*

bote *m. boat.*

botica *f. pharmacy.*

boticário *m. pharmacist, druggist.*

boxe *(x = ks) m. boxing.*

boxeador *(x = ks) m. boxer.*

boxear *(x = ks) to box.*

BRAÇO *m. arm.*

Eles ficaram com os braços cruzados. *They stayed there with their arms folded.*

bradar *to roar, to shout.*

BRANCO *white, pale, blank.*

Quero seis camisas brancas. *I want six white shirts.*

Você pode deixá-lo *(x = sh)* em branco. *You can leave it blank.*

Verso branco. *Blank verse.*

brando *adj. soft, smooth.*

brasa *f. live coal, ember.*

Eles estão sobre brasas. *They're very worried about it.*

BRASIL *m. Brazil.*

BRASILEIRO *adj. Brazilian; n. m. Brazilian.*

bravo *adj. brave, wild; bravo!*

BREVE *brief, short, soon, shortly.*

Até breve. *See you soon.*

Em breve. *Soon.*

Faça-o o mais breve possível! *Do it as soon as possible!*

brevidade *f. briefness, brevity.*

briga *f. quarrel, fight.*

brigada *f. brigade.*

brigar *to quarrel, to fight.*

brilhante *adj. brilliant, sparkling; n. m. diamond.*

brilhar *to shine, to sparkle.*

brincadeira *f. joke; jest, prank.*

Chega de brincadeiras! *That's enough joking!*

brincar *to joke; to play.*

Os meninos estão brincando. *The children are playing.*

Mas ele só estava brincando! *But he was only joking!*

brindar *to toast.*

brinde *m. toast; offering.*

brinquedo *m. toy.*

brisa *f. breeze.*

broche *m. clasp; brooch.*

brochura *f. brochure, pamphlet; paperback.*

bronze *m. bronze, brass.*

brotar *to bud; to produce; to burst out.*

brusco *adj. brusque, rude, rough.*

brutal *adj. brutal, rough.*

bruto *adj. brutal; rude.*

Foi um ato (acto) muito bruto. *It was a very brutal act.*

bruxaria *(x = sh) f. witchcraft.*

bruxo *(x = sh) m.* (**bruxa** *f.*) *sorcerer, medicine man; witch.*

budista *n. m. and f. Buddhist.*

bufão *m. braggart, joker.*

bufete *m. buffet, sideboard, dresser.*

bugia *f. wax candle.*

bugigangas *f. pl. trinkets, knickknacks.*

buraco *m. hole, opening.*

Buraco de fechadura. *Keyhole.*

burla *f. joke; trick; deceit.*

burlar *to joke, to jest; to trick; to deceive.*

burro *m. donkey, ass.*

busca *f. search, pursuit.*

Ele vai em busca de fama. *He's in pursuit of fame.*

buscar *to look for, to go for.*

busto *m. bust.*

buzina *f. horn (music, car, etc.).*

buzinar *to blow a horn; to honk a car horn.*

CÁ *here, this way.*

Venha cá! *Come here!*

cabana *f. hut, cabin.*

CABEÇA *f. head.*

Tenho dor de cabeça. *I have a headache.*

Dos pés à cabeça. *From head to foot.*

Isso não tem pés nem cabeça. *That doesn't make sense.*

cabeceira *f. head of a bed, table, or list.*

Mesa de cabeceira. *Bedside table.*

CABELO *m. hair.*

caber *to fit into; to have enough room; to contain.*

Não cabe mais nada no baú. *There's no more room in the trunk.*

cabide *m. coat hanger, hat rack, peg.*

cabina, cabine *f. cabin, booth.*
Cabina telefônica (cabine telefónica). *Telephone booth.*

cabo *m. tip, extremity, end; cape; handle; cable; rope; corporal.*
Ao cabo do dia. *At the end of the day.*
Ele nunca leva nada ao cabo. *He never finishes anything.*
Cabo da Boa Esperança. *Cape of Good Hope.*

caboclo *m.* Ⓑ. *backwoodsman; Brazilian Indian, half-breed; adj. copper-colored.*

cabra *f. female goat; m.* Ⓑ *half-breed; bandit; ruffian.*

caça *f. hunting; game.*

caçador *m. hunter.*

caçar *to hunt, to chase.*

cacarejar *to cackle; to chatter.*

caçarola *f. saucepan, casserole.*

cacau *m. cocoa, cacao.*

cacete *m. club, stick; adj. unpleasant, boring* Ⓑ.

cachaça *f. Brazilian sugar cane liquor or rum.*

cachimbo *m. pipe (for smoking).*

cachoeira *f. waterfall.*

cachorro *m. dog.*
Cachorro quente. *Hot dog.*

caçoar *to tease, to make fun of.*

CADA *adj. m. and f. each, every.*
Cada hora. *Each hour.*
Cada qual. *Each one. Every one.*
Cada vez que ele vem. *Each time he comes.*
Dar a cada um. *To give each one.*
Cada dia ele fala português melhor. *Every day he speaks Portuguese better.*

cadáver *m. corpse, cadaver.*

cadeia *f. chain.*

CADEIRA *f. chair.*

caderno *m. notebook.*

cadete *m. cadet.*

CAFÉ *m. coffee; coffeehouse.*
Uma xícara *(x = sh)* de café. *A cup of coffee.*
Café com leite. *Coffee with milk.*
Café preto. *Black coffee.*

CAFÉ DA MANHÃ *m. breakfast* Ⓑ.
Tomo o café da manhã às nove. *I have breakfast at nine o'clock.*

cafeteira *f. coffeepot.*

CAFEZINHO *m. small cup of black coffee* Ⓑ.

caída *f. fall, downfall.*

caído *adj. fallen.*

CAIR *to fall; to tumble down; to drop; to become, to fit.*

Caía chuva no telhado. *Rain was falling on the roof.*
Esse vestido lhe cai bem. *That dress looks good on you.*
O aniversário de João cai no mesmo dia que o meu. *John's birthday falls on the same day as mine.*

cais *m. dock, pier.*

CAIXA *(x = sh) f. box, case; chest; cabinet.*
Essa caixa é muito pequena. *That box is very small.*
Faça o favor de pagar na caixa. *Please pay the cashier.*

caixão *(x = sh) m. large box, chest; coffin.*

caixeiro *(x = sh) m. salesman, clerk.*

cajadada *f. blow with a stick.*

caju *m. cashew.*

cal *m. lime; whitewash.*

calabouço *m. jail, prison.*

calado *adj. quiet, silent, reserved.*

calamidade *f. calamity.*

calar *to keep quiet, to be silent; to conceal.*
Cale-se! *Be quiet!*

calçada *f. sidewalk; pavement.*

calçado *m. footwear, shoes.*

calção *m. shorts, trunks.*
Calção de banho. *Bathing trunks.*

calçar *to put on (shoes, socks, etc.); to tread on.*

calças *f. pl. trousers; panties.*

calcular *to calculate, to estimate, to presume.*

cálculo *m. computation, estimate; calculus.*

caldo *m. soup, broth; juice.*

calefação (calefacção) *f. heat, heating system.*

calendário *m. calendar, almanac.*

calibre *m. caliber; bore; gauge.*

caligrafia *f. penmanship, handwriting.*

calmo *adj. calm, quiet.*

calo *m. corn, callus.*

CALOR *m. heat, warmth.*
Sempre faz calor no verão. *It's always warm in the summer.*

calouro *m. beginner, freshman, greenhorn.*

calúnia *f. calumny, slander.*

caluniar *to slander.*

calvície *f. baldness.*

calvo *adj. bald; bare, barren.*

CAMA *bed; couch; layer.*
Fazer a cama. *To make the bed.*
Ele foi para a cama às dez. *He went to bed at ten.*

câmara *f. chamber; room; camera.*
Câmara municipal. *City council.*
Câmara cinematográfica. *Movie camera.*

camarada *m. and f. friend, companion.*

camarão *m. shrimp, prawn.*

camareira *f. chambermaid.*

camareiro *m. steward; room servant (hotel).*

camarote *m. box (theatre); cabin (ship).*

cambiar *to change, to exchange.*

câmbio *m. change, exchange.*

Câmbio exterior. *Foreign exchange.*

Eu perdi no câmbio. *I lost in the exchange.*

caminhão *m. truck.*

CAMINHAR *to walk; to march; to move along.*

CAMINHO *m. road, way, highway.*

Qual é o caminho mais curto para a cidade? *Which is the shortest way to the city?*

Todos os caminhos levam a Roma. *All roads lead to Rome.*

CAMISA *f. shirt, chemise.*

Ela me comprou três camisas. *She bought me three shirts.*

Eu prefiro trabalhar em mangas de camisa. *I prefer to work in shirtsleeves.*

camisaria *f. haberdashery; shirt factory.*

camisola *f. nightgown; undershirt* Ⓟ.

campainha *f. bell, buzzer.*

campeão *m. champion.*

campestre *adj. rural, rustic, country.*

campo *m. field, country; space.*

cana *f. cane, reed.*

Cana-de-açúcar. *Sugar cane.*

canal *m. canal; channel (maritime; TV).*

Passamos pelo canal do Panamá. *We went through the Panama Canal.*

canalha *m. rascal, scoundrel; f. rabble, mob.*

canário *m. canary.*

CANÇÃO *f. song.*

cancelar *to cancel.*

câncer *m. cancer (sign of the zodiac).*

cancioneiro *m. songbook.*

cancro *m. cancer (med.); chancre, canker.*

candeeiro *m. lamp; chandelier.*

candeia *f. oil lamp, lamp.*

candelabro *m. candelabrum.*

candidato *m. candidate.*

candidatura *f. candidacy.*

candidez *f. candor; simplicity.*

cândido *adj. candid, frank.*

caneca *f. mug.*

canela *f. cinnamon; shin.*

Gabriela, Cravo e Canela. *Gabriela, Clove and Cinnamon. (Title of a novel by Jorge Amado.)*

caneta *f. penholder, pen.*

Caneta esferográfica. *Ballpoint pen.*

Caneta-tinteiro. *Fountain pen.*

cânfora *f. camphor.*

cangaceiro *m. outlaw, bandit* Ⓑ.

canhão *m. cannon, gun; canyon.*

caniço *m. reed, rod.*

canino *adj. canine.*

Estou com uma fome canina. *I'm ravenous.*

canivete *m. penknife, pocketknife.*

canja *f. chicken soup with rice; a cinch, easy* Ⓑ.

É canja! *That's a cinch! That's easy!*

cano *m. pipe, tube.*

Os seus planos foram pelo cano a baixo. *His plans went down the drain.*

canoa *f. canoe.*

cansaço *m. weariness, fatigue.*

CANSADO *adj. tired, weary; tedious; annoying.*

Ficamos muito cansados. *We are very tired.*

cansar *to tire; to annoy, to bore.*

cansar-se *to get tired, to get annoyed, to become bored.*

cantador *m. singer (of popular songs).*

CANTAR *to sing.*

cântaro *m. pot, jar, pitcher.*

cantarolar *to hum.*

cântico *m. song, hymn.*

cantiga *f. popular song, ballad.*

cantina *f. canteen.*

canto *m. song; corner, nook.*

cantor *m. singer.*

CÃO *m. dog.*

Quem não tem cão, caça com gato. *One does the best one can. You have to make the best of things.*

capa *f. cape, cloak, coat; cover.*

Capa de chuva. *Raincoat.*

Capa de livro. *Book cover, binding.*

capacidade *f. capacity.*

capataz *m. foreman, boss.*

capaz *adj. capable, able.*

Ele é capaz de fazê-lo. *He's capable of doing it.*

capela *f. chapel.*

capelão *m. chaplain.*

capital *adj. principal, main; n. m. principal (money); capital (stock); n. f. capital (city).*

Quanto capital precisa para essa empresa? *How much capital do you need for that undertaking?*

Qual é a capital do estado? *What is the state capital?*

capitão *m. captain.*

capitólio *m. capitol.*

capítulo *m. chapter.*

capote *m. cape, cloak, overcoat.*

captar *to capture, to catch.*

capturar *to capture, arrest.*

CARA *f. face, look, appearance.*

Encontraram-se cara a cara. *They met face to face.*

Ele tem boa cara. *He looks like a decent guy.*

Você tem cara de fome. *You look like you're starving.*

Cara ou coroa? *Heads or tails?*

caranguejo *m. crab.*
caráter (carácter) *m. character.*
carbono *m. carbon; carbon paper.*
cárcere *m. jail, prison.*
cardápio *m. menu.*
cardeal *adj., n. m. cardinal.*
     Pontos cardeais. *Cardinal points.*
cardinal *adj. cardinal, principal.*
     Números cardinais. *Cardinal numbers.*
careca *adj. bald; n. m. bald person.*
CARECER *to lack, to need.*
carga *f. load, burden, freight, cargo.*
     O asno é animal de carga. *The donkey is a beast of burden.*
     Toda a carga chegou? *Did all of the cargo arrive?*
cargo *m. obligation, charge, responsibility; employment.*
     Alberto assumiu o cargo. *Albert took on the responsibility.*
carícia *f. caress.*
caridade *f. charity, pity.*
carimbar *to stamp, to seal.*
carinho *m. love, affection.*
carinhoso *adj. affectionate, kind.*
CARIOCA *adj. of the city of Rio de Janeiro; n. m. and f. inhabitant of Rio de Janeiro.*
     Ele é carioca da gema. *He's a real carioca.*
caritativo *adj. charitable.*
CARNAVAL *m. carnival.*
     É um samba de carnaval. *It's a carnival samba.*
CARNE *f. meat; flesh; pulp (of fruit).*
     Gosto mais de carne de vaca. *I like beef better.*
     Carne de carneiro. *Mutton.*
     Carne de vitela. *Veal.*
     Carne de porco. *Pork.*
     Nem carne nem peixe. *Neither fish nor fowl.*
carneiro *m. sheep.*
CARO *adj. expensive; dear (cherished).*
     Tudo é muito caro. *Everything is really expensive.*
     Meu caro amigo: *My dear friend:*
     Minha cara metade não concorda. *My better half does not agree.*
carpinteiro *m. carpenter; woodpecker.*
carregado *adj. loaded, heavy.*
carregar *to load, to burden.*
carreira *f. career, race (running).*
carreta *f. cart, wagon.*
carro *m. car, automobile; cart.*
     Carro-restaurante. *Dining car.*
     Carro eléctrico. *Streetcar* Ⓟ.
carroça *f. cart.*
CARTA *f. letter; map, chart; charter; playing card.*

     Nem uma carta recebi dele. *I didn't receive even one letter from him.*
     Carta registrada (registada). *Registered letter.*
     Carta expressa. *Special delivery letter.*
     Carta de crédito. *Letter of credit.*
     Carta de naturalização. *Naturalization papers.*
cartão *m. cardboard; card; calling card.*
     Ele me mandou (mandou-me) vários cartões (bilhetes) postais. *He sent me several postcards.*
     Deixei *(x = sh)* meu cartão. *I left my calling card.*
cartaz *m. poster, placard.*
carteira *f. wallet, pocketbook; portfolio; license.*
     Roubaram-me a carteira. *They stole my wallet.*
     Carteira de motorista. *Driver's license.*
carteiro *m. mailman, postman.*
cartilha *f. primer.*
carvalho *m. oak tree.*
carvão *m. coal, charcoal.*
CASA *f. house, home; firm, concern; room* Ⓟ.
     Ela mora na casa da tia. *She lives in her aunt's home.*
     Vamos para casa. *Let's go home.*
     Estarei em casa o dia todo. *I'll be home all day.*
     Eles estão em casa de João. *They're at John's house.*
     A casa editora ainda não me escreveu. *The publishing house did not write me yet.*
     O Presidente mora na Casa Branca. *The President lives in the White House.*
     Casa de banho Ⓟ. *Bathroom.*
casado *adj. married.*
casal *m. couple; married couple.*
casamento *m. marriage, wedding.*
casar *to marry.*
CASAR-SE *to get married.*
     Ela se casou com o filho do prefeito Ⓑ. *She married the mayor's son.*
casca *f. peel, husk, shell, bark.*
caseiro *adj. pertaining to the home, domestic; homemade.*
     É um remédio caseiro. *It's a home remedy.*
casimira *f. cashmere, woolen cloth.*
CASO *case, event.*
     É um caso raro! *It's a strange case!*
     Bem, vamos ao caso. *Well, let's get to the point.*
     Ele não faz caso de nada. *He doesn't pay attention to anything.*
     Caso que quer . . . *In case you want to . . .*
caspa *f. dandruff.*
castanha *f. chestnut.*
     Castanha-do-Pará. *Brazil nut.*

castiço *adj. pure; of good birth.*
castigar *to punish.*
castigo *m. punishment, penalty.*
casual *adj. accidental, casual.*
casualidade *f. chance, coincidence, accident.*
Eu o encontrei por casualidade. *I met him by chance.*
catálogo *m. catalog.*
catarata *f. cataract; waterfall.*
catedral *f. cathedral.*
catedrático *m. professor (especially of a university).*
categoria *f. category, class.*
catolicismo *m. Catholicism.*
católico *adj. Catholic.*
CATORZE *fourteen.*
caução *f. bond, bail, security.*
cauda *f. tail; end; extermity.*
Piano de cauda. *Grand piano.*
caudilho *m. chief, leader.*
CAUSA *f. cause, motive.*
Por causa disso, ninguém veio. *For that reason, nobody came.*
causar *to cause.*
Causou muito dano. *It caused great damage.*
cautela *f. caution, prudence.*
cauteloso *adj. cautious.*
cavala *f. mackerel.*
cavalaria *f. cavalry.*
cavaleiro *m. horseman, rider.*
cavalheiro *m. gentleman.*
cavalo *m. horse; knight (chess); jack (cards).*
cavar *to dig.*
caverna *f. cavern, cave.*
cavidade *f. cavity.*
cear *to eat supper (***ceio,*** etc.).*
cebola *f. onion.*
ceder *to grant; to give in, to yield.*
CEDO *early, soon.*
Ainda é muito cedo. *It's still too early.*
Mais cedo ou mais tarde. *Sooner or later.*
cedro *m. cedar.*
cédula *f. certificate, bill, promissory note.*
cego *adj. blind; n. m. blind person.*
cegonha *f. stork.*
cegueira *f. blindness.*
ceia *f. supper.*
CELEBRAR *to celebrate; to praise; to commemorate.*
Vamos celebrar a ocasião com uma festa no sábado. *We are going to celebrate the occasion with a party on Saturday.*
célebre *adj. famous; celebrated.*
célula *f. cell.*
CEM *hundred.*
Custa mais de cem dólares. *It costs more than a hundred dollars.*
cemento *m. cement.*

cemitério *m. cemetery.*
cena *f. scene; stage.*
Não gostei nada da primeira cena da peça. *I didn't like the first scene of the play at all.*
cenário *m. stage, setting, scenery.*
cenoura *f. carrot.*
censura *f. censorship; censure.*
censurar *to censor; to censure.*
CENTAVO *m. centavo; cent.*
centeio *m. rye.*
centelha *f. spark.*
centena *f. hundred, about a hundred.*
centenário *m. centenary.*
centésimo *adj. hundredth.*
centígrado *adj. centigrade.*
cêntimo *m. cent ($^1/_{100}$ euro).*
CENTO *hundred.*
Vasco da Gama chegou à India em mil quatrocentos e noventa e oito. *Vasco da Gama reached India in 1498.*
CENTRAL *adj. central; f. main office.*
América Central. *Central America.*
Onde é a central do correio? *Where is the main post office?*
CENTRO *m. center, middle; core; club, social circle.*
cera *f. wax.*
cerca *f. fence, hedge; enclosed land.*
cerca de *about, approximately.*
Creio que vi cerca de quarenta quadros modernos. *I believe I saw about forty modern paintings.*
cercar *to fence in, to enclose, to surround; to besiege.*
cereal *m. cereal.*
cérebro *m. brain, mind.*
cereja *f. cherry.*
cerejeira *f. cherry tree.*
cerimônia (cerimónia) *f. ceremony; formality.*
ceroulas *f. pl. long underwear, drawers.*
cerração *f. fog, mist.*
cerrado *adj. thick; dense; closed.*
cerrar *to close, to lock; to enclose.*
cerro *m. small hill.*
certeza *f. certainty.*
Temos certeza de que ele não vem hoje. *We are sure he is not coming today.*
Com certeza. *Of course.*
certidão *f. certificate.*
É preciso apresentar a certidão de nascimento. *You must show your birth certificate.*
certificado *m. certificate.*
certificar *to certify; to attest.*
CERTO *adj. sure, certain; right; true.*
Eu estou certo disso. *I'm sure of that.*
Está certo. *That's right.*

Certo amigo me disse isso. *A certain friend told me that.*

Nunca vai dar certo! *It'll never work!*

cerveja *f. beer, ale.*

cervejaria *f. brewery; beer hall.*

cervo *m. deer.*

cessar *to stop, to cease.*

cesto *m. basket.*

cetim *m. satin.*

céu *m. sky; heaven.*

cevada *f. barley.*

CHÁ *m. tea.*

Quer café ou prefere chá? *Do you want some coffee or do you prefer tea?*

Colher de chá. *Teaspoon.*

chácara *f. country house* Ⓑ.

chaleira *f. teakettle; m. and f. flatterer* Ⓑ.

chama *f. flame.*

chamada *f. call.*

Chamada interurbana. *Long-distance call.*

O professor sempre faz a chamada. *The teacher always calls the roll.*

CHAMAR *to call; to appeal; to name; to send for.*

O senhor chamou? *Did you call?*

Chamar pelo telefone. *To phone.*

Chame um táxi *(x = ks)*, por favor. *Please call a taxi.*

CHAMAR-SE *to be called, to be named.*

Como se chama ele? *What is his name?*

Ele se chama (chama-se) João Costa. *His name is John Costa.*

chaminé *f. chimney; smokestack.*

chão *m. floor, ground.*

chapa *f. plate, license plate.*

CHAPÉU *m. hat.*

Não sei onde deixei *(x = sh)* o chapéu. *I don't know where I left my hat.*

Chapéu de feltro. *Felt hat.*

Quando ela entrou, ele tirou o chapéu. *When she entered, he took off his hat.*

charlatão *m. quack, impostor.*

charque *m. beef jerky* Ⓑ.

charuto *m. cigar.*

chatear *to bore, to annoy.*

chato *adj. flat; boring.*

Ele é muito chato. *He's a big bore.*

CHAVE *f. key; wrench.*

Não posso abrir a porta sem a chave. *I can't open the door without the key.*

Chave de parafusos. *Screwdriver.*

Chave inglesa. *Monkey wrench.*

chávena *f. cup, teacup.*

chefe *m. and f. chief, director.*

CHEGADA *f. arrival.*

CHEGAR *to arrive, to come; to be enough.*

Quando chegaram? *When did you arrive?*

Chega para hoje. *That's enough for today.*

Chega aqui! *Get over here!*

Ele chegou a ser presidente da firma. *He got to be president of the firm.*

CHEIO *adj. full.*

Foi um dia bem cheio. *It was quite a full day.*

cheirar *to smell.*

cheiro *m. odor, smell.*

cheque *m. check.*

Quando viajo sempre levo comigo cheques de viagem. *When I travel I always take travelers' checks with me.*

chiado *m. squeaking, squealing, chirping.*

chiar *to squeak, to screech, to chirp.*

chifre *m. horn.*

chinela *f. house slipper.*

chinelo *m. slipper.*

chique *adj. chic, stylish.*

chiqueiro *m. pigpen.*

chispa *f. spark.*

chiste *m. joke, wisecrack.*

chita *f. calico, cotton cloth.*

choça *f. hut, shack.*

chocolate *m. chocolate.*

chofer *m. driver, chauffeur.*

Chofer de praça. *Cab driver, cabby.*

chope *m. draft beer* Ⓑ.

Chope-duplo. *A double-sized glass of draft beer; double-decker bus* Ⓑ.

choque *m. jolt, shock, collision.*

choramingar *to whimper, to whine.*

CHORAR *to cry, to weep, to mourn, to lament.*

Quando ouviram a notícia, choraram. *When they heard the news, they cried.*

Quem não chora não mama. *The squeaky wheel gets the most grease.*

choro *m. crying, weeping; type of Brazilian popular music.*

CHOVER *to rain.*

Se chover não vamos. *If it rains, we won't go.*

chumbo *m. lead.*

CHUVA *f. rain, rainfall.*

Há muita chuva em março (Março). *There is a lot of rainfall in March.*

chuveiro *m. shower.*

chuviscar *to drizzle.*

chuvisco *m. drizzle.*

cicatriz *f. scar.*

cicerone *m. and f. guide.*

ciclista *m. and f. cyclist.*

ciclone *m. cyclone.*

cidadania *f. citizenship.*

cidadão *m. citizen.*

CIDADE *f. city.*

Rio de Janeiro, cidade maravilhosa. *Rio de Janeiro, marvelous city.*

Em que cidade o senhor nasceu? *In what city were you born?*

cidra f. cider; citron.
ciência f. science.
ciente adj. aware, cognizant.
científico adj. scientific.
cifra f. figure, cipher, number; code.
cigano m. gypsy.
cigarra f. cicada.
cigarreira f. cigarette case.
CIGARRO m. cigarette.
cilindro m. cylinder, roller.
cima f. top, highest part.
   O livro está em cima da mesa. *The book is on top of the table.*
cimento m. cement.
CINCO five.
CINEMA m. movies; movie theater.
   Vamos ao cinema todos os domingos. *We go to the movies every Sunday.*
CINQÜENTA (CINQUENTA) fifty.
cinta f. belt, girdle, band.
cinto m. belt, sash.
cintura f. waist.
cinza f. ash, powder; adj. gray, ashen.
cinzeiro m. ashtray.
cinzento adj. gray, ashen.
cipreste m. cypress.
circo m. circus, ring.
circulação f. circulation.
circular to circulate.
círculo m. circle.
circunflexo (x = ks) adj. circumflex.
circunstância f. circumstance.
cirurgião m. surgeon.
cismar to think about, to ponder, to meditate.
   Em cismar sozinho à noite. *In meditation alone by night.*
cisne m. swan.
cita f. quotation, citation.
citação f. quotation, citation.
citar to quote, to cite.
ciúme m. jealousy.
   Acho que ele tem ciúmes dela. *I think he's jealous of her.*
ciumento adj. jealous.
   Ele é muito ciumento. *He is very jealous.*
civil adj. civil, civilian; courteous.
civilização f. civilization.
clamar to shout, to cry out.
claridade f. clearness; light; distinctness.
clarim m. bugle, trumpet.
clarinete m. clarinet.
CLARO adj. clear, bright; evident, intelligible, obvious; plain, frank; transparent, pure; light (color); n. m. blank, space.
   Escreva claro. *Write clearly.*
   Claro! *Of course!*
   Claro que sim! *Of course!*
   Claro que não! *Of course not!*

CLASSE f. class; kind; sort; order.
   É obra de primeira classe. *It's a top-notch work.*
clérigo m. clergyman, priest.
clero m. clergymen, clergy.
cliente m. and f. client; customer; patient.
clima m. climate.
clínica f. clinic.
cloaca f. sewer, cesspool, latrine.
clorofórmio m. chloroform.
clube m. club (social organization; nightspot).
cobertor m. blanket.
cobra f. snake.
cobrador m. collector.
COBRAR to charge, to collect, to receive (money).
   Quanto cobraram? *How much did they charge?*
   Ele está cobrando ânimo. *He is feeling much encouraged.*
cobre m. copper.
COBRIR to cover.
coçar to scratch; to thrash.
coceira f. itch; itchiness.
coche m. coach, carriage.
cochichar to whisper.
cochicho m. whispering, whisper.
cochilo m. nap, dozing; oversight Ⓑ.
coco m. coconut.
cócoras, f. pl. de cócoras squatting.
codorniz f. quail.
coelho m. rabbit.
   Matar dois coelhos com uma só cajadada. *To kill two birds with one stone.*
cofre m. safe, chest.
coincidência f. coincidence.
   Encontramo-nos por coincidência. *We met by chance.*
coincidir to coincide.
COISA (COUSA) f. thing, matter.
   Não há tal coisa. *There is no such thing.*
   Alguma coisa. *Something.*
   O senhor deseja outra coisa? *Do you want something else?*
   É a mesma coisa. *It's the same thing.*
   Será coisa de três dias. *It will take about three days.*
   Como vão as coisas? *How are things?*
coitado adj. poor, unfortunate; n. m. poor fellow, poor thing.
   Coitado de mim! *Poor me!*
cola f. glue.
colaboração f. collaboration.
colaborar to collaborate.
colar m. necklace, collar.
colcha f. bedspread.
colchão m. mattress.
coleção (colecção) f. collection.
colecionar (coleccionar) to collect.

colega *co-worker*

colégio *m. school (below college level— elementary or secondary).*

cólera *f. anger; cholera.*

colete *m. vest.*

colheita *f. crop, harvest.*

COLHER *f. spoon.*
Você esqueceu as colheres. *You forgot the spoons.*
Colher de café. *Coffee spoon.*
Colher de chá. *Teaspoon.*
Colher de sopa. *Soupspoon. Tablespoon.*

COLHER *to gather, to take, to obtain; to harvest; to pick.*
Quer colher-me algumas flores? *Would you pick some flowers for me?*

colibri *m. hummingbird.*

colina *f. hill.*

colmeia *f. beehive.*

colo *m. lap, neck.*

colocar *to place; to give employment to.*
Coloque tudo em seu lugar. *Put everything in its place.*
Meu pai o colocou numa casa de comércio. *My father got him a position in a business firm.*

colônia (colónia) *f. colony.*

colonial *adj. colonial.*

coluna *f. column, pillar.*

COM *with.*
Nós vamos com ele. *We are going with him.*
Com muito prazer. *Gladly. With great pleasure.*
Estamos com pressa. *We are in a hurry.*
Eles o prepararam com cuidado. *They prepared it carefully.*
Estou com frio. *I am cold.*

comandante *m. commander; captain of a ship.*

comando *m. command.*

comarca *f. district.*

combate *m. combat, military action.*
Pôr fora de combate. *To put out of action.*

combatente *adj. fighting; m. fighter, combatant.*
Não-combatente. *Noncombatant.*

combater *to combat, to fight.*

combinação *f. combination; slip (lady's garment).*

combinar *to combine.*

comboio *m. convoy; train* Ⓟ.

combustível *m. fuel.*

COMEÇAR *to begin, to commence.*
A que horas começa o programa? *At what time does the program begin?*

começo *m. beginning, start.*

comédia *f. comedy.*

comemoração *f. commemoration, celebration.*

comemorar *to commemorate, to celebrate.*

comentar *to comment on, to discuss.*
Ele gosta de comentar as notícias. *He likes to comment on the news.*

comentário *m. comment.*

COMER *to eat.*
Os meninos comem demais. *The children eat too much.*

comerciante *m. businessman.*

comerciar *to trade, to do business.*

comércio *m. business, trade, commerce.*

comestíveis *m. pl. food.*

cometer *to commit.*
Todos cometemos erros. *We all make mistakes.*

cometida *f. attack.*

cômico (cómico) *adj. comical, funny.*

comida *f. food.*
Comida e bebida. *Food and drink.*
Quarto e comida. *Room and board.*

comigo *with me.*
Quer ir comigo? *Do you want to go with me?*

comissão *f. commission, committee.*

comissário *m. commissioner.*

comitê (comité) *m. committee.*

comitiva *f. train, retinue.*

COMO *how, how much; as, like.*
Como vai o senhor? *How are you?*
Como se chama ela? *What is her name?*
Como o senhor quiser. *As you wish.*
Ele entrou como se estivesse em casa. *He came in as if he were in his own home.*

cômoda (cómoda) *f. dresser, chest of drawers.*

comodidade *f. comfort, ease; convenience.*
Este apartamento tem todas as comodidades. *This apartment has all the conveniences.*

cômodo (cómodo) *adj. comfortable, convenient.*

compadecer *to pity, to sympathize with.*

compaixão (x = sh) *f. compassion, pity, sympathy.*

companheiro *m. companion, comrade, colleague.*
Ele é meu companheiro de quarto. *He's my roommate.*
Eles sempre têm sido bons companheiros. *They have always been good companions.*

companhia *f. company; business firm.*
Gomes & Cia. *Gomes and Co.*

comparação *f. comparison.*

COMPARAR *to compare.*

comparecer *to appear; to attend a meeting.*

compartilhar *to share.*

compartimento *m. compartment; room.*

compatível *adj. compatible.*

compatriota *m. and f. compatriot.*

compensação *f. compensation.*

compensar *to compensate, to pay.*
competência *f. competence, ability; competition.*
competente *adj. competent, fit.*
competição *f. competition, rivalry; contest.*
competir *to compete, to contend; to behoove.*
  Compete a eles começar. *It is up to them to begin.*
complacente *adj. accommodating, agreeable, pleasing.*
complemento *m. complement.*
COMPLETAMENTE *completely.*
COMPLETAR *to complete, to finish.*
  Completar um trabalho. *To finish a task (job).*
COMPLETO *adj. complete, finished, full.*
  Por completo. *Completely.*
complicado *adj. complicated.*
complicar *to complicate.*
compor *to compose, to constitute.*
  Ele compôs dois poemas épicos. *He composed two epic poems.*
comportamento *m. behavior.*
comportar *to allow, to stand, to include.*
comportar-se *to behave, to act.*
composição *f. composition.*
compositor *m. composer; typesetter.*
composto *adj. composed, compound; n. m. compound, combination.*
compostura *f. composure; composition; falsity.*
compota *f. compote, preserves, stewed fruit.*
COMPRA *f. purchase.*
  Hoje vamos de compras. *We are going shopping today.*
comprador *m. buyer.*
COMPRAR *to buy.*
  Comprar a crédito. *To buy on credit.*
  Comprar a dinheiro. *To buy with cash.*
  Comprar a prestações. *To buy on installments.*
  Comprar por atacado. *To buy wholesale.*
  Eu comprei tudo muito barato. *I bought everything very cheap.*
COMPREENDER *to understand; to comprise, to include.*
  Compreende o que estou dizendo (a dizer)? *Do you understand what I am saying?*
  Não compreendi nada. *I didn't understand a thing.*
compreendido *adj. understood; including.*
compreensão *f. comprehension, understanding.*
compreensível *adj. comprehensible.*
compreensivo *adj. comprehensive.*
comprido *adj. long.*
comprimento *m. length.*

comprimir *to compress, to restrain, to repress.*
comprometer-se *to commit oneself.*
compromisso *m. compromise; engagement, commitment.*
comprovante *adj. confirming.*
comprovar *to prove, to confirm.*
compulsório *adj. compulsory.*
computador *m. computer.*
  Computador portátil. *Laptop computer.*
computadorizar *to computerize.*
computar *to compute.*
COMUM *adj. common.*
  Em comum. *In common.*
  De acordo comum. *By mutual consent.*
  Senso comum. *Common sense.*
comunicação *f. communication.*
  Telefonista, ponha-me em comunicação com o número . . . *Operator, connect me with number . . .*
comunicar *to communicate, to announce, to inform.*
comunidade *f. community.*
comunismo *m. communism.*
comunista *m. communist.*
conceber *to conceive.*
conceder *to grant.*
conceito *m. concept, idea.*
concelho *m. council of a municipality.*
concentrar *to concentrate.*
concepção *f. conception, idea.*
concernir *to concern.*
concerto *m. concert.*
concessão *f. concession.*
concha *f. shell.*
conciliação *f. conciliation.*
conciliar *to conciliate, to reconcile.*
conciso *adj. concise.*
concluir *to conclude, to finish; to settle.*
conclusão *f. conclusion.*
  Todos chegaram à mesma conclusão. *They all arrived at the same conclusion.*
concordância *f. agreement, harmony.*
concordar *to agree.*
concorrência *f. competition.*
concorrer *to compete; to concur.*
concreto *adj. concrete.*
concurso *m. contest, competition.*
conde *m. count.*
condecoração *f. decoration, medal.*
condenado *adj. condemned.*
condenar *to condemn, to convict; to disapprove.*
  Ele foi condenado ontem. *He was convicted yesterday.*
condição *f. condition.*
  Eles aceitaram sob a condição de que ele não voltasse. *They accepted on condition that he not return.*

Tudo está em boas condições. *Everything is in good order.*

condicionado *adj. conditioned.*
Com ar condicionado. *Air conditioned.*

condicional *adj. conditional.*

condimentar *to season.*

condiscípulo *m. classmate.*

condolência *f. condolence; sympathy.*
Aceite as minhas condolências. *Please accept my condolences.*

condor *m. condor.*

conduta *f. conduct, behavior.*

conduto *m. conduit, pipe; canal.*

condutor *m. conductor.*

CONDUZIR *to drive; to conduct; to carry; to lead.*
Este caminho conduz ao lago. *This road goes to the lake.*

confeitaria *f. confectionary, candy store.*

conferência *f. conference; lecture.*

conferencista *m. and f. lecturer.*

conferir *to confer, to bestow.*

confessar *to admit, to confess.*
Confesso que não pensei nisso. *I admit I didn't think of that.*

confiança *f. confidence, faith; familiarity.*
Ele é digno de confiança. *He is reliable.*
Eu lhe digo isto em confiança. *I'm telling you this in confidence.*
Todos têm confiança nele. *Everybody has confidence in him.*

confiar *to confide; to trust.*

confidência *f. confidence.*

confidencial *adj. confidential.*

confirmação *f. confirmation.*

confirmar *to confirm, to ratify.*

confissão *f. confession; acknowledgment.*

conflito *m. conflict, strife.*

conformar *to conform; to fit; to agree; to comply with.*

conformar-se com *to be satisfied with.*

CONFORME *according to; agreed.*
Estar conforme. *To be in agreement.*

conformidade *f. conformity; resemblance.*
De conformidade com. *In accordance with.*

confortante *adj. comforting.*

confortar *to comfort.*

confortável *adj. comfortable.*

conforto *m. comfort, ease.*

confundir *to confuse; to mistake.*

confundir-se *to become confused; to be perplexed.*

confusão *f. confusion, perplexity.*

confuso *adj. confused.*

congelar *to freeze.*

congestão *f. congestion.*

congratulação *f. congratulation.*

congratular *to congratulate.*

congregação *f. congregation.*

congresso *m. congress; assembly; conference.*

conhaque *m. cognac, brandy.*

CONHECER *to know, to understand, to be acquainted with.*
Você conhece Maria? *Do you know Maria?*
Não a conheço. *I don't know her.*
Vocês se conhecem? *Do you know each other?*
Muito prazer em conhecê-lo. *Very glad to know you.*

conhecido *adj. known; n. m. acquaintance.*
A obra dele é bem conhecida. *His work is well known.*

conhecimento *m. knowledge, understanding, acquaintance.*
Tudo chegou ao conhecimento de nossos amigos. *Everything came to the knowledge of our friends.*
Tomar conhecimento de. *To take notice of.*

conjetura (conjectura) *f. conjecture, guess.*

conjeturar (conjecturar) *to conjecture, to guess.*

conjugação *f. conjugation.*

conjugar *to conjugate.*

conjunção *f. conjunction.*

conjunto *adj. joint, united; n. m. whole.*

conjuração *f. conspiracy.*

conquista *f. conquest.*

conquistar *to conquer, to win over.*

consciência *f. conscience.*

consciente *adj. conscious, aware.*

conseguinte *adj. consequent; consecutive.*
Por conseguinte, perdemos. *Consequently, we lost.*

CONSEGUIR *to obtain, to attain, to get, to succeed in.*
Será difícil conseguir um aumento. *It will be difficult to get a raise.*
Não consegui convencê-lo. *I did not succeed in convincing him.*

conselheiro *m. member of a board (council); adviser; counselor.*

conselho *m. advice; council, advisory board.*
Seguirei sen conselho. *I will follow your advice.*
Conselho de ministros. *Cabinet.*
Conselho de guerra. *War council. Court-martial.*

consentimento *m. consent.*

consentir *to consent; to agree, to be willing; to tolerate.*
Você consente nisso? *Do you agree to that?*
Não consentirei nunca. *I'll never consent.*

consequência (consequência) *f. consequence.*
Em consequência. *Therefore. As a result.*

Você terá que aceitar as conseqüências. *You will have to accept the consequences.*

consertar *to fix, to repair.*
O senhor pode consertar meu relógio? *Can you fix my watch?*

conserto *m. repair, mending.*

conservação *f. conservation.*

conservador *adj., n. m. conservative.*

conservar *to conserve, to keep, to preserve.*
Ela não conserva nada. *She doesn't keep anything.*
Conserve à sua direita. *Keep to the right.*

conservas *f. preserves; canned food.*

consideração *f. consideration, regard.*

considerar *to consider, to take into account.*

considerável *adj. considerable, large.*

consignar *to consign, to assign.*

consigo *with him, with her, with you, with them.*
Eles o levaram consigo. *They took it with them.*

consistência *f. consistency; stability; firmness.*

consistente *adj. consistent, solid, firm.*

consistir *to consist, to be composed of.*

consoante *f. consonant.*

consolação *f. consolation.*

consolar *to console, to comfort.*

conspícuo *adj. conspicuous.*

constante *adj. constant.*

constar *to be evident; to consist of.*
Consta que eles nunca o fizeram. *The fact is that they never did it.*

constipação *f. a cold.*

constituição *f. constitution.*

constituir *to constitute.*

construção *f. construction, building.*

CONSTRUIR *to construct, to build.*

cônsul *m. consul.*

consulado *m. consulate.*

consulta *f. consultation.*

consultar *to consult, to seek advice.*
Você deve consultar um médico. *You should consult a doctor.*

consultório *m. doctor's office.*

consumidor *m. consumer.*

consumir *to consume, to use.*

consumo *m. consumption; expenditure.*
Artigos de consumo. *Consumer goods.*

CONTA *f. count; account; statement; bill; bead.*
Traga-me a conta, por favor. *Please bring me the bill.*
Ponha tudo na minha conta. *Charge it all to my account.*
Conta corrente. *Current account.*
Dar conta de. *To give an account of, to report.*
Tenha em conta que ele não sabe nada

disto. *Keep in mind that he knows nothing about this.*
Afinal de contas, que mais poderia eu ter feito? *After all, what more could I have done?*

contabilidade *f. bookkeeping, accounting.*

contador *m. accountant; purser; meter (gas, etc.).*

contagiar *to infect, to contaminate.*

contagioso *adj. contagious.*

conta-gotas *m. dropper.*

contaminar *to contaminate.*

CONTAR *to count; to tell.*
Você tem alguma coisa que me contar? *Do you have something to tell me?*
Vocês podem contar comigo. *You can count on me.*

contemplação *f. contemplation.*

contemplar *to comtemplate, to consider, to have in view.*

contemporâneo *adj., n. m. contemporary.*

contenda *f. quarrel, dispute, fight.*

contentamento *m. contentment.*

contentar *to please, to satisfy.*

CONTENTE *adj. content, happy, pleased.*
Ela está muito contente. *She is very happy.*

conter *to contain, to include, to hold.*

conter-se *to refrain, to restrain oneself.*

contestação *f. answer, reply.*

contestar *to contest; to reply.*

conteúdo *m. contents.*

contigo *with you (fam. sing.).*

contíguo *adj. contiguous; close, near.*

continente *m. continent.*

continuação *f. continuation.*

CONTINUAR *to continue.*

CONTO *m. story, tale; a thousand cruzeiros or escudos.*
Conto de fadas. *Fairy tale.*
Conto policial. *Detective story.*

CONTRA *against, contrary to, counter to.*
Ele o fez contra a sua vontade. *He did it against his will.*
Eu sou contra isso. *I am against that.*

contrabando *m. contraband; smuggling.*

contradição *f. contradiction.*
Ele diz o contrário do que sente. *He says the opposite of what he thinks.*
Ao contrário. *On the contrary.*

contradizer *to contradict.*

contrafazer *to counterfeit.*

contrafeito *adj. counterfeit.*

contrariar *to contradict; to annoy, to vex.*

contrariedade *f. mishap; disappointment; vexation.*

contrário *adj. contrary, opposite; n. m. opponent.*
Aconteceu-me o contrário. *The opposite happened to me.*

contra-senha *f. countersign; password.*
contrastar *to contrast.*
contraste *m. contrast.*
contratar *to engage, to hire; to bargain, to trade; to contract.*
contratempo *m. mishap, setback; disappointment.*
contrato *m. contract.*
contribuição *f. contribution; tax.*
contribuir *to contribute.*
controlar *to control* Ⓑ.
controle *m. control* Ⓑ.
   Fora do controle. *Out of control.*
contudo *nevertheless, however.*
conturbar *to trouble, to disturb.*
contusão *f. bruise, contusion.*
convalescença *f. convalescence.*
convenção *f. convention, agreement; pact.*
convencer *to convince.*
convencido *adj. convinced.*
conveniência *f. convenience, fitness.*
conveniente *adj. convenient, suitable.*
convento *m. convent.*
CONVERSA *f. conversation, talk, chatter.*
   Acho que é conversa demais. *In my opinion, that's enough chatter.*
   Conversa mole. *Idle chatter.*
CONVERSAÇÃO *f. conversation, talk.*
CONVERSAR *to chatter, to converse.*
   Tenho que conversar com você. *I have to talk to you.*
converter *to convert, to change.*
convés *m. deck (ship).*
convicção *f. conviction, belief, certainty.*
convidado *adj. invited; m. guest.*
convidar *to invite.*
convir *to suit; to agree.*
convite *m. invitation.*
cooperação *f. cooperation.*
cooperar *to cooperate.*
coordenar *to coordinate.*
copa *f. pantry; crown (hat); pl. hearts (cards).*
cópia *f. copy.*
   Tirar copias. *To make copies.*
copiadora *f. copier.*
   Copiadora de cor. *Color copier.*
copiar *to copy.*
COPO *m. glass (drinking); goblet, cup.*
   Por favor, um copo dágua. *A glass of water, please.*
coqueiro *m. coconut palm; palm tree.*
coquete *adj. coquettish; n. f. coquette.*
coquetel *m. cocktail, cocktail party* Ⓑ.
COR *f. color.*
   Esta cor está na moda. *This color is very stylish.*
   Esta cor vai bem com essa. *This color goes well with that one.*
   Cor fixa (x = ks). *Fast color.*

Cor viva. *Bright color*
Cor de laranja. *Orange.*
Um homem de cor. *A colored man.*
Ela vê tudo cor de rosa. *She sees everything through rose-colored glasses.*
CORAÇÃO *m. heart; core.*
   Com todo o meu coração. *With all my heart.*
   Mãos frias, coração quente. *Cold hands, warm heart.*
coragem *f. courage.*
   Coragem! *Have courage! Cheer up!*
corcovado *adj. humped; hunchbacked.*
corda *f. cord, rope; string; spring (watch).*
   Esqueci dar corda ao relógio. *I forgot to wind my watch.*
   Cordas vocais. *Vocal cords.*
cordão *m. cord, string, lace.*
   Cordões de sapato. *Shoelaces.*
cordeiro *m. lamb.*
cordel *m. twine, string, cord.*
cordial *adj. cordial, affectionate.*
cordilheira *f. mountain range.*
cordura *f. good sense.*
corneta *f. bugle, horn.*
corno *m. horn, antler.*
coro *m. choir, chorus.*
coroa *f. crown; wreath, garland.*
coroar *to crown; to complete.*
coronel *m. colonel.*
CORPO *m. body; corps.*
   Corpo e alma. *Body and soul.*
   Corpo diplomático. *Diplomatic corps.*
   Corpo de Paz. *Peace Corps.*
corredor *m. corridor; runner.*
correia *f. leather strap, leash, thong.*
CORREIO *m. mail; post office.*
   A que horas sai o correio? *At what time does the mail leave?*
   Correio aéreo. *Airmail.*
   Correio electronic. *E-mail.*
   Correio de voz. *Voice mail.*
corrente *adj. current, present (month); f. current; stream; draft (air).*
   Conta corrente. *Current account.*
   Recebi (a) sua estimada carta de 15 do corrente. *I have received your letter of the 15th of this month.*
   Sinto uma corrente de ar. *I feel a draft.*
   Estar ao corrente. *To be acquainted with. To be up-to-date on.*
   Corrente alternada. *Alternating current.*
   Corrente contínua. *Direct current.*
   Água corrente. *Running water.*
CORRER *to run; to flow; to elapse; to blow (wind); to draw (curtains).*
   Eles vêm correndo. *They come running.*
   Corra as cortinas. *Draw the curtains.*
correspondência *f. correspondence, mail.*

Eu estou em correspondência com eles. *I am in correspondence with them.*

correspondente *adj. corresponding.*

corresponder *to correspond.*

correto (correcto) *adj. correct.*

corrida *f. run, race, course.*

Corrida de cavalos. *Horse race.*

corrigir *to correct.*

corroborar *to corroborate.*

corromper *to corrupt.*

corrupção *f. corruption.*

corrupto *adj. corrupt.*

CORTAR *to cut; to cut off, to shorten.*

Esta faca não corta. *This knife doesn't cut.*

Vou cortar o cabelo. *I'm going to get a haircut.*

corte *m. cut; edge (knife); f. court, house of parliament, assembly; courting.*

cortejar *to court; to flatter.*

cortês *adj. courteous, gentle, polite.*

Ele é muito cortês. *He's very polite.*

cortesia *f. courtesy, politeness.*

cortiça *f. cork; bark.*

cortiço *m. beehive; tenement.*

cortina *f. curtain, screen.*

Cortina de ferro. *Iron curtain.*

Faça o favor de correr as cortinas. *Please draw the curtains.*

coruja *f. owl.*

corvo *m. crow, raven.*

coser *to sew.*

cosmético *adj. cosmetic.*

COSTA *f. coast, shore; pl. back.*

A costa atlântica. *The Atlantic coast.*

As costas da mão. *The back of the hand.*

Ele me deu as costas. *He turned his back on me.*

costela *f. rib; wife (fam.).*

costeleta *f. chop.*

Costeleta de porco. *Pork chop.*

costumado *adj. customary.*

costumar *to be accustomed, to be in the habit of; to accustom.*

costume *m. custom, habit, practice.*

costura *f. sewing.*

Máquina de costura. *Sewing machine.*

cotidiano *adj. daily.*

cotovelo *m. elbow.*

couraçado *adj. armored; n. m. battleship.*

couro *m. leather; hide; skin.*

cousa *f. see* **COISA.**

couve-flor *f. cauliflower.*

cova *f. cave, cavern.*

covarde *m. coward.*

cozer *to cook, to bake, to boil.*

cozinha *f. kitchen; cuisine.*

cozinhar *to cook.*

cozinheiro *m. cook, chef.*

crânio *m. skull, cranium.*

cravo *m. nail, tack; clove.*

Você deu no cravo. *You hit the nail on the head.*

crédito *m. credit; credence; reputation, standing.*

Comprar a crédito. *To buy on credit.*

Vender a crédito. *To sell on credit.*

Dar crédito. *To give credit.*

Carta de crédito. *Letter of credit.*

creme *m. cream.*

CRER *to believe, to think.*

Creio que sim. *I think so.*

Creio que não. *I think not.*

Ver é crer. *Seeing is believing.*

crescer *to grow, to increase.*

crescimento *m. growth, increase.*

criada *f. servant.*

criado *m. servant.*

CRIANÇA *f. child.*

criar *to create, to produce; to nurse; to rear; to bring up.*

criatura *f. creature, person.*

crime *m. crime.*

criminal *adj. criminal.*

criminoso *adj. criminal; n. m. outlaw, criminal.*

crioulo *adj. native; creole; n. m. creole, Portuguese dialect spoken in Cabo Verde.*

crise *f. crisis; depression.*

cristal *m. crystal.*

cristão *m. Christian.*

cristianismo *m. Christianity.*

critério *m. criterion.*

crítica *f. criticism, judgment, comment; review.*

A crítica não gostou da peça. *The critics did not like the play.*

criticar *to criticize, to judge.*

crítico *m. critic, reviewer.*

crônica (crónica) *f. chronicle; newspaper article or column.*

cronista *m. and f. chronicler; columnist.*

croquete *m. croquette.*

cruz *f. cross.*

cruzar *to cross; to cruise.*

CRUZEIRO *m. Brazilian monetary unit; large cross; cruise; cruiser (ship).*

Custa duzentos cruzeiros. *It costs 200 cruzeiros.*

Cruzeiro do Sul. *Southern Cross.*

cubano *adj. Cuban; m. Cuban.*

cubo *m. cube.*

cuecas *f. pl. men's undershorts.*

CUIDADO *m. care, attention; anxiety, worry.*

Cuidado! *Be careful!*

Ter cuidado. *To be careful.*

Cuidado com o cachorro! *Look out for the dog!*

Ao cuidado de . . . *Care of . . .*

cuidadoso *adj. careful.*

cuidar *to care, to take care, to mind, to look after.*

Quem cuida do jardim? *Who takes care of the garden?*

Cuide-se. *Take care of yourself.*

cujo *whose, of which, of whom.*

O professor Cândido, cujo livro sobre a literatura brasileira acaba de sair . . . *Professor Cândido, whose book on Brazilian literature has just come out . . .*

culpa *f. fault, guilt; sin.*

culpável *adj. guilty.*

cultivar *to cultivate; to till; to improve.*

No Brasil se cultiva (cultiva-se) muito o café. *Much coffee is grown in Brazil.*

Cultivar um talento. *To develop a talent.*

cultivo *m. farming, cultivation, tillage.*

culto *adj. well-educated; polished; n. m. worship, cult, religion.*

Ele é um homem culto. *He is a well-read man.*

cultura *f. culture; refinement.*

cultural *adj. cultural.*

cumprimentar *to greet; to congratulate.*

cumprimento *m. greeting, compliment.*

Meus cumprimentos. *My regards.*

cumprir *to carry out, to fulfill; to behoove.*

Ele sempre cumpre a palavra. *He always keeps his word.*

Eles cumpriram o curso em três anos. *They completed the course in three years.*

Cumpre-me avisá-lo . . . *I am pleased (it behooves me) to inform you . . . (business letter).*

cunha *f. wedge.*

cunhada *f. sister-in-law.*

cunhado *m. brother-in-law.*

cura *f. cure; m. priest.*

curar *to cure, to heal.*

curável *adj. curable.*

curiosidade *f. curiosity; oddity.*

curioso *adj. curious, inquisitive; strange, odd.*

Estou curioso por sabê-lo. *I'm anxious to know (it).*

cursar *to cross, to travel; to study at a university.*

curso *m. course, direction; current; course of studies.*

João fará o curso de filosofia. *John will study philosophy.*

curva *f. curve.*

custa *f. cost.*

À custa de. *At the cost of.*

CUSTAR *to cost.*

Quanto custam estes sapatos? *How much do these shoes cost?*

Custa-me crê-lo. *It's hard for me to believe it.*

Custe o que custar. *Cost what it may. Whatever the cost.*

custear *to defray expenses.*

custo *m. cost, price; difficulty.*

A todo custo. *At all costs.*

custódia *f. custody, guard, detention (legal).*

custodiar *to guard, to take into custody.*

custoso *adj. costly, expensive.*

cútis *f. skin, complexion.*

D

DA *(contr. of* **de** *+* **a***) of the, from the.*

O irmão da menina. *The girl's brother.*

Feche a porta da sala. *Close the door of the room.*

datilógrafa (dactilógrafa) *f. typist.*

datilógrafo (dactilógrafo) *m. typist.*

dádiva *f. gift, present.*

dadivoso *adj. liberal, generous.*

DAÍ *from there, of there; therefore.*

Daí a pouco. *A little later.*

dalém *from beyond* Ⓟ.

DALI *from there, of there; therefore.*

Saiu dali. *It came from over there.*

Dali a pouco. *A little later.*

dália *f. dahlia.*

dama *f. lady, dame.*

Jogo de damas. *Checkers.*

damasco *m. apricot; damask.*

danado *adj. spoiled, damaged.*

danar *to damage, to hurt.*

dança *f. dance.*

dançar *to dance.*

daninho *adj. harmful.*

dano *m. damage, loss; hurt, harm.*

DAQUELA *(contr. of* **de** *+* **aquela***) f. of that, from that.*

Não conheço nenhum professor daquela escola. *I don't know any teacher of that school.*

DAQUELE *(contr. of* **de** *+* **aquele***) m. of that, from that.*

O chapéu é daquele senhor. *The hat belongs to that man.*

DAQUI *(contr. of* **de** *+* **aqui***) from here, of here.*

Ele não é daqui. *He's not from this area.*

Daqui a oito dias. *In a week.*

DAQUILO *(contr. of* **de** *+* **aquilo***) of that, from that.*

DAR *to give; to show; to strike (hour); to hit; to take (a walk).*

Faça o favor de me dar (dar-me) o seu endereço. *Please give me your address.*

Eu lhe dou quatro dólares por esse livro. *I'll give you four dollars for that book.*
Vamos dar um passeio. *Let's take a walk.*
Vamos dar uma volta. *Let's go for a walk.*
Eu lhe dou (dou-lhe) as boas-vindas. *I welcome you.*
O relógio acaba de dar seis horas. *The clock has just struck six.*
Ele me deu as costas. *He turned his back on me.*
Vamos dar fim a todo isso. *We're going to put an end to all that.*
Isso me dá cuidado. *That worries me.* Ⓟ
Eles se dão muito bem. *They get along very well.*
Eu lhe dou (dou-lhe) a minha palavra. *I give you my word.*
É preciso dar corda ao relógio. *You must wind the watch.*
Você dá as cartas. *You deal.*
Eles vão dar uma festa no sábado. *They are going to have a party on Saturday.*
Eu dei com eles ontem. *I ran into (came upon) them yesterday.*
A mãe deu pancadas ao filho. *The mother struck her son.*
Dê-se pressa! *Hurry up!* Ⓟ
Dar um jeito. *To find a way, to finagle a solution.*
Dar-se conta de. *To realize.*
Dar à luz. *To give birth.*
Dar gritos. *To cry out.*
Dar os parabéns. *To congratulate.*
Dar a conhecer. *To make known.*
Tudo deu em nada. *It all came to naught.*
Dar de comer. *To feed.*
Dar de beber. *To give water to.*
Dar aula. *To conduct a class.*
Dá licença? *May I?*
dardo *m. dart.*
data *f. date.*
datar *to date.*
DE *of; from; for; by; on; to; with.*
Essa é a casa de meu amigo. *That's my friend's house.*
De quem é este livro? *Whose book is this?*
O que é feito dele? *What has become of him?*
O livro é dela. *The book is hers.*
Ele é do Brasil. *He's from Brazil.*
Eu sou de Lisboa. *I'm from Lisbon.*
Um copo d'água. *A glass of water.*
Uma casa de pedra. *A stone house.*
Uma xícara (x = sh) de café. *A cup of coffee.*
Máquina de costura. *Sewing machine.*
Está na hora do jantar. *It's time for dinner.*
De dia. *During the day.*
De noite. *At night.*

De nada. *Don't mention it.*
Ela está vestida de azul. *She is dressed in blue.*
De vez em quando. *From time to time.*
Aquela jovem de olhos azuis. *That girl with the blue eyes.*
Eles estão de pé. *They are standing.*
Carlos está de cama. *Charles is sick in bed.*
deão *m. dean.*
DEBAIXO *(x = sh) under, underneath.*
A carta estava debaixo dos papéis. *The letter was under the papers.*
debate *m. debate.*
debater *to debate, to discuss.*
débil *adj. feeble, weak.*
debilidade *f. feebleness, weakness.*
debilitar *to weaken, to debilitate.*
débito *m. debt.*
debruçar *to lean.*
debuxo *(x = sh) sketch.*
década *f. decade.*
decadência *f. decay, decadence; decline.*
decair *to decay, to decline, to die down.*
decano *m. dean.*
decente *adj. decent, honest; neat.*
decepção *f. disappointment.*
decidido *adj. decided; firm; determined.*
DECIDIR *to decide, to resolve, to determine.*
DECIDIR-SE *to decide, to make up one's mind.*
decifrar *to decipher, to decode.*
decímetro *m. decimeter.*
décimo *adj., n. m. tenth.*
Décimo primeiro. *Eleventh.*
Décimo segundo. *Twelfth.*
Décimo terceiro. *Thirteenth.*
Décimo quarto. *Fourteenth.*
Décimo quinto. *Fifteenth.*
Décimo sexto. *Sixteenth.*
Décimo sétimo. *Seventeenth.*
Décimo oitavo. *Eighteenth.*
Décimo nono. *Nineteenth.*
decisão *f. decision, determination.*
decisivo *adj. decisive.*
declaração *f. declaration.*
declarar *to declare, to state; to testify.*
Tem alguma coisa a declarar? *Do you have anything to declare (customs)?*
declinar *to decline.*
decoração *f. decoration; stage scenery.*
decorar *to decorate; to learn by heart, to memorize.*
decoro *m. decency, decorum, honor.*
decotado *adj. low-necked.*
decrescente *adj. decreasing.*
decrescer *to decrease.*
decrescimento *m. decrease.*
decretar *to decree.*

decreto *m. decree.*
dedal *m. thimble.*
dedicação *f. dedication.*
dedicado *adj. dedicated, devoted.*
dedicar *to dedicate; to devote.*
  Ele se dedicou à pintura. *He devoted himself to painting.*
dedicatória *f. dedication.*
DEDO *m. finger; toe.*
  Dedo mínimo. *Little finger.*
  Dedo indicador. *Index finger.*
  Dedo polegar. *Thumb.*
  Dedo médio. *Middle finger.*
  Dedo anular. *Ring finger.*
dedução *f. deduction.*
deduzir *to deduce, to understand.*
defeito *m. fault, defect.*
defeituoso *adj. defective.*
defender *to defend.*
defensiva *f. defensive.*
defensor *m. supporter, defender.*
defesa *f. defense.*
deficiência *f. deficiency.*
deficit *m. shortage, deficit.*
definição *f. definition, explanation.*
definido *adj. definite.*
definir *to define, to determine.*
definitivo *adj. definitive.*
deformação *f. deformation.*
deformar *to deform.*
deformidade *f. deformity.*
defraudar *to defraud, to swindle.*
defronte *facing.*
defunto *adj. deceased; n. m. deceased; dead person.*
degelo *m. thawing; thaw.*
degeneração *f. degeneration.*
degenerar *to deteriorate, to degenerate.*
degradante *adj. degrading.*
degradar *to degrade.*
degrau *m. step; rung (ladder); degree.*
degredar *to banish, to exile.*
DEITAR *to throw, to cast, to lay.*
  Isso é deitar lenha no fogo. *That's adding fuel to the fire.*
DEITAR-SE *to lie down, to go to bed.*
  Nós nos deitamos às dez. *We go to bed at ten.*
DEIXAR *(x = sh) to leave, to let; to quit, to give up.*
  Deixe-me vê-lo. *Let me see it.*
  Não nos deixaram entrar. *They did not let us enter.*
  Posso deixar meus livros aqui? *May I leave my books here?*
  Deixe para amanhã. *Leave it for tomorrow.*
  Deixe-me em paz! *Leave me alone!*
  Ele deixou de escrever-me. *He stopped writing me.*

  Ele deixou seu emprego. *He gave up his job.*
  Isso deixa muito a desejar. *That leaves much to be desired.*
  Não deixe de telefonar-me. *Don't fail (be sure) to telephone me.*
  Deixar um recado. *To leave a message.*
delegação *f. delegation.*
delegacia *f. delegacy.*
  Delegacia de polícia. *Police headquarters.*
delegado *m. delegate, deputy, commissioner.*
deleitar *to please, to delight.*
deleite *m. delight, pleasure.*
delgado *adj. thin, slender.*
deliberação *f. deliberation.*
deliberar *to deliberate.*
delicado *adj. delicate; dainty, nice; exquisite; fragile.*
delícia *f. delight, pleasure.*
delicioso *adj. delicious, delightful.*
  A sobremesa está deliciosa. *The dessert is delicious.*
delinqüente (delinquente) *m. delinquent, offender.*
delirar *to rave, to be delirious.*
delírio *m. delirium, raving; enthusiasm; frenzy.*
delito *m. misdemeanor, offense, crime.*
DEMAIS *other; rest; too much, too many.*
  Custa demais. *It costs too much.*
  Você bebe demais. *You drink too much.*
  Dois é bom; três é demais. *Two's company, three's a crowd.*
  Os demais. *The others; the rest.*
demanda *f. claim, demand, request; lawsuit.*
demandar *to demand, to claim; to take legal action; to enter a claim; to sue.*
demarcação *f. demarcation.*
demasiado *too much; too; excessive.*
demência *f. insanity, madness.*
demente *adj. insane, crazy.*
demissão *f. dismissal; firing; resignation.*
demitido *adj. dismissed; fired.*
demitir *to dismiss, to fire.*
demitir-se *to resign.*
democracia *f. democracy.*
democrata *m. and f. democrat.*
democrático *adj. democratic.*
demolição *f. demolition.*
demolir *to demolish.*
demônio (demónio) *m. devil, demon.*
  Como um demônio. *Like the devil.*
demonstração *f. demonstration.*
demonstrar *to demonstrate, to prove, to show.*
demora *f. delay.*
  Sem mais demora. *Without further delay.*
demorar(-se) *to delay, to tarry; to stay.*
  Você se demorou muito. *You are very late.*
denegar *to refuse, to deny.*

denominação f. denomination.
denominar to name.
denotar to denote, to indicate, to express.
densidade f. density.
denso adj. dense, thick.
dentadura f. denture, set of teeth.
dental adj. dental.
DENTE m. tooth.
    Escova de dentes. Toothbrush.
    Dente molar. Molar.
    Dor de dentes. Toothache.
    Dentes postiços. False teeth.
dentifrício m. toothpaste, dentifrice.
dentista m. and f. dentist.
DENTRO within, inside.
    Dentro de alguns dias. Within a few days.
    Dentro em pouco. In a short while.
    Que está acontecendo (a acontecer) lá
      dentro? What's going on inside there?
denúncia f. denunciation; accusation.
denunciar to denounce, to accuse; to give
    notice; to inform.
departamento m. department.
dependência f. dependence, dependency;
    annex.
DEPENDER to depend, be dependent on.
    Muito depende do que você faça. A great
      deal depends on what you do.
deplorar to deplore, to be sorry, to regret.
    Deploro muito o acontecido. I'm sorry
      about what happened.
deplorável adj. deplorable.
DEPOIS after, afterward, later.
    Dois dias depois. Two days later.
    Depois de pagar a conta ele saiu. After he
      payed the bill he left.
    Depois de amanhã. The day after
      tomorrow.
deportar to deport.
depositar to deposit, to place; to put in a safe
    place; to entrust.
    Eles depositaram o dinheiro. They
      deposited the money.
depósito m. deposit; depot; warehouse;
    reservoir; tank.
    Depósito de bagagem. Baggage room.
    Depósito de água. Water reservoir.
DEPRESSA fast; rapidly; in haste.
    Mais depressa! Faster!
    Depressa! Hurry!
depressão f. depression.
deprimir to depress.
deputado m. deputy, congressman.
derivar to derive.
derradeiro adj. last, final.
derramamento m. spilling, shedding.
derramar to spill; to shed; to scatter; to
    spread.
derredor around, about.

derreter to melt, to dissolve.
derribamento m. knocking down, felling.
derribar to demolish, to knock down, to bring
    down.
derrocar to overthrow; to demolish; to
    destroy.
derrota f. defeat, rout; ship's course.
derrotar to rout, to defeat.
derrubar to knock down, to bring down, to
    overthrow.
desabafar to free, to uncover; to unburden
    oneself.
desabitado adj. uninhabited, unoccupied.
desabitar to vacate.
desabotoar to unbutton.
desabrido adj. rude, insolent.
desabrigado adj. uncovered; without shelter;
    exposed.
desabrigar to uncover; to leave without
    shelter.
desabrigo m. lack of shelter.
desabrochar to unbutton, to unclasp, to
    unfasten; to open (flowers).
    Desabrochar-se. To free oneself.
desacerto m. mistake, error.
desacordo m. disagreement.
desacreditar to discredit.
desafiar to challenge, to defy.
desafinar to get out of tune, to play out of
    tune.
desafio m. challenge; competition.
desafogar-se to unburden oneself.
desafogo m. ease, relief.
desafortunado adj. unlucky, unfortunate.
desagradar to displease.
desagradável adj. unpleasant, disagreeable.
    Tudo isso foi muito desagradável. It was
      all very unpleasant.
desagradecer to be ungrateful.
desagradecido adj. ungrateful.
desagrado m. displeasure, discontent.
desagravar to vindicate, to avenge.
desagravo m. amends, vindication.
desaguamento m. drainage, draining.
desaguar to drain.
desairoso adj. clumsy, awkward.
desalentar to discourage.
desalento m. discouragement, dismay.
desalojar to dispossess, to evict; to dislodge;
    to drive out.
desalugado adj. vacant, unrented.
    Atualmente o apartamento está
      desalugado. At present, the apartment
      is vacant.
desalugar to vacate.
desamparado adj. abandoned.
desanimado adj. discouraged.
desanimar to discourage.
desânimo m. discouragement.

32

desaparecer *to disappear.*
  Meu cachorro desapareceu. *My dog disappeared.*

desapercebido *adj. unprepared, not ready.*

desaprovar *to disapprove of.*

desaproveitar *to misuse, not to make good use of.*

desarmado *adj. unarmed.*

desarmar *to disarm; to dismount, to take apart.*

desarrolhar *to uncork.*

desassossegar *to disturb.*

desassossego *uneasiness, restlessness.*

desastre *m. disaster, calamity.*

desatar *to untie, to loosen.*

desatento *adj. inattentive, thoughtless, negligent.*

desatino *m. lack of tact; folly, madness.*

desbaratar *to thwart, to upset (a plan); to destroy; to disperse, to rout, to spoil, to run.*

descabelado *adj. disheveled; hairless; impetuous.*

descalabro *m. calamity, great loss.*

descalçar *to take off shoes, gloves.*
  Ela se sentou e se descalçou (Ela sentou-se e descalçou-se). *She sat down and took her shoes off.*

descalço *adj. barefoot.*

descamisado *adj. shirtless.*

DESCANSAR *to rest.*
  O senhor não quer descansar um pouco? *Don't you want to rest a little?*

descanso *m. rest, calm, support.*

descarado *adj. brazen, impudent.*

descarga *f. discharge, unloading.*

descargo *m. discharge of an obligation.*

DESCARREGAR *to unload, to discharge; to fire (a gun).*
  Vão descarregar o navio amanhã. *They will unload the ship tomorrow.*

descarrilamento *m. derailment.*

descarrilar *to become derailed.*

descartar *to discard, to dismiss.*

descendência *f. descent, origin.*

descendente *adj. descendent; n. m. and f. descendant.*

descender *to descend from.*

descenso *m. descent.*

DESCER *to descend, to go down; to drop.*
  Desça já! *Come down right away!*

descoberta *f. discovery.*

descoberto *adj. discovered, uncovered; bareheaded.*

descobrimento *m. discovery.*

DESCOBRIR *to discover, to uncover; to find out; to disclose.*
  Descobrimos que não era verdade. *We found out that it was not true.*

O Brasil foi descoberto em mil e quinhentos. *Brazil was discovered in 1500.*

descolorido *adj. discolored, faded.*

descomedido *adj. immoderate; excessive; impolite; rude.*

descompor *to discompose, to disarrange.*

descompor-se *to become upset.*

descomposto *adj. out of order; upset.*

desconcertante *adj. disconcerting; confusing.*

desconcertar *to disturb, to confuse, to baffle.*

desconfiança *f. distrust.*

desconfiar *to distrust, to suspect.*
  Nós desconfiamos deles. *We distrust them.*

desconhecer *not to recognize, not to know; to ignore.*

desconhecido *adj. unknown; n. m. stranger.*
  Quem é aquele desconhecido? *Who is that stranger?*

desconhecimento *m. ignorance; ingratitude.*

desconsiderado *adj. thoughtless, inconsiderate.*

desconsolação *f. disconsolation.*

desconsolador *adj. disheartening, sad.*

descontar *to discount, to deduct.*

descontentamento *m. discontent, dissatisfaction.*

descontente *adj. discontented.*

descortês *adj. discourteous, impolite.*

descoser *to unstitch, to rip.*

descrédito *m. discredit.*

DESCREVER *to describe.*

descrição *f. description.*

descuidado *adj. careless; negligent; slovenly.*

descuidar *to neglect, to overlook.*
  Não descuide de preparar a lista. *Don't neglect to prepare the list.*

descuido *m. negligence, carelessness; omission, oversight.*

desculpa *f. excuse, apology.*

desculpar *to excuse, to pardon.*

DESCULPE! *Excuse me! Pardon me! I'm sorry!*

DESDE *since, after, from.*
  Ela está de cama desde ontem. *She's been (sick) in bed since yesterday.*
  Desde então. *Since then.*
  Desde criança. *From childhood.*
  Desde agora. *From now on.*
  Desde já. *Immediately, from now on.*

desdém *m. disdain, scorn, contempt.*

desdenhar *to disdain, to scorn.*

desdita *f. misfortune, calamity, unhappiness.*

desditado *adj. wretched; unfortunate; unhappy.*

desdizer *to retract, to deny, to contradict.*

DESEJAR *to desire, to wish.*
  Não desejo nada. *I don't want anything.*

João deseja falar com você. *John wants to talk to you.*

Eu lhe desejo felicidade. *I wish you happiness.*

desejável *adj. desirable.*

DESEJO *m. desire, wish.*

Esses são (os) meus desejos. *Those are my wishes.*

desejoso *adj. desirous.*

desembaraçar *to free, to disentangle.*

desembaraçar-se *to get rid of.*

desembarcadouro *m. landing place, dock.*

desembarcar *to disembark, to go ashore.*

desembarque *m. landing.*

desembolsar *to pay out, to disburse.*

desembolso *m. disbursement.*

desempacotar *to unpack.*

desempenhar *to perform; to accomplish; to carry out; to redeem, to take out of pawn; to free from debt.*

O ator principal desempenhou bem seu papel. *The main actor (the male lead) played his part well.*

desemprego *m. unemployment.*

desencantar *to disappoint, to disillusion.*

desenfreado *adj. unbridled, unrestrained.*

desenganado *disappointed, disillusioned.*

desenganar *to disappoint, to disillusion.*

desengano *m. disappointment, disillusionment.*

desenhar *to design, to sketch.*

desenho *m. design, sketch.*

desenlace *m. outcome, result, dénouement.*

O desenlace da peça é muito fraco. *The play's dénouement is very weak.*

desenredar *to disentangle.*

desenredo *m. outcome, result, dénouement.*

desenrolar *to unwind, to unroll.*

desentender *to misunderstand.*

desentendido *adj. not understanding; misunderstood.*

desentoar *to be out of tune.*

desenvoltura *f. ease, boldness; impudence.*

DESENVOLVER *to develop, to grow; to unfold.*

desenvolvido *adj. developed.*

desenvolvimento *m. development.*

desequilibrar *to unbalance.*

desertar *to desert.*

deserto *adj. deserted; n. m. desert.*

A cidade ficou deserta. *The city remained deserted.*

desertor *m. deserter.*

desesperação *f. desperation, despair; fury.*

desesperado *adj. hopeless; desperate; furious.*

desesperar *to despair; to exasperate.*

Isso me desespera. *That exasperates me.*

desespero *m. desperation, despair; fury.*

desfalecer *to faint; to weaken.*

desfalecimento *m. faint; weakness.*

desfazer *to undo; to take apart; to dissolve.*

Foi preciso desfazer a maior parte do que elas tinham feito. *It was necessary to undo most of what they had done.*

desfeito *adj. destroyed; in pieces; undone.*

desfiar *to ravel, to fray.*

desfigurar *to disfigure; to misshape; to distort.*

desfilar *to parade, to march in review.*

desfile *m. parade, review.*

desfolhar *to strip (as of leaves).*

desfrutar *to enjoy; to make fun of.*

desgastar *to wear out.*

desgaste *m. wear and tear.*

desgostar *to displease.*

desgosto *m. displeasure; sorrow.*

Ela sofreu muitos desgostos. *She suffered many sorrows.*

desgraça *f. misfortune, sorrow.*

Que desgraça! *What a misfortune!*

Por desgraça. *Unfortunately.*

Nunca uma desgraça vem só. *It never rains but it pours.*

desgraçado *adj. unfortunate, unlucky; unhappy; m. poor soul, wretch.*

Ele é um desgraçado. *He's a poor (unfortunate) soul.*

designar *to designate, to appoint.*

desígnio *m. design; plan.*

desigual *adj. uneven.*

desigualar *to make uneven.*

desigualdade *f. inequality; unevenness.*

desilusão *f. disillusion.*

desinfestar *to disinfest.*

desinfetante *adj., n. m. disinfectant.*

desinfetar *to disinfect.*

desinteresse *m. disinterest.*

desistir *to desist; to give up.*

desleal *adj. unfaithful; disloyal; bad-faith.*

deslealdade *f. unfaithfulness; disloyalty.*

desligado *adj. disconnected; off (light, radio, etc.).*

desligar *to disconnect; to turn off.*

Faça o favor de desligar o televisor. *Please turn off the TV.*

Espere um momento; não desligue. *Wait a minute; don't hang up (telephone).*

deslizar *to slip, to slide.*

deslize *m. slip, slipping.*

deslocação *f. dislocation; displacement.*

deslocar *to dislocate; to displace.*

deslumbramento *m. dazzling (great) light.*

deslumbrar *to dazzle, to daze.*

desmaiar *to faint, to turn pale.*

desmaio *m. faint, fainting spell; paleness.*

desmedido *adj. immoderate, excessive.*

desmemoriado *adj. forgetful.*

desmentir *to deny, to contradict.*

desmobiliar (desmobilar) *to remove the furniture.*

desmontar *to dismount; to take apart (a machine, etc.).*

desmoralizado *adj. demoralized.*

desmoralizar *to demoralize.*

desnatar *to skim (milk).*

desnudar *to undress, to bare.*

desnudo *adj. naked.*

desobedecer *to disobey.*

desobediência *f. disobedience.*

desobediente *adj. disobedient.*

desocupado *adj. not busy; unemployed.*
> Eu lhe falarei quando você estiver desocupado. *I'll speak to you when you are not busy.*

desocupar *to vacate, to empty.*

desonesto *adj. dishonest; indecent.*

desonra *f. dishonor; disgrace.*
> Ser pobre não é desonra. *Poverty is no disgrace.*

desonrar *to dishonor; to disgrace.*

desonroso *adj. dishonorable; disgraceful.*

desordem *f. disorder.*

desordenado *adj. disorderly, unruly.*
> A vida do Eduardo é bastante desordenada. *Edward's life is pretty wild.*

desorganizar *to disorganize.*

desorientar *to lead astray; to confuse.*

despachar *to dispatch, to forward, to expedite, to send.*

despedaçar *to tear or break into bits.*

despedida *f. farewell; dismissal.*
> A despedida foi uma ocasião muito triste. *The farewell was a very sad occasion.* Jantar de despedida. *Farewell dinner.*

despedir *to send away, to dismiss.*

despedir-se *to say farewell, to say good-bye to; to take leave.*
> Despedimo-nos deles na estação. *We said good-bye to them at the station.*

despeito *m. spite.*
> A despeito de. *In spite of.*

despejar *to empty; to throw out.*

despensa *f. pantry.*

desperdiçar *to waste.*

desperdício *m. waste.*

despertador *m. alarm clock.*

despertar *to awaken; to wake up.*

desperto *adj. awake.*

DESPESA *f. expense, cost.*
> Cada ano tenho ainda mais despesas. *Each year I have even more expenses.* Sempre há despesas imprevistas. *There are always some unforeseen expenses.*

DESPIR *to undress; to strip.*
> Ela se despiu e deitou-se. *She undressed and went to bed.*

despistar *to throw off the track, to mislead.*

despojar *to despoil; to strip.*

desposar *to marry.*

déspota *m. and f. despot.*

desprazer *to displease; displeasure.*

desprender *to unpin; to unfasten; to separate.*

desprendido *adj. unfastened; generous.*

despreocupado *adj. unconcerned.*

despreocupar *not to worry.*

desprezar *to despise, to scorn; to slight; to look down on.*

desprezo *m. contempt, scorn.*
> Todos o trataram com desprezo. *Everyone treated him with contempt.*

desproporcionado *adj. disproportionate, unequal.*

despropósito *m. nonsense, absurdity; excessive amount.*

desprovido *adj. lacking.*

desqualificar *to disqualify.*

desquitar *to free; to separate.*

desquitar-se *to separate legally.*

desquite *m. (kind of) legal separation.*
> O casamento terminou por desquite. *The marriage ended in separation.*

destacamento *m. detachment.*

destacar *to detach, to stand out.*

destapar *to uncover, to open.*

desterrado *adj. exiled, banished; n. m. exile.*

desterrar *to exile, to banish, to deport.*
> Alguns dos chefes foram desterrados. *Some of the leaders were exiled.*

destinar *to appoint; to destine.*

destinatário *m. addressee.*
> Escreva no envelope o nome do destinatário. *Write the name of the addressee on the envelope.*

destino *m. fate, destiny; destination.*
> Com destino a Lisboa. *Bound for Lisbon.*

destreza *f. skill.*

destro *adj. skillful, adroit.*

destróier (destruidor) *m. destroyer (ship).*

destruição *f. destruction.*

destruidor *adj. destructive; n. m. destroyer.*

destruir *to destroy.*
> É mais fácil destruir (do) que construir. *It is easier to destroy than to build.*

desumanidade *f. inhumanity.*

desumano *adj. inhumane, inhuman.*

desvanecer *to vanish; to dispel.*

desvantagem *f. disadvantage.*

desvantajoso *adj. disadvantageous.*

desvão *m. attic; hiding place.*

desvelar *to keep awake; to watch over; to unveil.*

desvelo *m. watching over; solicitude.*

desventurado *adj. unfortunate.*

desviar *to divert, to deviate, to dissuade.*
> Ele se desviou do assunto. *He digressed from the subject.*

desvio *m. deviation; detour.*
detalhe *m. detail.*
    Conte-me em detalhe o que aconteceu. *Tell me in detail what happened.*
    Detalhes biográficos. *Biographical data.*
detenção *f. detention.*
DETER *to detain, to hold back, to stop.*
    Meu amigo me deteve. *My friend detained me.*
detergente *adj., n. m. detergent.*
deteriorar *to deteriorate.*
determinação *f. determination, decision, courage.*
    Ele sempre fala com determinação. *He always speaks with conviction.*
determinado *adj. determined, resolute.*
determinar *to determine, to decide.*
determinar-se *to resolve, to make up one's mind.*
DETER-SE *to hold oneself back; to delay; to stop.*
detestar *to detest, to abhor.*
detestável *adj. detestable.*
detetive (detective) *m. detective.*
detido *adj. detained; arrested.*
    O ladrão foi detido pela polícia. *The thief was arrested by the police.*
DETRÁS *behind.*
    Detrás da porta. *Behind the door.*
    Falam dele por detrás. *They talk about him behind his back.*
DEUS *God.*
    Meu Deus! *Good Lord! Heavens!*
    Se Deus quiser. *God willing.*
    Pelo amor de Deus! *For heaven's sake!*
    Deus me livre! *Heaven forbid!*
    Graças a Deus! *Thank God!*
    O homem propõe e Deus dispõe. *Man proposes, and God disposes.*
    Deus lhe pague! *God bless you!*
DEVAGAR *slow, slowly.*
    Devagar se vai ao longe. *Easy does it.*
    Faça o favor de falar mais devagar. *Please speak more slowly.*
devastação *f. devastation.*
devastar *to devastate, to ruin.*
DEVER *to owe; should, must, ought; m. duty, task.*
    Quanto lhe devo? *How much do I owe you?*
    Devemos ir já. *We should go now.*
    Você devia comer mais. *You should eat more.*
    Que devemos fazer? *What should we do?*
    Ele sempre cumpre o seu dever. *He always does his duty.*
deveras *really, truly.*
devido *adj. due; owing to, on account of; proper.*

Devido à hora, não esperemos mais. *Owing to the time, let's not wait any longer.*
devoção *f. restitution, return.*
devolver *to return, to give back.*
    João nunca me devolveu o dinheiro. *John never returned the money to me.*
devorar *to devour, to consume.*
devoto *adj. devout, pious; devoted.*
DEZ *ten.*
DEZANOVE *nineteen* Ⓟ.
DEZASSEIS *sixteen* Ⓟ.
DEZASSETE *seventeen* Ⓟ.
DEZEMBRO *December.*
DEZENOVE *nineteen* Ⓑ.
DEZESSEIS *sixteen* Ⓑ.
DEZESSETE *seventeen* Ⓑ.
DEZOITO *eighteen.*
DIA *m. day.*
    Bom dia! *Good morning!*
    Que dia é hoje? *What day is it?*
    Daqui a cinco dias. *Five days from now.*
    Estarei em casa o dia todo. *I'll be home all day.*
    Eu o vejo todos os dias. *I see him every day.*
    De dia. *During the day.*
    Um dia sim um dia não. *Every other day.*
    No dia seguinte. *On the following day.*
    De dia em dia. *From day to day.*
    Dia feriado. *Holiday.*
    Dia de trabalho. *Workday.*
    Dia útil. *Workday. Weekday.*
    Dia de Ano Bom. *New Year's Day.*
    De quatro em quatro dias. *Every four days.*
    O dia todo. *All day long.*
    Dia de folga. *Day off.*
diabete, diabetes *m. and f. diabetes.*
diabo *m. devil.*
    Pobre diabo! *Poor devil! Poor fellow!*
    Pintar o diabo. *To raise the devil.*
diagnóstico *adj. diagnostic; n. m. diagnosis.*
diagrama *m. diagram, chart.*
dialeto (dialecto) *m. dialect.*
diálogo *m. dialog.*
diamante *m. diamond.*
diâmetro *m. diameter.*
DIANTE *before, in front, in the presence of.*
    Ele está esperando diante do clube. *He is waiting in front of the club.*
    Daqui em diante. *From now on.*
dianteira *f. front, lead.*
dianteiro *adj. leading, front; m. forward (sports).*
DIÁRIO *adj. daily; n. m. daily, daily newspaper; diary.*
    O diário ainda não chegou. *The paper isn't here yet.*

Eu gostaria de ver o diário dela. *I'd like to see her diary.*

diarréia (diarreia) *f. diarrhea.*

dicionário *m. dictionary.*

dieta *f. diet.*

difamação *f. defamation.*

difamar *to defame.*

DIFERENÇA *f. difference.*

Partir a diferença. *To split the difference.*

DIFERENTE *adj. different.*

diferir *to defer, to put off; to differ.*

DIFÍCIL *adj. difficult.*

A lição é muito difícil. *The lesson is very difficult.*

dificuldade *f. difficulty.*

dificultar *to make difficult, to obstruct.*

dificultoso *adj. difficult.*

difteria *f. diphtheria.*

difundir *to diffuse; to divulge; to broadcast.*

difusão *f. diffusion; broadcasting.*

digerir *to digest.*

digestão *f. digestion.*

dignar-se *to deign, to condescend.*

dignidade *f. dignity.*

digno *adj. deserving, worthy; honorable.*

Digno de confiança. *Trustworthy.*

digressão *f. digression.*

dilação *f. delay.*

dilatar *to put off, to delay; to expand.*

dilema *m. dilemma.*

dileto *adj. loved, beloved.*

diligência *f. diligence; legal arrangement; stagecoach.*

diligente *adj. diligent; active.*

diluir *to dilute.*

dilúvio *m. flood.*

dimensão *f. dimension.*

diminuir *to diminish, to decrease.*

diminutivo *adj. diminutive.*

diminuto *adj. diminutive, minute.*

dinamite *f. dynamite.*

dínamo *m. dynamo.*

dinheirão *m. large amount of money.*

DINHEIRO *m. money, currency.*

Dinheiro em caixa *(x = sh). Cash on hand.*

Estou sem dinheiro. *I'm broke.*

Dinheiro é um bom companheiro mas mal conselheiro. *Money is a good friend but a bad master.*

diploma *m. diploma.*

diplomacia *f. diplomacy.*

diplomático *adj. diplomatic.*

DIREÇÃO (DIRECÇÃO) *f. direction; address; guidance; management; administration.*

O volante de direção. *Steering wheel.*

Em direção a. *Toward.*

DIREITO *adj. straight, direct; proper; n. m.*

law, justice; claim, title; right; royalty; duty (import), tax.

À direita. *To the right. On the right.*

A mão direita. *The right hand.*

Faculdade de direito. *Law school.*

É preciso proteger os direitos do indivíduo. *It is necessary to protect the rights of the individual.*

Siga sempre direito. *Continue straight ahead.*

O senhor não tem direito a queixar-se *(x = sh). You have no right to complain.*

Direitos. *Rights. Fees. Duties.*

DIRETO (DIRECTO) *adj. direct, straight; nonstop; frank.*

Este trem (este comboio) é direto? *Is this a through train?*

DIRETOR (DIRECTOR) *adj. directing, managing; n. m. director, manager, administrator.*

Diretor de escola. *Principal (school).*

Diretor geral. *General manager.*

diretório (directório) *m. directory, directorate.*

DIRIGIR *to direct; to address; to conduct, to control, to guide; to drive.*

Vou dirigir-lhe uma carta. *I am going to write a letter to him.*

Ela sabe dirigir (um) automóvel? *Does she know how to drive a car?*

dirigir-se *to address oneself to, to speak to; to apply.*

A quem devo dirigir-me? *To whom should I apply?*

O senhor se dirige a nós? *Are you speaking to us?*

dirigível *m. dirigible.*

discar *to dial (telephone)* Ⓑ.

discernante *adj. discerning, discriminating.*

discernimento *m. discernment.*

discernir *to discern; to distinguish.*

disciplina *f. discipline.*

discípulo *m. disciple, follower; student.*

disco *m. disk; record (phonograph); dial (telephone).*

disco compacto *m. compact disk.*

Disco compacto em ROM. *CD-ROM.*

disco rígido *m. hard disk.*

discordante *adj. discordant.*

discórdia *f. discord, disagreement; dissension.*

discrepância *f. discrepancy.*

discrepar *to disagree, to differ.*

discreto *adj. discreet.*

discurso *m. speech.*

Fazer um discurso. *To make a speech.*

discussão *f. discussion; dispute.*

DISCUTIR *to discuss; to argue.*

disenteria *f. dysentery.*

disfarçar-se *to disguise.*

disfarce *m. disguise; mask.*

díspar *adj. unequal.*

disparar *to shoot, to fire, to discharge.*

disparatado *adj. nonsensical, absurd.*

disparatar *to blunder; to talk nonsense.*

disparate *m. nonsense.*

disparo *m. discharge, shot.*

dispendioso *adj. expensive, costly.*

dispensar *to dispense, to exempt; to bestow, to extend.*

dispensário *m. dispensary.*

disperso *adj. dispersed, scattered.*

disponível *adj. available.*

dispor *to dispose, to arrange, to provide for; to determine; to prepare; m. disposal.*
     Eu estou ao seu dispor. *I'm at your disposal.*
     Disponho de pouco tempo. *I have very little time now.*
     O homem põe, Deus dispõe. *Man proposes, God disposes.*

disposição *f. disposition; service; state of mind, condition.*
     Estou à sua disposição. *I'm at your disposal.*
     Ela está com disposição de aceitar. *She is inclined to accept.*

disposto *adj. disposed, ready, inclined; arranged.*
     Eles estão dispostos a fazê-lo. *They are inclined to do it.*
     Eu estou bem disposto. *I feel fine.*

disputa *f. dispute, quarrel; contest.*

disputar *to dispute, to quarrel.*

disquete *m. diskette, floppy disk.*

disseminar *to disseminate; to scatter.*

dissenção *f. dissension, strife.*

dissidente *adj. dissident; n. m. dissenter; nonconformist.*

dissimulação *f. dissimulation; pretense.*

dissimular *to pretend; to disguise.*

dissolver *to dissolve, to melt; to break up.*

dissuadir *to dissuade; to deter.*

DISTÂNCIA *f. distance.*
     É a pouca distância. *It's not far.*

DISTANTE *adj. far, distant.*

distinção *f. distinction; discrimination; difference.*
     Ele é um homem de grande distinção. *He is a very distinguished man.*
     Aqui é preciso fazer distinção. *It is necessary to make a distinction here.*

distinguir *to distinguish; to discriminate; to tell apart.*
     Não posso distinguir um do outro. *I can't tell one from the other.*

distinguir-se *to distinguish oneself.*

DISTINTO *adj. distinct; different; distinguished.*

Um homem distinto. *A man of distinction.*

distração (distracção) *f. distraction; absentmindedness.*

distraído *adj. inattentive, absentminded.*

distrair *to distract; to entertain.*

distrair-se *to enjoy oneself.*
     Ela se distraiu na festa. *She had a good time at the party.*

distribuição *f. distribution.*

distribuidor *adj. distributing; n. m. distributor.*

distribuir *to distribute; to divide; to allot, to allocate.*

distrito *m. district; region.*

disturbar *to disturb.*

distúrbio *m. disturbance.*

ditado *m. dictation; saying, proverb.*

ditador *m. dictator.*

ditar *to dictate.*
     Escreva o que vou ditar. *Write what I am going to dictate.*

dito *adj. said; n. m. saying.*
     Dito e feito. *No sooner said than done.*

ditongo *m. diphthong.*

divã *m. divan, couch.*

divagação *f. wandering, digression.*

divergência *f. divergence.*

diversão *f. diversion, amusement, recreation.*

diversidade *f. diversity, variety.*

DIVERSO *adj. different, diverse; pl. several, various.*
     Eu o vi em diversas ocasiões. *I saw him on several occasions.*

DIVERTIDO *adj. entertaining, amusing; funny.*
     Tudo isto é muito divertido. *This is all very amusing.*

divertimento *m. diversion, amusement; sport.*

DIVERTIR *to amuse, to divert, to entertain.*

DIVERTIR-SE *to amuse oneself, to have a good time.*
     Nós nos divertimos na festa. *We had a good time at the party.*
     Divirta-se! *Have a good time!*

dívida *f. debt.*
     Ela pagou todas as dívidas. *She paid all her debts.*
     Dívida ativa (activa). *Outstanding debt.*
     Contrair dívidas. *To incur debts.*

dividendo *m. dividend.*

DIVIDIR *to divide.*

divindade *f. divinity.*

divino *adj. divine; heavenly.*

divisa *f. motto, slogan; emblem.*

divisão *f. division; partition, compartment; section.*

divisar *to perceive, to catch sight of.*

divorciar *to divorce.*

divorciar-se *to get a divorce, to be divorced.*

divórcio *m. divorce.*
divulgar *to divulge, to disclose.*
DIZER *to say; to speak; to tell; m. saying.*
   Diga-me, por favor. *Please tell me.*
   Pode dizer-me onde é a estação? *Can you tell me where the station is?*
   Eu lhe direi. *I'll tell him.*
   Não me diga! *You don't say!*
   Que quer dizer esta palavra? *What does this word mean?*
   Dizer adeus. *To say good-bye.*
   Dizer bem (mal) de alguém. *To speak well (ill) of someone.*
   Para dizer a verdade . . . *To tell the truth . . .*
   Ouvi dizer que . . . *I heard that . . .*
DO *(contr. of* **de** + **o**) *of the, with the, from the.*
   Qual é a capital do estado? *What is the capital of the state?*
   Ele é do norte. *He's from the North.*
dó *m. do (music); pity; mourning.*
doação *f. donation, gift.*
doar *to give, to donate.*
DOBRAR *to turn; to double; to fold; to bend; to dub.*
   Dobrar (Virar) a esquina. *To turn the corner.*
   Dobre bem a carta. *Fold the letter well.*
doca *f. dock.*
DOCE *adj. sweet; agreeable, pleasant; n. m. candy; sweet.*
dócil *adj. docile; obedient; gentle.*
documentação *f. documentation.*
documento *m. document.*
doçura *f. sweetness; gentleness.*
DOENÇA *f. illness; malady.*
   Apanhar uma doença. *To catch a disease.*
   Doença contagiosa. *Contagious disease.*
DOENTE *adj. ill, sick; n. m. and f. sick person.*
   Ela está doente. *She is ill.*
doer *to ache, to pain.*
doido *adj. crazy, mad; n. m. madman; fool.*
doirado *adj. golden, gilded.*
DOIS *two.*
   Dois a dois. *Two by two.*
   De dois em dois meses. *Every two months.*
   Dois é bom, três é demais. *Two's company, three's a crowd.*
DÓLAR *m. dollar.*
dolência *f. sorrow, grief.*
dolorosa *f. bill (for a meal) (slang).*
doloroso *adj. painful.*
dom *m. gift; talent; dom (title).*
   Dom Pedro I foi o primeiro imperador do Brasil. *Dom Pedro I was the first emperor of Brazil.*
domar *to tame; to break in.*
doméstico *adj. domestic; n. m. servant.*

domicílio *m. residence, domicile.*
dominação *f. domination.*
dominante *adj. dominant.*
dominar *to dominate.*
DOMINGO *m. Sunday.*
   Domingo de Ramos. *Palm Sunday.*
   Domingo de Páscoa. *Easter Sunday.*
domínio *m. dominion; command; control.*
DONA *f. lady; title (used with the first name) meaning Mrs. or Miss.*
   Dona da casa. *Lady of the house.*
   Dona Ana. *Miss (or Mrs.) Anne.*
donaire *m. grace; elegance; witty saying.*
donativo *m. gift, donation.*
DONDE *(contr. of* **de** + **onde**) *from where, from which.*
   Donde é o senhor? *Where are you from?*
dono *m. owner.*
DOR *f. ache, pain, sorrow.*
   Dor de cabeça. *Headache.*
   Dor de dente(s). *Toothache.*
   Dor de garganta. *Sore throat.*
dormente *adj. dormant, sleeping; n. m. beam (house); cross tie (railroad).*
DORMIR *to sleep.*
   Dormiu bem? *Did you sleep well?*
   Eu não pude dormir. *I couldn't sleep.*
   Dormir como uma pedra. *To sleep like a log.*
   Dormir a sesta. *To take a nap.*
dormitar *to doze.*
dormitório *m. dormitory; bedroom* Ⓑ.
dose *f. dose.*
dotação *f. endowment; allocation.*
dotar *to allocate; to endow.*
dote *m. dowry; talent.*
dourado *adj. golden, gilded.*
doutor *m. doctor.*
doutrina *f. doctrine.*
DOZE *twelve.*
drama *m. drama.*
dramalhão *m. melodrama.*
dramático *adj. dramatic.*
dramatizar *to dramatize.*
dramaturgo *m. dramatist, playwright.*
drástico *adj. drastic.*
droga *f. drug.*
drogaria *f. drugstore, pharmacy.*
DUAS *(f. of* **dois**) *two.*
   Duas semanas. *Two weeks.*
   Às duas horas. *At two o'clock.*
duelo *m. duel.*
duende *m. ghost; goblin.*
duo *m. duo, duet.*
duodécimo *adj., n. m. twelfth.*
duplicado *adj. duplicate; n. m. duplicate, copy.*
duplicar *to duplicate; to repeat; to double.*
duplo *adj. double; duplicate; n. m. double.*

duque m. duke; deuce (cards).
duquesa f. duchess.
duração f. duration.
duradouro adj. durable; lasting.
DURANTE during.
　Durante o dia. During the day.
　Durante a noite. During the night.
　Durante algum tempo. For some time.
DURAR to last; to continue; to wear well.
　A viagem durou quatro dias. The trip
　　lasted four days.
durável adj. durable, lasting.
dureza f. hardness; harshness.
DURO adj. hard; difficult; firm; n. m. Spanish
　five pesos.
　A vida dele foi muito dura. His life was a
　　very difficult one.
　Não seja duro com ele. Don't be hard on
　　him.
　Pão duro. Tightwad.
DÚVIDA f. doubt.
　Sem dúvida. Without a doubt.
　Pôr em dúvida. To doubt.
DUVIDAR to doubt; to hesitate.
　Duvidamos que ela venha. We doubt she
　　will come.
duvidoso adj. doubtful; uncertain.
DUZENTAS f. two hundred.
DUZENTOS m. two hundred.
DÚZIA f. dozen.
　Por dúzia. By the dozen.

E

e (pron. as Eng. e in be) and.
　Maria e João chegaram tarde. Mary and
　　John arrived late.
ébrio adj. intoxicated, drunk.
economia f. economy, thrift.
　Economia política. Political economy.
econômico (económico) adj. economic;
　economical.
economizar to economize; to save.
edição f. edition, issue; publication.
edificar to construct, to build.
　Vão edificar uma nova escola. They are
　　going to build a new school.
edifício m. building.
　Este edifício é um edifício público. This
　　building is a public building.
editar to edit; to publish.
editor adj. publishing; n. m. publisher.
　Casa editora. Publishing house.
　O editor não aceitou o livro. The publisher
　　did not accept the book.
editorial adj. editorial; n. m. newspaper
　editorial; n. f. publishing house.

educação f. education; upbringing; training.
　Ele é um senhor de boa educação. He is a
　　man of good manners.
educar to educate; to bring up; to train.
　Ele é muito mal educado. He is very ill-
　　bred.
educativo adj. educational, instructive.
EFEITO m. effect, result, consequence;
　impression; pl. effects, assets, goods,
　belongings.
　As palavras causaram mau efeito. The
　　words had a bad effect.
　Com efeito, ela não sabe nada. In fact, she
　　doesn't know anything.
　Levar a efeito. To carry out. To put into
　　practice.
　Sem efeito. Without effect.
efetivo (efectivo) adj. effective; real; actual.
eficaz adj. effective; efficient.
eficiente adj. efficient; effective.
égua f. mare.
eis behold; here is; there is.
　Eis a razão. That's the reason.
　Eis porque não fomos. That's why we
　　didn't go.
eixo (x = sh) m. axle; axis.
ELA she; her; it.
　Ela não sabe nada. She doesn't know
　　anything.
　O vestido é para ela. The dress is for her.
elaboração f. elaboration.
elaborado adj. elaborate.
elaborar to elaborate; to work out.
ELAS f. they; them.
　Elas são irmãs. They are sisters.
elasticidade f. elasticity.
elástico adj. elastic; n. m. elastic; rubber band.
ELE he; him; it.
　Ele vem amanhã. He's coming tomorrow.
　A carta é para ele. The letter is for him.
electricidade Ⓟ (**eletricidade** Ⓑ) f. electricity.
eléctrico Ⓟ (**elétrico** Ⓑ) adj. electric.
elefante m. elephant.
eleger to elect; to choose.
eleição f. election; choice.
eleito adj. elected; selected.
　Carlos foi eleito presidente do clube.
　　Charles was elected president of the
　　club.
elementar adj. elementary; elemental.
elemento m. element; pl. rudiments, first
　principles.
elenco m. cast (theater); catalog; list; index.
　A peça é boa mas o elenco é muito ruim.
　　The play is good, but the cast is very
　　bad.
ELES m. they; them.
　Eles gostaram muito do filme. They liked
　　the film very much.

Eduardo partiu com eles. *Edward left with them.*

eletricidade (electricidade) *f. electricity.*

elétrico (eléctrico) *adj. electric.*

elevação *f. elevation.*

elevador *m. elevator; lift.*

O prédio tem elevador? *Does the building have an elevator?*

elevar *to elevate; to lift up.*

eliminação *f. elimination.*

eliminar *to eliminate.*

elo *m. link; tie.*

elogiar *to praise.*

elogio *m. praise, eulogy.*

eloqüência (eloquência) *f. eloquence.*

elucidação *f. elucidation, explanation.*

eludir *to elude, to evade.*

EM *in, into, on, at, by.*

Eu o tenho na mão. *I have it in my hand.*

O senhor chegou em boa hora. *You arrived at the right time.*

Entremos nesta loja. *Let's go into this store.*

Em que dia? *On what day?*

Ela está em casa. *She is home.*

Tudo foi em vão. *It was all in vain.*

Em geral. *In general. Generally.*

Em vez de. *Instead of.*

Em toda a parte. *Everywhere.*

Em meio de. *In the middle (midst) of.*

Em breve. *Soon.*

Em fim. *Finally.*

Em verdade. *In truth. Truly.*

Eu estava pensando nisso. *I was thinking about that.*

emagrecer *to become thin.*

embaixada *(x = sh) f. embassy.*

embaixador *(x = sh) m. ambassador.*

embaixo *(x = sh) below, under.*

Lá embaixo. *Down there.*

embandeirar *to deck out or decorate with flags.*

embaraçar *to embarrass; to hinder.*

embaraço *m. embarrassment; difficulty.*

embaralhar *to shuffle (cards); to mix.*

embarcação *f. vessel, ship, boat; embarkation.*

embarcar *to embark, to go aboard.*

Vamos embarcar em vinte minutos. *We are going aboard in twenty minutes.*

embargar *to embargo; to hinder.*

Sem embargo. *Nevertheless.*

embarque *m. embarkation; shipment.*

emblema *m. emblem, symbol.*

EMBORA *although; away.*

Vamos embora! *Let's go!*

Embora não tivéssemos dinheiro saímos de casa. *Although we did not have any money, we went out of the house.*

emborrachar-se *to become drunk.*

emboscada *f. ambush, trap.*

emboscar *to ambush.*

embriagar *to intoxicate; to enchant.*

embriagar-se *to become intoxicated; to become enchanted.*

embrulhar *to wrap up; to confuse; to disturb.*

embrulho *m. package; parcel; trick; swindle* Ⓑ.

Deixei *(x = sh)* os embrulhos na mesa. *I left the packages on the table.*

embrutecer *to brutalize; to make coarse.*

embrutecer-se *to be or to become stupid or coarse.*

embuste *m. lie; trick.*

embusteiro *m. liar; deceiver; cheater.*

embutido *adj. inlaid; n. m. inlaid work; mosaic.*

emendar *to amend, to correct.*

ementa *f. menu* Ⓟ.

emergência *f. emergency.*

emigração *f. emigration.*

emigrante *adj., n. m. and f. emigrant.*

eminente *adj. eminent.*

emissor *adj. issuing; n. m. transmitter.*

emissora *f. broadcasting station.*

emitir *to emit, to send forth; to issue (bonds); to utter; to broadcast.*

emoção *f. emotion.*

emocionante *adj. moving, touching.*

emocionar *to move, to excite.*

empachar *to stuff; to overload.*

empacotar *to package; to pack.*

empalmar *to palm; to pilfer.*

empanada *f. meat turnover.*

empapar *to soak.*

Ficamos empapados. *We were soaked.*

emparelhar *to pair; to join.*

empatar *to tie (score); to tie up (money).*

Os quadros empataram. *The teams tied.*

empate *m. tie, draw.*

empeçar *to entangle.*

empecilho *m. hindrance; difficulty.*

empenhar *to pawn; to pledge; to engage.*

Eu empenhei minha palavra. *I pledged (gave) my word.*

empenho *m. pledge, obligation; pawning; determination; persistence.*

Elas estudam com empenho. *They study diligently.*

empertigado *adj. haughty.*

empolgante *adj. thrilling, gripping.*

empório *m. trading center; grocery store* Ⓑ.

empreender *to undertake.*

empregado *adj. used, occupied; n. m. employee; servant.*

Isso foi bem empregado. *That was put to good use.*

Ela tem um empregado e duas empregadas.

She has one male servant and two maids.

EMPREGAR *to employ, to hire; to spend.*
Em que o senhor empregou a tarde? *How did you spend the afternoon?*
Empregamos dois dias em fazê-lo. *It took us two days to do it.*

EMPREGO *m. employment, job, occupation; use.*
Mário tem um bom emprego. *Mario has a good job.*

empresa *f. undertaking; enterprise; company.*

empresário *m. impresario; contractor; manager.*

emprestar *to lend.*
Emprestar de. *To borrow* Ⓑ.
Pedir emprestado. Tomar emprestado. *To borrow.*

empréstimo *m. loan.*

empurrar *to push, to shove.*

enamorar-se *to fall in love.*

encabeçar *to head, to direct; to start.*
Quem encabeçou a revolução? *Who headed the revolution?*

encadear *to chain; to link.*

encadernado *adj. bound (book).*
Eu prefiro o livro encadernado. *I prefer the book bound.*

encaixar *(x = sh) to fit; to inlay; to box, to put in a box; to come in handy.*
Isto encaixa sem dificuldade. *This fits easily.*

encalhar *to run aground; to stick.*

encaminhar *to guide, to direct.*

encaminhar-se *to take the road to; to set out for.*

encanamento *m. plumbing; pipelines.*

encanecer *to turn gray; to grow old; to mature.*

encantado *adj. charmed; delighted, enchanted.*

encantador *adj. charming, delightful, enchanting.*

encantamento *m. charm; delight; fascination; enchantment; marvel.*

encanto *m. charm; enchantment; delight; spell.*
Como por encanto. *As if by magic.*
Ela é um encanto de menina. *She is a charming little girl.*

encarar *to face; to look straight at.*
Temos que encarar o problema. *We have to face the problem.*

encarcerar *to imprison.*

encarecer *to raise the price; to entreat.*

encargo *m. charge; duty; tax.*
Os meus encargos vão crescendo. *My duties are growing.*

encarnado *adj. red; scarlet.*

encarregado *adj. in charge; n. m. person in charge.*

encarregar *to put in charge, to charge (with).*

encarregar-se *to take charge, to take care.*
Eu me encarrego de tudo. *I'll take care of everything.*

encenação *f. staging.*

encenador *m. director (theatre); producer (theatre).*

encenar *to stage (play); to display.*

enceradeira *f. floor waxer.*

encerar *to wax; to polish.*

encerrar *to close in; to enclose; to confine; to contain.*

encetar *to start; to begin.*
Encetar um assunto. *To broach a subject.*

encharcar *to drench; to soak.*

enchente *f. flood.*
As enchentes causam muito dano. *Floods cause great damage.*

ENCHER *to fill, to fill up.*
Encha o tanque. *Fill 'er up (fill up the tank).*

enchova *f. anchovy.*

enciclopédia *f. encyclopedia.*

encoberto *adj. covered; hidden.*
O céu está encoberto. *The sky is overcast.*

encobrir *to cover; to conceal.*

encolher *to shrink; to contract.*
Encolher os ombros. *To shrug the shoulders.*

encomenda *f. an order (purchase); commission.*

encomendar *to order; to commission.*
Ela encomendou os cinco volumes. *She ordered the five volumes.*

ENCONTRAR *to find; to meet; to meet by chance.*
O senhor encontrou o que procurava? *Did you find what you were looking for?*
Eles devem nos encontrar aqui. *They are to meet us here.*

ENCONTRAR-SE *to find oneself; to be; to meet.*
Eu me encontrei sozinho. *I found myself all alone.*
Vamos encontrar-nos amanhã. *We are going to meet tomorrow.*

ENCONTRO *m. meeting; encounter.*

encrenca *f. difficulty; obstacle.*
Deixe-me de encrencas. *I don't want any trouble.*

encrespar *to curl; to frizzle.*

encruzilhada *f. crossroads.*

endereçar *to address; to direct.*
Um momento. Vou endereçar esta carta. *Just a moment. I'm going to address this letter.*

endereço *m. address.*

endossar *to endorse.*

endurecer *to harden.*

energia *f. energy, power.*

enérgico *adj. energetic, active.*

enfadar *to irk, to annoy.*

enfado *m. displeasure; annoyance.*

enfartar *to glut; to stuff.*

ênfase *f. emphasis.*

enfático *adj. emphatic.*

enfeitar *to adorn, to decorate.*

enfermar *to become ill.*

Se ela continua assim vai enfermar. *If she continues that way, she is going to become ill.*

enfermeira *f. nurse.*

enfermeiro *m. male nurse; hospital orderly.*

enfermo *adj. sick; n. m. patient, sick person.*

ENFIM *finally, at last; in short.*

enforcar *to hang (a person).*

enfrear *to curb; to brake.*

É preciso enfrear nas colinas. *You have to use your brakes on the hills.*

enfrentar *to face; to confront.*

Temos que enfrentar o problema hoje. *We have to face the problem today.*

enfurecer *to become angry; to become furious.*

engaiolar *to cage; to lock up.*

engalanar *to decorate, to adorn.*

enganar *to deceive, to fool.*

enganar-se *to deceive oneself; to be mistaken.*

Sinto muito! Enganei-me. *I'm very sorry! I was mistaken.*

enganchar *to hook.*

engano *error, mistake; deceit.*

enganoso *adj. misleading; deceiving.*

engarrafar *to bottle.*

engendrar *to engender.*

engenharia *f. engineering.*

engenheiro *m. engineer; owner of a mill* Ⓑ.

engenho *m. ingenuity; skill; wit; mill.*

Engenho de açúcar. *Sugar mill.*

engolir *to swallow; to gulp down.*

Engula a pílula! *Swallow the pill!*

Faça o favor de falar mais alto e de não engolir as palavras. *Please speak louder, and do not swallow your words.*

engomar *to starch.*

engordar *to fatten; to grow fat.*

ENGRAÇADO *adj. amusing; funny.*

Não acho muito engraçado. *I don't think it's very funny.*

engraxar *(x = sh) to wax; to shine shoes, to grease.*

engraxate (engraxador) *(x = sh) bootblack.*

engrenagem *f. gear.*

enguia *f. eel.*

enjoado *adj. nauseated; carsick; seasick.*

enjoar *to nauseate; to feel nausea.*

enjôo *m. nausea; seasickness; car sickness.*

enlaçar *to join, to connect; to bind; to tie.*

enlace *m. union; marriage.*

Enlace matrimonial. *Marriage.*

enlatado *adj. canned.*

enlatar *to can (food).*

enlouquecer *to go mad; to drive mad.*

enojar *to nauseate; to feel nausea; to disgust.*

enojo *m. nausea; disgust.*

ENQUANTO *while.*

Enquanto nós estudávamos eles escreviam cartas. *While we studied, they wrote letters.*

Por enquanto. *For the time being.*

enredar *to entangle; to catch with a net.*

enredo *m. plot (of book); story; complication.*

O enredo do romance é muito fraco. *The novel's plot is quite weak.*

enriquecer *to enrich; to become rich.*

enrolar *to wind; to roll up; to wrap up.*

ensaboar *to soap; to lather.*

ensaiar *to try; to rehearse; to test.*

ensaio *m. trial; rehearsal; essay.*

Balão de ensaio. *Trial balloon.*

ensejo *m. opportunity; occasion.*

Aproveitamos o ensejo para . . . *We take this opportunity to . . .*

ensinamento *m. teaching, instruction.*

ENSINAR *to teach; to show; to train.*

Quer que lhe ensine? *Would you like me to teach you?*

ensino *m. teaching, instruction; training.*

ensurdecer *to deafen; to stun.*

ENTANTO *meanwhile.*

No entanto. *Nevertheless. However.*

ENTÃO *then; in that case; at that time.*

Então o senhor não quer ir comigo. *Then you don't want to go with me.*

Desde então. *Since that time.*

ENTENDER *to understand.*

Não entendi nada. *I didn't understand a thing.*

João entende disso. *John is familiar with that.*

Entendi mal. *I misunderstood.*

Ela me deu a entender que já era tarde. *She led me to believe that it was already too late.*

Não posso me entender com elas. *I can't come to an understanding with them.*

Agora nos entendemos. *Now we understand each other.*

entendimento *m. understanding.*

enternecer *to soften; to move to pity.*

enterrar *to bury.*

enterro *m. burial; interment; funeral.*

entidade *f. entity.*

entoação *f. intonation; tone.*

entoar *to tune; to intone; to be in tune.*

ENTRADA *f. entrance; entry; admission; ticket; entree.*

Quanto é a entrada? *How much is the admission?*

A entrada é gratuita. *(The) admission is free.*

Devemos comprar as entradas agora. *We should buy the tickets now.*

É proibida a entrada. *No admittance.*

Meia entrada. *Half-price ticket.*

ENTRAR *to enter; to go in; to fit.*

Entre! *Come in!*

Que não entre ninguém. *Don't let anybody in.*

Entramos no cinema às três. *We went into the movie theatre at three.*

Entrar com o pé direito. *To have a good start. To get off on the right foot.*

Ela entrou na universidade no ano passado. *She entered the university last year.*

Entrar por um ouvido e sair pelo outro. *To go in one ear and out the other.*

ENTRE *between; among.*

Fizeram-no entre os dois. *They did it between the two of them.*

Procure entre os papéis. *Look among the papers.*

Entre nós. *Between ourselves.*

Entre a espada e a parede. *Between a rock and a hard place.*

entreato (entreacto) *m. intermission.*

entrega *f. delivery; surrender.*

Entrega urgente. *Special delivery (mail).*

ENTREGAR *to deliver; to hand over.*

A quem entregou a carta? *To whom did you deliver the letter?*

entregar-se *to surrender; to give oneself up; to devote oneself (to).*

O criminoso se entregou à polícia. *The criminal gave himself up to the police.*

Entregar os pontos. *To give up.*

entregue *adj. delivered.*

entrementes *meanwhile.*

entremeter *to insert; to place between.*

ENTRETANTO *meanwhile; however.*

entretenimento *m. entertainment, amusement.*

entrevista *f. interview; conference.*

entrevistar *to interview.*

entristecer *to become sad.*

entusiasmar *to fill with enthusiasm.*

entusiasmar-se *to become enthusiastic.*

entusiasmo *m. enthusiasm.*

entusiasta *adj. enthusiastic; n. m. and f. enthusiast, fan.*

entusiástico *adj. enthusiastic.*

envasar *to bottle; to put in pots (flowers).*

envelhecer *to make old; to grow old.*

envelope *m. envelope.*

Não esqueça de escrever o endereço no envelope. *Don't forget to write the address on the envelope.*

envenenar *to poison.*

ENVIAR *to send; to dispatch.*

Envie-me uma dúzia. *Send me a dozen.*

Enviar por correio electrónico. *To e-mail.*

Enviar um fax. *To fax, to send a fax.*

envio *m. shipment; shipping.*

enviuvar *to become a widow or widower.*

envolver *to wrap up; to make into a package; to envelop; to surround.*

enxaguar *(x = sh) to rinse.*

época *f. epoch, age, era.*

equipa *f. team* Ⓟ.

equipamento *m. equipment.*

equipar *to equip; to furnish.*

equipe *f. team (business, etc.)* Ⓑ.

equivocação *f. mistake.*

equivocado *adj. mistaken.*

equivocar *to make a mistake; to mistake.*

equívoco *adj. equivocal; n. m. mistake; pun; misunderstanding.*

Acho que tudo foi um equívoco. *I believe it was all a misunderstanding.*

era *f. era; age; period.*

ereto (erecto) *adj. erect; upright.*

erguer *to erect, to raise.*

erigir *to erect, to build.*

errado *adj. wrong, in error.*

ERRAR *to err, to make a mistake.*

Errámos o caminho. *We lost our way.*

errata *f. erratum, error in writing or printing.*

ERRO *m. error, mistake.*

erudição *f. erudition, learning.*

erudito *adj. erudite, learned; n. m. scholar, erudite person.*

erva *f. herb, plant.*

Erva-mate. *Paraguay tea; maté.*

ervilha *f. pea.*

esbelto *adj. slim, slender; elegant.*

esboço *m. sketch; outline.*

escabroso *adj. rough; uneven; difficult.*

escada *f. stairs; staircase; ladder.*

Escada de incêndio. *Fire escape.*

Escada de mão. *Stepladder.*

Escada de serviço. *Service stairway.*

Escada rolante. *Escalator.*

escala *f. scale; ladder; stop.*

Em grande escala. *On a large scale.*

Porto de escala. *Port of call.*

escandir *to scan.*

escáner *m. scanner.*

escapar *to escape, to flee.*

escape *m. escape.*

escapo *adj. escaped; free.*

escarmentar *to punish; to reprimand.*

escárnio *m. scorn.*

escasso *adj. scarce, scanty.*

esclarecer *to clarify; to enlighten.*
escoamento *m. drainage.*
escoar *to drain; to flow.*
ESCOLA *f. school.*
   Escola elementar. *Elementary school.*
   Escola secundária. *Secondary school.*
ESCOLHER *to choose, to pick.*
escolhido *adj. chosen, select.*
escolta *f. escort.*
escoltar *to escort.*
escombros *m. pl. ruins.*
esconder *to hide, to conceal.*
escondido *adj. hidden.*
escorrer *to trickle; to drip.*
escoteira *f. girl scout.*
escoteiro *m. boy scout.*
ESCOVA *f. brush.*
   Escova de cabelo. *Hairbrush.*
   Escova de dentes. *Toothbrush.*
   Escova de roupa. *Clothes brush.*
escovar *to brush, to scrub.*
escravatura *f. slavery.*
escravidão *f. slavery.*
escravo *m. slave.*
ESCREVER *to write.*
   Escreva claramente. *Write clearly.*
   Como se escreve esta palavra? *How do you write (spell) that word?*
   Prefiro que escreva a carta à máquina. *I prefer that you type the letter.*
   Máquina de escrever. *Typewriter.*
   Escrever à maquina. *To type.*
escrito *adj. written; n. m. something written, writing.*
   Escrito à mão. *Handwritten.*
   Escrito à máquina. *Typewritten.*
   Pôr por escrito. *To put in writing.*
escritor *m. writer, author.*
escritório *m. office; study.*
escritura *f. writing; writ; document; deed.*
escrivão *m. notary, scribe.*
escrutínio *m. scrutiny; balloting; voting.*
escudo *m. shield.*
escurecer *to grow dark.*
escuridão *f. darkness.*
escusa *f. excuse.*
ESCUTAR *to listen; to heed.*
   Escute! *Listen!*
esfera *f. sphere.*
esforçar *to strengthen; to encourage.*
esforçar-se *to try hard, to endeavor, to strive.*
esforço *m. effort; endeavor.*
esfregar *to rub; to scrub; to scratch.*
esfriar *to cool off; to grow cold.*
esgotado *adj. exhausted; sold out; out of print.*

   Essa edição já está esgotada. *That edition is already sold out.*
esgotar *to drain; to exhaust.*
esgrima *f. fencing (sport).*
eslavo *adj. Slavic; Slav; n. m. Slav.*
esmagar *to overcome; to smash; to crush.*
esmaltar *to enamel.*
esmalte *m. enamel.*
   Esmalte de unhas. *Nail polish.*
esmerado *adj. carefully done; accomplished.*
esmerar *to do with great care; to perfect.*
esmero *m. care; perfection; neatness.*
esmolas *f. pl. alms.*
espaço *m. space, room.*
   Aqui não há espaço. *There's no room here.*
espada *f. sword.*
espaldar *m. back of a chair.*
espalhar *to spread; to scatter; to disseminate.*
espanhol *Spanish.*
espantar *to frighten, to drive away.*
espanto *m. fright.*
espantoso *adj. frightful.*
esparadrapo *m. adhesive tape.*
espargo *m. asparagus.*
espátula *f. spatula; letter opener.*
especial *adj. special.*
especialidade *f. specialty.*
especiarias *f. pl. spices.*
espécie *f. species; kind; sort.*
espectáculo ℗ (**espetáculo** Ⓑ) *m. spectacle, show.*
especulação *f. speculation.*
ESPELHO *m. mirror; looking glass.*
   Espelho retrovisor. *Rearview mirror.*
espera *f. wait, waiting.*
   Onde é a sala de espera? *Where is the waiting room?*
esperança *f. hope.*
ESPERAR *to wait for; to expect; to hope.*
   Assim o espero. *I hope so.*
   Espero que não. *I hope not.*
   Espero que sim. *I hope so.*
   Espere-me. *Wait for me.*
   Diga-lhe que espere. *Tell him to wait.*
   Espere um momento. *Wait a moment.*
esperto *adj. smart; alert; clever.*
   Ela é muito esperta. *She's very smart.*
espesso *adj. thick, dense.*
espetáculo (espectáculo) *m. spectacle, show.*
espiar *to spy on.*
espiga *f. spike; ear (corn).*
espinafre *m. spinach.*
espingarda *f. shotgun, rifle.*
espinha *f. spine; fishbone.*
espinho *m. thorn.*
espírito *m. spirit; mind; wit; soul.*
   Espírito prático. *Practical mind.*
   Ele é uma pessoa de espírito. *He is a man of wit.*

Espírito Santo. *Holy Spirit. Holy Ghost.*
espiritual *adj. spiritual.*
espirrar *to sneeze; to burst out.*
espirro *m. sneeze, sneezing.*
esplêndido *adj. splendid; excellent.*
esplendor *m. splendor, magnificence.*
esponja *f. sponge; parasite.*
esporte *m. sport.*
ESPOSA *f. wife, spouse.*
ESPOSO *m. husband, spouse.*
espreguiçadeira *f. chaise lounge, easy chair.*
espreguiçar-se *to stretch oneself out.*
espuma *f. foam, froth.*
Espuma de sabão. *Lather. Soapsuds.*
esquadra *f. squadron; squad; police station* Ⓟ.
ESQUECER *to forget; to neglect.*
Não esqueça o que lhe disse. *Don't forget what I told you.*
ESQUECER-SE *to forget.*
Ela se esqueceu de chamar. *She forgot to call.*
esquema *m. scheme, drawing.*
ESQUERDA *f. left, left side.*
À esquerda. *To the left.*
Esquerda, volver! *Left, face! (Military command).*
ESQUERDO *adj. left.*
esqui *m. ski.*
esquilo *m. squirrel.*
ESQUINA *f. corner (of a street).*
Dobrar (Virar) a esquina. *To turn the corner.*
A loja está na esquina. *The shop is on the corner.*
esquisito *adj. peculiar; odd; strange; unusual.*
esquivança *f. disdain, contempt.*
ESSA *f. that; that one; pl. those.*
Essa senhora. *That lady.*
Vamos por essa rua. *Let's go down that street.*
Essas coisas não me interessam. *Those things don't interest me.*
Prefiro estas a essas. *I prefer these to those.*
Ora essa! *Come on now!*
ESSE *m. that; that one; pl. those.*
Esse senhor. *That man.*
Esses meninos. *Those boys.*
Não quero esses; prefiro estes. *I don't want those; I prefer these.*
essência *f. essence.*
essencial *adj. essential.*
essoutro *that (other) one.*
ESTA *f. this; this one; pl. these.*
Esta senhora e aquele homem são irmãos. *This lady and that man are brother and sister.*
De quem é esta casa? *Whose house is this?*
Não gosto destas. *I don't like these.*

estabelecer *to establish.*
estabelecimento *m. establishment.*
estábulo *m. stable.*
ESTAÇÃO *f. station; season.*
Onde é a estação? *Where is the station?*
O inverno é a estação mais fria do ano. *Winter is the coldest season of the year.*
estacionamento *m. parking.*
Estacionamento proibido. *No parking.*
estacionar *to park; to stop.*
estada *f. stay; stop.*
estádio *m. stadium; stage, phase.*
ESTADO *m. state; condition.*
Em bom estado. *In good condition.*
Homem de estado. *Statesman.*
Estado-maior. *General staff.*
Estado de guerra. *State of war.*
Estados Unidos da América. *United States of America.*
estágio *m. period, phase; apprenticeship.*
estalagem *f. inn.*
estalar *to burst, to explode; to crack; to snap.*
estampa *f. picture, print.*
estampar *to stamp; to print.*
estampilha *f. small stamp; revenue stamp* Ⓑ.
estampilhar *to stamp; to put stamps on.*
estancar *to check; to stop.*
estância *f. dwelling, residence; station; stay.*
estanho *m. tin.*
estante *f. bookcase; lectern.*
ESTAR *to be.*
Estamos prontos. *We are ready.*
Elas estão cansadas. *They are tired.*
Que está fazendo? *What are you doing?*
Eles estão estudando. *They are studying.*
Eles estão a estudar Ⓟ. *They are studying.*
Onde está o seu irmão? *Where is your brother?*
Ele está no teatro. *He is at the theater.*
Deveríamos estar lá antes das nove. *We should be there before nine.*
A janela está aberta. *The window is open.*
Ela está de pé. *She is standing.*
Estou certo. *I am sure.*
Nós estamos de acordo. *We agree.*
Ela está doente. *She is sick.*
Estou para sair de viagem. *I am about to leave on a trip.*
Está bem. *Very well. Fine.*
Está na hora de partir. *It's time to leave.*
Estou com pressa. *I'm in a hurry.*
estátua *f. statue.*
estatura *f. stature.*
estatuto *m. statute, law.*
este *m. east.*
ESTE *m. this; this one; pl. these.*
Este senhor. *This man.*
Estes livros. *These books.*
Este é o meu. *This one is mine.*

Não quero estes. *I don't want these.*
estender *f. to extend; to stretch out.*
estenógrafa *f. stenographer.*
estenógrafo *m. stenographer.*
estiagem *f. dry weather, drought.*
esticar *to stretch.*
estilo *m. style.*
estima *f. esteem; appreciation.*
estimar *to esteem; to value.*
estimular *to stimulate.*
estímulo *m. stimulus.*
estio (Estio) *m. summer.*
estirar *to stretch, to extend.*
estirpe *f. stock; ancestry.*
estivador *m. stevedore, longshoreman.*
estojo *m. kit; case, box; set.*
Estojo de barba. *Shaving set.*
estômago *m. stomach.*
estoque *m. stock, supply* Ⓑ.
estorvar *to disturb; to hinder.*
estourar *to burst; to explode.*
ESTRADA *f. road, highway.*
Estrada de rodagem. *Highway.*
Estrada de ferro. *Railway.*
ESTRANGEIRO *adj. foreign; n. m. foreigner,*
alien; stranger.
Ela está no estrangeiro. *She is abroad.*
estranhar *to be surprised; to find strange.*
estranheza *f. strangeness; surprise.*
estranho *adj. strange; unusual; odd.*
Ele é um pouco estranho. *He's somewhat*
strange.
estratégia *f. strategy.*
estratégico *adj. strategic.*
estrear *to try or use for the first time; to make*
one's debut; to open (play).
estréia (estreia) *f. opening, première; first*
showing; debut.
A estréia de peça vai ser na sexta. *The play*
will open on Friday.
estreito *adj. narrow; n. m. strait.*
estrela *f. star.*
estremecer *to shake, to tremble.*
estremecimento *m. shaking, quiver.*
estribo *m. stirrup; running board.*
estropiar *to cripple; to deform.*
estrutura *f. structure.*
estudante *m. and f. student.*
ESTUDAR *to study.*
Os meus filhos não estudam bastante. *My*
children don't study enough.
estudioso *adj. studious.*
ESTUDO *m. study.*
Bolsa de estudos. *Scholarship.*
estufa *f. heating stove; hothouse.*
estupendo *adj. stupendous; wonderful.*
estupidez *f. stupidity.*
estúpido *adj. stupid; n. m. stupid person.*
eternidade *f. eternity.*

eterno *adj. eternal.*
ética *f. ethics.*
ético *adj. ethic, ethical.*
etiqueta *etiquette; ceremony; tag (on clothing,*
etc.).
euro *m. euro (currency in Portugal).*
europeu *adj. European.*
evacuação *f. evacuation.*
evacuar *to evacuate.*
evadir *to evade.*
evangelho *m. the Gospel.*
evaporar *to evaporate.*
evasão *f. evasion; escape.*
evasivo *adj. evasive.*
evento *m. event, happening.*
evidência *f. evidence; indication.*
evidente *adj. evident, obvious.*
EVITAR *to avoid.*
Quero evitar essa situação, se puder. *I*
should like to avoid that situation if
I can.
evitável *adj. avoidable.*
evocar *to evoke.*
evolução *f. evolution.*
exageração $(x = z)$ *f. exaggeration.*
exagerar $(x = z)$ *to exaggerate.*
exagero $(x = z)$ *m. exaggeration.*
exaltação $(x = z)$ *f. exaltation.*
exaltar $(x = z)$ *to exalt, to praise.*
exame $(x = z)$ *m. examination.*
Exame de admissão. *Admission*
examination.
Exame médico. *Medical examination.*
examinar $(x = z)$ *to examine; to inquire into;*
to investigate.
exasperação $(x = z)$ *f. exasperation.*
exasperar $(x = z)$ *to exasperate.*
exatidão (exactidão) $(x = z)$ *f. exactitude,*
exactness.
EXATO (EXACTO) $(x = z)$ *adj. exact;*
correct.
Exatamente. *Exactly.*
exceção *f. exception.*
exceder *to exceed.*
excelência *f. excellence.*
Vossa Excelência. *Your Excellency.*
excelente *adj. excellent; fine.*
excelentíssimo *adj. most excellent.*
excelso *adj. eminent; exalted.*
excepcional *adj. exceptional; unusual.*
excessivo *adj. excessive; too much.*
excesso *m. excess.*
Em excesso. *In excess. Excessively.*
exceto (excepto) *except.*
excetuar (exceptuar) *to except; to exempt; to*
exclude.
excitação *f. excitation; excitement.*
excitante *adj. exciting.*
excitar *to excite; to stimulate.*

excitável *adj. excitable.*
exclamação *f. exclamation.*
exclamar *to exclaim.*
excluir *to exclude; to keep out; to rule out.*
exclusão *f. exclusion.*
exclusivo *adj. exclusive.*
excursão *f. excursion, trip.*
execução *(x = z) f. execution; performance.*
executar *(x = z) to execute; to carry out.*
executivo *(x = z) adj. executive.*
exemplar *(x = z) adj. exemplary; n. m. copy; model.*
    Eu lhe mandarei um exemplar. *I'll send you a copy.*
EXEMPLO *(x = z) m. example, pattern.*
    Por exemplo. *For example.*
exercer *(x = z) to exercise; to carry out; to practice.*
    Exercer a medicina. *To practice medicine.*
exercício *(x = z) m. exercise; drill.*
    Fazer exercício. *To exercise.*
exército *(x = z) m. army.*
exibição *f. exhibition.*
exibir *(x = z) to exhibit.*
exigência *(x = z) f. exigency, urgent need.*
exigente *(x = z) adj. exigent, demanding.*
    Não seja tão exigente. *Don't be so demanding.*
exigir *(x = z) to demand; to require; to exact.*
    As circunstâncias o exigem. *The situation requires it.*
exilar *(x = z) to exile.*
exílio *(x = z) m. exile.*
existência *(x = z) f. existence; stock of goods* Ⓟ.
existente *(x = z) adj. living, existent.*
EXISTIR *(x = z) to exist, to be.*
    Não existe tal coisa. *No such thing exists.*
ÊXITO *(x = z) m. success; hit (song, etc.); result; outcome.*
    Eles tiveram bom êxito. *They were a big success.*
exortar *(x = z) to exhort; to urge.*
expandir *to expand; to spread out.*
expansão *f. expansion.*
expectativa *f. expectation; hope.*
expedição *f. expedition; shipment.*
expediente *adj. expeditious; n. m. expedient; office hours.*
expedir *to expedite; to dispatch, to send.*
expelir *to expel.*
experiência *f. experience; trial.*
experimentar *to experience; to experiment.*
experimento *m. experience; experiment.*
experto *adj. expert; n. m. expert.*
expirar *to expire; to die; to exhale.*
explicação *f. explication.*
EXPLICAR *to explain.*
    Deixe-me explicá-lo. *Let me explain it.*

explicativo *adj. explanatory.*
explicável *adj. explainable.*
explícito *adj. explicit.*
exploração *f. exploration.*
explorador *m. explorer.*
explorar *to explore.*
explosão *f. explosion; outburst.*
expoente *m. and f. exponent.*
expôr *to expound; to explain; to make clear; to expose.*
exportação *f. export.*
exportador *adj. exporting; n. m. exporter.*
    Casa exportadora. *Exporting firm.*
exportar *to export.*
exposição *f. exposition, show, exhibition; exposure.*
expositor *m. exhibitor; expositor.*
exposto *adj. exposed; liable to.*
    Está exposto das dez às quatro horas. *It is being shown from ten to four o'clock.*
expressão *f. expression.*
expresso *adj. express; clear; n. m. express (train); special delivery.*
exprimir *to express.*
expulsão *f. expulsion.*
expulsar *to expel, to eject, to throw out.*
expulso *adj. expelled, expulsed.*
extensão *f. extension; extent.*
    Em toda extensão. *In every sense.*
extensivo *adj. extensive; far-reaching.*
extenso *adj. extensive; vast.*
extenuação *f. extenuation.*
extenuar *to extenuate.*
exterior *adj. exterior; foreign.*
extinguir *to extinguish, to put out.*
extra *extra.*
extrair *to extract, to pull out.*
extra-oficial *adj. unofficial; off the record.*
extraordinário *adj. extraordinary.*
    É um caso extraordinário. *It's an unusual case.*
extratar *to extract.*
extrato (extracto) *m. extract.*
extravagância *f. folly, extravagance.*
extravagante *adj. extravagant; odd.*
extraviado *adj. lost, missing; astray.*
extraviar *to mislead; to mislay.*
extravio *m. loss; deviation; straying.*
extremidade *f. extremity; very end.*
extremo *adj. extreme; last; n. m. extreme; end.*

F

fá *n. musical note.*
fã *m. and f. fan (follower).*
fábrica *f. factory; mill; plant.*
    Preço de fábrica. *Factory price.*

Marca de fábrica. *Trademark.*

fabricação *f. manufacturing; manufacture.*

fabricante *m. and f. manufacturer; maker.*

fabricar *to manufacture, to make; to build.*

fábula *f. fable; story, tale.*

fabuloso *adj. fabulous; incredible.*

FACA *f. knife.*

façanha *f. deed; accomplishment.*

facão Ⓑ **facção** Ⓑ *and* Ⓟ *. f. faction.*

face *f. face; side.*

O negócio tem duas faces. *There are two sides to the matter.*

fachada *f. façade.*

FÁCIL *easy.*

Parece fácil mas é difícil. *It looks easy, but it's difficult.*

Facilmente. *Easily.*

É fácil de aprender. *It's easy to learn.*

facilidade *f. ease, facility.*

facilitar *to facilitate, to make easy.*

facsimile *m. facsimile, fax.*

FACTO Ⓟ (**FATO** Ⓑ) *m. fact; occurrence.*

faculdade *f. faculty; school (in a university, etc.).*

Faculdade de direito. *Law school.*

fada *f. fairy.*

Conto de fadas. *Fairy tale.*

fadista *m. and f. singer and player of fados; ruffian.*

FADO *m. fate, destiny; Portuguese popular folk song.*

faina *f. task, chore.*

faixa *(x = sh) f. sash; strip.*

faixar *(x = sh) to bind; to tie up.*

fala *f. speech; language.*

falador *adj. talkative; n. m. talker; gabber.*

FALAR *to speak, to talk.*

O senhor fala português? *Do you speak Portuguese?*

Eu falo português. *I speak Portuguese.*

Aqui se fala inglês. *English is spoken here.*

Fale! *Speak!*

Fale mais devagar. *Speak slower.*

Desejo falar com o gerente. *I wish to speak to the manager.*

Gostaria de falar-lhe sobre um assunto importante. *I would like to speak to you about an important matter.*

Fale mais alto. *Speak louder.*

De que estão falando? *What are they talking about?*

Falemos nisso agora mesmo. *Let's talk about that right now.*

falecer *to die.*

Ele faleceu no ano passado. *He died last year.*

falha *f. fault, flaw.*

falhar *to fail; to miss.*

falho *adj. faulty; defective.*

falsear *to falsify; to distort.*

falsidade *f. falsehood; untruth.*

falsificação *f. falsification; forgery.*

falsificar *to falsify.*

falso *adj. false; incorrect.*

Alarme falso. *False alarm.*

Chave falsa. *Skeleton key.*

FALTA *f. need, lack; absence; fault, defect; mistake.*

Temos que desculpar as faltas dele. *We must excuse his faults.*

Eu corrigirei as faltas. *I'll correct the mistakes.*

Sem falta. *Without fail.*

Estamos com falta de água. *We are short of water.*

Perdemos tudo por falta de dinheiro. *We lost everything for lack of money.*

FALTAR *to need, to lack; to be absent; to fail.*

Aqui faltam três livros. *Three books are missing here.*

Ela faltou à aula hoje. *She missed class today.*

Era o que faltava! *That's the last straw!*

Faltam vinte minutos para as duas. *It's twenty minutes to two.*

Ele nunca falta à palavra. *He never goes back on his word.*

falto *adj. lacking, wanting.*

fama *f. fame, reputation, rumor, report.*

FAMÍLIA *f. family.*

familiar *adj. familiar, pertaining to the family; m. and f. close friend; relative.*

faminto *adj. hungry, famished.*

famoso *adj. famous.*

fanático *adj. fanatic.*

fanfarrão *adj. boasting, bragging; n. m. braggart.*

fantasia *f. fantasy, fancy; fancy dress, carnival costume* Ⓑ*.*

fantasma *m ghost, phantasm.*

fantástico *adj. fantastic.*

fantoche *m. puppet.*

farda *f. uniform.*

fardo *m. bale; parcel, bundle.*

faringe *f. pharynx.*

farinha *f. flour, meal.*

Farinha de trigo. *Wheat flour.*

farmacêutico *m. pharmacist, druggist.*

farmácia *f. pharmacy, drugstore.*

faro *m. lighthouse; sense of smell (animal).*

farofa *f. a dish made of manioc meal, meat, eggs, vegetables, etc.*

farol *m. lighthouse; beacon; headlight.*

Farol verde. *Green light.*

Farol vermelho. *Red light. Stoplight.*

farrapo *m. rag; ragamuffin.*

farroupilha *m. ragamuffin.*

farsa *f. farce.*

farsante *m. and f. actor, actress in farces; joker.*

farsista *adj. joking; n. m. and f. joker, clown.*

fartar *to fill with, to satiate.*

farto *adj. satiated, full; abundant.*
Estou farto disto. *I'm sick of this.*

fascinar *to fascinate, to charm.*

fase *f. phase; aspect.*

fastidioso *adj. boring, annoying.*

fastígio *m. apex, summit.*

fastio *m. boredom; lack of appetite.*

fatal *adj. fatal.*

fatalidade *f. fate, destiny; fatality.*

fatia *f. slice.*
Uma fatia de pão. *A slice of bread.*

fatigador *adj. tiring; boring.*

fatigante *adj. tiring.*

fatigar *to tire; to annoy.*

FATO (FACTO) *m. fact, occurrence; man's suit* Ⓟ.
De fato. *As a matter of fact.*
O fato é que já é tarde. *The fact is that it is already too late.*

fator (factor) *m. factor; agent.*

fátuo *adj. fatuous; foolish.*

fatura (factura) *f. invoice, bill.*
Aqui tem a fatura. *Here is the invoice.*

faturar (facturar) *to bill, to invoice.*

fauna *f. fauna.*

fausto *adj. happy; fortunate; n. m. pageantry.*

FAVA *f. a kind of bean.*
Mandar às favas. *To send someone packing.*

favela *f. slum* Ⓑ.

favelado *m. slum dweller* Ⓑ.

FAVOR *m. favor; service; good graces; letter.*
É um grande favor que me faz. *It's a great favor you are doing me.*
Por favor. *Please.*
Faça o favor de chamar-me às sete. *Please call me at seven.*
Recebemos seu favor de 5 do corrente. *We are in receipt of your favor (letter) of the 5th of this month.*

favorável *adj. favorable.*

favorecer *to favor; to help.*

favorito *adj. favorite.*

fax *m. fax, facsimile.*
Enviar um fax. *To send a fax.*
Receber um fax. *To receive a fax.*

fazenda *f. farm; plantation; estate; cloth, material.*
Fazenda de café. *Coffee plantation.*
Fazenda de lã. *Woolen cloth.*

fazendeiro *m. farmer, planter; owner of fazenda.*

FAZER *to make; to do; to cause; to be (cold, etc.)*

Faça o favor de dar-me o mapa. *Please give me the map.*
Permite-me fazer-lhe algumas perguntas? *May I ask you some questions?*
Fazem bom pão aqui. *They make good bread here.*
Que faço? *What shall I do?*
Faça como quiser. *Do as you wish.*
Que está fazendo (a fazer)? *What are you doing?*
Que havemos de fazer? *What are we to do?*
Já está feito. *It's already done.*
O navio faz água. *The ship leaks.*
Hoje faço vinte anos. *I am twenty years old today.*
Faço a barba com gilete. *I shave with a safety razor.*
Ela faz a cama todas as manhãs. *She makes her bed every morning.*
Faça chamar o médico. *Have the doctor called* Ⓟ.
Vamos fazer uma viagem no verão (Verão). *We're going on a trip in the summer.*
O deputado fez um discurso. *The congressman made a speech.*
Fazer gazeta. *To play hookey (from school).*
Fazer greve. *To go on strike.*
Fazer a chamada. *To call the roll.*
Fazer caso de. *To pay attention to.*
Fazer o papel. *To play the part.*
Fazer mal. *To do evil, harm.*
Fazer compras. *To go shopping.*
Fazer economias. *To save.*
Fazer exercício. *To exercise.*
Fazer frio. *To be cold (weather).*
Fazer calor. *To be warm (weather).*
Faz bom tempo. *The weather is good.*
Faz mau tempo. *The weather is bad.*
Fazer falta. *To need; to be lacking.*
Fazer alto. *To stop.*
Fazer parte de. *To belong to; to take part in.*
Fazer fila. *To stand in line.*
Não faz mal. *Never mind.*
Fazer um passeio. *To go for a walk.*

FÉ *f. faith; certificate.*
Ela o fez de boa fé. *She did it in good faith.*
Ele o disse de má fé. *He said it in bad faith (deceitfully).*
A fé católica. *The Catholic religion.*

febre *f. fever.*
Febre amarela. *Yellow fever.*

FECHADO *adj. closed; shut; finished.*
A porta não está fechada. *The door is not closed.*

FECHAR *to close; to shut; to finish.*
Amanhã vou fechar a conta. *Tomorrow I am going to close my account.*
Feche a porta à chave. *Lock the door.*

fecundo *adj. fruitful, productive, fecund.*
feder *to smell bad, to stink.*
federação *f. federation.*
FEIJÃO *m. bean, beans.*
feijoada *f. a popular dish made of black beans, meat, vegetables, etc.*
feio *adj. ugly; unpleasant.*
feira *f. fair; market.*
feiticeira *f. witch.*
feiticeiro *m. wizard.*
feitio *m. pattern; style; workmanship.*
FEITO *adj. made; done; finished; n. m. act; fact; deed.*
　　Mal feito. *That was wrong. Poorly done (made).*
　　Bem feito. *Well done.*
　　Dito e feito. *No sooner said than done.*
　　Feito! *Agreed!*
　　Já feito. *Already made; Ready-made.*
　　Feito sob medida. *Tailor-made.*
　　Feito à mão. *Handmade.*
　　Feito à máquina. *Machine-made.*
feitor *m. administrator; manager; foreman.*
feitura *f. workmanship; work.*
felicidade *f. happiness.*
felicitação *f. congratulation.*
　　Felicitações! *Congratulations!*
felicitar *to congratulate, to felicitate.*
FELIZ *adj. happy; fortunate.*
　　Feliz Ano Novo! *Happy New Year!*
　　Feliz Natal! *Merry Christmas!*
　　Foi o dia mais feliz da minha vida. *It was the happiest day of my life.*
　　Somos muito felizes. *We are very happy.*
　　Felizmente. *Happily. Fortunately.*
fêmea *f. female.*
feminino *adj. feminine.*
fenômeno *m. phenomenon.*
fera *f. wild beast.*
féria *f. wages; pl. holiday, vacation.*
　　Vamos passar as férias nas montanhas. *We are going to spend our vacation in the mountains.*
feriado *m. holiday.*
ferido *adj. wounded, injured; n. m. wounded person.*
　　Ele foi ferido no braço. *He was wounded in the arm.*
　　O ferido está muito melhor. *The wounded man is much better.*
ferir *to wound, to injure, to hurt.*
fermentação *f. fermentation; ferment.*
fermentar *to ferment; to leaven.*
fermento *leaven, yeast.*
feroz *adj. ferocious, fierce; cruel.*
ferradura *f. horseshoe.*
ferragens *f. pl. hardware.*
ferramenta *f. tool.*
ferreiro *m. blacksmith.*

férreo *adj. iron, ferrous.*
FERRO *m. iron; electric iron.*
　　Passar a ferro. *To iron (clothes).*
　　Estrada de ferro. *Railroad.*
ferrovia *f. railroad.*
ferroviário *adj. railroad.*
ferrugem *f. rust.*
fértil *adj. fertile, fruitful.*
ferver *to boil; to seethe.*
fervor *m. fervor, zeal.*
FESTA *f. feast; party; celebration; holiday.*
　　Dona Maria vai dar uma festa no sábado. *Dona Maria is going to give a party on Saturday.*
　　Boas Festas! *Merry Christmas! Happy New Year!*
festejar *to celebrate, to party; to praise.*
festividade *f. festival.*
festivo *adj. festive, merry.*
FEVEREIRO *m. February.*
　　O segundo mês do ano é fevereiro (Fevereiro). *February is the second month of the year.*
fiado *adj. on credit.*
　　Ela não gosta de comprar fiado. *She doesn't like to buy on credit.*
fiador *m. guarantor; bondsman.*
fiambre *m. cold meats.*
fiança *f. bail, bond; security; deposit.*
fiar *to trust, to confide; to sell on credit; to spin, to weave.*
　　Todos nós fiamos nele. *All of us trust him.*
fibra *f. fiber; filament.*
　　Fibro de vitro. *Fiberglass.*
FICAR *to remain, to stay; to be; to become.*
　　Não quero ficar mais aqui. *I don't want to stay here any longer.*
　　João ficou com os tios. *John stayed with his aunt and uncle.*
　　Quando lhe expliquei a situação ele ficou convencido. *When I explained the situation to him he was convinced.*
　　Ela ficou pálida. *She turned pale.*
　　Eu fico com este. *I'll take this one.*
　　Ficamos sem dinheiro. *We ran out of money.*
　　Hoje ela ficou em casa. *Today she stayed home.*
　　Fique com o troco. *Keep the change.*
　　Ela ficou doente. *She became ill.*
ficção *f. fiction.*
ficha *f. index card, file card; chip (poker).*
fichar *to record, to file.*
fichário *m. file cabinet; card index.*
fidelidade *f. fidelity; loyalty.*
　　De alta fidelidade. *High fidelity.*
fiel *adj. faithful, loyal; accurate.*
fígado *m. liver; courage.*
figo *m. fig.*

figueira *f. fig tree.*
figura *f. figure, form, appearance; image.*
figurar *to figure; to appear.*
fila *f. line; row; rank.*
    Em fila. *In line. In a row.*
    Fazer fila. *To line up; To stand in line.*
    Primeira fila. *First row. Front rank.*
filar *to seize, to grasp, to sponge, to mooch.*
filé *m. fillet (meat, fish).*
fileira *f. line, row; tier; rank.*
filete *m. fillet; thread (screw).*
FILHA *f. daughter, child.*
    Eles têm três filhas e um filho. *They have three daughters and one son.*
FILHO *m. son, child; pl. children.*
    Não temos filhos. *We don't have any children.*
    Tal pai, tal filho. *Like father, like son.*
filiação *f. filiation; relationship.*
filial *adj. filial; n. f. branch office or store.*
filipino *Philippine.*
filmar *to film.*
FILME *m. film; movie.*
    Não gostei do filme. *I didn't like the film.*
filosofia *f. philosophy.*
filósofo *m. philosopher.*
filtrar *to filter, to strain.*
filtro *m. filter, strainer.*
FIM *end; object, purpose, aim.*
    No fim do mês. *At the end of the month.*
    Em fins de junho (Junho). *Toward the end of June.*
    Dar fim a. *To finish.*
    Por fim. *Finally. At last.*
    Sem fim. *Endless. Endlessly.*
    A fim de. *In order that.*
    No fim das contas. *After all.*
finado *adj., n. m. deceased.*
    Dia de Finados. *All Souls' Day.*
FINAL *adj. final; n. m. end.*
    Parte final. *Last part.*
    No final das contas. *After all. In the end.*
    Finalmente. *Finally.*
finalizar *to finish, to conclude.*
finanças *f. pl. finances; public funds.*
financeiro *adj. financial; n. m. financier.*
findar *to finish, to end.*
fineza *f. fineness; delicacy; courtesy.*
    Agradeço muito a sua fineza. *I appreciate your courtesy very much.*
fingir *to pretend.*
finlandês *adj. Finnish; n. m. Finn.*
fino *adj. fine, delicate; cunning; keen; polite.*
fio *m. thread, string; filament; edge (knife).*
    Fio de pérolas. *String of pearls.*
    Dias a fio. *Days on end.*
    Ela perdeu o fio da conversa. *She lost the thread of the conversation.*
FIRMA *f. firm; business concern; signature.*

Ela trabalha com uma firma norte-americana. *She works for an American (North American) firm.*
firmar *to sign, to endorse; to make firm; to secure.*
firme *adj. firm, fast, stable, secure, resolute.*
    Ele se mantem firme. *He holds his ground.*
fiscal *adj. fiscal; n. m. inspector; controller.*
física *f. physics.*
físico *adj. physical; n. m. physicist; physique.*
    Ele tem um defeito físico. *He has a physical defect.*
fisiologia *f. physiology.*
fisionomia *f. appearance; look.*
FITA *f. ribbon; movie film; tape.*
    Fita de máquina de escrever. *Typewriter ribbon.*
fitar *to stare at.*
fixar *(x = ks) to fix, to fasten; to determine; to stare.*
fixo *(x = ks) adj. fixed, set; fast (of color).*
flagrante *adj. flagrant; red-handed; n. m. snapshot.*
    Em flagrante. *In the act. Red-handed.*
flamejar *to flame.*
flamengo *adj. Flemish; n. m. Fleming; flamingo.*
flâmula *f. small flame; pennant; streamer.*
flanela *f. flannel.*
flauta *f. flute.*
flecha *f. arrow, dart.*
flertar *to flirt.*
flexível *adj. flexible, pliable.*
FLOR *f. flower, blossom.*
    Estar em flor. *To be in bloom.*
    Na flor da idade. *In the prime of life.*
florescer *to blossom, to bloom.*
floresta *f. forest.*
florista *m. and f. florist.*
fluente *adj. fluent, flowing.*
fluido *adj. fluid; fluent; n. m. fluid.*
fluminense *adj. of the State of Rio de Janeiro; m. and f. native of the State of Rio de Janeiro.*
flutuar *to float; to fluctuate.*
foca *f. seal, sea lion.*
focalizar *to focus, to focalize.*
focinho *m. snout; nose.*
foco *m. focus.*
    Em foco. *In focus.*
fogão *m. cooking stove.*
FOGO *m. fire.*
    Abrir fogo. *To open fire.*
    Pegar fogo. *To catch fire.*
    Armas de fogo. *Firearms.*
    Fogos de artifício. *Display of fireworks.*
    Não há fumaça sem fogo. *Where there's smoke there's fire.*
fogoso *adj. fiery, impetuous.*

fogueira *f. bonfire; blaze.*

foguete *m. rocket; missile; firecracker; lively person* Ⓑ.

fôlego *m. breath, wind.*

    Sem fôlego. *Out of breath.*

folga *f. rest, leisure.*

    Dia de folga. *Day off.*

folgar *to rest; to take it easy; to amuse oneself.*

FOLHA *f. leaf; sheet; blade.*

    A árvore não tem mais folhas. *The tree has no more leaves.*

    Virar a folha. *To change the subject.*

    Folha de estanho. *Tinfoil.*

    Uma folha de papel. *A sheet of paper.*

    Folha de faca. *Knife blade.*

folhagem *f. foliage.*

folhear *to thumb through, to glance at.*

folhetim *m. serial publication.*

folheto *m. pamphlet.*

folia *f. gaiety, merrymaking.*

fólio *m. folio.*

FOME *f. hunger.*

    Estou com fome (Tenho fome). *I am hungry.*

    Estar com (Ter) uma fome canina. *To be ravenous.*

    Estou morrendo (a morrer) de fome. *I'm starving.*

fomentar *to foment, to encourage.*

fonética *f. phonetics.*

fonógrafo *m. phonograph, record player.*

FONTE *f. spring, fountain; source.*

    Eu sei de boa fonte. *I have it on good authority.*

FORA *outside, out.*

    Há mais gente fora de que dentro. *There are more people outside than inside.*

    Fora! *Get out!*

    Estar fora. *To be absent. To be out.*

    Fora disso. *Besides that.*

    Fora de si. *Beside oneself. Frantic.*

    Deite fora. *Throw it away.*

forasteiro *adj. foreign; strange; n. m. foreigner; stranger.*

FORÇA *f. force, strength, power.*

    À força. *By force.*

    À força de. *By dint of.*

    Força motriz. *Motive power.*

    Forças armadas. *Armed forces.*

forçar *to force, to compel, to oblige.*

forçoso *adj. forceful; compelling; compulsory.*

FORMA *f. form, shape; manner, way; mold; pattern.*

    A forma desta caixa (x = sh) é interessante. *The shape of this box is interesting.*

    Em forma de "U." *U-shaped.*

    De nenhuma forma! *By no means!*

    Desta forma. *In this way.*

    Fora de forma! *Dismissed! (Military.)*

    Última forma! *As you were! (Military.)*

formação *f. formation.*

formal *adj. formal.*

formalidade *f. formality.*

formar *to form, to shape.*

    Os alunos formaram um círculo. *The students formed a circle.*

formar-se *to graduate.*

    O filho dela se formou em direito. *Her son graduated in law.*

formatura *f. graduation, commencement.*

formidável *adj. formidable; excellent; wonderful; terrific.*

    Ela é formidável. *She's wonderful.*

formiga *f. ant.*

formoso *adj. beautiful; handsome; lovely; fine.*

formosura *f. beauty.*

fórmula *f. formula; blank form; recipe.*

    Faça o favor de preencher esta fórmula Ⓟ. *Please fill out this form.*

formular *to formulate.*

formulário *m. blank form, application form.*

    Primeiro é preciso preencher este formulário. *First you must fill out this form.*

fornalha *f. oven; furnace.*

fornecer *to furnish, to provide.*

forno *m. oven; furnace.*

forrar *to line (a garment, etc.); to cover.*

    O sobretudo está forrado. *The overcoat is lined.*

forro *adj. free, freed; m. lining; pudding.*

fortalecer *to fortify.*

fortaleza *f. fortress, stronghold; fortitude, strength.*

FORTE *adj. strong, powerful; n. m. fort; strong point.*

    Caixa-forte (x = sh). *Strongbox. Safe.*

    Ele sempre joga forte. *He always plays hard.*

    O irmão dela é muito forte. *Her brother is very strong.*

fortificação *f. fortification.*

fortificar *to fortify, to strengthen.*

fortuito *adj. fortuitous, accidental.*

fortuna *f. fortune.*

    Boa fortuna. *Good luck.*

    Por fortuna. *Fortunately.*

fósforo *m. phosphorous; match (to light with).*

fossa *f. pit; hole.*

fotografar *to photograph.*

fotografia *f. photography; photograph, photo, picture.*

foz *f. mouth (of a river).*

fracalhão *m. weakling, coward.*

fração (fracção) *f. fraction.*

fracassar *to fail.*

fracasso *m. failure.*

fraco *adj. lean, thin; weak; n. m. weakling; weakness.*

frade *m. friar, monk.*

fragate *f. frigate.*

frágil *adj. fragile, brittle; weak, frail.*

fragmento *m. fragment.*

fragrância *f. fragrance, pleasing odor.*

fragrante *adj. fragrant.*

frágua *f. forge.*

framboesa *f. raspberry.*

francês *adj. French; n. m. Frenchman; French language.*

FRANCO *adj. frank, free, open, plain; n. m. franc.*
　　Ele não foi franco conosco. *He was not frank with us.*
　　Porto franco. *Free port.*
　　Franco de porte. *Postpaid.*
　　Entrada franca. *Admission free.*

frango *m. chicken.*
　　Frango assado. *Roast chicken.*

franqueado *adj. franked; free.*

franquear *to frank, to free from charges; to prepay; to facilitate.*
　　Franqueou as cartas? *Did you put stamps on the letters?*
　　Franquear a passagem. *To clear the way.*

franqueza *f. frankness, sincerity.*
　　Fale com franqueza. *Speak frankly.*

franquia *f. franchise; exemption from duties (taxes).*

fraqueza *f. weakness.*

frasco *m. flask, bottle.*

frase *f. phrase, sentence.*
　　Frase feita. *Idiom. Common expression.*

fraternidade *f. fraternity, brotherhood.*

fraude *f. fraud.*

FREAR Ⓑ *to put on the brakes; to slow down; to curb.*
　　Freie! *Put on the brakes!*

freguês *m. customer, client.*

frei *m. friar.*

FREIO *m. brake; check, curb; bit.*
　　Freio de mão. *Hand brake.*
　　Freio de emergência. *Emergency brake.*

freira *f. nun, sister.*

frenético *adj. mad, frantic.*

FRENTE *f. front; façade; appearance.*
　　Na frente de. *In front of.*
　　Frente a frente. *Face to face.*
　　Bem em frente. *Straight ahead.*
　　Porta da frente. *Front door.*

freqüência (frequência) *f. frequency.*
　　Eles se viam com freqüência. *They saw one another frequently.*

freqüente (frequente) *adj. frequent.*

FRESCO *adj. cool; fresh; wet (paint); n. m. fresh air; fresco (painting).*

A água está fresca. *The water is cool.*
　　Tomar o fresco. *To go out for some fresh air.*
　　Tinta fresca. *Wet paint.*
　　Ar fresco. *Fresh air.*

frescura *f. freshness; coolness.*

fretar *to freight; to charter.*

frete *m. freight; cargo.*

fricassé *m. fricassee.*

fricção *f. friction, rubbing.*

friccionar *to rub, to massage.*

frigir *to fry; to bother.*

frigorífico *m. refrigerator* Ⓟ; *freezer.*

FRIO *adj. cold, cool; n. m. cold.*
　　Estou com frio (Tenho frio). *I am cold.*
　　Está frio hoje. *It's cold today.*
　　Sangue frio. *Cold blood.*
　　Tempo frio. *Cold weather.*

friorento *adj. sensitive to cold.*

fritada *f. fried dish.*

fritar *to fry.*

frito *adj. fried.*
　　Batatas fritas. *Fried potatoes.*
　　Estou frito. *I'm in trouble. I'm in a mess* Ⓑ.

fronha *f. pillowcase; pillow.*

fronte *f. forehead; front.*

fronteira *f. frontier, border.*

frota *f. fleet.*
　　Frota mercante. *Merchant fleet.*

frouxo ($x = sh$) *adj. loose; slack; flabby.*

frugal *adj. frugal, thrifty.*

frustrar *to frustrate.*

FRUTA *f. fruit.*

frutífero *adj. fruitful.*

frutificar *to bear fruit.*

FRUTO *m. fruit; result; profit.*
　　Em dois anos vai dar fruto. *In two years it will show results.*

fubá *m. Brazilian cornmeal.*

fuga *f. escape, flight.*
　　Em fuga. *In flight.*
　　Pôr em fuga. *To put to flight. To rout.*

fugaz *adj. fleeting, transitory.*

fugir *to flee, to escape, to run away.*

fugitivo *adj., n. m. fugitive.*

fulano *m. person; So-and-So; John Doe.*
　　Fulano de Tal. *So-and-So. John Doe.*
　　Fulano, Beltrano e Sicrano. *Tom, Dick, and Harry.*

fulgir *to glow, to shine.*

fulgor *m. brilliance, glow.*

fumaça *f. smoke.*
　　Não há fumaça sem fogo. *Where there's smoke there's fire.*

fumador *adj. smoking; n. m. smoker.*

FUMAR *to smoke.*
　　Ela fuma demais. *She smokes too much.*

fumo *m. smoke; tobacco* Ⓑ; *fumes.*

Quero fumo para cachimbo. *I want some pipe tobacco.*

função *f. function, performance.*

funcionar *to function; to work; to run (machine).*

Esta máquina não funciona. *This machine doesn't work.*

Funcionar bem. *To be in good working condition.*

funcionário *m. functionary; employee.*

Funcionário público. *Government employee.*

fundação *f. foundation.*

fundador *m. founder.*

fundamental *adj. fundamental.*

fundamento *m. foundation, base, ground; reason.*

Sem fundamento. *Groundless.*

Faltar de fundamento. *To be without foundation or reason.*

fundar *to found, to base.*

Foi fundada em 1965. *It was founded in 1965.*

fundear *to anchor.*

fundição *f. foundry; casting, melting.*

fundir *to melt; to fuse.*

FUNDO *adj. deep; bottom; base; background; n. m. pl. funds.*

Fundo duplo. *Double bottom.*

Artigo de fundo. *Main article in a newspaper.*

Conhecer a fundo. *To know well.*

Fundos públicos. *Public funds.*

fúnebre *adj. funereal; sad.*

funeral *adj. funeral, funereal; n. m. funeral.*

funesto *adj. fatal; fateful.*

funil *m. funnel.*

furacão *m. hurricane.*

furar *to penetrate, to break through.*

Furar uma festa. *To crash a party.*

furgão *m. baggage car; van.*

fúria *f. fury, rage, fit of madness.*

furioso *adj. furious, mad, frantic.*

furor *m. fury.*

furtar *to steal; to cheat.*

Furtar-se ao dever. *To shirk one's responsibility.*

Não furtarás. *Thou shalt not steal.*

furto *m. theft.*

fusão *fusion; union.*

fusível *m. fuse.*

fuso *m. spindle, spool; screw; zone (time).*

futebol *m. soccer.*

futebolista *m. and f. soccer fan; soccer player.*

fútil *adj. futile.*

FUTURO *adj. future; n. m. future; fiancé.*

Em futuro próximo. *In the near future.*

Ela nos apresentou seu futuro. *She introduced her fiancé to us.*

fuzil *m. rifle.*

gabardina *f. gabardine.*

gabinete *m. cabinet; study; laboratory; ministry.*

Gabinete de leitura. *Reading room.*

gado *m. cattle, livestock.*

gaiola *f. cage.*

gaita *f. fife; harmonica; "dough," money ⓑ; useless things ⓑ.*

Não tenho gaita. *I don't have any money.*

Gaita galega. *Bagpipe.*

gaiteiro *m. player of fife, harmonica, or bagpipe.*

gaivão *m. swift (bird).*

gaivota *f. seagull, gull; fool ⓑ.*

gala *f. gala occasion; fine or formal dress.*

De gala. *Full or formal dress.*

Fazer gala de. *To boast of; to show off.*

galã *m. main romantic lead (theatre); lover.*

galantaria *f. gallantry; politeness.*

galante *adj. gallant; polite.*

galantear *to court; to compliment.*

galão *m. gallon; stripe (uniform).*

galego *adj. Galician; n. m. Galician; a Portuguese person in Brazil (not complimentary) ⓑ.*

galeria *f. gallery; arcade.*

galgo *m. greyhound.*

Correr como um galgo. *To rush, to hurry along.*

galhardete *m. pennant, streamer, banner.*

galho *m. branch (tree).*

galhofa *f. something funny; joke; fun.*

galicismo *m. Gallicism.*

galinha *f. chicken, hen; coward ⓑ.*

Deitar-se com as galinhas. *To go to bed with the chickens: To retire early.*

Muita galinha e poucos ovos. *Much talk and little action.*

galinheiro *m. chicken coop; gallery (theatre).*

galo *m. rooster, cock.*

Ao cantar do galo. *At dawn.*

Missa do galo. *Midnight mass.*

galocha *f. galochas, rubber overshoes.*

galopar *to gallop.*

galope *m. gallop.*

gamão *m. backgammon.*

gamo *m. deer, stag.*

gana *f. desire, craving; hate.*

gancho *m. hook; hairpin.*

ganhador *adj. winning; n. m. winner.*

GANHAR *to gain; to earn; to win; to reach.*

Como ganhar amigos. *How to win friends.*
Quanto dinheiro ganhou? *How much money did you earn?*
Não ganhamos. *We did not win.*
Ele não pode ganhar a vida. *He can't make a living.*
ganho *adj. gained, earned; n. m. profit, gain.*
ganso *m. goose, gander.*
garage Ⓑ, **garagem** *f. garage.*
garantia *f. guarantee; guaranty; security.*
Garantia por escrito. *Written guarantee.*
garantir *to guarantee; to vouch for.*
garção *m. waiter* Ⓑ.
gardênia (gardénia) *f. gardenia.*
GARFO *m. fork.*
gargalhada *f. burst of laughter.*
GARGANTA *f. throat; gorge.*
Dor de garganta. *Sore throat.*
Estou com ele pela garganta. *I've had enough of him.*
garota *f. young girl* Ⓑ.
garoto *m. boy; urchin.*
garra *f. claw; finger; hand.*
GARRAFA *f. bottle.*
Uma garrafa de cerveja. *A bottle of beer.*
gás *m. gas.*
Gás lacrimogêneo (lacrimogénio). *Tear gas.*
gasolina *f. gasoline.*
gasosa *f. soda pop.*
gasoso *adj. gaseous.*
GASTAR *to spread; to wear out; to use.*
Gastei todo o dinheiro que me deu. *I spent all the money you gave me.*
Não gaste o tempo com ela. *Don't waste your time with her.*
Os meninos gastam tudo em pouco tempo. *The children wear everything out in a short time.*
GASTO *adj. spent; worn out; n. m. cost, expense.*
Todo o dinheiro foi gasto em dois meses. *All the money was spent in two months.*
Houve muitos gastos. *There were many expenses.*
gata *f. cat.*
gatilho *m. trigger.*
gatinha *f. kitten.*
Andar de gatinhas. *To crawl on all fours.*
GATO *m. cat; clever person; slip, error.*
Não dé carne ao gato. *Don't give the cat meat.*
Não compre gato por lebre. *Don't buy a pig in a poke.*
Eles vivem como cão e gato. *They fight like cats and dogs.*
Quem não tem cão, caça com gato. *You have to make the best of things.*
Ela cometeu um gato. *She pulled a boner.*

gauchesco *adj. Gaucho* Ⓑ.
gaúcho *adj. of Rio Grande do Sul in Brazil; n. m. native of Rio Grande do Sul; also type of cowboy of Uruguay and of Argentina.*
gaveta *f. drawer (desk).*
A carta está na gaveta da mesa. *The letter is in the drawer of the table.*
gavião *m. hawk; sly person* Ⓑ; *ladies' man* Ⓑ: *children's game* Ⓟ.
gazeta *f. gazette, newspaper.*
geladeira *f. icebox, refrigerator.*
gelado *adj. frozen; icy; cold; n. m. sherbet; ice cream; cold drink.*
gelar *to freeze; to frighten.*
gelatina *f. gelatin; jelly.*
geléia (geleia) *jelly, jam.*
gelo *m. ice; indifference.*
Gelo seco. *Dry ice.*
gema *f. yolk (egg); core.*
Carioca da gema. *A true carioca (native of the city of Rio de Janeiro).*
gêmeo (gémeo) *m. twin.*
gemer *to moan; to creak.*
gemido *m. groan; sigh.*
general *m. general (military rank).*
GÊNERO (GÉNERO) *m. class, kind, sort; gender; pl. goods.*
O gênero humano. *Mankind.*
Gêneros alimentícios. *Foodstuffs.*
generosidade *f. generosity.*
generoso *adj. generous, liberal.*
gengibre *m. ginger.*
gengiva *f. gum (mouth).*
gênio (génio) *m. genius; talent; nature, disposition; temperament.*
Ele tem mau gênio. *He has a bad temper.*
genro *m. son-in-law.*
GENTE *f. people; personnel; one, they, we.*
Há muita gente hoje. *There are many people (here) today.*
A gente não faz isso. *One doesn't do that.*
gentil *adj. kind; polite; courteous.*
gentileza *f. kindness; courtesy.*
Agradeço muito a sua gentileza. *I am very grateful for your kindness.*
gentio *adj. and n. m. gentile, pagan, heathen.*
genuíno *adj. genuine, real.*
geografia *f. geography.*
geometria *f. geometry.*
geração *f. generation.*
gerador *adj. generating; n. m. generator.*
GERAL *adj. general.*
Em geral. *In general. Generally.*
Minas Gerais. *Minas Gerais ("General Mines"), name of a state in Brazil.*
gerânio *m. geranium.*
gerar *to generate.*
gerência *f. management, administration.*

gerente *m. manager, administrator.*
gerigonça *f. jargon; slang.*
germânico *adj. Germanic.*
germe *m. germ.*
germinar *to germinate.*
gerúndio *m. gerund.*
gesticular *to gesticulate.*
gesto *m. gesture.*
gigante *adj. giant; n. m. giant.*
gilete *f. safety razor.*
     Não uso navalha, só gilete. *I don't use a straight razor, just a safety razor.*
ginásio *m. high school; gymnasium.*
girar *to rotate, to turn; to circulate.*
girassol *m. sunflower.*
gíria *f. slang; jargon.*
giro *m. turn; stroll; terrific* Ⓟ *(slang).*
giz *m. chalk.*
     Sem giz não so pode escrever no quadro negro. *We can't write on the blackboard without chalk.*
glacial *adj. glacial; cold.*
globo *m. globe, ball.*
glória *f. glory; fame.*
gloriar *to glorify.*
glorioso *adj. glorious.*
glosa *f. comment; criticism.*
goiaba *f. guava.*
goiabada *f. guava paste.*
goiano *adj., n. m. of the state of Goiás in Brazil.*
gol *m. goal (sports).*
gola *f. collar; throat.*
golfe *m. golf.*
     Tacos de golfe. *Golf clubs.*
golfo *m. gulf.*
     Gôlfo do México. *Gulf of Mexico.*
GOLPE *m. blow; coup.*
     De golpe. *Suddenly; All at once.*
     De um só golpe. *At one stroke; With one blow.*
     Um golpe de sorte. *A lucky blow or stroke.*
     Golpe de estado. *Coup d'état.*
     Golpe de mestre. *Master stroke.*
     Golpe de mar. *Surf, heavy sea.*
goma *f. gum; starch.*
     Goma de mascar. *Chewing gum.*
GORDO *adj. fat; n. m. fat person.*
     O pai dele é muito gordo. *His father is very fat.*
gordura *f. fat; grease; stoutness.*
gorila *m. gorilla.*
gorjear *to warble.*
gorjeta *f. tip (money).*
gorro *m. cap.*
GOSTAR *to like; to taste.*
     Gosto muito dele. *I like him very much.*
     Gosto mais deste. *I prefer this one.*

     Eu gostaria de ver a peça. *I should like to see the play.*
GOSTO *m. liking; taste; pleasure.*
     Ela tem bom gosto. *She has good taste.*
     Isto é muito a meu gosto. *This is very much to my taste.*
gostoso *adj. tasty, delicious.*
gota *f. drop (liquid); gout.*
     Gota a gota. *Drop by drop.*
     Elas se parecem como duas gotas d'água. *They are as alike as two peas in a pod.*
     Essa foi a gota d'água que fez transbordar o copo. *That was the straw that broke the camel's back.*
gotejar *to trickle, to drip.*
governador *m. governor.*
governante *adj. governing, ruling; n. m. ruler; governor.*
governar *to govern, to rule; to control.*
     E ela quem governa em casa. *She rules the house.*
governo *m. government; control.*
     O novo governo é forte. *The new government is strong.*
gozar *to enjoy.*
     Elas gozam de boa saúde. *They enjoy good health.*
gozo *m. joy; enjoyment.*
gozoso *adj. joyful, merry.*
GRAÇA *f. grace; favor; pardon; wit; charm; name; pl. thanks.*
     Graças a Deus. *Thank God.*
     Eu terminei tudo, graças à sua ajuda. *I finished everything, thanks to your help.*
     Não acho graça nisso. *I don't think that's funny.*
     Tem graça. *That's funny.*
     Lançar graças. *To crack jokes.*
     Qual é sua graça? *What is your name?*
gracejar *to joke.*
     Ele sempre está gracejando (está a gracejar). *He's always joking.*
gracioso *adj. gracious; witty.*
grade *f. grating; grille; latticework.*
gradual *adj. gradual.*
graduar *to grade, to classify; to graduate.*
graduar-se *to graduate (school).*
gráfica *f. writing; spelling.*
gráfico *adj. graphic; n. m. graph; chart.*
gralha *f. crow; jay; magpie; chatterbox, gossip, misprint.*
grama *f. grass; gram.*
gramática *f. grammar.*
grampear *to staple; to clip.*
     Máquina de grampear. *Stapler.*
grampo *m. staple; clip; pin; cramp.*
granada *f. grenade.*

GRANDE *adj. great, large, tall.*
A casa dele é muito grande. *His house is very large.*
Ele é um grande artista. *He is a great artist.*

grandeza *f. greatness.*

grandioso *adj. grandiose, magnificent.*

granizar *to hail.*

granizo *m. hail.*

granja *f. farm.*

grão *m. grain; kernel.*

gratidão *f. gratitude.*

gratificação *f. gratuity, tip.*

gratificar *to reward; to tip.*

grátis *free (at no cost).*

grato *adj. grateful; pleasant.*
Fico-lhe muito grato. *I remain gratefully yours. I am very grateful to you.*

gratuito *adj. free (at no cost).*

grau *m. degree.*
Dez graus abaixo *(x = sh)* de zero. *Ten degrees below zero.*
Por graus. *By degrees.*

gravado *adj. engraved; recorded.*

gravador *adj. engraving; recording; n. m. engraver; recorder; tape recorder.*

gravar *to engrave; to record.*
O professor gravou duas fitas. *The professor recorded two tapes.*

GRAVATA *f. necktie.*
Vou levar seis gravatas na mala. *I'm going to take six neckties in my bag.*
Eu prefiro gravata-borboleta. *I prefer a bow tie.*

grave *adj. grave, serious.*
Foi muito grave. *It was very serious.*
Acento grave. *Grave accent mark.*

gravidade *f. seriousness, gravity.*

gravura *f. etching; engraving; picture.*

graxa *(x = sh) f. grease; shoe polish.*

graxento *(x = sh) adj. greasy.*

grego *adj. Greek.*

grelha *f. grill.*

grelhar *to grill, to broil.*

grêmio (grémio) *m. guild, society.*

greve *f. strike.*
Os operários entraram em greve. *The workers went on strike.*

grevista *m. and f. striker.*

grifo *m. italics.*
Leia a parte em grifo. *Read the part in italics.*

grilo *m. cricket.*

gripe *f. grippe, influenza.*

grisalho *adj. grayish; grizzled.*

gritar *to shout, to scream.*
Quem gritou? *Who cried out?*

gritaria *f. shouting; hubbub.*

grito *m. shout, scream.*
Grito de guerra. *Battle cry.*

groselha *f. currant; gooseberry.*

grosseiro *adj. coarse, rude, impolite.*

grosso *adj. thick; coarse.*

grou *m. crane (bird).*

grua *f. crane (bird); crane, derrick.*

grudar *to glue, to paste, to stick together.*

grude *m. glue, paste.*

grunhido *m. grunt.*

grunhir *to grunt.*

GRUPO *m. group.*
Vamos dividi-los em quatro grupos diferentes. *We are going to divide them into four different groups.*

gruta *f. grotto, cave.*

guarda *m. and f. guard; watch; guardian; watchman.*
Guarda de honra. *Guard of honor.*
Quem está de guarda? *Who is on duty?*

guarda-chuva *m. umbrella.*
Hoje não precisamos de guarda-chuva. *We don't need an umbrella today.*

guarda-livros *m. and f. bookkeeper.*

guarda-marinha *m. midshipman.*

guardanapo *m. napkin.*

GUARDAR *to keep; to guard; to take care of.*
Guarde o dinheiro no banco. *Keep your money in the bank.*
Ela não sabe guardar segredo. *She doesn't know how to keep a secret.*

guarda-roupa *m. wardrobe; cloakroom.*

guarnecer *to trim; to garnish; to garrison.*

guarnição *f. trim; garrison; crew.*
Todos os membros da guarnição estão a bordo. *All the members of the crew are aboard.*

guatemalteco *adj., n. m. Guatemalan.*

GUERRA *f. war.*
Fazer guerra. *To wage war.*
Guerra civil. *Civil war.*
Guerra atômica (atómica). *Nuclear war.*
Guerra fria. *Cold war.*

guerreiro *adj. warlike; m. warrior.*

GUIA *m. guide, leader; guidebook; directory; f. guidance; permit, bill.*
Gostaria dos serviços dum guia. *I'd like to have the services of a guide.*
Não tem guia da cidade? *Don't you have a guidebook of the city?*

guianês *adj., n. m. Guianan.*

guiar *to guide, to direct; to drive.*
O senhor sabe guiar? *Do you know how to drive?*

guichê (guichet, guichê) *m. window (ticket, information).*
Guichê de informações. *Information window.*

guisa *f. guise.*
À guisa de. *Like.*

H

guisado *m. stew.*
guisar *to stew.*
guitarra *f. guitar.*
guitarrista *m. and f. guitarist.*

hã *ha!*
hábil *adj. able; clever; capable.*
  Ele é muito hábil. *He is very clever.*
habilidade *f. ability, skill.*
habilitado *adj. able; qualified.*
habilitar *to qualify; to enable.*
habitação *f. dwelling, residence.*
habitante *m. and f. inhabitant, resident.*
  É uma cidade de vinte mil habitantes. *It is a city of twenty thousand inhabitants.*
habitar *to inhabit.*
hábito *m. habit, custom; dress, garb.*
  Ele tinha o hábito de levantar-se cedo. *He was in the habit of getting up early.*
  Ela tinha esse mau hábito. *She had that bad habit.*
  O hábito não faz o monge. *Clothes don't make the man.*
habituar *to accustom.*
habituar-se *to become accustomed.*
haitiano *adj. and n. m. Haitian.*
hálito *m. breath.*
  Mau hálito. *Bad breath.*
hangar *m. hangar.*
harmonia *f. harmony.*
harpa *f. harp.*
haste *f. pole, rod.*
hastear *to hoist (flag).*
havaiano *adj. Hawaiian; n. m. Hawaiian.*
havana *m. and f. Havana cigar.*
HAVER *to have (auxiliary verb; however, today "ter" is replacing it in this use); to be, to exist; there to be.*
  Há. *There is. There are.*
  Havia. *There was. There were.*
  Houve. *There was. There were.*
  Haverá. *There will be.*
  Haveria. *There would be.*
  Haja. *There may be.*
  Que haja. *Let there be.*
  Houvesse. *There might be.*
  Se houvesse. *If there were.*
  Há havido. *There has (have) been.*
  Havia havido. *There had been. There would have been.*
  Haveria havido. *There would have been.*
  Há que. *It is necessary.*
  Haverá que. *It will be necessary.*
  Houve que. *It was necessary.*
  Há de ser. *It must be.*

Hei de partir amanhã. *I'm to leave tomorrow.*
Há pouco tempo. *A short while ago.*
Ela havia escrito a carta? *Had she written the letter?*
Ontem não houve aulas. *There were no classes yesterday.*
Deve haver cartas para mim. *There must be some letters for me.*
Há uma semana que a vi. *I saw her a week ago.*
Que há de novo. *What's new?*
O que é que há? *What's the matter?*
Haja o que houver. *Come what may.*
Não há remédio. *It can't be helped.*
Vai haver muita gente lá. *There will be many people there.*
Não há de quê. *Don't mention it.*
hebreu *adj., n. m. Hebrew.*
hectare *m. hectare.*
hediondo *adj. hideous, repugnant.*
hélice *m. and f. propeller.*
hemisfério *m. hemisphere.*
hera *f. ivy.*
herança *f. inheritance, legacy, heritage.*
herdar *to inherit.*
herdeiro *m. heir.*
hereditário *adj. hereditary.*
herói *m. hero.*
heróico *adj. heroic.*
hesitar *to hesitate.*
  Ela hesitou em fazê-lo. *She hesitated in doing it.*
hidráulico *adj. hydraulic.*
hidroavião *m. seaplane.*
hidrofobia *f. hydrophobia, rabies.*
hiena *f. hyena.*
hífen *m. hyphen.*
higiene *f. hygiene.*
higiênico (higiénico) *adj. hygienic, sanitary.*
hino *m. hymn; anthem.*
  Hino nacional. *National anthem.*
hipérbole *f. hyperbole.*
hipermercado *m. large supermarket.*
hipertensão *f. hypertension.*
hipnotismo *m. hypnotism.*
hipnotizar *to hypnotize.*
hipocrisia *f. hyprocrisy.*
hipócrita *adj. hypocritical; n. m. and f. hypocrite.*
hipódromo *m. racetrack, hippodrome.*
hipopótamo *m. hippopotamus.*
hipoteca *f. mortgage.*
hipotecar *to mortgage.*
hispânico *adj. Hispanic.*
hispano-americano *adj. Spanish-American; n. m. Spanish-American.*
  Literatura hispano-americana. *Spanish-American literature.*

HISTÓRIA *f. history; story.*
  História antiga. *Ancient history.*
  História moderna. *Modern history.*
  Não me conte mais histórias! *Don't tell me any more stories!*
historiador *m. historian.*
histórico *adj. historic.*
HOJE *m. today.*
  Hoje é segunda-feira. *Today is Monday.*
  Qual é o programa de hoje? *What's today's program?*
  De hoje em diante. *From now on.*
  Hoje em dia. *Nowadays.*
  De hoje a oito dias. *In a week.*
  Hoje à noite. *Tonight. This evening.*
  Hoje à tarde. *This afternoon.*
holandês *adj., n. m. Dutch.*
holofote *m. searchlight.*
HOMEM *m. man.*
  Homem de bem. *Honest man.*
  Homem do mundo. *Man of the world.*
  Homem de letras. *Man of letters.*
  Homem de negócios. *Businessman.*
  Homem de Estado. *Statesman.*
  O homem põe e Deus dispõe. *Man proposes, God disposes.*
homenagem *f. homage, honor, respects.*
  Prestar homenagem. *To render homage to.*
homenzarrão *m. very large man.*
homossexual *m., f. homosexual.*
hondurenho *adj., n. m. Honduran.*
honesto *adj. honest; sincere.*
honra *f. honor, respect.*
  Em honra de. *In honor of.*
honradez *f. honesty, integrity.*
honrar *to honor.*
HORA *f. hour; time.*
  Que horas são? *What time is it?*
  São duas horas e meia. *It's two thirty.*
  À que horas começa a festa? *What time does the party begin?*
  Está na hora de jantar. *It's time for dinner.*
  Hora de verão. *Daylight saving time.*
  Ele chegou na hora. *He arrived on time.*
horário *m. schedule; timetable.*
horizontal *adj. horizontal.*
horizonte *m. horizon.*
horrível *adj. horrible.*
horror *m. horror.*
horroroso *adj. horrible, frightful, dreadful.*
horta *f. vegetable garden.*
hospedagem *f. lodging; board.*
hospedar *to lodge.*
hóspede *m. and f. guest.*
hospício *m. asylum (hospital).*
hospital *m. hospital.*
hospitalizar *to hospitalize.*
hóstia *f. Host (communion bread).*
hostil *adj. hostile.*

hostilidade *f. hostility.*
hostilizar *to antagonize.*
hotel *m. hotel.*
hoteleiro *m. hotelman, innkeeper.*
humanidade *f. humanity, mankind.*
humanitário *adj. humanitarian, philanthropic.*
HUMANO *adj. human, humane; n. m. man, human being.*
  Um ser humano. *A human being.*
humildade *f. humility.*
humilde *adj. humble.*
humilhado *adj. humiliated.*
humilhante *adj. humiliating.*
humilhar *to humiliate; to humble.*
HUMOR *m. humor; disposition.*
  Estar de bom humor. *To be in a good mood.*
  Estar de mau humor. *To be in a bad mood.*
humorado *adj. humored.*
  Mal humorado. *Bad-tempered.*
humorista *m. and f. humorist.*
húngaro *adj. Hungarian; n. m. Hungarian.*
hurra! *hurrah!*

I

iaiá *f. missy, miss* Ⓑ.
iate *m. yacht.*
ibérico *adj., n. m. Iberian.*
ibero *adj., n. m. Iberian.*
içar *to hoist.*
  Içar a bandeira. *To hoist the flag.*
ida *f. departure; one-way (ticket).*
  Bilhete de ida e volta. *Round-trip ticket.*
IDADE *f. age; time, period.*
  Idade de ouro. *Golden Age.*
  Idade Média. *Middle Ages.*
  Certidão de idade. *Birth certificate.*
  Que idade o senhor tem? *How old are you?*
ideal *adj., n. m. ideal.*
idealizar *to idealize.*
idear *to think of, to conceive; to devise; to plan.*
IDÉIA (IDEIA) *f. idea.*
  Não tenho a mínima idéia. *I haven't the slightest idea.*
  É uma boa idéia. *It's a good idea.*
  Mais tarde ela mudou de idéia. *Later she changed her mind.*
idem *the same, ditto.*
idêntico *adj. identical, the same.*
identidade *f. identity.*
  O senhor tem os seus documentos de identidade? *Do you have your identification papers?*
identificação *f. identification.*

identificar *to identify.*
idioma *m. language.*
idiota *adj. idiotic; n. m. and f. idiot, fool.*
idiotice *f. foolishness, foolish thing.*
idiotismo *m. idiocy.*
ídolo *m. idol.*
idoso *adj. aged, old.*
ignomínia *f. infamy; disgrace.*
ignorância *f. ignorance.*
ignorante *adj. ignorant; unaware; n. m. ignoramus, ignorant person.*
     Ela estava ignorante do que acontecia. *She was unaware of what was happening.*
     Ele é um ignorante. *He's an ignoramus.*
ignorar *to be ignorant of, not to know, to be unaware.*
     Ignoro seu nome. *I don't know his name.*
IGREJA *f. church.*
IGUAL *adj. equal; similar, like; even.*
     Vamos dividi-lo em partes iguais. *We'll divide it in equal parts.*
     Não ter igual. *To be matchless. To have no equal.*
     Nunca vi coisa igual. *I never saw anything like it.*
     Cada qual com seu igual. *Birds of a feather flock together.*
igualar *to equalize, to make even; to compare.*
igualdade *f. equality.*
     Igualdade de condições. *Equal terms.*
ilegal *adj. illegal.*
ilegítimo *adj. illegitimate.*
ilegível *adj. illegible.*
ileso *adj. unharmed, safe.*
iletrado *adj., n. m. illiterate.*
ilha *f. island, isle.*
ilimitado *adj. unlimited.*
iludir *to deceive.*
iluminação *f. illumination.*
iluminar *to illuminate.*
ilusão *f. illusion.*
ilusivo *adj. illusive.*
ilustração *f. illustration.*
ilustrar *to illustrate; to explain.*
ilustrar-se *to acquire knowledge; to become distinguished.*
ilustre *adj. illustrious, celebrated.*
imagem *f. image, figure.*
imaginação *f. imagination.*
IMAGINAR *to imagine, to think, to suspect.*
     Imagine! *Just imagine!*
     Não posso imaginar tal coisa! *I can't imagine such a thing!*
imbecil *adj. imbecileic; n. m. imbecile.*
imediação *f. immediacy; pl. environs.*
imediatamente *immediately.*
imediato *adj. immediate; near; m. second in command.*
imenso *adj. immense.*

imigração *f. immigration.*
imigrante *adj., n. m. immigrant.*
imigrar *to immigrate.*
imitação *f. imitation.*
imitar *to imitate; to mimic.*
imoderado *adj. immoderate.*
imoral *adj. immoral.*
imortal *adj. immortal.*
imóvel *adj. immobile; n. m. real estate* Ⓑ*.*
impaciência *f. impatience.*
impacientar *to make impatient, to exasperate.*
impaciente *adj. impatient, restless.*
ímpar *adj. odd, uneven (number).*
     Número ímpar. *Odd number.*
imparcial *adj. impartial, unbiased.*
impávido *adj. fearless.*
impedimento *m. impediment, hindrance, obstacle.*
impedir *to hinder, to prevent.*
     A linha está impedida Ⓟ. *The line (telephone) is busy.*
impenetrável *adj. impenetrable.*
imperador *m. emperor.*
imperativo *adj., n. m. imperative.*
imperfeito *adj. imperfect, faulty; n. m. imperfect (tense).*
império *m. empire, domain.*
     Império Romano. *Roman Empire.*
impermeabilizar *to waterproof.*
impermeável *adj. waterproof; n. m. raincoat.*
     Hoje vou levar o impermeável. *I'm going to take my raincoat today.*
impertinente *adj. impertinent.*
impessoal *adj. impersonal.*
ímpeto *m. impetus.*
impetuoso *adj. impetuous.*
ímpio *adj. wicked, impious; n. m. impious person.*
implicar *to implicate; to imply.*
implícito *adj. implicit.*
implorar *to implore.*
imponente *adj. imposing.*
IMPOR *to impose; to command.*
     Impor respeito. *To command respect.*
     Impor condições. *To impose conditions.*
     Impor um imposto. *To levy a tax.*
importação *f. importation, import.*
IMPORTÂNCIA *f. importance.*
     Não tem importância. *It doesn't matter.*
     Sem importância. *Unimportant.*
IMPORTANTE *adj. important.*
     Isto é importante. *This is important.*
IMPORTAR *to import; to matter, to be important; to amount to.*
     Esta casa importa café do Brasil. *This firm imports coffee from Brazil.*
     Que importa? *What does it matter?*
     Não importa. *It doesn't matter. Never mind.*

Importa muito. *It matters a lot. It's very important.*

Não me importa. *It makes no difference to me.*

Em quanto importa a conta? *How much is the bill? How much does the bill come to?*

importunar *to annoy, to bother.*

imposição *f. imposition.*

impossibilidade *f. impossibility.*

impossibilitar *to make impossible, to preclude.*

IMPOSSÍVEL *adj. impossible.*

É impossível. *It's impossible. It can't be done.*

imposto *adj. imposed, set; n. m. tax, duty.*

Imposto de renda. *Income tax.*

Isento de imposto. *Tax-free.*

impreciso *adj. vague, not clear.*

imprensa *f. press.*

impressão *f. impression; printing, edition.*

impressionar *to impress; to move; to affect.*

impresso *adj. printed; n. m. printed document.*

impressora *f. printer (machine).*

Impressora a laser. *Laser printer.*

Impressora de cor. *Color printer.*

imprevisto *adj. unforeseen, unexpected; sudden.*

Ele chegou de imprevisto. *He arrived unexpectedly.*

imprimir *to print, to imprint.*

impróprio *adj. improper, unfit, unbecoming.*

improvável *adj. unlikely, improbable.*

improvisar *to improvise.*

improviso *adj. unexpected; impromptu.*

De improviso. *Unexpectedly.*

imprudência *f. imprudence, lack of prudence.*

impulsionar *to impel; to drive; to urge.*

impulso *m. impulse.*

impunidade *f. impunity.*

impureza *f. impurity, contamination.*

impuro *adj. impure, contaminated.*

imputar *to impute, to attribute.*

imunizar *to immunize.*

imutável *adj. fixed, unchangeable.*

inaceitável *adj. inadmissible; unacceptable.*

inadaptável *adj. not adaptable.*

inadequado *adj. inadequate.*

inadmissível *adj. inadmissible.*

inadvertido *adj. inadvertent.*

inalterável *adj. unalterable, unchangeable.*

inativo (inactivo) *adj. inactive.*

inauguração *f. inauguration.*

inaugurar *to inaugurate, to begin.*

incansável *adj. untiring.*

incapacidade *f. incapacity, inability, incompetence.*

incapaz *adj. incapable, incompetent.*

Ela é incapaz de fazê-lo. *She is incapable of doing it.*

incendiar *to set on fire.*

incêndio *m. fire.*

incerteza *f. uncertainty.*

incerto *adj. uncertain.*

incessante *adj. incessant, continual, ceaseless.*

inchar *to swell, to puff up.*

incidente *adj., n. m. incident.*

incisão *f. incision.*

inciso *adj. incised, cut.*

incitar *to incite, to stimulate.*

inclemência *f. inclemency.*

A inclemência do tempo não nos permitiu sair. *The bad weather kept us at home.*

inclinação *f. inclination, tendency.*

inclinar *to incline, to bend.*

inclinar-se *to incline; to bow.*

INCLUIR *to include, to enclose.*

Está incluído o vinho? *Is the wine included?*

inclusive *inclusively.*

inclusivo *adj. inclusive.*

incluso *adj. included; enclosed.*

incoerente *adj. incoherent.*

incógnito *adj. incognito; unknown.*

incombustível *adj. incombustible.*

incomodar *to disturb, to inconvenience, to bother.*

Não se incomode. *Don't bother.*

incômodo (incómodo) *adj. uncomfortable, inconvenient.*

incomparável *adj. matchless, without equal.*

incompatível *adj. incompatible.*

incompetência *f. incompetency.*

incompleto *adj. incomplete, unfinished.*

incompreensível *adj. incomprehensible.*

inconcebível *adj. inconceivable, unthinkable.*

incondicional *adj. unconditional.*

inconfidência *f. disloyalty.*

incongruência *f. incongruity.*

inconsciência *f. unconsciousness; lack of conscience.*

inconsciente *adj. unconscious; unaware.*

inconstância *f. inconstancy, fickleness.*

inconstitucional *adj. unconstitutional.*

inconveniente *adj. unseemly, inopportune; n. m. inconvenience, difficulty.*

incorporar *to incorporate.*

incorreto (incorrecto) *adj. incorrect, inaccurate, wrong, improper.*

incorrigível *adj. incorrigible.*

incredulidade *f. incredulity, disbelief.*

incrédulo *adj. incredulous; n. m. unbeliever.*

incremento *m. increment, increase.*

increpar *to reproach, to rebuke.*

incrível *adj. incredible, unbelievable.*

Mas isso é incrível! *But that's incredible!*

incubadora *f. incubator.*

incubar *to incubate, to hatch.*
inculcar *to inculcate.*
inculpar *to blame.*
inculto *adj. uncultivated; uncultured.*
incumbência *f. duty, charge, mission.*
incumbir *to commit, to entrust.*
incurável *adj. incurable.*
indagar *to inquire, to investigate.*
indecente *adj. indecent, shameful.*
indecisão *f. indecision, vacillation.*
indeciso *adj. undecided, vacillating, hesitant.*
indefeso *adj. defenseless.*
indefinido *adj. indefinite.*
indelével *adj. indelible.*
indenização *f. indemnity, reparation.*
indenizar *to indemnify, to reimburse.*
independência *f. independence.*
    Dia de Independência. *Independence Day.*
independente *adj. independent.*
indesejável *adj., n. m. and f. undesirable.*
indeterminado *adj. indeterminate; undecided.*
indevido *adj. improper.*
índex *m. index; index finger; pl. indices.*
indiano *adj., n. m. and f. Indian (from India).*
INDICAR *to indicate, to point out.*
    Faça o favor de me indicar o caminho.
        Please show me the way.
índice *m. index, table of contents.*
    Índice de preços. *Price index.*
    Índice de mortalidade. *Death rate.*
indício *m. indication, sign, mark, clue.*
indiferença *f. indifference.*
indiferente *adj. indifferent.*
indígena *adj., n. m. and f. native.*
indignar *to irritate, to annoy, to anger.*
indigno *adj. unworthy, undeserving, shameful.*
índio *adj., n. m. Indian (native peoples of North and South America).*
indireto (indirecto) *adj. indirect.*
indiscreto *adj. indiscreet.*
indiscrição *f. indiscretion.*
indiscutível *adj. unquestionable.*
indispensável *adj. indispensable, essential.*
indispor *to indispose, to upset.*
indisposição *f. indisposition.*
individual *adj. individual.*
indivíduo *m. individual, person.*
índole *f. disposition, nature.*
indulgência *f. indulgence.*
indulgente *adj. indulgent.*
indústria *f. industry.*
industrial *adj. industrial; n. m. and f. industrialist.*
induzir *to induce, to influence.*
ineficácia *f. inefficacy.*
ineficaz *adj. inefficacious, ineffectual.*
inegável *adj. undeniable.*
inépcia *f. ineptitude.*
inepto *adj. inept.*

inequívoco *adj. unmistakable, clear.*
inércia *f. inertia.*
inerte *adj. inert; inactive.*
inesgotável *adj. inexhaustible.*
inesperado *adj. unexpected.*
    Inesperadamente. *Suddenly. Unexpectedly.*
inesquecível *adj. unforgettable.*
inevitável *adj. inevitable, unavoidable.*
inexatidão (inexactidão) *(x = z) f. inaccuracy.*
inexato (inexacto) *(x = z) adj. inexact, inaccurate.*
inexperto *adj. inexpert, inexperienced.*
inexplicável *adj. inexplicable.*
infalível *adj. infallible.*
infamar *to defame, to malign.*
infame *adj. infamous.*
infâmia *f. infamy.*
infância *f. childhood.*
infantaria *f. infantry.*
infante *adj., n. m. and f. infant.*
infantil *adj. infantile, childish.*
infatigável *adj. tireless.*
infecção (infeção) *f. infection.*
infeccionar (infecionar) *to infect, to contaminate.*
infeliz *adj. unhappy; unfortunate; n. m. unhappy, unfortunate person.*
    Ele é infeliz. *He is unhappy.*
    Infelizmente. *Unfortunately.*
inferior *adj. inferior, lower; subordinate; n. m. inferior person; subordinate.*
    É uma fazenda de qualidade inferior. *The material is of inferior quality.*
inferioridade *f. inferiority.*
inferir *to infer, to conclude.*
inferno *m. hell, inferno.*
infestar *to infest; to overrun.*
infiel *adj. unfaithful.*
ínfimo *adj. lowest.*
infinidade *f. infinity.*
infinito *adj. infinite.*
inflação *f. inflation.*
inflamação *f. inflammation.*
inflamar *to inflame.*
inflamável *adj. inflammable.*
inflar *to inflate.*
influência *f. influence.*
    Ele tem muita influência no governo. *He is quite influential in the government.*
influenciar *to influence.*
INFLUIR *to influence, to inspire.*
INFORMAÇÃO *f. information; inquiry, investigation.*
    Eu não recebi essa informação. *I did not receive that information.*
informalidade *f. informality.*
INFORMAR *to inform; to report.*
    Ela não me informou disso. *She did not inform me about that.*

informática *f. computer science.*
informe *adj. formless; n. m. information.*
infortunado *adj. unfortunate.*
infração (infracção) *f. infraction, infringement.*
infreqüência (infrequência) *f. infrequence.*
infreqüente (infrequente) *adj. infrequent.*
infringir *to infringe, to violate.*
infrutuoso *adj. unsuccessful, fruitless.*
infundado *adj. unfounded, groundless.*
infundir *to infuse, to instill.*
ingênuo (ingénuo) *adj. ingenuous.*
INGLÊS *adj. English; n. m. Englishman; English language.*
    Fala-se inglês. *English is spoken here.*
    Ela não fala inglês. *She does not speak English.*
    Ele é inglês. *He is English.*
ingratidão *f. ingratitude.*
ingrato *adj. ungrateful.*
ingressar *to enter.*
ingresso *m. entry, entrance; admission ticket* Ⓑ.
inicial *adj., n. f. initial.*
iniciar *to initiate, to begin.*
iniciativa *f. initiative.*
    Tomar a iniciativa. *To take the initiative.*
início *m. beginning.*
    De início. *At first.*
inimigo *adj., n. m. enemy.*
iniqüidade (iniquidade) *f. iniquity, wickedness.*
injúria *f. insult; injury; offense.*
injustiça *f. injustice.*
injusto *adj. unjust, unfair.*
inocência *f. innocence.*
inocente *adj. innocent.*
inodoro *adj. odorless.*
inofensivo *adj. inoffensive, harmless.*
inolvidável *adj. unforgettable.*
inoportuno *adj. inopportune, untimely.*
inovar *to innovate.*
inquebrantável *adj. unbreakable; tenacious, unyielding.*
inquérito *m. inquiry; inquest.*
inquietar *to disturb, to cause anxiety.*
inquieto *adj. restless, uneasy.*
    Ela passou toda a noite inquieta. *She was restless all night.*
inquirir *to inquire.*
insalubre *adj. unsanitary, unhealthful.*
insano *adj. insane, mad.*
inscrever *to inscribe; to register; to sign up.*
inscrever-se *to register (at a school, etc.); to sign up.*
inscrição *f. inscription, registration.*
inseguro *adj. uncertain; insecure.*
insensatez *f. foolishness.*
insensato *adj. foolish; insane.*

insensível *adj. insensitive, impassive.*
inseparável *adj. inseparable.*
inserir *to insert; to introduce.*
inseticida (insecticida) *f. insecticide.*
inseto (insecto) *m. insect.*
insidioso *adj. insidious, treacherous.*
insigne *adj. famous, noted.*
insígnia *f. badge; pl. insignia.*
insignificante *adj. insignificant.*
insinuar *to insinuate, to hint.*
insipidez *f. insipidity; lack of flavor (taste); flatness.*
insípido *adj. insipid; tasteless.*
insistência *f. insistence, persistence.*
insistir *to insist.*
    Insistimos em que ela venha. *We insist that she come.*
insolação *f. sunstroke.*
insolência *f. insolence, rudeness.*
insolente *adj. insolent, rude.*
insolvente *adj. insolvent.*
insônia (insónia) *f. insomnia.*
inspeção (inspecção) *f. inspection.*
inspecionar (inspeccionar) *to inspect, to examine.*
inspetor (inspector) *m. inspector, supervisor.*
inspiração *f. inspiration.*
inspirar *to inspire; to inhale.*
    Ele inspira confiança. *He inspires confidence.*
instalação *f. installation; pl. fixtures.*
instalar *to install, to set up.*
instância *f. instance; request.*
    Em última instância. *As a last resort.*
instantâneo *adj. instantaneous, immediate; n. m. snapshot.*
INSTANTE *adj. instant; urgent; n. m. instant, moment.*
    Espere um instante. *Wait a minute.*
    A cada instante. *Every minute; All the time.*
instar *to urge, to press.*
instaurar *to establish, to initiate.*
instinto *m. instinct.*
instituição *f. institution.*
instituir *to institute, to establish.*
instituto *m. institute.*
instrução *f. instruction; education.*
    Instrução pública. *Public education.*
    Instrução primária. *Elementary education.*
    Instrução secundária. *Secondary education.*
    Instruções de manejo. *Operating instructions.*
instruir *to instruct, to teach.*
instrumento *m. instrument.*
    Que instrumento você toca? *What instrument do you play?*
    Instrumento de sopro. *Wind instrument.*
instrutivo *adj. instructive.*

instrutor *m. instructor, teacher.*
insubordinado *adj. insubordinate.*
insubordinar-se *to rebel, to revolt.*
insuficiência *f. insufficiency.*
insuficiente *adj. insufficient.*
insultar *to insult.*
insulto *m. insult, offense.*
insuperável *adj. insuperable, insurmountable.*
intato (intacto) *adj. intact, untouched.*
integral *adj. integral, whole.*
  Pão integral. *Whole wheat bread.*
integrar *to integrate.*
integridade *f. integrity.*
íntegro *adj. entire, whole; upright, honest.*
inteirar *to complete.*
inteirar-se *to become informed.*
inteiro *adj. entire, complete.*
inteletual (intelectual) *adj., n. m. and f. intellectual.*
inteligência *f. intelligence; understanding.*
INTELIGENTE *adj. intelligent, bright.*
  Ela é muito inteligente. *She is very intelligent.*
inteligível *adj. intelligible.*
intemperado *adj. intemperate.*
intempérie *f. rough or bad weather.*
INTENÇÃO *f. intention, intent.*
  Ele tinha segundas intenções. *He had ulterior motives.*
  Ter boas intenções. *To have good intentions; To mean well.*
  Ter más intenções. *To have bad intentions; Not to mean well.*
  Ter a intenção de. *To intend to.*
intendência *f. quartermaster (corps); administration.*
intendente *m. quartermaster; superintendent.*
intensidade *f. intensity.*
intenso *adj. intense.*
intentar *to try, to attempt; to intend.*
intento *adj. intent, purpose.*
intercalar *to intercalate, to insert.*
intercâmbio *m. interchange, exchange.*
interceder *to intercede, to plead (in another's behalf).*
interceptar *to intercept; to block.*
INTERESSANTE *adj. interesting.*
  Este romance é muito interessante. *This novel is very interesting.*
INTERESSAR *to interest, to concern.*
  Isso não me interessa. *That doesn't interest me.*
INTERESSAR-SE *to be concerned; to become interested.*
  Não me interesso por isso. *I'm not interested in that.*
INTERESSE *m. interest.*
  Ele não mostra o menor interesse. *He doesn't show the slightest interest.*

interino *adj. provisional, temporary, acting.*
INTERIOR *adj. interior, internal; n. m. interval, inside; country (rural)* Ⓑ.
  Ministério do Interior. *Department of the Interior.*
interligar *to network (computers).*
intermediar *to intermediate.*
intermediário *adj., n. m. intermediary.*
intermédio *adj. intermediate; n. m. intermediary; intervention; interlude.*
internacional *adj. international.*
internar *to intern.*
interno *adj. internal, interior; n. m. intern; boarding student.*
  Para uso interno. *For internal use.*
interpor *to interpose.*
interpretação *f. interpretation.*
interpretar *to interpret.*
  Acho que o senhor interpretou mal. *I believe you misunderstood.*
intérprete *m. and f. interpreter.*
interrogação *f. interrogation, questioning; question; inquiry; question mark.*
interrogar *to interrogate, to question.*
  Não me interrogue mais. *Don't question me any longer.*
interrogatório *m. interrogation, examination.*
INTERROMPER *to interrupt.*
  Foi preciso interromper o trabalho. *It was necessary to interrupt the work.*
interrupção *f. interruption.*
  Sem interrupção. *Without stopping.*
interruptor *m. switch (electric).*
interurbano *adj. interurban; n. m. long-distance telephone call.*
intervalo *m. interval; intermission.*
  Podemos falar no intervalo. *We can talk during the intermission.*
intervir *to intervene, to mediate.*
intestino *adj. intestinal, internal; n. m. intestine.*
intimar *to summon; to order; to inform.*
intimidade *f. intimacy, closeness, friendship.*
intimidar *to intimidate, to frighten.*
íntimo *adj. intimate, close.*
  Eles eram amigos íntimos. *They were very close friends.*
intitular *to entitle, to give a name to.*
intolerância *f. intolerance.*
intolerante *adj. intolerant.*
intolerável *adj. intolerable, unbearable.*
intoxicação *(x = ks) f. intoxication, poisoning.*
intranquilo (intranquilo) *adj. restless.*
intransigência *f. intransigence.*
intransigente *adj. intransigent, uncompromising, unyielding.*
intransitável *adj. impassable.*
intratável *adj. hard to deal with, stubborn, unsociable.*

intrepidez *f. intrepidity, courage.*
intrépido *adj. intrepid, fearless.*
intricado *adj. intricate, complicated.*
intriga *f. intrigue, plot.*
   Fazer intriga. *To plot.*
intrigante *adj. intriguing, scheming; n. m. and*
   f. intriguer, schemer.
introdução *f. introduction.*
introduzir *to introduce (not people; see*
   apresentar), *to initiate.*
   O professor introduziu uma nova teoria.
     The professor introduced (brought out)
     a new theory.
intromissão *f. interference.*
intruso *adj. intrusive; n. m. intruder.*
intuição *f. intuition.*
inumano *adj. inhuman, cruel.*
inundar *to flood, to overflow.*
INÚTIL *adj. useless; fruitless; futile.*
   É inútil fazer a viagem. *There's no use (in)*
     taking the trip.
   Ele é um homem inútil. *He's good for*
     nothing. He can't do anything.
inutilidade *f. uselessness, inutility.*
inutilizar *to spoil, to ruin, to disable.*
INUTILMENTE *uselessly, in vain.*
   Fizemos a viagem inutilmente. *We took the*
     trip in vain.
invadir *to invade.*
   Portugal foi invadido nos primeiros anos
     do século dezenove (dezanove).
     Portugal was invaded in the early
     years of the nineteenth century.
invalidar *to invalidate, to nullify; to render*
   void.
inválido *adj. invalid, disabled; n. m. invalid.*
invariável *adj. invariable, constant.*
invasão *f. invasion.*
inveja *f. envy.*
invejar *to envy.*
invenção *f. invention.*
inventar *to invent.*
inventário *m. inventory.*
invento *m. invention.*
invernar *to spend the winter, to hibernate.*
INVERNO *m. winter.*
   Não gosto nada do inverno (Inverno). *I*
     don't like winter at all.
inverossímil *adj. unlikely, improbable.*
inverter *to invert, to reverse; to invest.*
investigação *f. investigation.*
investigar *to investigate.*
invisível *adj. invisible; n. m. the invisible;*
   lady's fine hair net; fine hairpin.
iodo *m. iodine.*
IR *to go; to move; to be.*
   Vamos! *Let's go!*
   Já vou! *I'm coming!*
   Vou para casa. *I'm going home.*

Vá embora! *Go away!*
Não posso ir. *I can't go.*
Como vai? *How are you?*
Vou bem, obrigado. *I'm fine, thank you.*
Como vão as coisas? *How are things?*
   How is everything?
Ela vai muito melhor. *She is much better.*
Vamos ver. *Let's see.*
Vamos, chega. *Come on now, that's enough.*
A situação vai de mal a pior. *The situation*
   is going from bad to worse.
Ir a pé. *To walk. To go on foot.*
Ir a cavalo. *To ride. To go on horseback.*
Ir de carro. *To drive. To go by car.*
Ir de avião. *To fly. To go by plane.*
Ir a bordo. *To go aboard.*
João foi à cidade. *John went downtown.*
O chapéu lhe vai bem. *The hat looks good*
   on you.
Acho que vai chover. *I think it's going to*
   rain.
Devagar se vai ao longe. *Easy does it.*
Água vem, água vai. *Easy come, easy go.*
ira *f. anger, rage.*
   Acesso de ira. *Fit of rage.*
iracundo *adj. irascible.*
irlandês *adj. Irish; n. m. Irishman.*
IRMÃ *f. sister.*
   Ele tem duas irmãs. *He has two sisters.*
IRMÃO *m. brother.*
ironia *f. irony.*
irônico (irónico) *adj. ironic.*
irradiar *to irradiate; to broadcast; to be on*
   the air.
irreal *adj. unreal.*
irreflexão *(x = ks) f. thoughtlessness.*
irregular *adj. irregular.*
irresponsabilidade *f. irresponsibility.*
irresponsável *adj. irresponsible.*
irrigar *to irrigate.*
irritar *to irritate, to exasperate.*
irrompível *adj. unbreakable.*
isentar *to exempt, to free.*
isolado *adj. isolated.*
isolar *to isolate, to separate.*
isqueiro *m. cigarette lighter.*
ISSO *that.*
   Isso mesmo. *That's it.*
   Por isso. *Therefore.*
   Que é isso? *What's that?*
   Isso não me importa. *That makes no*
     difference to me.
   Nem por isso. *Don't mention it. Not at all.*
   Só faltava isso. *That's the last straw.*
ISTO *this.*
   Que é isto? *What's this?*
   Para que serve isto? *What's this for?*
   Tudo isto é muito interessante. *All this is*
     very interesting.

Por isto. *Therefore.*
Com isto. *Herewith.*
Isto é. *That is. Namely.*
Além disso. *Besides. Furthermore.*
italiano *adj., n. m. Italian.*
itinerário *m. itinerary.*
iugoslavo *adj., n. m. Yugoslav.*

J

JÁ *already; now, immediately; ever.*
Já me falaram nisso. *They already spoke to me about that.*
Venha já. *Come right now.*
Já esteve na capital? *Were you ever in the capital?*
Já não. *No longer.*
Já vou! *I'm coming!*
Já que. *Since. Inasmuch as.*
Desde já. *Immediately.*
jaça *f. fault, imperfection.*
jacaré *m. alligator.*
jacente *adj. lying down, recumbent.*
jacinto *m. hyacinth.*
jactância *f. boasting.*
jactar-se *to boast, to brag.*
jamais *never.*
JANEIRO *m. January; year.*
Ela tem sessenta janeiros. *She is sixty years old.*
JANELA *f. window.*
A janela de meu quarto é grande. *The window in my room is large.*
jangada *f. raft; sailing raft used in northeastern Brazil.*
JANTAR *m. dinner; to have dinner, to dine.*
Jantamos às sete. *We dine at seven.*
Sala de jantar. *Dining room.*
Jantar fora. *To dine out.*
O jantar está na mesa. *Dinner is served.*
japonês *Japanese.*
jaqueta *f. jacket.*
jaquetão *m. double-breasted jacket.*
jarda *f. yard (36 inches).*
JARDIM *m. garden.*
Jardim botânico. *Botanical garden.*
Jardim da infância. *Kindergarten.*
Jardim público. *Public park.*
Jardim zoológico. *Zoo.*
jardineira *f. female gardener; small table; small bus* Ⓑ.
jardineiro *m. male gardener.*
jarra *f. jar, vase.*
jarro *m. pitcher, jug.*
jato (jacto) *jet, stream.*
Jato de luz. *Flash of light.*
Avião a jato. *Jet plane.*

javali *m. wild boar.*
jazer *to lie, to repose.*
Aqui jaz. *Here lies.*
jazida *f. mineral deposit, bed; resting place.*
jazz *m. jazz.*
JEITO *m. manner, way; aptitude; special knack or ability.*
Ela tem jeito para professora. *She is especially talented at teaching.*
Com jeito. *Skillfully. Adroitly.*
Dar um jeito. *To find a way. To finagle a solution.*
jejuar *to fast.*
jejum *m. fast, fasting.*
Dia de jejum. *Fast day.*
Em jejum. *Fasting.*
jérsei *m. jersey (sweater)* Ⓑ.
jesuíta *m. Jesuit.*
Jesus, Jesus Cristo *m. Jesus, Jesus Christ.*
jibóia *f. boa constrictor.*
joalharia (joalheria) *f. jewelry store.*
jocoso *adj. jocose, funny.*
JOELHO *m. knee.*
De joelhos. *On one's knees. Kneeling.*
Pôr-se de joelhos. *To kneel.*
jogada *f. play, move (in a game); throwing, casting.*
Foi uma boa jogada. *It was a good play (in a game).*
jogador *m. player; gambler.*
JOGAR *to play (game); to gamble; to cast, to throw.*
No Brasil e em Portugal jogam futebol. *In Brazil and in Portugal they play soccer.*
Ele perdeu todo o dinheiro jogando. *He lost all his money gambling.*
Jogue isso fora! *Throw that out!*
JOGO *m. game; play; gambling; set.*
Jogo de cartas. *Card game.*
Jogo de azar. *Game of chance.*
Jogo de damas. *Checkers.*
Jogo do bicho. *Brazilian lottery, numbers game* Ⓑ.
Jogo de palavras. *Play on words.*
Casa de jogo. *Gambling house.*
joguete *m. toy, plaything.*
jóia *f. jewel, gem; pl. jewelry.*
jornada *f. journey; short trip.*
JORNAL *m. newspaper; diary; journal.*
Banca de jornais. *Newsstand* Ⓑ.
jornaleiro *m. day laborer; newsboy.*
jornalismo *m. journalism.*
jornalista *m. and f. journalist; newspaper man or woman.*
jorro *m. torrent, outpouring.*
A jorros. *In torrents.*
JOVEM *adj. young; n. m. young man; n. f. young lady.*

Quem é essa jovem? *Who's that young lady?*

Não conheço esse jovem. *I don't know that young man.*

jubilação *f. jubilation, rejoicing; retirement of a teacher.*

jubilar *to rejoice; to retire.*

judeu *adj. Jewish; n. m. Jew.*

judicial *adj. judicial.*

juiz *m. judge; arbiter; referee; umpire.*

Juiz de paz. *Justice of the peace.*

Juiz de direito. *District judge.*

juízo *m. judgment; opinion; decision; good judgment; mind.*

Você perdeu o juízo? *Have you lost your mind?*

Ele é um homem de juízo. *He's a man of good judgment.*

Chamar a juízo. *To summon to court.*

Dia de juízo. *Judgment day.*

julgado *adj. tried; sentenced; n. m. judicial district.*

julgamento *m. judgment, sentence; trial.*

julgar *to judge; to suppose, believe.*

Julgo que será assim. *I believe that's the way it will be.*

JULHO *m. July.*

jumento *m. donkey.*

JUNHO *m. June.*

júnior *adj. junior.*

junta *f. board, council, junta, committee; junction, union, coupling; joint.*

A que horas foi a junta? *What time did the meeting take place?*

Junta administrativa. *Administrative council.*

Junta de comércio. *Board of trade.*

Junta universal. *Universal joint.*

JUNTAR *to join, to unite; to assemble, to gather; to amass.*

Os dois exércitos juntaram forças. *The two armies joined forces.*

junto *adj. joined; close.*

Deixe *(x = sh)* tudo junto à porta. *Leave it all by the door.*

Fizemos o trabalho juntos. *We did the work together.*

Junto de. *Next to; Near.*

juramento *m. oath, vow.*

jurar *to swear, to take an oath.*

Juro que sim. *I swear it is so.*

júri *m. jury.*

juros *m. pl. interest.*

Juros compostos. *Compound interest.*

justiça *f. justice; fairness; law.*

Fazer justiça. *To do justice. To be just.*

Levar à justiça. *To bring to justice.*

justificar *to justify.*

JUSTO *adj. just; fair; exact; tight; close-fitting.*

Isso não é justo. *That's not fair.*

Este chapéu é muito justo. *This hat is too tight.*

Uma parte justa. *A fair share.*

juventude *f. youth.*

L

la *it, her, you (after verb forms ending in r, s, or z).*

LÁ *over there, there.*

LÃ *f. wool.*

LÁBIO *m. lip.*

Lamber os lábios. *To smack one's lips.*

laborar *to work, to cultivate.*

laboratório *m. laboratory.*

laborioso *adj. laborious; hardworking.*

lacerar *to lacerate, to mangle.*

laço *m. lasso; loop; trap; tie.*

Cair no laço. *To fall into a trap.*

lacônico (lacónico) *adj. laconic, brief.*

ladear *to be or go alongside; to dodge.*

Ele ladeou a questão. *He dodged the issue.*

ladeira *f. slope; hillside.*

Ladeira abaixo *(x = sh). Downhill.*

Ladeira acima. *Uphill.*

ladino *adj. shrewd, crafty, cunning.*

LADO *m. side; party, faction.*

Sente-se a meu lado. *Sit next to me.*

Ao outro lado da rua. *Across the street. On the other side of the street.*

Ela mora na casa do lado. *She lives next door.*

Por outro lado. *On the other hand.*

Não cabe de lado. *It won't fit sideways.*

Trabalharam lado a lado. *They worked side by side.*

Olhar de lado. *To look askance at. To look down at.*

De todos os lados. *From all sides. From all directions.*

Conheço muito bem seu lado fraco. *I know his weakness very well.*

Eu estou do lado de você. *I am on your side.*

ladrão *m. thief, robber.*

ladrar *to bark.*

ladrido *m. barking, bark.*

lagarta *f. caterpillar.*

lagarto *m. lizard.*

lago *m. lake, pond.*

lagoa *f. lagoon, pond.*

lagosta *f. lobster.*

LÁGRIMA *f. tear; teardrop.*

Lágrimas de alegria. *Tears of joy.*

Lágrimas de crocodilo. *Crocodile tears.*

laguna *f. lagoon.*

lama *f. mud.*

lamentar *to lament, to regret, to deplore.*

lamentável *adj. lamentable, regrettable, deplorable.*
    É lamentável. *It's regrettable.*

lâmina *f. lamina, blade.*

LÂMPADA *f. lamp; lightbulb.*
    Lâmpada de mesa. *Table lamp. Desk lamp.*
    Lâmpada néon. *Neon bulb.*
    Lâmpada elétrica (eléctrica). *Electric lightbulb.*
    Lâmpada de rádio. *Radio tube.*
    Mudar uma lâmpada. *To change a lightbulb.*

lançamento *m. launching; throwing, casting.*

LANÇAR *to launch; to throw; to cast; to eject.*
    Lançar à água. *To launch (a ship).*
    Lançar fora. *To throw out.*
    Ele se lançou aos pés dela. *He threw himself at her feet.*
    Lançar um livro. *To publish a book.*
    Lançar mão de. *To take hold of. To resort to.*

lance *m. throwing, casting; incident; predicament.*

lancha *f. launch, motorboat.*

lânguido *adj. languid, listless.*

lanterna *f. lantern.*
    Lanterna elétrica (eléctrica) de mão. *Flashlight.*

lápide *f. a flat stone with an inscription; tombstone.*

LÁPIS *m. pencil.*

lapso *m. lapse; slip.*

lar *m. hearth; home.*

LARANJA *f. orange.*

laranjada *f. orangeade.*

laranjeira *f. orange tree.*

lareira *f. hearth, fireplace.*

largar *to release; to cast off.*

LARGO *adj. wide; ample.*
    Um metro de largo. *A meter wide. One meter in width.*

largura *f. width; extent.*

laringe *m. and f. larynx.*

laringite *f. laryngitis.*

lástima *f. pity, compassion.*
    É uma lástima! *That's too bad!*
    Que lástima! *What a pity!*

lastimar *to feel sorry for; to regret.*

lastimável *adj. lamentable, deplorable.*

lastro *m. ballast.*

LATA *f. tin; tin can.*
    Lata de lixo (x = sh). *Garbage can.*
    Latas de conservas. *Canned goods.*
    Abridor de latas. *Can opener.*

lateral *adj. lateral.*

latido *m. barking, bark.*

latifúndio *m. large landed estate.*

latim *m. Latin.*

latino *adj. Latin.*

latino-americano *adj., n. m. Latin-American.*

latir *to bark, to yelp.*

latitude *f. latitude.*

lavadeira *f. washerwoman; washing machine.*

lavagem *f. washing; wash.*

lavanderia *f. laundry (place where clothes are washed).*

LAVAR *to wash; to bathe; to clean.*
    Lave as mãos antes de jantar. *Wash your hands before dinner.*
    Lavar a seco. *To dry-clean.*

lavatório *m. lavatory; washbasin.*

lavável *adj. washable.*

lavrador *m. farmer.*

lavrar *to cultivate, to till; to cut; to work.*

laxante *(x = sh) adj. laxative; n. m. laxative.*

lazer *m. leisure.*

leal *adj. loyal.*

lealdade *f. loyalty.*

leão *m. lion.*

lebre *f. hare.*
    Comprar gato por lebre. *To buy a pig in a poke.*

lecionar (**leccionar**) *to teach, to give lessons; to lecture.*

legal *adj. legal; all right, permissible; "cool."*
    Tudo legal. *Everything's cool.*

legalizar *to legalize; to validate.*

legar *to bequeath; to delegate.*

legenda *f. legend; inscription.*

legendário *adj. legendary.*

legião *f. legion.*

legislação *f. legislation.*

legislar *to legislate.*

legislatura *f. legislature.*

legitimar *to legitimate, to legalize.*

legítimo *adj. legitimate, authentic.*

legível *adj. legible.*

légua *f. league (measure of distance).*

legume *m. vegetable.*

LEI *f. law, act; rule.*
    Lei das médias. *Law of averages.*
    Lei de oferta e procura. *Law of supply and demand.*

leitão *m. suckling pig.*

LEITE *m. milk.*
    Leite condensado. *Condensed milk.*
    Leite magro. *Skim milk.*
    Tirar leite de vaca morta. *To draw blood from a stone. ("To extract milk from a dead cow.")*

leiteiro *m. milkman.*

leiteria *f. dairy.*

leito *m. bed.*

leitor *m. reader.*

leitura *f. reading; reading matter.*

lema *m. motto; slogan.*

LEMBRANÇA *f. remembrance; reminder; souvenir; pl. regards, greetings.*
Lembranças à sua irmã! *Give my regards to your sister!*
LEMBRAR *to remember, to recall; to remind.*
LEMBRAR-SE *to remember, to recall.*
Não me lembro. *I don't remember.*
Ela não se lembra disso. *She doesn't remember that.*
leme *m. rudder, helm.*
LENÇO *m. handkerchief.*
lençol *m. sheet (bed).*
lenda *f. legend, tale.*
lenha *f. firewood.*
Deitar lenha ao fogo. *To add fuel to the fire.*
lenhador *m. woodcutter.*
lenho *m. tree trunk.*
lentamente *adv. slowly.*
lente *m. teacher, professor; lens.*
lentidão *f. slowness.*
LENTO *adj. slow.*
leoa *f. lioness.*
leopardo *m. leopard.*
LER *to read.*
Leia em voz alta. *Read aloud.*
Você leu este romance? *Did you read this novel?*
lesão *f. lesion, injury; wrong.*
lesar *to hurt; to wound; to injure; to wrong.*
leste *m. east.*
LETRA *f. letter; lyrics; handwriting.*
Letra maiúscula. *Capital letter.*
Letra minúscula. *Small letter.*
Não me lembro da letra dessa canção. *I don't remember the lyrics of that song.*
Ela tem boa letra. *She has good handwriting.*
Ao pé da letra. *Literally.*
Letra de câmbio. *Bill of exchange.*
letrado *adj. learned, erudite; n. m. scholar; lawyer.*
letreiro *m. inscription; sign; label; poster.*
levantamento *m. raising; uprising, revolt.*
LEVANTAR *to raise, to lift, to pick up; to suspend.*
Levantar a voz. *To raise the voice.*
Levantar o pano. *To raise the curtain (theatre).*
Levantar a mão. *To raise one's hand.*
Levantar a mesa. *To clear the table.*
Levantar os ombros. *To shrug the shoulders.*
Levantar a sessão. *To adjourn the meeting.*
LEVANTAR-SE *to get up.*
A que horas se levanta? *At what time do you get up?*
Levanto-me às sete. *I get up at seven.*

LEVAR *to carry, to take; to wear; to bear; to need.*
Leve-me ao seu chefe. *Take me to your leader.*
Leve este livro a seu pai. *Take this book to your father.*
Quanto tempo vai levar? *How long will it take?*
Levar a cabo. *To carry out. To bring about.*
Eles levam boa vida. *They lead a good (easy) life.*
Levar em conta. *To take into account.*
Levar pau. *To fail (an examination).*
Levar à força. *To take by force.*
leve *adj. light (weight); slight.*
leviano *adj. frivolous; imprudent.*
léxico *(x = ks) m. lexicon.*
lha *(contr. of* **ihe + a**) *it to him, to her, to you, etc.*
LHE *to him, to her, to you, to it.*
lho *(contr. of* **lhe + o**) *it to him, to her, to you, etc.*
liar *to tie, to bind.*
liberação *f. liquidation, discharge.*
liberal *adj., n. m. and f. liberal.*
liberar *to release.*
LIBERDADE *f. liberty, freedom.*
Tomar a liberdade. *To take the liberty.*
libertador *adj. liberating; n. m. liberator.*
libertar *to liberate, to free.*
libra *f. pound.*
LIÇÃO *f. lesson.*
Dar lições. *To give lessons.*
LICENÇA *f. permission; leave; license; permit.*
Com licença. *Excuse me. May I?*
Dá licença? *Excuse me. May I?*
Pedir licença. *To ask for leave; To ask for permission.*
Licença de motorista. *Driver's license.*
licenciado *m. person holding a master's degree.*
licenciar *to license; to allow; to grant leave of absence.*
lícito *adj. lawful; licit.*
licor *m. liqueur, liquor.*
lidar *to combat, to fight.*
líder *m. leader* Ⓑ.
lido *adj. read; well-read.*
liga *f. league.*
Liga das Nações. *League of Nations.*
ligado *adj. connected; on (TV, radio, etc.).*
LIGAR *to join, to connect; to tie, to bind; to turn on (radio, etc.).*
A ferrovia liga as duas cidades. *The railroad joins the two cities.*
Ligue-me com . . . *Connect me with . . .*
Faça o favor de ligar o rádio. *Please turn on the radio.*

ligeireza *f. lightness; quickness.*
LIGEIRO *adj. light (weight); quick, swift.*
lilás *adj., n. m. lilac.*
lima *f. file (tool); lime.*
   Lima de unhas. *Nail file.*
limão *m. lemon.*
limar *to file, to make smooth; to polish.*
limitação *f. limitation, limit.*
limitado *adj. limited.*
limitar *to limit; to restrain; to border on.*
limite *m. limit; boundary, border.*
   Tudo tem os seus limites. *There's a limit to everything.*
limoeiro *m. lemon tree.*
limonada *f. lemonade.*
LIMPAR *to clean, to cleanse; to clear.*
   Limpar a garganta. *To clear the throat.*
limpeza *f. cleaning; cleanliness.*
LIMPO *adj. clean; neat; clear.*
   Quero uma toalha limpa. *I want a clean towel.*
   Estou limpo. *I'm broke.*
linácea *f. flax.*
lince *m. and f. lynx.*
linchar *to lynch.*
lindar *to delimit; to border.*
linde *m. limit, boundary.*
LINDO *adj. pretty, beautiful.*
   Como ela é linda! *How pretty she is!*
líneo *adj. linen.*
LÍNGUA *f. tongue; language.*
   Língua portuguesa. *Portuguese language.*
   Língua materna. *Mother tongue.*
   Língua românica. *Romance language.*
   Tenho na ponta da língua. *I have it on the tip of my tongue.*
linguagem *f. language.*
lingüista (linguista) *m. and f. linguist.*
LINHA *f. line; row; string, thread.*
   Linha, por favor. *Line, please (telephone).*
   Linha interurbana. *Long-distance line.*
   Linha ferroviária. *Railway.*
   Linha aérea. *Airline.*
   Manter em linha. *To keep in line.*
   Linha reta. *Straight line.*
linimento *m. liniment.*
linóleo *m. linoleum.*
linotipista *m. and f. linotypist.*
linotipo *m. linotype.*
liqüidação (liquidação) *f. liquidation.*
liqüidar (liquidar) *to liquidate.*
líquido (líqüido) *adj. liquid; net (profit, etc.); n. m. liquid.*
lírico *adj. lyric.*
lírio *m. lily.*
LISBOETA *adj. of Lisbon; n. m. and f. person from Lisbon.*
liso *adj. smooth, even.*
   Cabelo liso. *Straight hair.*

lisonja *f. praise, flattery.*
lisonjear *to praise, to flatter; to please.*
lisonjeiro *adj. flattering; pleasing; n. m. flatterer.*
LISTA *f. list; stripe; directory; menu.*
   Lista telefônica (telefónica). *Telephone book.*
   Lista negra. *Blacklist.*
literário *adj. literary.*
literato *m. man of letters.*
literatura *f. literature.*
litigar *to litigate.*
litígio *m. litigation, lawsuit.*
litoral *adj. coastal; n. m. coastline.*
litro *m. liter.*
lituano *adj., n. m. Lithuanian.*
livrar *to free.*
   Deus me livre! *God forbid!*
livraria *f. bookstore.*
LIVRE *adj. free (unimpeded).*
   Quando você estiver livre falaremos. *When you are free, we'll talk.*
   Livre a bordo. *Free on board.*
   Ao ar livre. *In the open air.*
   Tradução livre. *Free translation.*
   Verso livre. *Free verse.*
livreiro *m. bookseller.*
LIVRO *m. book.*
   Livro brochado. *Paperback.*
   Livro caixa (x = sh) *Cash book.*
   Livro de bolso. *Pocket book.*
   Livro de consulta. *Reference book.*
lixo (x = sh) *m. garbage.*
lo *(form taking the place of pronoun o after a verb form ending in r, s or z) him, you, it.*
lobo *m. wolf.*
lôbrego *adj. murky, dark; sad.*
lóbulo *m. lobule, lobe.*
local *adj. local; m. place.*
localidade *f. locality, place.*
localizar *to localize, to locate.*
loção *f. lotion, wash.*
locomoção *f. locomotion.*
locutor *m. speaker, announcer.*
lodo *m. mud, mire.*
lógico *adj. logical, reasonable.*
LOGO *right away, immediately; soon; shortly.*
   Até logo. *So long. See you soon.*
   Desde logo. *At once.*
   Logo depois. *Soon after.*
   Logo que. *As soon as.*
lograr *to obtain, to get; to attain; to manage; to succeed.*
   Elas lograram fazê-lo. *They managed to do it.*
LOJA *f. shop, store; lodge.*
   Loja de miudezas. *Notions shop.*
lona *f. canvas.*

londrino *adj. of London; n. m. Londoner.*
LONGE *far, distant.*
　　É muito longe! *It's too far!*
　　É longe daqui? *Is it far from here?*
　　Devagar se vai ao longe. *Slow and steady wins the race.*
　　Bem longe. *Really far.*
　　Longe disso. *Far from it.*
longitude *f. longitude.*
longo *adj. long.*
lotação *f. capacity; small bus* Ⓑ.
lotado *adj. filled full (capacity); crowded.*
lotar *to fill to capacity.*
lote *m. lot, piece of land; share.*
loteria *f. lottery.*
louça *f. dishes, chinaware.*
louco *adj. crazy, mad, insane; n. m. madman.*
　　Ele está louco. *He's crazy.*
　　Ele está louco por ela. *He's crazy about her. He's madly in love with her.*
loucura *f. madness, insanity; folly.*
　　Isso é uma loucura. *That's absurd. That's crazy.*
louro *adj. blond.*
louvar *to praise.*
LUA *f. moon.*
　　Lua nova. *New moon.*
　　Lua-de-mel. *Honeymoon.*
luar *m. moonlight.*
lubrificante *adj. lubricating; n. m. lubricant.*
lubrificar *to lubricate.*
lucrativo *adj. lucrative, profitable.*
lucro *m. profit, gain.*
　　Lucros e perdas. *Profits and losses.*
LUGAR *m. place, site; seat; occasion.*
　　Ponha as coisas em seu lugar. *Put things in their place.*
　　Eu em seu lugar não iria. *If I were you (in your place), I would not go.*
　　A que horas terá lugar? *At what time will it take place?*
　　Em lugar de. *Instead of.*
　　Dar lugar a. *To give cause for. To give occasion for.*
　　Em primeiro lugar. *In the first place.*
lume *m. fire; light.*
luminoso *adj. shining, luminous.*
lunático *adj., n. m. lunatic.*
lusiada *adj., n. m. and f. Lusitanian, Portuguese.*
LUSITANO *adj., n. m. Lusitanian, Portuguese.*
LUSO *adj., n. m. Lusitanian, Portuguese.*
　　Luso-brasileiro. *Luso-Brazilian. Portuguese-Brazilian.*
lustrar *to polish, to shine.*
lustre *m. luster, gloss; splendor.*
luta *f. fight, struggle, battle.*

　　A luta pela vida. *The struggle for existence.*
lutador *m. fighter, wrestler.*
lutar *to fight, to wrestle, to struggle.*
luto *m. mourning; grief, sorrow.*
　　De luto. *In mourning.*
LUVA *f. glove; coupling.*
　　Assentar como uma luva. *To fit like a glove.*
luxo *(x = sh) m. luxury.*
　　Edição de luxo. *Deluxe edition.*
luxuoso *(x = sh) adj. luxurious, deluxe.*
LUZ *f. light.*
　　Acenda a luz. *Turn the light on.*
　　Apague a luz. *Put the light out. Turn the light off.*
　　Luz elétrica (eléctrica). *Electric light.*
　　Dar à luz. *To give birth to.*
luzir *to shine, to brighten.*

M

ma *(contr. of* **me** *+* **a**) *it to me, her to me, you to me.*
MÁ *adj. f. bad, evil.*
　　Não é má idéia (ideia). *That's not a bad idea.*
　　Má fama. *Ill repute.*
　　De má vontade. *Unwillingly.*
MAÇÃ *f. apple.*
　　Maçã-de-Adão. *Adam's apple* Ⓟ.
macaco *m. monkey; jack (for lifting).*
macarrão *m. macaroni.*
machacaz *adj. cunning, sly.*
machado *m. ax.*
machete *m. machete; small guitar.*
macho *adj. male, masculine; vigorous; n. m. male, male animal.*
machucar *to pound; to bruise.*
maciço *adj. massive; compact; solid; firm.*
macio *adj. soft, smooth; gentle.*
maconha *f. marijuana.*
mácula *f. stain, spot; dishonor.*
macumba *f. voodoo ceremony of Brazil* Ⓑ.
MADEIRA *f. wood, lumber, timber.*
　　A caixa *(x = sh)* é de madeira. *The box is made of wood.*
madeireiro *m. lumber dealer.*
madeirense *adj. of the island of Madeira; n. m. and f. person from the island of Madeira.*
madeixa *(x = sh) f. lock of hair; skein.*
madrasta *f. stepmother.*
madre *f. nun.*
madressilva *f. honeysuckle.*
madrileno *adj. of Madrid; n. m. person from Madrid.*

madrinha *f. godmother; sponsor; maid of honor.*

madrugada *f. dawn, early morning.*
De madrugada. *At dawn.*

madrugador *m. early riser.*

madrugar *to get up early; to get ahead of.*
A quem madruga, Deus ajuda. *The early bird catches the worm.*

madurar *to ripen, to mature.*

madureza *f. maturity, ripeness.*

maduro *adj. ripe, mature.*
A fruta ainda não está madura. *The fruit isn't ripe yet.*

MÃE *f. mother.*

magia *f. magic.*

mágico *adj. magic, magical; marvelous.*

magistério *m. teaching profession; teaching position.*

magistrado *m. magistrate.*

magnânimo *adj. magnanimous.*

magnésia *f. magnesia.*

magnético *adj. magnetic.*

magnífico *adj. magnificent, excellent, wonderful.*

magnitude *f. magnitude.*

magno *adj. great.*

magnólia *f. magnolia.*

mago *adj. magic; m. magician; wizard.*

mágoa *f. sorrow; anguish.*

MAGRO *adj. thin.*

MAIO *m. May.*

maionese *f. mayonnaise.*

MAIOR *adj. greater, greatest; bigger, larger; adult, of age.*
A major parte. *Most. The majority.*
Este é maior do que aquele. *This one is larger than that one.*
Maior de idade. *Of age.*
Estado maior. *General staff (military).*

maioria *f. majority, plurality.*

MAIS *more; any more; besides; n. m. rest; most.*
Mais ou menos. *More or less.*
Deseja mais alguma coisa? *Would you like something else?*
Quer mais café? *Would you like more coffee?*
Nada mais? *Is that all? Nothing else?*
Não há mais. *There is (there are) no more.*
Não tenho mais. *I don't have any more.*
Ela é mais inteligente (do) que ele. *She is more intelligent than him.*
É a coisa mais fácil do mundo. *It's the easiest thing in the world.*
Mais adiante. *Further on.*
A casa é mais longe. *The house is farther.*
São mais de dez horas. *It's after ten o'clock.*
Mais depressa! *Faster!*

Mais devagar! *Slower!*
Fale mais alto, por favor. *Speak louder, please.*
Os mais dos alunos não estudam bastante. *Most students don't study enough.*
O mais cedo possível. *As soon as possible.*
Tenho mais de quinze. *I have more than fifteen.*
Vou trabalhar mais dez anos. *I'm going to work ten more years.*
Mais tarde. *Later. Later on.*
Não querem estudar mais. *They don't want to study any longer.*
Nunca mais. *Never again.*

maiúscula *adj. capital (letter); n. f. capital letter.*

majestade *f. majesty.*

majestoso *adj. majestic, imposing.*

MAL *badly, poorly; hardly; as soon as; n. m. evil; harm; disease, illness.*
O livro está mal escrito. *The book is poorly written.*
De mal a pior. *From bad to worse.*
Fazer mal. *To do harm. To do wrong.*
Estar mal de saúde. *To be ill.*
Não faz mal. *It doesn't matter. Don't bother.*
O paletó me fica mal. *The jacket doesn't fit right.*
Eu me sinto mal hoje. *I don't feel well today.*
Ela mal me falou. *She hardly spoke to me.*
Mal-agradecido. *Ungrateful.*
Menos mal. *Not so bad.*

mala *f. suitcase, bag; trunk (of a car).*
Fazer as malas. *To pack.*

malária *f. malaria.*

malbaratar *to squander; to sell at a loss.*

malcriado *ill-mannered, impolite.*

maldade *f. wickedness.*

maldição *f. curse.*

maldizer *to damn; to curse.*

malefício *m. evil act; witchcraft.*

maleita *f. malaria.*

mal-estar *m. indisposition; discomfort.*

maleta *f. handbag, suitcase.*

malfalante *adj. slandering; n. m. and f. slanderer.*

malfeitor *m. malefactor, criminal.*

malgastar *to squander, to waste.*

malhar *to hammer, to beat.*
Malhar o ferro enquanto está quente. *To strike while the iron is hot.*

mal-humorado *adj. ill-humored, peevish.*

malícia *f. malice; cunning.*

malicioso *adj. malicious; cunning.*

malignar *to corrupt.*

maligno *adj. malignant.*

mal-intencionado *adj. malicious, evil-minded.*

malsão *adj. unhealthy, unhealthful.*
maltratar *to treat roughly, to mistreat, to abuse; to harm.*
maltrato *m. ill-treatment.*
maluco *adj. crazy, insane; m. madman.*
malvado *adj. wicked.*
mamã *f. mamma, mother; wet nurse* Ⓑ.
MAMÃE *f. mommy, mother* Ⓑ.
mamar *to suck; to take the breast.*
mamífero *adj. mammalian; m. mammal.*
mana *f. sis, sister.*
manancial *m. fountain, spring; source.*
manar *to flow, to ooze.*
mancha *f. stain, spot, blemish.*
   Mancha solar. *Sunspot.*
manchar *to stain, to spot, to soil.*
manchete *f. headline* Ⓑ.
manco *adj. crippled, lame; n. m. cripple.*
mandado *m. order, command; writ.*
   A mandado de. *By order of.*
MANDAR *to send; to order, to command; to govern.*
   Mande-o à minha casa. *Send it to my home.*
   Mandei que chamassem o médico. *I had them call the doctor.*
   Quem manda aqui? *Who's in charge here?*
   Mandar às favas. *To send someone packing.*
   Mandar aviar uma receita. *To have a prescription filled.*
mandatário *adj. mandatory; n. m. attorney; agent; proxy.*
mandato *m. mandate, order.*
mandíbula *f. jaw.*
mandioca *f. manioc, cassava.*
mando *m. command, authority, control.*
mandolina *f.* **mandolin** *m. mandolin.*
MANEIRA *f. manner, way, method.*
   Faça desta maneira. *Do it this way.*
   Faça de qualquer maneira. *Do it any way you can.*
   Não há maneira de fazê-lo. *There's no way to do it.*
   De maneira que o senhor não vem? *So you're not coming?*
   De maneira nenhuma. *By no means.*
   Escreva-o de maneira que se possa ler. *Write it so that it can be read.*
   Da mesma maneira. *In the same way.*
   Boas maneiras. *Good manners.*
manejar *to handle; to manage; to govern.*
manejo *m. management; handling.*
MANGA *f. sleeve; glass funnel; waterspout.*
   Em mangas de camisa. *In shirtsleeves.*
MANHÃ *f. morning, forenoon.*
   Ontem de manhã. *Yesterday morning.*
   Amanhã de manhã. *Tomorrow morning.*
   Hoje de manhã. *This morning.*

   Todas as manhãs. *Every morning.*
manhoso *adj. skillful, cunning.*
mania *f. mania; whim; obsession.*
maníaco *adj. maniacal; n. m. maniac; crackpot.*
manicômio (manicómio) *m. insane asylum.*
manifestação *f. manifestation, demonstration.*
manifestar *to manifest; to state; to reveal.*
manifesto *adj. manifest, clear; obvious.*
manipulação *f. manipulation, handling.*
manipular *to handle, to manipulate; to manage.*
manivela *f. crank; lever; handle.*
manjar *m. food; coconut pudding* Ⓑ.
mano *m. brother.*
mansão *m. mansion.*
manso *adj. tame, gentle, meek.*
manta *f. blanket; cloak; neckerchief.*
MANTEIGA *f. butter; flattery.*
   Pão e manteiga. *Bread and butter.*
mantel *m. tablecloth.*
manter *to maintain, to support; to keep up; to uphold.*
   Manter ordem. *To maintain order.*
   Manter correspondência. *To keep up a correspondence.*
   Manter a palavra. *To keep one's word.*
manter-se *to carry on, to remain, to keep.*
   Manter-se firme. *To remain firm.*
mantimento *m. maintenance, support.*
manto *m. mantle, cloak.*
manual *adj. manual; n. m. manual, handbook.*
manuelino *adj. of D. Manuel I of Portugal, esp. referring to the architecture of the period (early 16th century).*
manufaturar (manufacturar) *to manufacture.*
manuscrito *adj. handwritten; n. m. manuscript.*
manutenção *f. support, maintenance.*
MÃO *f. hand.*
   Ter à mão. *To have at hand.*
   Ter na mão. *To have in the hand.*
   Apertar a mão de alguém. *To shake hands with someone.*
   Aperto de mão. *Handshake.*
   Mão esquerda. *Left hand.*
   Mão direita. *Right hand.*
   Pedir a mão de. *To ask for the hand of (in marriage).*
   Estar em boas mãos. *To be in good hands.*
   Vir às mãos. *To come to blows.*
   Lavar as mãos. *To wash one's hands.*
   De boa mão. *On good authority.*
   As mãos cheias. *Liberally. Abundantly.*
   Feito à mão. *Made by hand.*
   De primeira mão. *Firsthand.*
   Mãos à obra! *Let's get to work!*
   Dar a mão a. *To shake hands with.*

mapa *m. map, chart.*
mapa-múndi *m. world map.*
MÁQUINA *f. machine, engine.*
    Máquina de escrever. *Typewriter.*
    Máquina de lavar. *Washing machine.*
    Máquina de lavar louça. *Dishwasher.*
    Máquina fotográfica. *Camera.*
    Máquina de fax. *Fax machine.*
    Máquina de contestacão. *Answering machine.*
maquinaria *f. machinery.*
maquinista *m. machinist; engineer.*
MAR *m. sea.*
    Fazer-se ao mar. *To sail. To put to sea.*
    Por mar. *By sea.*
maracá *m. maraca (musical instrument).*
maranha *f. entanglement.*
maranhense *adj. and n. m. and f. of the state of Maranhão, in Brazil.*
maravilha *f. marvel, wonder.*
maravilhoso *adj. marvelous, wonderful.*
    Cidade maravilhosa. *Marvelous city (literary description of Rio).*
marca *f. mark; brand; make; sign.*
    Marca registrada (registada). *Registered trademark.*
MARCAR *to mark; to brand.*
    Vamos marcar a data. *Let's set the date.*
    Marquemos a hora. *Let's decide on a time.*
marceneiro *m. cabinetmaker.*
marcha *f. march.*
    Praticar marcha. *To go hiking.*
marchar *to march.*
marco *m. window frame, door frame; boundary mark; mark (German monetary unit).*
MARÇO *m. March.*
maré *f. tide.*
mareado *adj. seasick.*
marear *to get seasick.*
marfim *m. ivory.*
margarida *f. daisy.*
margarina *f. margarine.*
margem *f. margin, border, edge; shore, bank (river).*
marido *m. husband.*
marinha *f. navy.*
    Marinha mercante. *Merchant marine.*
    Marinha de guerra. *Navy.*
marinheiro *m. sailor, seaman.*
mariposa *f. moth.*
marítimo *adj. maritime.*
marmelada *f. marmalade.*
marmita *f. dinner pail; mess kit.*
mármore *m. marble.*
marquês *m. marquis.*
marrom *adj. brown* Ⓑ; *n. m. brown color* Ⓑ.
martelar *to hammer.*
martelo *m. hammer.*

mártir *m. and f. martyr.*
MAS *but, yet, however.*
    Eu esperei duas horas mas ela não chegou. *I waited for two hours, but she did not arrive.*
    Ela é não só bela mas também inteligente. *She is not only pretty but also intelligent.*
    Nem mas nem meio mas. *No ifs, ands, or buts.*
mascar *to chew.*
máscara *f. mask, disguise.*
mascote *f. mascot.*
masculino *adj. masculine.*
    Gênero (género) masculino. *Masculine gender.*
massa *f. dough; mass.*
mastigar *to chew.*
mata *f. forest, woods.*
mata-borrão *m. blotting paper.*
matadouro *m. slaughterhouse.*
matança *f. slaughter.*
MATAR *to kill, to murder.*
    Matar o tempo. *To kill time.*
    Matar a fome. *To satisfy one's hunger.*
mate *m. maté (a kind of tea).*
matemática *f. mathematics.*
matemático *m. mathematician.*
matéria *f. matter, material; subject.*
    Matéria-prima. *Raw material.*
material *adj. material; n. m. material, equipment.*
materializar *to materialize.*
maternal *adj. maternal.*
maternidade *f. maternity.*
materno *adj. maternal, motherly.*
matiz *m. shade (of color).*
mato *m. woods, forest, thicket; country (rural).*
matrícula *f. matriculation, registration.*
matricular *to matriculate, to register.*
    Em que universidade se matriculou? *At what university did you register?*
matrimonial *adj. matrimonial.*
matrimônio (matrimónio) *m. marriage, matrimony.*
matuto *m. backwoodsman, hillbilly.*
MAU (f. MÁ) *adj. bad, wicked; ill; poor.*
    Mau tempo. *Bad weather.*
    Ele é mau. *He's bad.*
    Mau humor. *Bad humor.*
mausoléu *m. mausoleum.*
máximo *(x = ss) adj. maximum, highest, greatest; n. m. maximum.*
    Máxima altura. *Highest point; Peak.*
    Qual é o preço máximo? *What is the top price?*
    Até o máximo. *To the utmost.*
maxixe *(x = sh) m. gherkin; Brazilian dance.*

ME *me; to me; myself.*

João me deu o livro. *John gave me the book.*

Dê-me o endereço, por favor. *Give me the address, please.*

Eu me levanto às seis. *I get up at six.*

Primeiro vou lavar-me. *First I'm going to wash (myself).*

meão (f. meã) *adj. average, mean.*

mecânico *adj. mechanical; n. m. mechanic.*

mecanismo *m. mechanism, machinery.*

mecha *f. wick, fuse.*

medalha *f. medal.*

mediação *f. mediation, intervention.*

mediador *m. mediator, go-between.*

mediano *adj. median, medium.*

mediante *by means of, by virtue of.*

mediar *to mediate, to intercede.*

medicina *f. medicine, remedy.*

médico *adj. medical; n. m. physician, doctor.*

MEDIDA *f. measure, measurement; rule.*

Medida padrão. *Standard measure.*

Tomaram-se as medidas necessárias. *The necessary measures were taken.*

Feito sob medida. *Tailor-made. Made to order.*

A medida que ele falava, ela escrevia o que ele dizia. *As he spoke, she wrote what he said.*

médio *adj. mean, medium, average; n. m. half-back (soccer).*

Classe média. *Middle class.*

Médio direito. *Right halfback.*

medíocre *adj. mediocre.*

mediocridade *f. mediocrity.*

medir *to measure.*

Medir as palavras. *To measure one's words.*

meditação *f. meditation.*

meditar *to meditate.*

medo *m. fear, dread.*

Ele está com medo Ⓑ. *He is afraid.*

Elas têm medo dele. *They are afraid of him.*

medula *f. medulla, marrow; pith, essence.*

MEIA *f. stocking; sock.*

Quer meias de lã ou de algodão? *Do you want wool or cotton stockings?*

MEIO *adj. and adv. half, halfway, mean; n. m. sing. and pl. means.*

Quero meio quilo de café. *I want half a kilo of coffee.*

Às duas e meia. *At two thirty.*

Meio irmão. *Half brother.*

Está meio cheio. *It's half full.*

Meio dólar. *Half dollar.*

Meios legais. *Legal means.*

Por meio de. *By means of.*

Meio de transporte. *Means of transportation.*

Por qualquer meio. *By any means.*

MEIO-DIA *m. noon.*

Ao meio-dia. *At noon.*

mel *m. honey.*

Lua-de-mel. *Honeymoon.*

melaço *m. molasses.*

melancia *f. watermelon.*

melancólico *adj. sad, melancholy.*

melão *m. melon.*

MELHOR *adj. and adv. better, best.*

Sinto-me melhor. *I feel better.*

Ele é o melhor aluno de todos. *He's the best student of all.*

Ela fala português melhor de que ele. *She speaks Portuguese better than he does.*

Talvez isso seja melhor. *Perhaps that would be better.*

Eu fiz o melhor que pude. *I did the best I could.*

Eu farei o melhor possível. *I'll do the best I can.*

Tanto melhor! *So much the better!*

Tanto melhor se ela não vem. *So much the better if she doesn't come.*

É melhor que você dirigir. *You better drive.*

Ele está um tanto melhor. *He's somewhat better.*

Cada vez melhor. *Better and better.*

Ele é o meu melhor amigo. *He's my best friend.*

melhora *f. improvement.*

melhorar *to improve.*

O tempo está melhorando (está a melhorar). *The weather is getting better.*

Melhorar de saúde. *To get better (health).*

melodia *f. melody.*

membrana *f. membrane, tissue.*

membro *m. member; part.*

memorável *adj. memorable.*

MEMÓRIA *f. memory; memoir; memorandum.*

Ela tem uma memória extraordinária. *She has an extraordinary memory.*

Eu não tenho boa memória. *I don't have a good memory.*

Aprenda-o de memória. *Learn it by heart.*

Em memória de . . . *In memory of . . .*

menção *f. mention.*

mencionar *to mention.*

mendigar *to beg.*

mendigo *m. beggar.*

menear *to move; to stir; to shake; to wag.*

MENINA *f. child, girl, young lady.*

MENINO *m. child, boy, young man.*

Ele é um menino muito inteligente. *He's a very intelligent boy.*

MENOR *adj. smaller; younger; least; n. m. and f. minor.*

Ele é menor. *He's a minor. He's underage.*

MENOS *adj. and adv. less; least; minus; except.*

É mais ou menos a mesma coisa. *It's more or less the same thing.*

Todos foram menos eu. *Everyone went but me.*

Estaremos lá às sete menos um quarto. *We'll be there at a quarter to seven.*

Não irei a menos que você me acompanhe. *I won't go unless you go with me (accompany me).*

Pelo menos. *At least.*

Menos mal. *Not so bad. It could be worse.*

Estarei em casa em menos de dez minutos. *I'll be home in less than ten minutes.*

Mais dia, menos dia. *Sooner or later.*

Cada vez menos. *Less and less.*

Menos que nunca. *Less than ever.*

menoscabo *m. disdain, contempt; belittlement.*

menosprezar *to belittle, to disparage; to disdain.*

menosprezo *m. belittlement; scorn.*

mensageiro *m. messenger.*

mensagem *f. message.*

Eu não recebi mensagem alguma. *I didn't receive any message at all.*

mensal *adj. monthly.*

mensalidade *f. monthly allowance; monthly payment.*

menta *f. mint (flavor).*

mental *adj. mental.*

mentalidade *f. mentality.*

MENTE *f. mind, understanding.*

Tenha-o sempre em mente. *Always bear it in mind.*

mentecapto *adj. crazy.*

mentir *to lie.*

mentira *f. lie, falsehood.*

mentiroso *adj. lying, false, deceitful; n. m. liar.*

menu *m. menu.*

mercado *m. market, marketplace.*

Mercado de valores. *Stock market.*

mercadologia *f. marketing.*

mercador *m. merchant, dealer.*

mercadoria *f. commodity, merchandise, goods.*

mercante *adj. merchant, commercial; n. m. merchant.*

Navio mercante. *Merchant ship.*

Marinha mercante. *Merchant marine.*

mercê *f. favor; reward; mercy.*

Estar à mercê de. *To be at the mercy of.*

mercearia *f. grocery store.*

mercenário *adj. mercenary.*

merecer *to deserve, to merit.*

merecido *adj. deserved.*

merenda *f. light lunch, snack.*

merendar *to have a snack, to eat a light lunch.*

merengue *m. meringue.*

mergulhar *to dive, to plunge.*

meridiano *adj., n. m. meridian.*

mérito *m. merit, worth, value.*

mero *adj. mere, only, pure, simple.*

MÊS *m. month.*

Há dois meses. *Two months ago.*

O mês que vem. *Next month.*

O mês passado. *Last month.*

Todos os meses. *Every month.*

MESA *f. table; board, committee.*

Ponha a mesa. *Set the table.*

Os convidados se sentaram à mesa. *The guests sat down at the table.*

mesclar *to mix, to blend, to mingle.*

MESMA *adj. f. same, equal, self.*

Ela mesma o disse. *She said so herself.*

Ele já não é a mesma pessoa. *He's no longer the same person.*

Somos da mesma idade. *We're of the same age.*

MESMO *adj. and adv. same.*

O mesmo dia. *The same day.*

É o mesmo homem que vi ontem. *He's the same man I saw yesterday.*

Eu mesmo o farei. *I'll do it myself.*

Agora mesmo. *Right now.*

Ali mesmo. *Right there. In that very place.*

Eu espero aqui mesmo. *I'll wait right here.*

Mesmo assim, não vou. *Even so, I won't go.*

Hoje mesmo o faço. *This very day I'll do it.*

Não é o mesmo. *It's not the same (thing).*

Ao mesmo tempo. *At the same time.*

É mesmo? *Is that so?*

É isso mesmo! *That's it (exactly)!*

Para mim é o mesmo. *It's all the same to me.*

Por isso mesmo não vamos. *For that very reason we're not going.*

mesquinho *adj. niggardly, stingy.*

mestiço *adj. and n. m. of mixed blood, mestizo.*

mestre *m. and f. teacher; master; expert.*

Cópia mestre. *Master copy.*

meta *f. goal; end, object, aim.*

metade *f. half; middle, center.*

Dê-me a metade. *Give me half.*

Cara metade. *Better half. Wife.*

Eu fui só a metade do caminho a pé. *I went only half of the way on foot.*

metafísica *f. metaphysics.*

metáfora *f. metaphor.*

metal *m. metal.*

metálico *adj. metallic.*

metalurgia *f. metallurgy.*

metamorfose *f. metamorphosis.*

metediço *adj. meddlesome.*

meteorito *m. meteorite.*
meteoro *m. meteor.*
meteorologia *f. meteorology.*
METER *to put; to put in, to insert.*
  Meter a mão no bolso. *To put one's hand in one's pocket.*
  Não consigo meter a chave na fechadura. *I can't get the key in the lock.*
  Meter-se com. *To get mixed up with. To interfere.*
  Meter-se em camisa de onze varas. *To get into a difficult situation.*
metódico *adj. methodical.*
método *m. method.*
metralhadora *f. machine gun.*
METRO *m. meter (39.37 inches).*
metrópole *f. metropolis.*
MEU *adj., pro. m. my, mine; pl.* **meus.**
  Meu livro. (O meu livro). *My book.*
  Meus livros. (Os meus livros.) *My books.*
  Este lenço não é meu. *This handkerchief is not mine.*
  Eles são amigos meus. *They're friends of mine.*
  Isto é meu. *This is mine. This belongs to me.*
  O prazer é todo meu. *The pleasure is all mine.*
  Meus senhores: *Gentlemen:*
  A meu ver. *In my opinion.*
mexer *(x = sh) to stir; to disturb.*
mexer-se *(x = sh) to stir oneself, to move.*
mexicano *(x = sh) adj., n. m. Mexican.*
micróbio *m. microbe, germ.*
microcomputador *m. microcomputer.*
microcosmo *m. microcosm.*
microfilmar *to microfilm.*
microfilme *m. microfilm.*
microfone *m. microphone.*
microonda *f. microwave.*
  Forno de microondas. *m. microwave oven.*
microprocessador *m. microprocessor.*
microscópio *m. microscope.*
migalha *f. crumb; bit.*
migrar *to migrate.*
MIL *thousand.*
  Mil novecentos e sessenta e seis. *1966.*
  Dois mil dólares. *Two thousand dollars.*
  Duas mil casas. *Two thousand houses.*
milagre *m. miracle, marvel.*
milagroso *adj. miraculous.*
milésimo *adj., n. m. thousandth.*
milha *f. mile.*
  Quantas milhas são daqui a Chicago? *How many miles is it from here to Chicago?*
milhão *m. million.*
MILHO *m. corn.*
miligrama *m. milligram.*
milímetro *m. millimeter.*

milionário *adj., n. m. millionaire.*
militante *adj. militant.*
militar *adj. military; n. m. military man, soldier.*
  Serviço militar. *Military service.*
  Escola militar. *Military academy.*
mil-réis *m. former monetary unit of Brazil, replaced by the cruzeiro* Ⓑ.
MIM *me, myself (after a prep.).*
  Para mim. *For me.*
  Para mim tanto faz. *It's all the same to me.*
  Ai de mim! *Poor me!*
mimar *to pamper, to spoil (person).*
mina *f. mine.*
mineral *adj., n. m. mineral.*
mingau *m. a soft, mushy food; porridge.*
MINHA *(f. of* **meu**) *adj. and pro. my, mine; pl.* **minhas.**
  Esta gravata é minha. *This tie is mine. This is my tie.*
  Ela é uma amiga minha. *She is a friend of mine.*
  Minhas senhoras: *Ladies:*
  Minha casa é sua. *Make yourself at home. You're always welcome here.*
miniatura *f. miniature.*
mínimo *adj. minimum, least, smallest; n. m. minimum.*
  Não tenho a mínima idéia (ideia). *I haven't the slightest idea.*
  Este é o preço mínimo. *This is the lowest price.*
MINISTÉRIO *m. cabinet; ministry; a department of the government.*
  Ministério de Educação e Saúde. *Department of Education and Welfare.*
  Ministério da Guerra. *War Department.*
  Ministério da Marinha. *Navy Department.*
  Ministério da Aeronáutica. *Air Force Department.*
  Ministério da Fazenda. *Treasury Department.*
MINISTRO *m. minister; secretary (of government department).*
  Ministro da Agricultura. *Secretary of Agriculture.*
minoria *f. minority.*
minuta *f. note, memorandum.*
MINUTO *m. minute.*
  Espere um minuto! *Wait a minute!*
miolo *m. core, interior; pl. brains.*
míope *adj. myopic, nearsighted.*
mirar *to look, to behold, to gaze at.*
miserável *adj. miserable, wretched; miserly.*
miséria *f. misery; destitution.*
  Eles vivem na miséria. *They live in abject poverty.*
misericórdia *f. mercy.*
MISSA *f. mass.*

Missa cantada. *High mass.*
Missa do galo. *Midnight mass (Christmas).*
Ouvir missa. *To attend mass.*
missão *f. mission.*
missionário *m. missionary.*
mistério *m. mystery.*
misterioso *adj. mysterious.*
misto *adj. mixed.*
Colégio misto. *Coeducational school.*
mistura *f. mixture.*
misturar *to mix.*
mitigar *to mitigate, to ease.*
mito *m. myth.*
mitologia *f. mythology.*
miudeza *f. pl. details; odds and ends; notions.*
Loja de miudezas. *Notions shop.*
miúdo *adj. small; n. m. small child, kid* Ⓟ.
Dinheiro miúdo. *Small change.*
mo (*contr. of* **m** + **o**) *it to me, you to me, him to me.*
Ela escreveu-mo. *She wrote it to me.*
Eles mos mandaram. *They sent them to me.*
mobilar, (mobiliar) *to furnish (apartment, etc.).*
mobília *f. furniture.*
mobiliário *adj. of furniture; n. m. furniture.*
MOÇA *f. girl, young lady.*
moção *f. motion, movement; parliamentary motion.*
mochila *f. knapsack, backpack.*
mocidade *f. youth.*
MOÇO *m. boy, young man.*
Moço de recados. *Messenger.*
moda *f. fashion, style; manner.*
Os chapéus de palha estão fora de moda? *Are straw hats out of style?*
Estar na moda. *To be in style.*
A última moda. *The latest style.*
modalidade *f. modality; form.*
modelo *m. model; pattern.*
modem *m. modem.*
moderação *f. moderation.*
moderado *adj. moderate.*
moderar *to moderate; to restrain.*
MODERNO *adj. modern.*
Métodos modernos. *Modern methods.*
Arte moderna. *Modern art.*
modéstia *f. modesty.*
modesto *adj. modest.*
módico *adj. moderate, reasonable.*
É um preço módico. *It's a reasonable price.*
modificar *to modify, to alter.*
modismo *m. idiom.*
modista *f. dressmaker.*
MODO *m. mode, method, manner; mood.*
É o melhor modo de fazê-lo. *It's the best way to do it.*
Deste modo. *This way.*

De modo que. *So that.*
Fale de modo que todos possam ouvir. *Speak so that all can hear.*
De nenhum modo. *By no means. In no way. Not at all.*
Do mesmo modo. *In the same way.*
Modo condicional. *Conditional mood.*
moeda *f. money; coin.*
Papel moeda. *Paper currency. Bills.*
Pagar na mesma moeda. *To give as good as you get.*
mofa *f. mockery, derision.*
mofar *to mock, to deride.*
mofino *adj. unfortunate, unhappy.*
mogno (mógono) *m. mahogany.*
moído *adj. ground, crushed; worn out, exhausted.*
moinho *m. mill.*
mola *f. spring coiled metal; motivating force.*
Mola de relógio. *Watch spring.*
molde *m. mold, pattern, model.*
moldura *f. molding; picture frame.*
molecada *f. gang of boys, street urchins.*
moleque *m. urchin; black boy* Ⓑ.
molestar *to disturb, to trouble, to bother, to annoy; to tease.*
moléstia *f. illness; discomfort.*
molesto *adj. bothersome; uncomfortable; annoying.*
molhar *to wet, to moisten, to dampen.*
Molhar a garganta. *To wet one's whistle.*
molho *m. gravy, sauce.*
Molho de salada. *Salad dressing.*
molusco *m. mollusk, shellfish.*
momentâneo *adj. momentary.*
MOMENTO *m. moment, instant.*
Não tenho nem um momento livre. *I don't have even a free moment.*
Espere um momento. *Wait a moment.*
A qualquer momento. *At any moment.*
De um momento para outro. *From one moment to the next.*
monarca *m. and f. monarch.*
monarquia *f. monarchy.*
mondar *to weed; to prune.*
monge *m. monk.*
monólogo *m. monologue.*
monopólio *m. monopoly.*
monopolizar *to monopolize.*
monotonia *f. monotony.*
monótono *adj. monotonous.*
monstro *m. monster.*
monstruosidade *f. monstrosity.*
monstruoso *adj. monstrous.*
monta *f. amount, total.*
De pouca monta. *Of little importance.*
montanha *f. mountain.*
montar *to mount; to ride (horseback); to*

amount to; to assemble; to set (a precious stone).

Montar a cavalo. *To get on a horse. To ride a horse.*

A quanto monta a conta? *How much does the bill come to?*

Monte esta máquina. *Assemble this machine.*

monte m. *mountain, hill; pile.*

montra f. *shopwindow, showcase.*

monumental adj. *monumental.*

monumento m. *monument.*

morada f. *dwelling, residence.*

morador m. *resident, inhabitant.*

moral adj. *moral;* n. m. *morality; morale;* n. f. *morals, ethics.*

morango m. *strawberry.*

MORAR *to dwell, to reside, to live.*

Onde o senhor mora? *Where do you live?*

mordedura f. *bite.*

morder *to bite.*

morena adj. *dark-complexioned;* n. f. *brunette.*

moreno adj. *dark-complexioned;* n. m. *brunet.*

moribundo adj. *dying.*

MORRER *to die.*

Ele morreu de fome. *He died of hunger.*

morro m. *hill, mound.*

Morro abaixo (x = sh). *Downhill.*

Morro acima. *Uphill.*

mortal adj. *mortal, fatal.*

mortalidade f. *mortality, death rate.*

MORTE f. *death.*

Morte súbita. *Sudden death.*

morteiro m. *mortar.*

mortificação f. *mortification.*

mortificar *to humiliate, to mortify; to vex.*

MORTO adj. *dead;* m. *dead person.*

Estou morto de fome. *I'm famished. I'm starved.*

Ele está morto. *He is dead.*

mosca f. *fly; a bore.*

moscatel m. *muscatel (grape or wine).*

moscovita adj. and n. m. and f. *Muscovite, Russian.*

mosquito m. *mosquito.*

mostarda f. *mustard.*

mostra f. *exhibition, show; pl. gestures.*

À mostra. *On view.*

mostrador m. *face, dial (clock, watch, etc.); showcase.*

MOSTRAR *to show; to exhibit; to prove.*

Ela me mostrou as costas. *She turned her back on me.*

mostruário m. *showcase.*

motivar *to motivate.*

motivo m. *motive, reason; motif.*

Sem motivo. *Groundless. Unfounded.*

motocicleta f. *motorcycle.*

MOTOR m. *motor, engine.*

Não chegamos a tempo porque o motor falhou. *We didn't arrive on time because the motor stalled.*

motorista m. and f. *motorist, driver.*

MÓVEL adj. *movable;* n. m. *a piece of furniture; motive.*

MOVER *to move.*

movimentar *to move, to get moving.*

movimento m. *movement, motion; traffic.*

Há muito movimento nesta rua. *There is a lot of traffic on this street.*

Pôr em movimento. *To set in motion.*

mucama, mucamba both Ⓑ f. *Mammy.*

muçulmano adj., n. m. *Muslim.*

muda f. *change, move.*

mudança f. *change, moving out.*

MUDAR *to change, to alter; to remove; to move out or away.*

Eu mudei de parecer. *I've changed my mind.*

Vamos mudar de casa. *We're going to move.*

Mudar de roupa. *To change clothes.*

Mudar de idéia. *To change one's mind.*

Quando ela chegou eles mudaram de conversa. *When she arrived, they changed the subject.*

mudo adj. *mute, silent.*

mugir *to moo; to roar.*

MUITO adj. and adv. *much, very much, very;* pl. *many, too many.*

Muito dinheiro *A lot of money.*

Ela escreve muito. *She writes a great deal.*

Muito mais barato. *Much cheaper.*

Muitos livros. *Many books.*

Isto é muito melhor. *This is much better.*

Com muito prazer. *Gladly. With much pleasure.*

Agradeço muito. *I appreciate it very much.*

Há muito tempo. *A long time ago.*

Está muito frio hoje. *It's very cold today.*

Não muito. *Not much.*

Ainda falta muito. *There's still a lot missing. There's still a lot to be done.*

Muito bem! *Fine! Excellent!*

Muitas vezes. *Often. Frequently.*

Muito obrigado. *Thank you very much.*

mula f. *female mule.*

muleta f. *crutch.*

MULHER f. *woman, wife.*

Mulher de casa. *Housewife.*

mulo m. *male mule.*

multa f. *fine, penalty.*

multar *to fine.*

multidão f. *multitude, crowd.*

multiplicar *to multiply.*

multiplicidade f. *multiplicity.*

múltiplo adj. *multiple.*

MUNDO *m. world; multitude; great quantity.*
  Ela quer ver o mundo. *She wants to see the world.*
  Tenho que comprar um mundo de coisas. *I have to buy a whole lot of things.*
  Todo o mundo quer ir. *Everybody wants to go.*
  O mundo todo. *The whole world.*
munheca *f. wrist.*
munição *f. ammunition.*
municipal *adj. municipal.*
municipalidade *f. municipality; city council.*
município *m. municipality.*
muralha *wall (around a city, etc.); rampart.*
murmurar *to murmur; to whisper; to gossip.*
murmúrio *m. murmur, whisper.*
muro *m. wall.*
murro *m. blow, punch.*
músculo *m. muscle.*
museu *m. museum.*
  Que dias o museu está aberto? *What days is the museum open?*
  O museu de Arte Moderna. *The Museum of Modern Art.*
MÚSICA *f. music.*
  Música clássica. *Classical music.*
  Música popular. *Popular music.*
  Música de dança. *Dance music.*
musical *adj. musical.*
músico *adj. musical (said of people); n. m. musician.*
mutável *adj. changeable.*
mutilar *to mutilate.*
mútuo *adj. mutual.*

N

NA *(contr. of* **em** + **a***) in the, on the, at the.*
  Na cidade. *In the city.*
na *(form of object pronoun* **a** *when used after a verb ending in a nasal sound) it, her, you.*
  Compraram-na. *They bought it.*
nabo *m. turnip.*
NAÇÃO *f. nation.*
  Nações Unidas. *United Nations.*
nacional *adj. national.*
nacionalidade *f. nationality.*
NADA *nothing; not at all.*
  Não desejo nada. *I don't want anything.*
  Nada de novo. *Nothing new.*
  Nada mais. *Nothing more. Nothing else.*
  De nada. *Don't mention it.*
  Não vale nada. *It's worthless.*
  Nada disso. *None of that. Not at all.*
  Não sei nada disso. *I don't know anything about it.*

Antes de mais nada. *First of all.*
Nada de queixas *(x = sh). No complaining! Let's have no complaints.*
Eu não tenho nada com isso. *I have nothing to do with that.*
Ou tudo ou nada. *All or nothing.*
nadador *m. swimmer.*
nadar *to swim, to float.*
  Ela sabe nadar? *Does she know how to swim?*
nado *m. swimming.*
  Nado de peito. *Breast stroke.*
naipe *m. suit (cards).*
namorado *adj. in love; m. lover, suitor, boyfriend.*
namorar *to court, to go out with.*
namoro *m. love affair, courtship.*
NÃO *no, not.*
  Não falo espanhol. *I don't speak Spanish.*
  Eu tive que dizer que não. *I had to say no.*
  Ainda não. *Not yet.*
  Não sei. *I don't know.*
  Não a conheço. *I don't know her.*
  Não quer sentar-se? *Won't you have a seat? Won't you sit down?*
  Não há ninguém na sala. *There's no one in the room.*
  Não tenho mais. *I don't have any more.*
  Já não. *No longer. Not any more.*
  Não tenho muito tempo. *I don't have much time.*
  Não há de quê. *Don't mention it. You're welcome.*
  Não importa. *It doesn't matter.*
  Não me diga! *You don't say! Don't tell me!*
  A não ser que. *Unless.*
  Não obstante. *Nevertheless. Notwithstanding.*
  Acho que não. *I don't think so.*
  Ela não disse palavra. *She didn't say anything.*
  Não? *or* Não é? *or* Não é verdade? *Isn't that so?*
  Não faz mal. *Don't bother. It's all right.*
  Pois não! *Certainly! Of course!*
napolitano *adj. Neapolitan; n. m. Neapolitan.*
NAQUELA *(contr. of* **em** + **aquela***) f. in that, on that, in that one, on that one.*
  Não há ninguém naquela sala. *There is no one in that room.*
NAQUELE *(contr. of* **em** + **aquele***) m. in that, on that, in that one, on that one.*
  Naquele ano. *In that year.*
NAQUILO *(contr. of* **em** + **aquilo***) in that, on that.*
narcótico *adj., n. m. narcotic.*
NARIZ *m. nose.*
  Nariz aquilino. *Aquiline nose.*

Ele mete o nariz em tudo. *He pokes his nose into everything.*

Torcer o nariz. *To turn up one's nose.*

Assoar o nariz. *To blow one's nose.*

narração *f. account, narration, story.*

narrar *to narrate, to relate.*

NASCER *to be born; to bud; to rise (sun); to originate.*

Ele nasceu em São Paulo mas os pais dele nasceram em Lisboa. *He was born in São Paulo, but his parents were born in Lisbon.*

nascimento *m. birth; origin, source.*

nata *f. cream; the best part.*

natação *f. swimming.*

natal *adj. natal, native; n. m. Christmas.*

natalício *adj., n. m. birthday.*

nativo *adj. native.*

natural *adj. natural, native; n. m. native.*

Os alimentos naturais são saudáveis. *Natural foods are healthful.*

NATURALMENTE *of course, naturally.*

natureza *f. nature.*

naturismo *m. naturalism; back-to-nature movement.*

naturista *m. naturalist; believer in the back-to-nature movement.*

naufragar *to be shipwrecked; to fail.*

naufrágio *m. shipwreck; failure.*

náusea *f. nausea.*

náutica *f. navigation.*

náutico *adj. nautical.*

naval *adj. naval.*

navalha *f. razor; knife.*

navegação *f. navigation; shipping.*

navegador *m. navigator.*

navegante *m. navigator, seafarer.*

navegar *to navigate; to sail.*

navegável *adj. navigable.*

navio *m. ship.*

Navio mercante. *Merchant ship.*

Navio de guerra. *Warship.*

neblina *f. fog, mist.*

NECESSÁRIO *adj. necessary.*

É necessário fazê-lo hoje. *It must be done today.*

NECESSIDADE *f. necessity; need.*

Não há necessidade de registrar a carta. *It's not necessary to register the letter.*

A necessidade faz lei. *Necessity is its own law.*

necessitado *adj. poor, needy; n. m. person in need.*

NECESSITAR *to need; to be in need.*

Necessita mais alguma coisa? *Do you need anything else?*

necrologia *f. necrology, obituary.*

nefasto *adj. ill-fated; ominous.*

NEGAR *to deny; to refuse; to disown.*

Não o negue. *Don't deny it.*

Não o nego. *I don't deny it.*

Ele se negou a fazê-lo. *He refused to do it.*

negativa *f. refusal.*

negativo *adj. negative.*

Uma resposta negativa. *A negative answer. An answer in the negative.*

negligência *f. negligence, neglect.*

negligente *adj. negligent, careless.*

negociante *m. merchant, trader, businessman.*

negociar *to negotiate.*

NEGÓCIO *m. business; affair; transaction.*

Fazer bons negócios. *To do good business.*

Fazer mau negócio. *To get a bad deal.*

Abandonar os negócios. *To retire from business.*

Homem de negócios. *Businessman.*

Mulher de negócios. *Businesswoman.*

NEGRO *adj. black; gloomy; n. m. Negro.*

Vestir-se de negro. *To dress in black.*

Ele vê tudo negro. *He always looks on the dark side. He takes a gloomy view of everything.*

NELA *(contr. of* em + ela*) f. in it, on it, in her, on her.*

NELE *(contr. of* em + ele*) m. in it, on it, in him, on him.*

NEM *neither, either, nor, not.*

Não vou nem com você nem com ele. *I won't go either with you or with him.*

Nem meu irmão nem eu fomos. *Neither my brother nor I went.*

Nem sempre. *Not always.*

Nem sequer. *Not even.*

Nem mais nem menos. *Exactly. Neither more nor less.*

Nem peixe *(x = sh)* nem carne. *Neither fish nor fowl.*

NENHUM *not any, no, none, any.*

Nenhum homem. *No man.*

De modo nenhum. *By no means. No way.*

A nenhum preço. *Not at any price.*

Nenhuma das meninas. *None of the girls.*

Nenhum de nós. *None of us.*

Estar a nenhum. *To be broke* Ⓑ.

nervo *m. nerve.*

Nervo ótico (óptico). *Optic nerve.*

Ela é uma pilha de nervos. *She's a bundle of nerves.*

nervoso *adj. nervous.*

NESSA *(contr. of* em + essa*) f. in that, on that, in that one, on that one.*

Ponha o livro nessa mesa. *Put the book on that table.*

NESSE *(contr. of* em + esse*) m. in that, on that, in that one, on that one.*

Nesse caso eu não vou. *In that case, I won't go.*

NESTA (*contr. of* **em** + **esta**) *f. in this, on this, in this one, on this one.*
Não foram a outra cidade; ficaram nesta. *They did not go to another city; they stayed in this one.*

NESTE (*contr. of* **em** + **este**) *m. in this, on this, in this one, on this one.*
Não está nesse, está neste. *It's not in that one, it's in this one.*

neto *m. grandchild.*

neurótico *adj. neurotic.*

neutral *adj. neutral.*

neutro *adj. neutral, neuter; n. m. neuter.*

nevar *to snow.*
Está nevando (a nevar). *It's snowing.*

neve *m. snow.*

nevoeiro *m. fog.*

nicaraguano *adj., n. m. Nicaraguan.*

nicotina *f. nicotine.*

NINGUÉM *nobody, anybody, no one, anyone, none.*
Ninguém veio. *Nobody came.*
Ele nunca fala mal de ninguém. *He never says anything bad about anyone.*
Um joão-ninguém. *A nobody.*

ninho *m. nest.*

NISSO (*contr. of* **em** + **isso**) *in that, of that.*

NISTO (*contr. of* **em** + **isto**) *in this, of this.*

nítido *adj. clear, bright, sharp.*

nível *m. level.*

NO (*contr. of* **em** + **o**) *in the, on the, at the.*
No livro. *In the book.*

no (*form of object pronoun* **o** *when used after a verb ending in a nasal sound*) *it, him, you.*
Viram-no ontem. *They saw him yesterday.*

nó *m. knot; tie; joint; knuckle.*

nobre *adj. noble; n. m. nobleman.*

nobreza *f. nobility.*

noção *f. notion, idea.*

nocivo *adj. harmful.*

nogueira *f. walnut tree; walnut (wood).*

NOITE *f. night, evening.*
Boa noite. *Good evening. Good night.*
Hoje à noite. *Tonight.*
Ontem à noite. *Last night.*
Todas as noites. *Every night.*
De noite. *At night. In the evening.*
À meia-noite. *At midnight.*

noivado *m. engagement; wedding.*

noivar *to get engaged; to be engaged.*
Carlos noivou-se com uma Americana. *Charles got engaged to an American girl.*

noivo *m. sweetheart, boyfriend, fiancé, bridegroom.*
Os noivos. *The newlyweds.*

nojo *m. nausea; disgust.*

NOME *m. name; noun.*

Ponha aqui o nome e o endereço (a direcção). *Put your name and address here.*
Eu a conheço de nome. *I know her by name.*
Nome de batismo (baptismo). *Baptismal name.*
Nome de família. *Family name. Last name.*
Qual é o seu nome? *What is your name?*
Nome coletivo (colectivo). *Collective noun.*

nomeação *f. nomination, appointment.*

nomear *to appoint, to nominate; to name.*
Ele foi nomeado diretor (director). *He was appointed director.*

nonagésimo. *adj., n. m. ninetieth.*

nono *adj., n. m. ninth.*

nora *f. daughter-in-law.*

nordeste *adj., n. m. northeast.*

norma *f. norm, rule, standard, model.*

normal *adj. normal.*

normalidade *f. normality, normalcy.*

noroeste *adj., n. m. northwest.*

NORTE *adj., n. m. north.*
Norte América. *North America.*

norte-americano *adj., n. m. North American.*

norueguês *adj., n. m. Norwegian.*

NOS *us, to us, ourselves.*
Levantamo-nos imediatamente. *We got up immediately.*
Elas não nos disseram nada. *They didn't say anything to us.*
Eles não nos deixaram entrar. *They did not let us enter.*

NÓS *we, us.*
Nós vamos hoje; elas vão amanhã. *We are going today; they are going tomorrow.*
Estes livros são para nós? *Are these books for us?*

NOSSO *our.*
Nossa cidade. *Our town.*
Nossa irmã. *Our sister.*
Nosso irmão. *Our brother.*
De quem é? É nossa. *Whose is it? It's ours.*

NOTA *f. note; grade, mark.*
Tomar nota. *To take note.*
Nota promissória. *Promissory note.*
O aluno recebeu boas notas. *The student received good grades.*
Digno de nota. *Noteworthy.*

notar *to note, to notice.*
Não notei nada. *I didn't notice anything.*

notário *m. notary.*

notável *adj. notable; worthy of notice.*
Ele é um homem notável. *He's an outstanding man.*

NOTÍCIA *f. a piece of news, information; notice; pl. news.*

Boa notícia. *A piece of good news.*
As notícias do dia. *The news of the day.*
Más notícias. *Bad news.*

notificação *f. notification.*

notificar *to notify, to inform.*

notório *adj. well-known, evident.*

noturno (nocturno) *adj. nocturnal, night, in the night.*

novato *m. novice, beginner.*

NOVE *nine.*

novecentos *nine hundred.*

novela *f. novelette, novel.*

novelista *m. and f. novelist.*

NOVEMBRO *m. November.*

NOVENTA *ninety.*

noviço *m. novice, apprentice.*

NOVIDADE *f. novelty; news.*
Há alguma novidade? *Anything new?*
Não há novidade. *Nothing new.*
A última novidade. *The latest thing.*
Cheio de novidades. *Full of airs.*

NOVO *adj. new.*
Esse chapéu é novo? *Is that hat new? Is that a new hat?*
Que há de novo? *What's new?*
É preciso fazê-lo de novo. *It's necessary to do it again. It has to be done again.*
Feliz Ano Novo! *Happy New Year!*
O irmão mais novo. *The younger brother.*

noz *f. nut; walnut.*

nu *adj. naked, nude, bare.*

nublado *adj. cloudy.*

nublar *to become cloudy, to cloud.*

nuca *f. nape (neck).*

nuclear *adj. nuclear.*

núcleo *m. nucleus.*

nulidade *f. nullity; nonentity; incompetent person.*

nulo *adj. null, void; n. m. worthless person.*

NUM *(contra. of* **em** + **um**) *in a, on a, to a.*
Num livro. *In a book.*

NUMA *(contr. of* **em** + **uma**) *in a, on a, to a.*
Numa mesa. *On a table.*

numerar *to number.*

NÚMERO *m. number, figure.*
O número de meu telefone é . . . *My telephone number is . . .*
Escreva o número. *Write the number.*
Números arábicos. *Arabic numerals.*
Números pares. *Even numbers.*
Números ímpares. *Odd numbers.*
Número cardinal. *Cardinal number.*
Número ordinal. *Ordinal number.*
Sem número. *Countless. Endless.*

NUNCA *never; ever.*
Nunca! *Never!*
Nunca vou ao cinema. *I never go to the movies.*
Quase nunca. *Hardly ever.*

Nunca mais. *Never again.*
Mais vale tarde do que nunca. *Better late than never.*

nupcial *adj. nuptial.*

núpcias *f. pl. nuptials, wedding.*

nutrição *f. nutrition, nourishment.*

nutrir *to nourish, to feed.*

nutritivo *adj. nutritious, nourishing.*

nuvem *f. cloud.*

O

O *m. the; it, him.*
O livro. *The book.*
Comprei-o. *I bought it.*
Eu não o vi. *I didn't see him.*
Nós não os vimos. *We did not see them.*
Os alunos estão na escola. *The students are in school.*

obcecado *adj. obsessed.*

obedecer *to obey.*
Ele sempre obedece. *He always obeys.*

obediência *f. obedience.*

obediente *adj. obedient.*

obeso *adj. obese, fat.*

objetar (objectar) *to object, to oppose.*

OBJETO (OBJECTO) *m. object, thing; purpose, aim.*
Por fim ele logrou seu objeto. *At last he reached his goal.*
Objeto direto (directo): *Direct object.*

oblíquo *adj. oblique.*

OBRA *f. work (of art, etc.); book; deed; action.*
É uma obra em quatro volumes. *The work is in four volumes.*
Obra-prima. *Masterpiece.*
Obras públicas. *Public works.*
Obra de arte. *Work of art.*
Obra de consulta. *Reference book. Reference work.*
Obra dramática. *Dramatic work. Play.*
Mãos à obra! *Let's get to work! To work!*

obrar *to work; to act; to operate.*

obreiro *m. worker, workman.*

obrigação *f. obligation, duty.*

OBRIGADO *adj. obliged, thankful; thanks, thank you.*
Muito obrigado. *Thank you very much.*

obrigar *to oblige.*

obrigatório *adj. obligatory.*

obscurecer *to darken, to grow dark.*

obscuridade *f. obscurity.*

obscuro *adj. obscure, dark.*
Uma noite obscura. *A dark night.*

obsequiar *to oblige, to favor.*

obséquio *m. favor, kindness.*

Agradeço muito o seu obséquio. *Thank you for your kindness.*

observar *to observe, to notice; to obey.*
É preciso observar as regras. *One must follow the rules.*

observatório *m. observatory.*

obsessão *f. obsession.*

obstáculo *m. obstacle.*

obstinado *adj. obstinate.*

obstruir *to obstruct, to block.*
Obstruir o tráfico. *To block traffic.*

obtenção *f. attainment.*

OBTER *to obtain, to get; to attain.*
Ele obteve um bom emprego. *He got a good job.*

obturador *m. shutter (camera); plug, stopper.*

obtuso *adj. obtuse, blunt.*

obus *m. howitzer.*

óbvio *adj. obvious, evident.*

OCASIÃO *f. occasion, opportunity.*
Eu perdi uma boa ocasião. *I missed a good opportunity.*
Eu irei na primeira ocasião que tiver. *I'll go the first chance I have.*
Em outra ocasião. *Some other time.*
Por ocasião de. *On the occasion of.*

ocasionar *to cause, to bring about.*

ocaso *m. setting (sun); decline.*

oceano *m. ocean.*
Oceano Atlântico. *Atlantic Ocean.*
Oceano Pacífico. *Pacific Ocean.*

ocidental *adj. western, occidental.*

ócio *m. idleness, leisure.*

ociosidade *f. idleness, leisure.*

ocioso *adj. idle; lazy.*

octagésimo *eightieth.*

ocorrência *f. event.*

ocorrer *to happen, to occur.*
Não me ocorreu. *It didn't occur to me.*

oculista *m. and f. optician.*

óculos *m. pl. eyeglasses.*
Usar óculos. *To wear glasses.*

ocultar *to conceal, to hide.*

oculto *adj. concealed, hidden.*

ocupação *f. occupation, business; occupancy.*

OCUPADO *adj. busy; occupied; engaged.*
Estou muito ocupado. *I am very busy.*

OCUPAR *to occupy; to take possession of.*
Os móveis ocupam muito lugar. *The furniture takes up a lot of space.*

odiar *to hate.*

ódio *m. hatred.*

odioso *adj. hateful.*

OESTE *m. west.*

ofender *to offend.*

ofensa *f. offense.*

ofensiva *f. offensive.*
Tomar a ofensiva. *To take the offensive.*

OFERECER *to offer; to present.*

Ele me ofereceu dois dólares pelo livro. *He offered me two dollars for the book.*

oferecimento *m. offer.*

oferta *f. offer, offering; gift.*
É a última oferta. *It's the last (final) offer.*
Oferta e procura. *Supply and demand.*

oficial *adj. official; n. m. official, officer.*

oficina *f. workshop.*

ofício *m. job, occupation.*

oh *oh.*

oi *popular Brazilian greeting; corresponds to "hi," "hiya."*

oitavo *adj., n. m. eighth.*

OITENTA *eighty.*

OITO *eight.*
De hoje a oito dias. *A week from today.*

oitocentos *eight hundred.*

olá *hello!*

óleo *m. oil.*
Óleo de amendoim. *Peanut oil.*
Óleo combustível. *Fuel oil.*

olfato *m. sense of smell, smell.*

olhada *f. glance, look.*
Dar uma olhada. *To take a look.*

olhadela *f. glimpse, glance, look.*

OLHAR *to look at, to glance at, to watch; n. m. glance, look.*
Ele olhou para ela. *He looked at her.*
Olhar com bons olhos. *To look upon with favor.*

OLHO *m. eye; attention, care.*
Eu tenho os olhos cansados de tanto ler. *My eyes are tired from reading so much.*
Olho de agulha. *Eye of a needle.*
Num abrir e fechar de olhos. *In the blink of an eye.*
Quatro olhos vêem mais que dois. *Two heads are better than one.*

oliva *f. olive.*

olor *m. fragrance, odor.*

oloroso *adj. fragrant.*

olvidar *to forget.*

olvido *m. forgetfulness.*

ombro *m. shoulder.*
Encolher os ombros. *To shrug the shoulders.*

omelete, omeleta *f. omelet.*

omissão *f. omission.*

omitir *to omit, to leave out.*
Você omitiu a primeira parte. *You left out the first part.*

onça *f. ounce; wildcat.*
Tempo da onça. *Long ago.*
Amigo da onça. *False friend.*

onda *f. wave.*
Onda curta. *Shortwave (radio).*
Onda sonora. *Sound wave.*

ONDE *where.*

Onde está a tinta? *Where is the ink?*
Onde vendem romances brasileiros? *Where do they sell Brazilian novels?*
De onde (or donde) é o seu professor? *Where is your teacher from?*
ondular *to wave.*
ônibus (autocarro) *m. bus.*
ONTEM *yesterday.*
Eles chegaram ontem. *They arrived yesterday.*
ONZE *eleven.*
opa! *wow!*
opaco *adj. opaque; dull.*
opção *f. option, choice.*
ópera *f. opera.*
operação *f. operation.*
operar *to operate (medical); to produce, to work.*
operário *m. worker, workman.*
opinar *to give an opinion.*
opinião *f. opinion.*
Esta é a opinião de todos. *Everyone is of this opinion.*
Eu mudei de opinião. *I changed my opinion.*
opôr *to oppose.*
opôr-se *to oppose.*
Eu me oponho a essa resolução. *I am against that resolution.*
oportunidade *f. opportunity.*
Esta é uma boa oportunidade. *This is a good opportunity.*
oportuno *adj. opportune.*
oposição *f. opposition.*
opositor *adj. opposing; n. m. opponent, competitor.*
oposto *adj. opposed, opposite, contrary.*
opressão *f. oppression.*
opressivo *adj. oppressive.*
opressor *m. oppressor.*
oprimir *to oppress.*
optar *to choose.*
óptico, ótico (óptico) *adj. optic, optical; m. optician.*
ora *now, well.*
Ora! *Well!*
Por ora. *For the time being.*
oração *f. prayer; speech; clause, sentence.*
orador *m. speaker, orator.*
oral *adj. oral.*
orar *to pray; to ask for.*
orçamento *m. budget.*
ORDEM *f. order; method; rule.*
Às suas ordens. *At your service.*
Por ordem de . . . *By order of . . .*
Chamar à ordem. *To call to order.*
Em ordem. *In order.*
A ordem do dia. *The order of the day.*
Fora de ordem. *Out of order.*

ordenado *m. salary.*
ordenança *f. ordinance; m. and f. orderly (military).*
ordenar *to order, to command; to ordain; to arrange.*
ordenhar *to milk.*
ordinal *adj. ordinal.*
ordinário *adj. ordinary, common.*
orelha *f. ear.*
Orelha dum livro. *Flap of a book.*
órfão *m. orphan.*
orgânico *adj. organic.*
organismo *m. organism.*
organização *f. organization.*
organizar *to organize, to form, to arrange.*
órgão *m. organ.*
orgulho *m. pride.*
orgulhoso *adj. proud, haughty.*
oriental *adj. oriental, eastern; n. m. Oriental.*
orientar *to orient.*
orientar-se *to orient oneself, to get one's bearings.*
É difícil orientar-se nesta cidade. *It is difficult to get one's bearings in this city.*
ORIENTE *m. orient, east.*
origem *f. origin, source.*
original *adj. original.*
originalidade *f. originality.*
originar *to cause, to originate.*
ornamento *m. ornament, decoration.*
ornar *to adorn.*
orquestra *f. orchestra.*
ortografia *f. spelling.*
orvalho *m. dew.*
osso *m. bone.*
Em carne e osso. *In the flesh. In person.*
ostentar *to display, to show off, to boast.*
ostra *f. oyster.*
ótico *adj. optical; otic.*
otimismo (optimismo) *m. optimism.*
otimista (optimista) *m. optimist.*
ótimo (óptimo) *adj. excellent, wonderful.*
Ótimo! *Excellent! Great!*
OU *or, either.*
Compre-me dois ou três. *Buy me two or three.*
OURO *m. gold, money; pl. diamonds (cards).*
Sim, tenho um relógio de ouro. *Yes, I have a gold watch.*
ousar *to dare.*
OUTONO *m. autumn, fall.*
outorgar *to grant; to agree to.*
OUTRO *adj. other, another.*
Não quero este, quero outro. *I don't want this one; I want the other one.*
Prefiro os outros. *I prefer the other ones.*
Outro dia. *Another day.*
No outro dia. *The other day.*

Outra garrafa de cerveja! *Another bottle of beer!*

Outra vez. *Again.*

Outras vezes. *Other times.*

OUTUBRO *m. October.*

OUVIDO *m. hearing; ear.*

Dor de ouvido. *Earache.*

Ela tem ouvido para música. *She has an ear for music.*

Entrar por um ouvido e sair pelo outro. *To go in one ear and out the other.*

ouvinte *m. and f. listener; auditor.*

OUVIR *to hear, to listen.*

Não ouço nada. *I can't hear a thing.*

Não ouvi o despertador. *I didn't hear the alarm clock.*

Ouvir missa. *To hear mass.*

Ouvimos dizer que ela é atriz. *We heard that she's an actress.*

ovação *f. ovation.*

oval *adj. oval.*

ovelha *f. sheep.*

OVO *egg.*

Ovos duros. *Hard-boiled eggs.*

Ovos estrelados. *Fried eggs.*

Ovos mexidos *(x = sh). Scrambled eggs.*

A clara do ovo. *The white of the egg.*

A gema do ovo. *The yolk of the egg.*

oxalá *(x = sh) let's hope; God willing.*

Oxalá não esteja chovendo. *Let's hope it's not raining.*

P

pá *f. shovel, spade; blade (propeller).*

Pá de hélice. *Propeller blade.*

pacato *adj. quiet, peaceful.*

paciência *f. patience.*

Tenha paciência. *Be patient. Have patience.*

Estou perdendo (a perder) a paciência. *I'm losing my patience.*

paciente *adj., n. m. and f. patient.*

pacífico *adj. peaceful; mild.*

PACOTE *m. package, bundle.*

pacto *m. pact, agreement.*

pactuar *to reach an agreement, to sign a pact.*

padaria *f. bakery.*

padecer *to suffer, to bear.*

padecimento *m. suffering.*

padeiro *m. baker.*

padrão *m. standard; pattern (sewing, etc.).*

Padrão de vida. *Standard of living.*

padrasto *m. stepfather.*

padre *m. priest, Father.*

Padre-nosso. *Our Father. The Lord's Prayer.*

Padre Tomás. *Father Thomas.*

padrinho *m. godfather; best man; sponsor.*

paga *f. payment; pay, wages, fee.*

pagador *m. payer, paymaster, teller.*

pagamento *m. payment; pay.*

Pagamento adiantado. *Payment in advance.*

Dia de pagamento. *Payday.*

Pagamento a (em) prestações. *Payment in installments.*

pagão *adj. pagan; n. m. pagan.*

PAGAR *to pay, to pay for.*

Quanto lhe pagaram? *How much did they pay you?*

Pagar na mesma moeda. *To pay back in the same coin. To give as good as you get.*

Pagar uma visita. *To pay a visit.*

Pagar a prestações. *To pay in installments.*

Pagar caro. *To pay dearly.*

PÁGINA *f. page (book).*

Em que página está? *On what page is it?*

pago *adj. paid; m. pay, wages.*

PAI *m. father; pl. parents.*

Tal pai, tal filho. *Like father, like son.*

pai-de-santo *m. priest of Afro-Brazilian ritual; medicine man* .

painel *m. panel.*

pairar *to hover.*

país *m. country (nation).*

paisagem *f. landscape, view.*

paisano *adj. civilian; m. civilian; fellow countryman.*

À paisano. *In civilian clothes. In plainclothes.*

paixão *(x = sh) f. passion.*

palácio *m. palace.*

paladar *m. palate; taste.*

PALAVRA *f. word; promise.*

Que quer dizer esta palavra? *What does this word mean?*

Ele me tirou a palavra da boca. *He took the words right out of my mouth.*

Não falte à sua palavra. *Don't go back on your word.*

Peço a palavra? *May I have the floor?*

Ele me deu a sua palavra. *He gave me his word.*

Em poucas palavras. *In short. In a few words.*

Cumprir a palavra. *To keep one's word.*

Em toda a extensão da palavra. *In the full sense of the word.*

Não dizer sequer uma palavra. *Not to say a word.*

palavrão *m. a curse word, an ugly word.*

palco *m. stage.*

palestino *adj., n. m. Palestinian.*

palestra *f. talk, conversation, lecture.*

PALETÓ *n. man's jacket, coat.*

palha *f. straw.*

Chapéu de palha. *Straw hat.*
palhaço *m. clown.*
pálido *adj. pale.*
palito *m. toothpick.*
palma *f. palm; pl. applause.*
Bater palmas. *To applaud. To clap.*
palmada *f. slap.*
palmeira *f. palm tree.*
palmo *m. span (of the hand).*
palpável *adj. palpable, evident.*
pálpebra *f. eyelid.*
palpitar *to beat, to throb, to palpitate.*
palrar *to chatter.*
paludismo *m. malaria.*
pampa *f. pampa, treeless plain.*
panamenho *adj., n. m. Panamanian.*
pança *f. paunch, belly.*
pancada *f. blow; hit.*
pandeireta *f. small tambourine.*
pandeiro *m. tambourine.*
pane *f. breakdown (due to motor).*
panela *f. pot, pan.*
panfleto *m. pamphlet.*
pânico *adj., n. m. panic.*
PANO *m. cloth, material; curtain (theatre).*
Pano de mesa. *Tablecloth.*
panorama *m. panorama, landscape, view.*
panqueca Ⓑ *f. pancake.*
pantalha *f. lampshade; screen.*
pântano *m. swamp, marsh.*
panteísmo *m. pantheism.*
pantomima *f. pantomime.*
PÃO *m. bread.*
Pão com manteiga. *Bread and butter.*
O pão nosso de cada dia. *Our daily bread.*
pãozinho *m. roll (bread).*
PAPA *m. Pope.*
PAPÁ *m. papa, daddy.*
papagaio *m. parrot; kite.*
PAPAI *m. papa, daddy.*
Papai Noel. *Santa Claus.*
PAPEL *m. paper; role.*
Preciso duma folha de papel. *I need a sheet of paper.*
Escreva-o neste papel. *Write it on this paper.*
Há papel de escrever na gaveta. *There's some writing paper in the drawer.*
Papel moeda. *Paper currency. Bills.*
Papel de seda. *Tissue paper.*
Papel carbono. *Carbon paper.*
Papel de embrulho. *Wrapping paper.*
Papel em branco. *Blank paper.*
Saco de papel. *Paper bag.*
Desempenhar um papel. *To play a role. To play a part.*
papelão *m. cardboard.*
papelaria *f. stationery shop.*
paquete *m. steamship.*

PAR *adj. equal; par; even (number); n. m. pair, couple; peer.*
O cruzeiro e o escudo estavam ao par. *The cruzeiro and the escudo were at par.*
Um par de luvas. *A pair of gloves.*
Números pares e ímpares. *Even and odd numbers.*
Ela é uma senhora sem par. *There's nobody like her. She's the greatest.*
PARA *for, to, until, about, in order to, toward.*
Para quê? *What for? For what purpose?*
Para quem é isto? *Who is this for?*
Esta carta é para o senhor. *This letter is for you.*
Para que serve isto? *What's this for? What's this good for?*
Deixemos *(x = sh)* para amanhã. *Let's leave (it) for tomorrow.*
Ela tem talento para a música. *She has a gift for music.*
Vou agora para não chegar tarde. *I'm leaving now in order not to arrive late.*
Quando sai o trem (comboio) para a capital? *When does the train for the capital leave?*
Para sempre. *Forever.*
Para onde foram? *Where did they go?*
Para cá e para lá. *To and fro.*
parabéns *m. pl. congratulations.*
parábola *f. parable; parabola.*
pára-brisa *m. windshield.*
pára-choque *m. bumper (car).*
PARADA *f. stopping place; stop, halt; pause; parade; wager.*
Ponto de parada (paragem). *Stopping place.*
Parada de ônibus Ⓑ (Paragem de autocarro Ⓟ). *Bus stop.*
Cinco minutos de parada. *Five minutes' stop.*
paradeiro *m. whereabouts.*
parado *adj. stopped, still.*
paradoxo *(x = ks) m. paradox.*
paraense *adj., n. m. and f. of the state of Pará in Brazil.*
parafuso *m. screw.*
Chave de parafuso. *Screwdriver.*
PARAGEM *f. stopping place; stop.*
Paragem de autocarro Ⓟ (Parada de ônibus Ⓑ). *Bus stop.*
parágrafo *m. paragraph.*
paraguaio *adj., n. m. Paraguayan.*
paraibano *adj., n. m. of the state of Paraíba in Brazil.*
paraíso *m. paradise.*
paralelo *adj. and m. parallel.*
paralisar *to paralyze.*
paralisia *f. paralysis.*
paralítico *adj. and m. paralytic.*

paranaense *adj., n. m. and f. of the state of Paraná in Brazil.*

parapeito *m. parapet, rampart; windowsill.*

pára-quedas *m. parachute.*

pára-quedista *m. parachutist.*

PARAR *to stop, to halt, to stay; to bet.*
Por que paramos aqui? *Why are we stopping here?*
Pare em frente da estação. *Stop in front of the station.*
(O) meu relógio parou. *My watch stopped.*
Quando vai parar de chover? *When is it going to stop raining?*
Em que hotel pararam? *At what hotel did you stay?*
Sem parar. *Continuously.*

pára-raios *m. lightning rod.*

parasita *m. and f. parasite.*

pára-sol *m. parasol.*

parceiro *m. partner.*

parcela *f. parcel, portion.*

parcelado *adj. divided.*

parcelar *to parcel out.*

parceria *f. partnership.*

parcial *adj. partial.*

parcialidade *f. partiality, bias.*

parco *adj. economical, thrifty.*

pardo *adj. brown, dark; n. m. mulatto.*

PARECER *to appear, to seem, to look; n. m. opinion; appearance.*
Que lhe parece? *What do you think (of it)?*
Parece-me muito caro. *It seems awfully expensive to me.*
Ao que parece. *Apparently.*
Parece que vai chover. *It looks as if it's going to rain.*
Dê-me o seu parecer. *Give me your opinion.*
Eu também sou do mesmo parecer. *I'm also of the same opinion.*
Ela se parece muito com a tia. *She looks very much like her aunt.*

parecido *adj. similar, like.*

PAREDE *f. wall.*
As paredes têm ouvidos. *The walls have ears.*
Estar entre a espada e a parede. *To be between a rock and a hard place.*

parelha *f. matching item, pair.*

PARENTE *m. relative, relation.*
Não tenho parentes nesta cidade. *I don't have family in this city.*

parêntese *m. parenthesis.*
Parênteses quadrados. *Brackets.*

parir *to give birth.*

parisiense *adj., n. m. and f. Parisian.*

parlamento *m. parliament.*

paróquia *f. parish.*

paroquiano *m. parishioner.*

parque *m. park.*
Parque de diversões. *Amusement park.*

parreira *f. trellised grapevine.*

parreiral *m. grape arbor; arbor.*

PARTE *f. part, portion, share; side; role; party (dispute).*
Em que parte da cidade mora? *In what part of the city do you live?*
Cada um pagou a sua parte. *Each one paid his share.*
Trago isto da parte do senhor Nunes. *This is from Mr. Nunes.*
Cumprimente João da minha parte. *Say hi to John for me.*
Li a maior parte do livro. *I read most of the book.*
O senhor o viu (viu-o) em alguma parte? *Did you see him anywhere?*
Em nenhuma parte. *Nowhere.*
Em parte. *In part. Partly.*
Em grande parte. *Largely. In large part.*
Em toda parte. *Everywhere.*
Dar parte. *To inform. To notify.*
Por toda parte. *Everywhere.*
Por minha parte. *For my part. As far as I'm concerned.*

participação *f. participation; share; announcement.*
Participação de casamento. *Marriage announcement.*

participar *to participate, to take part; to share; to announce, to inform, to notify.*
Vocês participaram no jogo? *Did you take part in the game?*
Não poderemos participar da festa. *We won't be able to attend the reception.*

particípio *m. participle.*
Particípio passado. *Past participle.*
Particípio presente. *Present participle.*

particular *adj. particular, private; m. pl. particulars, details.*
Em particular. *In private. In particular.*
Escola particular. *Private school.*

particularidade *f. particularity, peculiarity.*

PARTIDA *f. departure; item, entry; game, match.*
Ponto de partida. *Starting point. Point of departure.*
Uma partida de xadrez (x = sh). *A game of chess.*
Partida dobrada. *Double entry (account).*

partidário *adj., n. m. partisan, follower, supporter.*
Ser partidário de. *To be in favor of.*
Máquina partidária. *Party machinery.*

PARTIDO *adj. divided, split, broken; n. m. party; advantage; side.*
Está partido! *It's broken!*

Que partido vamos tomar? *Which side are we going to take?*

O Partido Democrático. *The Democratic party.*

O Partido Republicano. *The Republican party.*

O Partido Trabalhista. *The Labor party.*

PARTIR *to divide, to split; to leave; to cut; to break.*

O avião está para partir. *The plane is about to leave.*

Vamos partir na sexta. *We are going to leave on Friday.*

Preciso duma faca para partir o pão. *I need a knife to cut the bread.*

A partir de hoje. *From today on.*

Parti-me a perna em criança. *I broke my leg as a child.*

parto *m. childbirth.*

parvo *n. m. blockhead; adj. foolish.*

Páscoa *f. Easter; Passover.*

pasmar *to bewilder; to amaze.*

passa *f. raisin.*

passadiço *m. walkway; passageway.*

PASSADO *adj. past, done; n. m. past; past tense.*

O ano passado. *Last year.*

A semana passada. *Last week.*

Esqueçamos o passado. *Let's forget the past.*

Um bife bem passado. *A well-done steak.*

Mal passado. *Rare (meat).*

passageiro *adj. passing, transitory; m. passenger; traveler.*

passagem *f. passage; fare.*

Passagem de ida e volta. *A round-trip ticket.*

Quanto custa a passagem? *What is the fare?*

passaporte *m. passport.*

PASSAR *to pass, to go by, to go across; to come over, to come in; to spend (time); to approve; to happen.*

Passe-me o sal, por favor. *Please pass the salt.*

Passe por aqui. *Come this way.*

Pode passar por meu escritório amanhã? *Can you drop by my office tomorrow?*

Ele passa por brasileiro mas é americano. *He passes for a Brazilian, but he's an American.*

Os anos passam rapidamente. *The years go by quickly.*

Passe bem. *Good-bye. Take it easy.*

Passar por alto. *To overlook. To omit.*

Passar a ferro. *To iron. To press (clothes).*

Muitos dias ele passava fome. *Many days he would go hungry.*

Passar um telegrama. *To send a telegram.*

Como tem passado? *How have you been?*

pássaro *m. bird.*

Mais vale um pássaro na mão que dois voando (a voar). *A bird in the hand is worth two in the bush.*

passatempo *m. pastime, amusement.*

passe *m. pass, permit; free ticket.*

PASSEAR *to walk, to take a walk; to ride.*

PASSEIO *m. walk, stroll; ride; trip.*

Dar um passeio. *To go for a walk.*

passivo *adj. passive; n. m. liability.*

PASSO *m. step; pass; passageway; gait.*

Está a dois passos daqui. *It's only a few steps from here.*

Passo a passo. *Step by step.*

A cada passo. *At every step. Frequently.*

Ao passo que. *While. As.*

Quem vai dar o primeiro passo? *Who will take the first step?*

pasta *f. paste; dough; briefcase.*

Pasta de dente(s). *Toothpaste.*

pastagem *f. pasture.*

pastel *m. pastry; pastel.*

pastelaria *f. pastry shop.*

pasteleiro *m. pastry cook.*

pastilha *f. lozenge, drop.*

pasto *m. pasture; food.*

pastor *m. shepherd; pastor.*

pata *f. paw; foot; female duck.*

Pata anterior. *Foreleg.*

Pata posterior. *Hind leg.*

Meter a pata. *To put your foot in your mouth. To make a blunder.*

patente *adj. patent, obvious; f. patent; privilege.*

patife *n. m. lowlife, scoundrel, "piece of work."*

patim *m. skate.*

Patins de rodas. *Roller skates.*

Patins de gelo. *Ice skates.*

patinar *to skate.*

pátio *m. patio, courtyard, yard.*

pato *m. drake, male duck.*

patranha *f. lie, fib.*

patrão *m. master; skipper; employer; boss; landlord.*

pátria *f. fatherland, native country.*

patriota *m. and f. patriot.*

patriotismo *m. patriotism.*

patrocinar *to patronize (a business, etc.); to sponsor.*

patrono *m. patron, sponsor.*

patrulha *f. patrol.*

PAU *adj. boring; n. m. pole, stick, club; wood.*

Pau de bandeira. *Flagpole.*

A meio pau. *At half-mast.*

Ele levou pau. *He failed (an examination)* Ⓑ.

paulista *adj., n. m. and f. of the state of São Paulo in Brazil.*

paulistano *adj., n. m. of the city of São Paulo in Brazil.*

pausa *f. pause.*

pauta *guidelines; ruled lines.*

pavão *m. peacock.*

pavilhão *m. pavilion; tent; pennant.*

pavimento *m. pavement.*

pavio *m. wick.*
　Pavio de vela. *Candlewick.*
　De fio a pavio. *From beginning to end.*

pavor *m. fear, terror.*

PAZ *f. peace.*
　Por que não fazem as pazes? *Why don't you make up? Why don't you bury the hatchet?*
　Em paz. *In peace.*
　Deixe-me *(x = sh)* em paz! *Leave me alone!*

PÉ *m. foot; footing; base; basis.*
　A pé. *On foot.*
　Ao pé da colina. *At the foot of the hill.*
　De *(or* em*)* pé. *Standing. On foot.*
　Ao pé da letra. *Literally.*
　Pôr-se em pé. *To stand up.*
　Ficar de pé. *To remain standing. To stand (including agreements, etc.).*
　Isso não tem pés nem cabeça. *I can't make heads or tails of that.*
　Ele se levantou (levantou-se) com o pé esquerdo. *He got up on the wrong side of the bed.*

peão *m. pedestrian; peon; pawn (chess).*

PEÇA *f. piece, part; room; article; joke, trick; play (drama).*
　Peça por peça. *Piece by piece.*
　Quantas peças (divisões) tem o apartamento? *How many rooms does the apartment have?*
　A peça é em três atos (actos). *The play has three acts.*
　Pregar uma peça. *To play a trick or practical joke.*

pecado *m. sin.*

pecar *to sin, to do wrong.*

pecuário *adj. of cattle; n. m. cattleman.*

peculiar *adj. peculiar, individual.*

peculiaridade *f. peculiarity.*

PEDAÇO *m. bit, piece*
　Fazer em pedaços. *To break into pieces.*

pedagogo *m. pedagogue, teacher.*

pedal *m. pedal.*

pedestal *m. pedestal, support.*

pedestre *adj., n. m. and f. pedestrian.*

pedido *adj. ordered; asked for; n. m. order, demand, request.*
　O pedido chegou ontem. *The order arrived yesterday.*
　Fazer um pedido. *To order (goods). To place an order.*
　A pedido de. *At the request of.*

PEDIR *to ask for; to demand; to order (goods); to beg.*
　Ela me pediu que lhe fizesse um favor. *She asked me to do her a favor.*
　Pedir licença. *To ask permission.*
　Peço a palavra. *May I have the floor?*
　Pedir informações. *To inquire. To ask for information.*
　Pedir desculpas. *To apologize.*
　Pedir emprestado. *To borrow.*

PEDRA *f. stone, rock; blackboard; gem.*
　Pedras preciosas. *Precious stones.*
　Duro como uma pedra. *Hard as (a) stone.*
　Não deixar pedra sobre pedra. *Not to leave one stone on top of another.*

pedreiro *m. bricklayer; stonemason.*

PEGAR *to glue; to stick; to grasp, to take hold of; to catch.*
　Ele pegou na pasta e saiu. *He took his briefcase and left.*
　Ela já pegou no sono. *She's already fallen asleep.*
　Pegar fogo. *To catch fire.*
　Pegue e pague. *Cash and carry.*

PEITO *m. chest; breast; bosom; heart, courage.*
　Não o tome a peito. *Don't take it to heart.*
　Ele é um homem de peito. *He is a courageous man.*

PEIXE *(x = sh) m. fish (in water).*

pelado *adj. plucked, bare, bald; penniless.*

pelar *to peel, to skin; to rob; to grow bald.*

pele *f. skin; hide; fur.*
　Salvar a pele. *To save one's skin.*

peleja *f. fight, struggle.*

pelejar *to fight, to struggle.*

peleteria *f. furrier's, fur shop.*

película *f. film.*

PELO *(contr. of* **por** *+* **o***) for the, through the.*
　Pelo amor de Deus. *For the love of God.*
　Pelo contrário. *On the contrary.*

pêlo *m. fur, fuzz.*
　Montar em pelo. *To ride bareback.*
　Em pelo. *Naked.*

pelota *f. pellet; soccer ball.*

pelotão *m. platoon; group.*

PENA *f. feather; writing pen; penalty, punishment; grief, sorrow.*
　Desenho a bico de pena. *Pen-and-ink drawing.*
　Pena de morte. *Death sentence.*
　É (uma) pena! *That's too bad!*
　Ter pena de. *To feel sorry for.*
　Que pena! *What a pity!*
　Não vale a pena. *It's not worth it. It's not worth the trouble.*

penal *adj. penal.*
penalidade *f. penalty.*
penalizar *to distress, to pain; to penalize.*
pendão *m. pennant, flag.*
pendente *adj. hanging; pending; n. m. pendant, earring.*
pender *to hang; to be pending.*
pendurar *to hang, to suspend; to pawn* Ⓑ*; to put on your credit card/account* Ⓑ*.*
penetrante *adj. penetrating, piercing.*
penetrar *to penetrate; to comprehend.*
penha *f. rock, cliff, bluff.*
penhor *m. pawn, pledge.*
    Dar em penhor. *To pawn. To pledge.*
    Casa de penhores. *Pawnshop.*
península *f. peninsula.*
penitência *f. penitence; penance.*
penitente *adj., n. m. and f. penitent.*
penoso *adj. painful, distressing; arduous.*
pensador *adj. thinking; n. m. thinker.*
pensamento *m. thought, idea.*
pensão *f. pension; board; boardinghouse.*
PENSAR *to think; to consider; to intend.*
    Pense antes de falar. *Think before you speak.*
    Sem pensar. *Without thinking.*
    Ela está pensando (a pensar) nas férias. *She's thinking about her vacation.*
    Pensamos estar no cinema às oito. *We expect to be at the movie theater at eight.*
pensativo *adj. pensive, thoughtful.*
pensionista *m. and f. pensioner, boarder.*
PENTE *m. comb.*
penteado *m. coiffure, hairdo, hairstyle.*
    Que penteado prefere? *Which hairstyle do you prefer?*
pentear *to comb.*
penúltimo *adj. penultimate, next to last.*
penúria *f. penury, poverty.*
pepino *m. cucumber.*
PEQUENO *adj. little, small; n. m. child.*
    Ele é muito pequeno. *He's quite small.*
    Como estão os pequenos? *How are the little ones?*
PÊRA *f. pear.*
peral *m. pear orchard.*
perante *before, in the presence of.*
percal *m. percale.*
perceber *to perceive, to understand, to "get."*
    Dar a perceber. *To imply.*
    Percebemos o que queriam fazer. *We understood what they wanted to do.*
    Não o percebo. *I don't get it.*
percentagem *f. percentage.*
percepção *f. perception.*
percha *f. perch, pole.*
percorrer *to traverse, to cover (distance); to search through.*

perda *f. loss; damage; waste.*
    A perda foi grande. *The loss was heavy. It was a great loss.*
    Perda total. *Total loss.*
perdão *f. pardon.*
    Perdão! *I'm sorry! Excuse me!*
PERDER *to lose; to spoil; to miss.*
    Perdi a caneta. *I lost my pen.*
    Estamos perdendo (a perder) tempo. *We're losing time. We're wasting time.*
    Perder de vista. *To lose sight of.*
    Você perdeu uma boa oportunidade. *You missed a good opportunity.*
    Perdemos a paciência. *We lost patience. We lost our patience.*
    Ele perdeu o avião. *He missed the plane.*
    Depressa! Não há tempo a perder. *Hurry! There's no time to lose.*
    Perder a vez. *To lose one's turn.*
perdição *f. perdition; ruin.*
perdido *adj. lost; ruined.*
perdiz *f. partridge.*
PERDOAR *to excuse, to pardon, to forgive.*
    Perdoe-me. *Pardon me. Excuse me.*
    Perdoe a demora. *Pardon the delay.*
perdurar *to last a long time; to endure.*
perecer *to perish, to die.*
    O menino pereceu de fome. *The child died of hunger.*
peregrino *m. pilgrim.*
perfeição *f. perfection, excellence.*
PERFEITO *adj. perfect; excellent.*
    É um trabalho perfeito. *It's a perfect piece of work.*
perfídia *f. perfidy, treachery.*
perfil *m. profile; outline.*
perfumaria *f. perfume shop.*
perfume *m. perfume; scent, fragrance.*
perfurar *to perforate, to penetrate.*
PERGUNTA *f. question.*
    Fazer perguntas. *To ask questions.*
PERGUNTAR *to ask, to inquire.*
    Por que me pergunta isso? *Why do you ask me that?*
    Ela lhe perguntou (perguntou-lhe) alguma coisa? *Did she ask you something?*
    Quem perguntou por mim? *Who asked for me?*
perícia *f. skill.*
perigo *m. danger, peril.*
    Não há perigo. *There's no danger.*
perigoso *adj. dangerous.*
periódico *adj. periodic, periodical; n. m. periodical.*
periodista *m. and f. journalist, newspaper writer.*
período *m. period, span of time.*
perito *adj. expert, experienced, skillful; n. m. expert; appraiser.*

permanecer *to remain, to stay; to continue.*
Quanto tempo vai permanecer fora da cidade? *How long will you be out of town?*

permanência *f. permanence; stay.*

PERMANENTE *adj. permanent.*

permeável *adj. permeable.*

PERMISSÃO *f. permission; permit; authorization; consent.*
Ter permissão. *To have permission.*

PERMITIR *to permit, to let, to allow.*
Permita-me. *Allow me.*
Permite que lhe faça uma pergunta? *May I ask you a question?*

permuta *f. permutation; exchange; barter.*

PERNA *f. leg.*
Estirar as pernas. *To stretch one's legs.*

pernambucano *adj., n. m. of the state of Pernambuco in Brazil.*

pernicioso *adj. pernicious, injurious, harmful.*

pérola *f. pearl.*

perpendicular *adj., n. f. perpendicular.*

perpetrar *to perpetrate.*

perpetuar *to perpetuate.*

perpetuidade *f. perpetuity.*

perpétuo *adj. perpetual, everlasting.*

perplexidade $(x = ks)$ *f. perplexity, bewilderment.*

perplexo $(x = ks)$ *adj. perplexed, bewildered, puzzled.*
Fico perplexo. *I'm puzzled.*

persa *adj., n. m. and f. Persian.*

perscrutar *to scrutinize, to scan.*

perseguição *f. persecution; pursuit.*

perseguir *to persecute; to pursue; to harass.*

perseverança *f. perseverance.*

perseverar *to persevere, to persist.*

persignar-se *to cross oneself, to make the sign of the cross.*

persistência *f. persistence.*

persistente *adj. persistent, firm.*

persistir *to persist.*

personagem *m. and f. personage; character (in book, play).*

personalidade *personality.*

perspetiva (perspectiva) *f. perspective.*

perspicácia *f. perspicacity.*

perspicaz *adj. perspicacious, acute.*

perspirar *to perspire.*

persuadir *to persuade, to convince.*

persuasão *f. persuasion.*

pertencer *to belong.*
Não me pertence. *It doesn't belong to me.*

pertinente *adj. pertinent.*

PERTO *near.*
Fica perto. *It's close. It's nearby.*
Fica perto da escola. *It's near the school.*

perturbar *to perturb, to disturb.*

peru *m. turkey.*

peruano *adj., n. m. Peruvian.*

perversão *f. perversion.*

perversidade *f. perversity.*

perverso *adj. perverse, wicked.*

perverter *to pervert.*

pesadelo *m. nightmare.*

pesado *adj. heavy; tedious, tiresome.*
O ferro é pesado. *Iron is heavy.*
É um trabalho pesado. *It's hard work.*

pêsames *m. pl. condolences.*

PESAR *to weigh; to cause regret or sorrow; n. m. grief, sorrow; regret.*
Quanto pesa a caixa $(x = sh)$? *How much does the box weigh?*
Pesar as palavras. *To weigh one's words.*
É com grande pesar que lhe escrevo. *It is with great sorrow that I write you.*

pesca *f. fishing; catch.*

pescado *m. catch of fish; fish (after it has been caught; see* peixe*).*

pescar *to fish; to catch.*
Pescar em águas turvas. *To fish in troubled waters.*

pescaria *f. fishing.*

pescoço *m. neck.*

peso *m. weight; burden; importance; peso (money).*
Peso líquido. *Net weight.*
Peso bruto. *Gross weight.*
Peso pesado. *Heavyweight (boxing).*

pesquisa *f. research, investigation.*

pêssego *m. peach.*

pessimismo *m. pessimism.*

pessimista *adj. pessimistic; n. m. and f. pessimist.*

péssimo *adj. very bad, terrible.*

PESSOA *f. person.*
Ela é muito boa pessoa. *She's a very nice person. She's a wonderful person.*
Pessoa de bem. *Fine person.*
Ela apareceu em pessoa. *She was there in person.*

pessoal *adj. personal, private; n. m. personnel.*
Viva, pessoal, apressamo-nos! *OK, people, let's get moving!*

pestana *f. eyelash; fringe, edging.*
Queimar as pestanas. *To burn the midnight oil.*

peste *f. plague, pestilence; pest.*

petição *f. petition; claim.*

petróleo *m. petroleum.*

pia *f. washbasin; sink; font.*
Pia da cozinha. *Kitchen sink.*

piada *f. joke, wisecrack.*

pianista *m. and f. pianist.*

piano *m. piano.*

piar *to peep (as a baby chick).*

picada *f. sting; prick; dive (airplane).*

picante *adj. hot, highly seasoned; sharp; caustic; n. m. appetizer.*

pica-pau *m. woodpecker.*

picar *to bite, to sting; to prick; to itch; to chop; to nibble; to spur; to be hot (pepper, etc.); to dive (airplane).*
Picou-me uma abelha. *A bee stung me.*
Picar carne. *To chop (up) meat.*

pícaro *adj. crafty, sly.*

pico *m. peak, summit; spine; thorn; sting; a bit.*
Subiram ao pico mais alto. *They climbed to the highest peak.*
Ficaram lá um mês e pico. *They stayed there a little more than a month.*

piedade *f. piety; pity; mercy.*

pigarrear *to clear the throat.*

pigarro *m. frog in the throat.*

pijama *m. pajamas.*

pilar *m. pillar, column, post.*

pilha *f. pile, heap; battery (in a car, etc.).*
Pilha sêca (seca). *Dry battery.*

pilhéria *f. joke, gag.*

piloto *m. pilot.*
Piloto de provas. *Test pilot.*

pílula *f. pill.*

pimenta *f. pepper.*

pincel *m. brush.*

pindorama *m. country of palms* Ⓑ.

pingar *to drip, to leak.*

pingue-pongue *m. Ping-Pong.*

pinha *f. pinecone; sweetsop, sugar apple (a tropical fruit)* Ⓑ.

pinheiro *m. pine tree.*

pinho *m. pine (wood).*

pino *m. peg; pin; apex.*
Pino mestre. *Kingpin.*
No pino de. *At the peak of.*

pinta *f. spot; mole, beauty mark.*

pintado *adj. painted; spotted, speckled, freckled.*

pintar *to paint; to describe.*
Que está pintando (a pintar)? *What are you painting?*
Pintar a óleo. *To paint in oil.*
Pintar o sete. *To raise hell.*

pintor *m. painter.*

pintura *f. painting.*
Pintura a óleo. *Oil painting.*

pio *adj. pious; n. m. peep, chirp.*

piolho *m. louse.*

pioneiro *m. pioneer.*

PIOR *adj. and adv. worse, worst.*
O doente está pior. *The patient is worse.*
Isso é o pior. *That's the worst of it.*
Ainda pior. *Worse yet.*
A situação vai de mal a pior. *The situation is going from bad to worse.*
Cada vez pior. *Worse and worse.*

piorar *to worsen.*

piquenique *m. picnic.*

pirâmide *f. pyramid.*

pirata *m. pirate.*

pires *m. sing. and pl. saucer, saucers.*

pisada *f. footstep; footprint.*

pisar *to tread, to step on; to press; to walk.*

piscar *to wink, to blink.*
Ele piscou para ela. *He winked at her.*

piscina *f. swimming pool.*

piso *m. floor, ground; tread; gait.*

pista *f. track; landing strip; trail, clue.*
Seguir a pista. *To follow the trail.*
Pista de corridas. *Race track.*

pistão *m. piston; cornet.*

pistola *f. pistol, gun.*

pitoresco *adj. picturesque.*

placa *f. plate (metal); plaque; badge.*
Placa de licença. *License plate.*

placar *to placate, to appease; n. m. placard, poster; badge.*

plaina *f. carpenter's plane.*

plana *f. category, class.*

planalto *m. plateau.*

planejar *to plan.*

planeta *m. planet.*

planície *f. plain.*

plano *adj. smooth, even; n. m. plane; plan.*
Primeiro plano. *Foreground.*
Último plano. *Background.*
Geometria plana. *Plane geometry.*

planta *f. plant; plan.*
Planta anual. *Annual plant.*

plantação *f. plantation; planting.*

plantar *to plant; to drive into the ground.*
Vamos plantar algumas árvores perto da casa. *We're going to plant some trees near the house.*

plástica *f. plastic art; plastic surgery.*

plástico *adj., n. m. plastic.*

plataforma *f. platform.*

plátano *m. plane tree; sycamore.*

platéia (plateia) *f. orchestra section (theatre); audience.*

platina *f. platinum.*

platino *adj. of the River Plate region.*

pleito *m. lawsuit; dispute.*

PLENO *adj. full, complete.*
Plenos poderes. *Full powers.*
Em pleno dia. *In broad daylight.*

pluma *f. feather, plume; feather pen.*

plural *adj., n. m. plural.*

pneu *m. tire (on a car, etc.).*

pneumático *adj. pneumatic.*

pó *m. dust; powder.*
Pó de arroz. *Face powder.*

POBRE *adj. poor; n. m. and f. poor person; beggar.*
Ele é muito pobre. *He is very poor.*
Pobre homem! *Poor man! Poor fellow!*

pobreza f. poverty, need.

poço m. well; shaft (elevator, mine, etc.); pit.
Poço de petróleo. Oil well.

podar to prune.

PODER to be able; can; may; n. m. power;
authority; command.
Em que posso servi-lo? What can I do for
you? (How) may I help you?
Não posso ir. I can't go.
Não pode ser! That can't be! That's
impossible!
Eu fiz o melhor que pude. I did the best I
could.
Quem tem o poder nesse país? Who has
the power in that country?
Poder executivo. Executive power.
Plenos poderes. Full powers.
Não posso com eles. I can't deal with
them.
Posso entrar?—Pode. May I come in?—
You may.

poderoso adj. mighty, powerful.

podre adj. rotten; corrupt.

podridão f. rottenness; corruption.

poeira f. dust.

poema m. poem.

poesia f. poetry.

poeta m. poet.

POIS as, since; so; well; then; why; now;
indeed.
Pois faça-o. Then do it.
Pois vamos. Then let's go.
Pois bem. Well then.
Pois é. That's it. Of course.
Pois não! Of course! Certainly!

polaco adj. Polish; n. m. Pole.

polar adj. polar.
Estrela polar. North Star.

polca f. polka.

polcar to dance the polka.

polegada f. inch.

polegar m. thumb; big toe.

poleiro m. perch; top gallery of theater;
peanut gallery ⑧.

polêmica (polémica) f. polemics; controversy.

polêmico (polémico) adj. polemic, polemical.

polícia f. police force; m. policeman.
Polícia militar. Military police.

policial adj. police; n. m. policeman, officer.
Romance policial. Detective story.

polido adj. polished, bright.

polígamo adj. polygamous; n. m. polygamist.

polimento m. polishing; polish.

poliomielite f. poliomyelitis.

polir to polish.

política f. politics; political science; policy.
Política econômica. Economic policies.
Política social. Social policies.

político adj. political; n. m. politician.

Ter influência política. To have good
political connections.
Economia política. Political economy.

pólo pole; polo.

polonês adj. Polish; n. m. Polish person.

poltrona f. easy chair; orchestra seat.

pólvora f. powder, gunpowder.

pomada f. pomade.

pomar m. orchard.

pombo m. pigeon, dove.
Pombo de barro. Clay pigeon.

pômulo (pómulo) m. cheek.

ponche m. punch (drink).

ponderação f. consideration, reflection.

ponderar to ponder, to weigh.

PONTA f. point; tip.
Ter na ponta da língua. To have on the tip
of the tongue.
Nas pontas dos pés. On tiptoe.

pontapé m. kick.

pontaria f. aim, aiming.

ponte f. bridge.
Ponte suspensa. Suspension bridge.
Ponte levadiça. Drawbridge.

ponteiro m. pointer; hand (clock).

pontiagudo adj. pointed, sharp.

PONTO m. point; dot; period; place; stitch;
prompter.
Ponto de partida. Starting point. Point of
departure.
Ponto final. Period.
Ponto e vírgula. Semicolon.
Dois pontos. Colon.
Seis pontos cinco. 6.5.
Ponto por ponto. Point by point.
Estarei lá às sete horas em ponto. I'll be
there at seven o'clock sharp.
Ponto cardeal. Cardinal point (N, S, E, W
on compass).
Ponto culminante. Climax.
Ponto fraco. Weakness. Weak point.
Estávamos a ponto de sair quando
chegaram. We were about to leave
when they arrived.
Até certo ponto é verdade. To a certain
extent it is true.

pontual adj. punctual.

popa f. stern.
A popa. Aft.
De proa à popa. From stem to stern.

popular adj. popular.
E uma canção popular. It's a popular
song.

popularidade f. popularity.

pôquer ⑧ m. poker.

POR for; by; through; about.
Por correio aéreo. By airmail.
Ganharam por dois pontos. They won by
two points.

Dom Casmurro foi escrito por Machado de Assis. Dom Casmurro *was written by Machado de Assis.*

Entrem pela porta principal. *Enter through the main door.*

Pode pasar pela casa? *Can you pass by the house?*

Por mês. *By the month.*

Por muito tempo. *For a long time.*

Pela manhã. *In the morning.*

Pela tarde. *In the afternoon.*

Pela noite. *In the evening.*

Por agora. *For the present.*

Por dentro. *On the inside.*

Por fora. *On the outside.*

Por conseguinte. *Consequently.*

Por fim. *Finally.*

Por quê? *Why?*

Por toda parte. *Everywhere.*

Por Deus! *Heavens! For heaven's sake!*

Por outro lado. *On the other hand.*

Por exemplo *(x = z). For example.*

Por volta (de). *Around. About.*

Por pouco. *Almost. Nearly.*

Por meio de. *By means of.*

Por atacado. *Wholesale.*

Por aqui. *This way.*

Por acaso. *By chance.*

Por favor. *Please.*

Eu não votei por ele. *I didn't vote for him.*

PÔR *to put; to set (table); to put on; to lay (eggs).*

Ponha o livro na mesa. *Put the book on the table.*

Pôr a mesa. *To set the table.*

Pôr ovos. *To lay eggs.*

Pôr à prova. *To put to the test.*

Pôr em execução *(x = z). To carry out. To execute.*

Pôr em dúvida. *To doubt. To question.*

Pôr mãos à obra. *To get to work.*

Pôr em liberdade. *To free.*

Pôr uma gravata. *To put on a tie.*

Pôr por escrito. *To put in writing.*

Pôr os pontos nos ii. *To dot the i's and cross the t's.*

Pôr mel em boca de asno. *To cast pearls before swine.*

O homem põe e Deus dispõe. *Man proposes, God disposes.*

porão *m. hold (ship), basement* Ⓑ.

porca *f. sow; nut (for bolt).*

porção *f. portion, part, share; many, much* Ⓑ.

Dividir em porções. *To divide. To share.*

porcelana *f. porcelain; chinaware.*

porco *adj. dirty, filthy; n. m. pig. pork.*

porém *however, but, nevertheless.*

porfia *f. insistence, obstinacy.*

porfiado *adj. stubborn, obstinate.*

porfiar *to persist.*

pormenor *m. detail.*

PORQUE *because, on account of, for, as, since.*

Ela não veio porque estava ocupada. *She didn't come because she was busy.*

Porque era tarde ficamos em casa. *Since it was late, we stayed home.*

porquê *m. reason, the why, why.*

Não sei porquê. *I don't know why.*

porqueiro *m. swineherd.*

pôr-se *to start, to begin, to get.*

Pôr-se a falar. *To begin to speak.*

Pôr-se de joelhos. *To get on one's knees.*

PORTA *f. door, doorway; gate.*

Abra a porta. *Open the door.*

Feche a porta. *Close the door.*

Feche a porta à chave quando sair. *Lock the door when you leave.*

Porta-malas. *Car trunk.*

Porta principal. *Main entrance. Main door.*

Porta giratória. *Revolving door.*

porta-aviões *m. aircraft carrier.*

portador *m. bearer, carrier; porter, messenger.*

portal *m. portal, doorway.*

portão *m. large door, gate.*

portar *to carry; to reach a port; to arrive.*

portar-se *to behave.*

Portar-se mal. *To behave badly.*

portaria *f. reception desk.*

portátil *adj. portable.*

Máquina de escrever portátil. *Portable typewriter.*

Computador portátil. *Laptop computer.*

porte *m. transportation; freight cost; department; postage.*

Quanto é o porte? *How much is the postage?*

Porte pago. *Postpaid.*

porteiro *m. doorman; janitor.*

portenho *adj., n. m. of the city of Buenos Aires.*

portento *m. wonder, portent, prodigy.*

portentoso *adj. prodigious, marvelous.*

porto *m. port, harbor; port (wine).*

Porto de escala. *Port of call.*

portuense *adj., n. m. of the city of Porto in Portugal.*

PORTUGUÊS *adj., n. m. Portuguese.*

Eu falo português. *I speak Portuguese.*

Uma gramática de português. *A Portuguese grammar.*

Ele é português mas ela não é portuguesa. *He is Portuguese, but she is not Portuguese.*

porvir *m. future.*

pós-guerra *adj. postwar; n. m. postwar period.*

POSIÇÃO *f. position, place, situation.*
 Posição firme. *A firm stand. A firm position.*
positivo *adj. positive, sure, certain.*
posse *f. possession, ownership; pl. possessions; wealth.*
 Homem de posses. *A man of means.*
possessão *f. possession.*
possibilidade *f. possibility.*
POSSÍVEL *adj. possible.*
 Não será possível fazê-lo. *It won't be possible to do it.*
 Farei quanto me for possível. *I'll do as much as I can.*
 O mais cedo possível. *As soon as possible.*
possuir *to possess, to have.*
posta *f. slice; post, mail.*
 Posta-restante. *General delivery.*
postal *adj. postal; n. m. postcard.*
 Cartão postal (bilhete postal). *Postcard.*
posteridade *f. posterity.*
posterior *adj. posterior, rear, back.*
POSTO *adj. put, placed; set (table, sun); n. m. place, post, station.*
 Posto de gasolina. *Gas station.*
 Posto militar. *Military post.*
 Posto naval. *Naval station.*
póstumo *adj. posthumous.*
postura *f. posture, position.*
potável *adj. potable.*
potência *f. power, strength, force.*
 As grandes potências. *The Great Powers.*
potentado *m. potentate, ruler.*
potente *adj. potent, powerful, mighty.*
potro *m. colt.*
POUCO *adj. and adv. little; small; scanty; n. m. a little, a small part; pl. a few.*
 Quer um pouco de café? *Would you like some coffee?*
 Ela sabe um pouco de tudo. *She knows a little about everything.*
 Fica-me muito pouco dinheiro. *I have very little money left.*
 Ele chegará dentro de pouco (tempo). *He'll be here shortly.*
 Poucas vezes. *A few times.*
 Gosto um pouco. *I like it a bit.*
 Aos poucos. *Little by little.*
 Acho um pouco caro. *I think it's rather (a little) expensive.*
 Há pouco. *A short while ago.*
 Tenho uns poucos. *I have a few.*
poupar *to save, to economize.*
 Vou poupar o meu dinheiro. *I'm going to save my money.*
pousar *to set down; to put; to stay, to lodge.*
POVO *m. people; public.*
 O povo português. *The Portuguese people.*
povoação *f. population; town, settlement.*

povoar *to populate; to stock.*
PRAÇA *f. plaza, square; market; enlisted man.*
 Vamos dar uma volta pela praça. *Let's take a stroll around the square.*
 Carro de praça. *Taxi.*
prado *m. meadow, pasture, field.*
praga *f. plague; curse.*
praia *f. beach, shore.*
pranto *m. weeping, crying.*
prata *f. silver; silverware.*
prateleira *f. shelf.*
prática *f. practice; exercise; talk.*
 A prática faz o mestre. *Practice makes perfect.*
praticante *adj. practicing; n. m. practitioner; apprentice.*
praticar *to practice; to do (a hobby, etc.).*
 Ela pratica bordado. *She does embroidery.*
prático *adj. practical; skilled; experienced (worker); n. m. harbor pilot.*
PRATO *m. dish, plate; course (meal).*
 Este prato é gostoso. *This dish is delicious.*
 Qual é o prato do dia? *What's today's special?*
 Prato fundo. *Soup plate.*
 Prato raso. *Dinner plate.*
 Do prato à boca se perde a sopa. *The best laid plans often go awry.*
praxe *(x = sh) f. custom, habit.*
 De praxe. *Usual. Customary.*
PRAZER *to please; m. pleasure, enjoyment.*
 Tenho muito prazer em conhecê-lo. *I am very glad to know you.*
 O prazer é todo meu. *The pleasure is all mine.*
 Foi um prazer vê-lo de novo. *It was a pleasure to see you again.*
prazo *m. term; period of time.*
 Comprar a prazo. *To buy on time. To buy on the installment plan.*
 Prazo de entrega. *Time of delivery.*
preâmbulo *m. preamble, introduction.*
 É um preâmbulo interessante. *It's an interesting preface.*
 Deixe *(x = sh)* de preâmbulos e diga o que quer. *Stop beating around the bush and tell me what you want.*
precário *adj. precarious.*
precaução *f. precaution.*
precaver *to forewarn, to caution.*
precedência *f. precedence.*
precedente *adj. preceding; n. m. precedent.*
preceder *to precede.*
preceito *m. precept, rule.*
preciosidade *f. preciousness; precious or beautiful thing.*
precioso *adj. precious, dear.*
 Pedras preciosas. *Precious stones.*

precipício *m. precipice.*
precipitação *f. precipitation.*
precipitado *adj. precipitate, hasty.*
precipitar *to precipitate; to hurry; to rush on.*
precisão *f. precision, accuracy; necessity.*
Instrumento de precisão. *Precision instrument.*
PRECISAR *to need; to specify.*
Preciso duma dúzia. *I need a dozen.*
Precisamos (de) estudar mais. *We must study more.*
PRECISO *adj. necessary; exact.*
É preciso pagar hoje. *It is necessary to pay today.*
É preciso que cheguemos antes da seis. *It is necessary that we arrive before six.*
Não é preciso. *It's not necessary.*
PREÇO *m. price; value.*
Por que preço? *At what price?*
Preço fixo. *Fixed price.*
Preço de fábrica. *At cost.*
A qualquer preço. *At any price.*
Preço de ocasião. *Bargain price.*
Preço de varejo. *Retail price.*
Abaixar *(x = sh)* o preço. *To lower the price.*
preconceito *m. prejudice.*
Preconceito de raça. *Racial prejudice.*
predição *f. prediction.*
predicar *to preach.*
predileção *f. predilection, preference.*
Ter predileção por. *To have a fondness for. To have a preference for.*
prédio *m. building, house; land.*
É um prédio de dois andares. *It's a building with two floors.*
predisposto *adj. predisposed, inclined.*
predizer *to predict, to foretell.*
predominar *to predominate, to prevail.*
preencher *to fill (out).*
Faça o favor de preencher este formulário. *Please fill out this form.*
Preencher uma vaga. *To fill a vacancy.*
prefácio *m. preface, introduction.*
prefeito (administrador do concelho) *m. mayor, administrator.*
prefeitura (câmara municipal) *f. city hall.*
preferência *f. preference, choice.*
De preferência. *Preferably.*
Ter preferência. *To take preference. To have priority.*
preferido *adj. preferred, favorite.*
PREFERIR *to prefer.*
Qual prefere? *Which do you prefer?*
Prefiro este. *I prefer this one.*
preferível *adj. preferable.*
É preferível ir pessoalmente. *It's better to go in person.*
prefixo *(x = ks) m. prefix.*

prega *f. crease, fold.*
pregar *to nail; to fasten; to stick; to preach.*
Pregar um prego. *To drive a nail.*
Pregar uma peça emalguém. *To play a trick on someone.*
Não preguei os olhos. *I didn't sleep a wink.*
prego *m. nail.*
preguiça *f. laziness.*
preguiçoso *adj. lazy.*
O João é muito preguiçoso. *John is very lazy.*
pré-histórico *adj. prehistoric.*
prejuízo *m. harm, damage; loss.*
preliminar *adj. preliminary.*
prelo *m. printing press.*
prelúdio *m. prelude.*
prematuro *adj. premature.*
premeditação *f. premeditation.*
premeditar *to premeditate.*
premiar *to reward.*
PRÊMIO *m. prize, reward; premium.*
Ela ganhou o prêmio. *She won the prize.*
prenda *f. gift, present; talent.*
prendar *to present with.*
prendedor *m. clasp; fastener.*
Prendedor de gravata. *Tie clip.*
PRENDER *to fasten; to catch; to arrest.*
Quem prendeu o ladrão? *Who arrested (caught) the thief?*
prenhe *adj. pregnant.*
prensa *f. printing press; press.*
Prensa hidráulica. *Hydraulic press.*
preocupação *f. preoccupation, concern, worry.*
preocupar *to preoccupy, to concern.*
Eles estão muito preocupados. *They are quite concerned.*
preparação *f. preparation.*
preparado *adj. prepared; preparation (medicinal).*
PREPARAR *to prepare, to get ready.*
Primeiro temos que preparar a lição. *First we have to prepare the lesson.*
preparativo *adj. preparative; n. m. pl. preparations.*
Estamos fazendo (a fazer) os preparativos para a viagem. *We're making preparations for the trip.*
preparatório *adj. preparatory.*
preponderância *f. preponderance.*
preponderar *to prevail.*
preposição *f. preposition.*
presa *f. prey, capture; female prisoner; fang; claw.*
prescindir *to do without, to dispense with.*
prescrever *to prescribe.*
presença *f. presence.*
Presença de espírito. *Presence of mind.*

presenciar *to be present; to witness, to see.*
  Acabamos de presenciar . . . *We've just witnessed . . .*
PRESENTE *adj. present; n. m. gift, present; present time; present tense.*
  Presente! *Present! Here!*
  Presente de aniversário. *Birthday gift.*
  A presente serve para dizer-lhe . . . *(in a letter) This is to inform you . . .*
presépio *m. stable; crèche, Nativity scene.*
preservação *f. preservation.*
preservar *to preserve; to maintain; to keep.*
presidência *f. presidency.*
presidente *m. president; chairman.*
presidiário *m. convict.*
presídio *m. penitentiary, prison.*
presidir *to preside, to direct.*
preso *adj. imprisoned, arrested; n. m. prisoner, convict.*
  Preso em flagrante. *Caught in the act.*
  Ele foi preso como cúmplice. *He was arrested as an accomplice.*
  Está preso! *You're under arrest!*
PRESSA *f. haste, speed, hurry.*
  Estou com pressa (tenho pressa). *I'm in a hurry.*
  Sem pressa. *Leisurely.*
  Por que tanta pressa? *Why the rush?*
pressagiar *to predict, to foretell.*
presságio *m. prediction; omen.*
pressentimento *m. presentiment, premonition.*
prestar *to lend; to aid; to pay (attention).*
  Prestar atenção. *To pay attention.*
  Você me prestou um bom serviço. *You rendered me a great service.*
  Não presta para nada. *It's not good for anything.*
prestes *adj. ready.*
presteza *f. quickness, speed, promptness.*
prestígio *m. prestige.*
prestigioso *adj. famous; influential.*
presumido *adj. vain, conceited; n. m. conceited person.*
presumir *to presume, to assume; to be conceited.*
presunção *f. presumption; conceit.*
presunto *m. ham.*
pretendente *n. m. and f. candidate, claimant; n. m. suitor.*
pretender *to claim, to intend.*
  Pretendemos visitar o Brasil. *We intend to visit Brazil.*
pretensão *f. pretension.*
pretensioso *adj. pretentious; n. m. pretentious person.*
pretexto *(x = sh) m. pretext.*
PRETO *adj. black; dark; difficult.*
  Vestir de preto. *To wear black.*
prevalecer *to prevail.*

prevenção *f. prevention; prejudice.*
prevenir *to prevent; to warn.*
  Estamos prevenidos. *We're prepared. We've been forewarned.*
prever *to foresee; to anticipate.*
  Ele previu essa dificuldade. *He expected (foresaw) that difficulty.*
prévio *adj. previous, prior.*
  Aviso prévio. *Previous notice.*
  Questão prévia. *Previous question (parliamentary procedure).*
previsão *f. foresight, prevision.*
previsto *adj. foreseen, expected.*
prezado *adj. dear, esteemed.*
  Prezado Senhor: *Dear Sir:*
primário *adj. primary.*
  Escola primária. *Elementary school. Primary school.*
PRIMAVERA *f. spring (season).*
PRIMEIRO *adj., n. m. first; foremost.*
  Traga-nos primeiro a sopa. *Bring us the soup first.*
  Bilhete de primeira. *First-class ticket.*
  Eles moram na primeira casa. *They live in the first house.*
  De primeira ordem. *First-rate.*
  A primeira vez. *The first time.*
  O primeiro do mês. *The first of the month.*
  Primeiro andar. *First floor.*
  Em primeiro lugar. *In the first place.*
  Primeiro ministro. *Prime minister.*
  Primeiro prêmio (prémio). *First prize.*
  Primeiros socorros. *First aid.*
  O romance está escrito na primeira pessoa. *The novel is written in the first person.*
  Primeiro plano. *Foreground.*
primitivo *adj. primitive.*
primo *adj. prime; n. m. cousin.*
  Número primo. *Prime number.*
  Obra prima. *Masterpiece.*
  Ela é prima de João. *She is John's cousin.*
primor *m. beauty; excellence.*
princesa *f. princess.*
PRINCIPAL *adj. principal, main, chief; n. m. principal.*
  Quem tem o papel principal? *Who has the main role?*
  O principal é acabar este trabalho antes da sexta. *The main (most important) thing is to finish this work before Friday.*
príncipe *m. prince.*
principiante *adj. beginning; n. m. and f. beginner.*
PRINCÍPIO *m. beginning, origin; principle.*
  No princípio parecia-me fácil. *It seemed easy to me at first.*
  Pagam no princípio de mês. *They pay the first part of the month.*

Em princípio não me parece má idéia (ideia). *In principle it doesn't seem like a bad idea.*

prioridade *f. priority.*

prisão *f. imprisonment; prison.*

prisioneiro *m. prisoner.*

privação *f. privation, want.*

privada *f. toilet.*

privado *adj. private, confidential.*
Vida privada. *Private life.*

privar *to deprive.*

privilegiado *adj. privileged.*

privilégio *m. privilege.*

pró *m. pro; argument for.*
Os prós e os contras. *The pros and cons.*
Em pró de. *In favor of.*

proa *f. bow (ship).*

probabilidade *f. probability.*

PROBLEMA *m. problem.*

procaz *adj. insolent, impudent, bold.*

procedência *f. origin, source; validity.*

procedente *adj. coming or proceeding from; logical.*

proceder *to proceed; to act, to behave; m. behavior, conduct.*
Ele procedeu corretamente (correctamente). *He acted properly.*
Proceda com muito cuidado. *Proceed very carefully.*

procedimento *m. procedure; method.*

processar *to sue; to indict.*

processo *m. process, procedure; lawsuit.*

proclamação *f. proclamation.*

proclamar *to proclaim; to promulgate.*
Nesse mesmo dia proclamaram a paz. *They declared peace on that very day.*

procriar *to procreate.*

procura *f. search; demand.*
Oferta e procura. *Supply and demand.*
Ela está à procura duma boa gramática de português. *She is looking for a good Portuguese grammar.*

PROCURAR *to look for, to seek; to try.*
Estou procurando (a procurar) o chapéu. *I'm looking for my hat.*
Procure estar na esquina às nove. *Try to be on the corner at nine.*

prodígio *m. wonder, marvel.*

prodigioso *adj. prodigious, marvelous.*

produção *f. production, output.*

produtivo *adj. productive.*

produto *m. product, yield.*
Produtos alimentícios. *Food products. Food.*

PRODUZIR *to produce, to turn out; to yield.*
Essa fábrica produz automóveis. *That factory produces (turns out) automobiles.*

proeza *f. prowess; accomplishment.*

profanação *f. profanation.*

profanar *to profane.*

profano *adj. profane, irreverent; worldly.*

profecia *f. prophecy.*

proferir *to utter, to say.*
Ele proferiu um discurso. *He delivered an address.*

professar *to profess, to declare openly; to teach.*

professor *m. professor, teacher.*
Professor particular. *Private tutor.*

profeta *m. prophet.*

profético *adj. prophetic.*

profissão *f. profession; declaration.*
Seu nome e profissão, por favor. *Your name and profession, please.*

profissional *adj. professional.*

profundidade *f. profundity, depth.*
200 metros de profundidade. *200 meters deep.*

PROFUNDO *adj. profound, deep; intense.*
Silêncio profundo. *Deep silence.*
O poço é muito profundo. *The well is very deep.*

prognosticar *to prognosticate, to forecast.*

prognóstico *adj. prognostic; n. m. forecast; prognosis.*

PROGRAMA *m. program; plan.*
O program não foi muito bom. *The program was not very good.*

progredir *to progress, to advance.*

progresso *m. progress.*
Ordem e progresso. *Order and progress.*

proibição *f. prohibition.*

proibido *adj. prohibited, forbidden.*
É proibido fumar. *No smoking.*
É proibida a entrada. *No admittance.*

PROIBIR *to prohibit, to forbid.*
Proibo-lhe de fazer isso. *I forbid you to do that.*

projetado (projectado) *adj. projected, planned.*

projetar (projectar) *to project, to plan.*

projetil, projétil (projéctil) *m. projectile, missile.*

projeto (projecto) *m. project, plan.*

proletariado *m. proletariat.*

proletário *adj. proletarian.*

prólogo *m. prologue.*

prolongação *f. prolongation, extension.*

prolongar *to prolong, to extend.*

promessa *f. promise.*

PROMETER *to promise.*
Mas você prometeu fazê-lo. *But you promised to do it.*
Ele nunca cumpre o que promete. *He never does what he promises.*

prometido *adj. promised; m. promise; fiancé.*
Cumprir o prometido. *To keep a promise.*

promoção *f. promotion.*
promover *to promote, to advance.*
promulgar *to promulgate, to publish.*
pronome *m. pronoun.*
prontidão *f. promptness; swiftness.*
PRONTO *adj. ready, prepared.*
   Estamos prontos. *We are ready.*
prontuário *m. handbook.*
pronúncia *f. pronunciation.*
   Ela tem uma boa pronúncia. *She has good pronunciation. Her pronunciation is good.*
pronunciar *to pronounce; to utter; to give (a speech).*
   A senhora pronuncia muito bem o português. *You pronounce Portuguese very well.*
   Pronunciar (uma) sentença. *To pronounce sentence.*
propagação *f. propagation, dissemination.*
propaganda *f. propaganda, advertisement.*
propagandista *m. and f. propagandist.*
propagar *to propagate; to spread (news, etc.).*
propender *to tend, to incline to.*
propensão *f. propensity, tendency.*
propenso *adj. inclined, disposed.*
propício *adj. propitious, favorable.*
   Um momento propício. *A favorable moment.*
proponente *adj., n. m. and f. proponent.*
propor *to propose; to suggest.*
   Proponho ir vê-lo. *I intend to go to see him.*
   O homem propõe, Deus dispõe. *Man proposes, God disposes.*
proporção *f. proportion.*
proporcionar *to provide, to supply; to proportion, to adjust.*
proposição *f. proposition, proposal.*
propósito *m. purpose, intention.*
   Fizemos isso de propósito. *We did it on purpose.*
   A propósito. *By the way.*
   A propósito de. *Regarding. With regard to.*
proposta *f. proposal, proposition.*
proposto *adj. proposed.*
propriedade *f. property; ownership; propriety.*
   Acabo de comprar essa propriedade. *I've just bought that property.*
   Propriedade literária. *Copyright.*
proprietário *m. proprietor, owner, landlord.*
PROPRIO *adj. own; proper, fit, suitable.*
   Essas foram suas próprias palavras. *Those were his/her own words.*
   Esse é um jogo próprio de meninos. *That's a game (suitable) for children.*
prorrogação *f. prorogation, extension.*
prorrogar *to extend (time), to prolong.*
prorromper *to break out, to burst out.*

prosa *f. prose; chatter, gab* Ⓑ.
prosaico *adj. prosaic.*
prosista *m. and f. prose writer; chatterer* Ⓑ.
prosperar *to prosper, to thrive; to be successful.*
prosperidade *f. prosperity.*
próspero *adj. prosperous; successful.*
   Próspero ano novo! *Happy New Year!*
prospeto (prospecto) *m. prospectus; prospect.*
prosseguir *to pursue, to carry on, to go on, to continue, to proceed.*
   Prossiga! *Continue!*
prostrar *to prostrate.*
protagonista *m. and f. protagonist.*
proteção (protecção) *f. protection; support.*
proteger *to protect; to support.*
protestante *adj. protesting, Protestant; n. m. and f. protestor; Protestant.*
protestar *to protest.*
protesto *m. protest, objection; expression.*
   Sob protesto. *Under protest.*
   Com os protestos de minha alta consideração. *Sincerely yours.*
protetor (protector) *m. protector.*
PROVA *f. proof; test, examination; proof sheet; fitting (of garments).*
   Recebi duas provas. *I received two proofs.*
   À prova de fogo. *Fireproof.*
   Prova oral. *Oral test.*
   Prova escrita. *Written test.*
provado *adj. proven, tried.*
PROVAR *to try; to taste; to prove; to try on.*
   Prove este vinho. *Try this wine.*
PROVÁVEL *adj. probable, likely.*
   É pouco provável. *It's not likely.*
   É provável que venha amanhã. *It's likely that he will come tomorrow.*
PROVEITO *m. profit; benefit, advantage.*
   Tirar proveito. *To derive profit from. To turn to advantage.*
   Bom proveito! *(said at meals). Enjoy your meal! Bon appétit!*
proveitoso *adj. profitable, beneficial.*
prover *to provide, to furnish, to supply.*
provérbio *m. proverb.*
providência *f. providence, precaution; pl. steps, measures.*
   Tomar providências. *To take steps. To take measures.*
província *f. province.*
provir *to derive from, to come from.*
provisão *f. provision, supply; pl. provisions.*
   Provisões de guerra. *Munitions.*
provisional *adj. provisional, temporary.*
provisório *adj. provisional, temporary.*
provocação *f. provocation.*
provocador *adj. provocative; n. m. instigator, troublemaker.*
provocar *to provoke, to vex.*

PRÓXIMO *(x = s) adj. near, next, neighboring; m. neighbor, fellowman.*
Na próxima semana. *Next week.*
Amar o próximo. *To love one's neighbor.*
prudência *f. prudence, moderation.*
prudente *adj. prudent, cautious.*
pseudônimo (pseudónimo) *m. pseudonym.*
psicanálise *f. psychoanalysis.*
psicologia *f. psychology.*
psicólogo *m. psychologist.*
psicótico *psychotic.*
psique *m. psyche.*
psiquiatra *m. and f. psychiatrist.*
psiquiatria *f. psychiatry.*
psíquico *adj. psychic.*
psiu! *pst! shh!*
pua *f. sharp point, prong; bit (drill).*
publicação *f. publication.*
publicar *to publish, to announce.*
Ele publicou uma série de artigos sobre a literatura brasileira. *He published a series of articles about Brazilian literature.*
publicidade *f. publicity.*
PÚBLICO *adj. public; n. m. public; audience.*
Biblioteca pública. *Public library.*
Em público. *In public.*
O público não gostou da peça. *The audience did not like the play.*
pudim *m. pudding.*
pudor *m. modesty, shyness; propriety.*
pugilista *m. pugilist, boxer.*
pugna *f. struggle, fight.*
pular *to jump.*
pulga *f. flea.*
Andar com a pulga atrás da orelha. *To be suspicious. To smell a rat.*
pulmão *m. lung.*
pulmonia *f. pneumonia.*
pulo *m. jump, skip.*
Quando ela ouviu a notícia deu pulos de alegria. *When she heard the news, she jumped with joy.*
Em dois pulos. *Right away. In two shakes of a lamb's tail.*
Dar um pulo na casa de alguém. *To drop in on someone.*
pulôver Ⓑ *m. pullover, sweater.*
pulsar *to pulsate, to beat.*
pulseira *f. bracelet.*
Relógio-pulseira. *Wristwatch.*
pulso *m. pulse; wrist; force, strength.*
Deixe-me tomar-lhe o pulso. *Let me take your pulse.*
pum! *Bang! Boom!*
pundonor *m. dignity, self-respect.*
pungente *adj. pungent, acute.*
pungir *to prick, to pierce; to torment; to afflict.*

punhado *m. handful, a few.*
Um punhado de soldados defenderam a posição. *A handful of soldiers defended the position.*
punhal *m. dagger.*
punhalada *f. a stab; stab wound.*
punho *m. fist, wrist; cuff; handle.*
De próprio punho. *In one's own handwriting.*
punição *f. punishment.*
punir *to punish.*
pupilo *m. ward; protegé.*
purê (puré) *m. purée.*
Purê de batatas. *Mashed potatoes.*
pureza *f. purity.*
purga *f. purge; laxative.*
purgação *f. purge; purification.*
purgante *adj., n. m. purgative.*
purgar *to purge; to cleanse.*
purgatório *m. purgatory.*
purificar *to purify.*
puro *adj. pure, clean; plain.*
É a pura verdade. *That's the plain truth.*
púrpura *f. crimson, purple.*
pusilânime *adj. fainthearted, cowardly; n. m. and f. coward, wimp.*
pútrido *adj. rotten, putrid.*
putrificar *to putrefy, to rot.*
puxa! *(x = sh) Gosh! Golly!*
puxar *(x = sh) to pull; to haul; to take after, to resemble.*
Puxar conversa. *To strike up a conversation.*
Puxa-saco. *Apple-polisher* Ⓑ.

Q

quadra *f. square area; quatrain; series of four; quarter; block (of street)* Ⓑ*; court (sports).*
quadragésimo *adj., n. m. fortieth.*
quadrado *adj. square.*
Um metro quadrado. *One square meter.*
quadrilha *f. a squadron; a gang; a square dance.*
Uma quadrilha de ladrões. *A gang of thieves.*
quadro *m. picture; painting; team; board.*
Quadro negro. *Blackboard.*
Quadro a óleo. *Oil painting.*
Quadro de avisos. *Bulletin board.*
QUAL *which; what; which one; like; as.*
Qual prefere o senhor? *Which (one) do you prefer?*
Quais são os do senhor? *Which (ones) are yours?*
Cada qual. *Each one.*

qualidade *f. quality; kind; grade.*
qualquer *adj. any.*
 A qualquer hora. *At any time.*
 Ele é capaz de qualquer coisa. *He is capable of anything.*
 De qualquer maneira. *By any means. Anyhow.*
QUANDO *when.*
 Quando vai partir? *When are you going to leave?*
 Quando o senhor quiser. *Whenever you wish.*
 Até quando? *Until when?*
 De quando em quando. *From time to time.*
 De vez em quando. *From time to time.*
 Quando ela chegou, ele já tinha partido. *When she arrived, he had already left.*
quantia *f. sum, amount.*
quantidade *f. quantity, amount.*
QUANTO *how much; how; as much as; all that.*
 Quanto? *How much?*
 Quantos? *How many?*
 A quantos do mês estamos? *What day of the month is it?*
 Quanto é? *How much is it?*
 Compre quantos livros você quiser. *Buy as many books as you like.*
 Quanto mais lhe dou, mais me pede. *The more I give him, the more he asks for.*
 Quanto antes. *As soon as possible.*
 Quanto a mim, não irei nunca. *As for me, I'll never go.*
quão *adv. how, as.*
QUARENTA *forty.*
quaresma *f. Lent.*
QUARTA, *f. Wednesday.*
QUARTA-FEIRA *f. Wednesday.*
quarteirão *m. city block.*
quartel *m. barracks; quarter.*
 Quartel-general. *General headquarters.*
QUARTO *adj. fourth, m. quarter, fourth; room, bedroom.*
 Estarei lá às dez menos um quarto. *I'll be there at a quarter to ten.*
 Às quatro e um quarto. *At a quarter past four.*
 Quarto de solteiro. *Single bedroom.*
 Quarto de casal. *Double bedroom.*
QUASE *almost, nearly.*
 Quase nunca leio o jornal. *I hardly ever read the newspaper.*
 Quase sempre. *Almost always.*
 Quase nunca. *Hardly ever.*
QUATRO *four.*
 São quatro horas. *It's four o'clock.*
QUATROCENTOS *four hundred.*
QUE *what, how; that, which; who, whom; than.*

Que deseja? *What do you want?*
Que é isto? *What's this?*
Que horas são? *What time is it?*
Por que me chamou? *Why did you call me?*
De que está falando (a falar)? *What are you talking about?*
Que pena! *What a pity! Too bad!*
Não sei o que disseram. *I don't know what they said.*
Isso é o que eu digo. *That's what I say.*
Maria disse que o faria. *Mary said she would do it.*
Vale mais do que o senhor pensa. *It's worth more than you think.*
Espero que sim. *I hope so.*
Ela é mais inteligente (do) que ele. *She is more intelligent than he is.*
Temos que partir. *We have to leave.*
quê *(used as an interjection or as an interrogative when it stands alone or in final position) what! why! why? something.*
 Por quê? *Why? (For what reason?)*
 Para quê? *Why? (For what purpose?)*
 Não há de quê. *Don't mention it. You're welcome.*
quebra *f. break; crash; bankruptcy.*
quebradiço *adj. fragile, brittle.*
quebrado *adj. broken; ruptured; m. fraction.*
quebra-luz *m. lampshade.*
quebrantar *to break; to wear out.*
QUEBRAR *to break; to burst; to weaken.*
 Quebrar a palavra. *To break one's word.*
queda *f. fall; inclination.*
 Queda de água. *Waterfall.*
 Ela tem queda para as letras. *She has a bent for literature.*
quedar *to stay.*
QUEIJO *m. cheese.*
queimado *adj. burned.*
 Cheira a queimado. *It smells like something's burning.*
queimar *to burn; to parch; to sell at reduced prices; to get angry.*
 Queimar as pestanas. *To burn the midnight oil.*
queixa *(x = sh) f. complaint; protest.*
 Apresentar queixa. *To lodge a complaint.*
 Ter motivo de queixa. *To have grounds for complaint.*
queixar-se *(x = sh) to complain.*
 Eles se queixaram das condições nas escolas. *They complained about conditions in the schools.*
queixo *(x = sh) m. chin; jaw.*
queixoso *(x = sh) adj. constantly complaining.*
QUEM *who, whom; whoever; those who.*
 Quem é ele? *Who is he?*
 Quem são os outros convidados? *Who are the other guests?*

Quem fala? *Who's speaking?*

Para quem é esta caixa *(x = sh)? Who is this box for?*

De quem é? *Whose is it?*

Quem fala assim não conhece o problema. *Whoever says that doesn't know the problem.*

QUENTE *warm, hot.*

Está muito quente hoje. *It's very hot today.*

quer *whether, or.*

Quer ele aceite quer não aceite, eu vou continuar. *Whether he accepts or not, I'm going to continue.*

Quer sim, quer não. *Whether yes or no.*

querença *f. affection, fondness; wish, desire.*

QUERER *to wish, to want, to desire; to like.*

Que quer o senhor? *What do you want? What would you like?*

O senhor quer ver o apartamento? *Do you want (would you like) to see the apartment?*

Eu não o quero. *I don't want it.*

Se o senhor quiser. *If you wish.*

Faça como quiser. *Do as you wish.*

Como quiser. *As you wish.*

Quero comprar um relógio. *I want to buy a watch.*

Não quero mais. *I don't want any more.*

Que quer dizer esta palavra? *What does this word mean?*

Sem querer. *Unintentionally.*

Queira Deus. *God willing.*

Querer é poder. *Where there's a will, there's a way.*

querido *adj. dear, beloved.*

Querida filha. *Beloved daughter.*

QUESTÃO *f. question; dispute; matter.*

Eles resolveram a questão. *They settled the matter.*

Eis a questão. *That's the point.*

questionar *to question.*

questionável *adj. questionable, debatable.*

quiçá *perhaps.*

QUIETO *adj. quiet, still.*

Fique quieto! *Be quiet!*

quilate *m. carat; caliber.*

quilha *f. keel.*

quilo *m. kilo, kilogram.*

quilograma *m. kilogram.*

quilômetro (quilômetro) *m. kilometer.*

química *f. chemistry.*

químico *adj. chemical; m. chemist.*

quimono *m. kimono.*

QUINHENTOS *five hundred.*

quinina *f. quinine.*

qüinquagésimo *adj., n. m. fiftieth.*

QUINTA *f. Thursday; farm; country house.*

QUINTA-FEIRA *f. Thursday.*

quintal *m. backyard.*

QUINTO *adj. fifth.*

O quinto andar. *The fifth floor.*

quintuplicar *to quintuple.*

quíntuplo *adj. quintuple, fivefold.*

QUINZE *fifteen.*

Dentro de quinze dias. *Within fifteen days. In two weeks.*

quinzena *f. period of fifteen days, two weeks.*

quiosque *m. kiosk, stand (for newspapers, etc.).*

quitanda *f. vegetable market or shop.*

quitandeiro *m. greengrocer, operator of a quitanda.*

quitar *to free, to release.*

quite *adj. even, clear.*

Estamos quites. *We're even.*

quota *f. quota; share, portion.*

R

rã *f. frog.*

rábano *m. radish.*

rabi *m. rabbi.*

rabo *m. tail.*

De cabo a rabo. *From head to tail. From end to end.*

raça *f. race; breed.*

Raça humana. *Human race.*

Cavalo de raça. *Thoroughbred horse.*

ração *f. ration.*

racemo *m. bunch (grapes).*

raciocinar *to reason.*

racciocínio *m. reasoning.*

racional *adj. rational; reasonable.*

racionar *to ration.*

racista *m. and f. racist.*

radar *m. radar.*

radiação *f. radiation.*

radiador *m. radiator.*

radiar *to radiate; to shine.*

radical *adj. radical; n. m. and f. radical.*

RÁDIO *m. radio; radius; radium.*

Aparelho de rádio. *Radio set.*

Rádio portátil. *Portable radio.*

radioatividade (radioactividade) *f. radioactivity.*

radiodifusão *f. radio broadcasting; radio broadcast.*

radioemissora *f. radio station.*

radiografia *f. radiography; X-ray photography.*

radiouvinte *m. and f. radio listener.*

raia *f. line; ray.*

Passar as raias. *To go too far.*

raiar *to line; to radiate, to shine; to dawn.*

Estaremos iá no raiar do dia. *We'll be there at daybreak.*

rainha *f. queen.*

RAIO *m. ray, beam; spoke (wheel); lightning; thunderbolt; misfortune; radius.*
Raio de sol. *A ray of sunlight.*
Raios X. *X rays.*
Como um raio. *Like a flash.*
Raio de ação (acção). *Sphere of action.*

raiva *f. anger, rage; rabies.*
Ela estava pálida de raiva. *She was livid with rage.*

raivar *to be furious, to be angry, to rage.*
Raivar por. *To be "dying to." To be extremely eager or anxious for something.*

raivoso *adj. furious, angry; mad.*

raiz *f. root.*
Lançar raizes. *To take root.*
Raiz quadrada. *Square root.*

raja *f. stripe, streak.*

rajado *adj. striped, streaked.*

ralar *to grate; to annoy.*

ralhar *to scold; to nag; to get angry.*

rama *f. branches; foliage.*
Algodão em rama. *Raw cotton.*

ramal *m. branch, line, extension.*

ramificação *f. ramification.*

ramo *m. branch; limb; bunch (flowers).*
Não sei nada desse ramo da família. *I don't know anything about that branch of the family.*
Domingo de Ramos. *Palm Sunday.*

rampa *f. ramp, slope.*

rancho *m. mess (military); hut; a group of strollers.*

ranço *adj. rancid.*

ranger *to gnash; to creak.*
Quando ouviu isso, ele rangeu os dentes. *When he heard that, he gnashed his teeth.*

rapado *adj. scraped; close-cropped.*

rapariga *f. prostitute Ⓑ; young lady Ⓟ.*

RAPAZ *m. young man; fellow.*

rapidez *f. rapidity, swiftness.*

RÁPIDO *adj. rapid, fast, swift; n. m. express train; messenger service; rapids.*
Vou tomar o rápido. *I'm going to take the express.*

raposa *f. fox.*
Cova de raposa. *Foxhole.*

raposo *m. fox.*

raptar *to abduct, to kidnap; to rob.*

rapto *m. kidnapping, abduction; robbery.*

raqueta *f. racket (tennis).*

rareza *f. rarity.*

raridade *f. rarity.*

raro *adj. rare, unusual.*
Ele é um homem muito raro. *He's a very unusual man.*
Raras vezes. *Rarely. Seldom.*

rascante *adj. bitter, sour.*

rascar *to scratch.*

rascunho *m. draft, preliminary copy.*

rasgadura *f. tear, rip.*

rasgão *m. tear, rip.*

rasgar *to tear, to rip.*
Rasgar em pedaços. *To tear to pieces.*

rasgo *m. tear, rip; flash of wit; noble deed.*
Rasgo de eloqüência (eloquência). *Burst of eloquence.*

raso *flat, even, level; n. m. flat land.*
Soldado raso. *Private (military).*

raspar *to scrape; to rasp; to ease.*

rasteiro *adj. low; creeping.*
Planta rasteira. *Creeping plant.*

rasto *m. track, trail; trace, sign, clue; footprint.*
Andar de rasto. *To crawl.*

rata *f. rat; blunder.*

ratificação *f. ratification.*

ratificar *to ratify, to sanction.*

rato *m. rat, mouse; thief.*
Calado como um rato. *Quiet as a mouse.*

ratoeira *f. mousetrap; trick.*

ratoneiro *m. petty thief.*

RAZÃO *f. reason; cause; rate; right.*
Ter razão. *To be right.*
Não ter razão. *To be wrong.*
O senhor tem razão. *You are right.*
Ela não tem razão. *She's wrong.*
À razão de. *At the rate of.*
Dar ouvidos à razão. *To listen to reason.*
Idade da razão. *Age of discretion.*
Perder a razão. *To lose one's reason.*

razoamento *m. reasoning.*

razoar *to reason, to argue.*

razoável *adj. reasonable, fair.*

ré *f. female defendant or criminal; stern.*
Marcha à ré. *Reverse speed.*
À ré. *Astern.*

reabastecer *to replenish, to restock.*

reabilitar *to rehabilitate.*

reação (reacção) *f. reaction.*

reacionário (reaccionário) *adj. and m. reactionary.*

real *adj. real; actual; royal; n. m. monetary unit.*

realçar *to enhance; to intensify.*

realidade *f. reality; fact.*
Na realidade. *Actually. In fact.*

realismo *m. realism.*

realista *adj. realistic; royalist; n. m. and f. realist; royalist.*

realizar *to realize, to accomplish, to fulfill.*
Ele realizou o que tinha projetado (projectado). *He accomplished what he had planned.*

reaparecer *to reappear.*

reator (reactor) *m. reactor.*

rebaixamento *(x = sh) m. reduction, lowering.*
rebaixar *(x = sh) to reduce, to lower, to diminish.*
Esta semana rebaixaram os preços. *This week they lowered prices.*
rebanho *m. flock, herd.*
rebater *to repel; to refute; to discount (note); to return (sports).*
rebelar *to rebel, to revolt.*
rebelde *adj. rebellious; defiant; n. m. and f. rebel.*
rebelião *f. rebellion.*
rebentar *to burst.*
rebocador *m. plasterer; tugboat.*
reboque *m. tow, towing; trailer.*
Levar a reboque. *To take in tow.*
rebuçar *to hide; to muffle up.*
rebuscar *to search; to glean.*
recado *m. message; errand; pl. greetings.*
Tem algum recado para mim? *Do you have a message for me?*
Dê-lhe meus recados. *Give him my regards.*
recaída *f. relapse.*
recair *to fall back; to relapse.*
recalcar *to trample, to read; to repress.*
recalcitrar *to oppose, to resist.*
recanto *m. nook; retreat.*
recatado *adj. prudent, modest, sober.*
recatar-se *to be cautious.*
recato *m. caution.*
RECEAR *to fear.*
Receio que ele não venha. *I'm afraid he won't come.*
RECEBER *to receive, to accept.*
Hoje recebi duas cartas. *I received two letters today.*
receio *m. fear; doubt.*
receita *f. prescription; recipe; receipts, income.*
Aviar uma receita. *To fill a prescription.*
Receita bruta. *Gross income.*
Receita líquida. *Net income.*
receitar *to prescribe.*
recém-chegado *adj. newly arrived; n. m. newcomer.*
RECENTE *adj. recent, new, fresh; modern.*
Um acontecimento recente. *A recent event.*
Recentemente. *Recently.*
recepção *f. reception.*
receptor *m. receiver.*
rechonchudo *adj. fat, chubby.*
recibo *m. receipt.*
Pode me dar (dar-me) um recibo? *Can you give me a receipt?*
recife *m. reef.*
Recife de coral. *Coral reef.*
recinto *m. enclosed area; enclosure.*

recipiente *adj. recipient, receiving; m. receiver, container.*
reciprocar *to reciprocate.*
reciprocidade *f. reciprocity.*
recíproco *adj. reciprocal, mutual.*
Reciprocamente. *Reciprocally.*
recital *f. recital.*
recitar *to recite, to relate.*
reclamação *f. reclamation, complaint.*
reclamante *m. and f. claimant.*
reclamar *to complain, to protest.*
reclamo *m. claim, complaint.*
recluso *adj. confined; n. m. recluse; convict.*
recobrar *to recover, to regain.*
Recobrar a saúde. *To regain one's health.*
RECOLHER *to pick up; to gather; to collect.*
Ela recolheu todos os documentos. *She gathered all the documents.*
recomendação *f. recommendation.*
Carta de recomendação. *Letter of recommendation.*
RECOMENDAR *to recommend, to advise; to command; to entrust.*
Aquele amigo que você recomendou recebeu o emprego. *That friend you recommended received the job.*
recomendável *adj. recommendable.*
recompensa *f. reward, compensation.*
recompensar *to recompense, to reward.*
reconciliação *f. reconciliation.*
reconciliar *to reconcile.*
RECONHECER *to recognize; to admit; to examine; to appreciate.*
O senhor reconhece esta letra? *Do you recognize this handwriting?*
Reconheço que tudo é como ele indicou. *I admit that everything is as he indicated.*
reconhecimento *m. recognition; acknowledgment; appreciation, gratitude; reconaissance.*
reconstituinte *m. tonic.*
reconstrução *f. reconstruction.*
reconstruir *to reconstruct, to rebuild.*
recopilar *to compile, to collect.*
recordação *f. remembrance.*
recordar *to remember, to recall.*
Não posso recordar o nome dele. *I don't recall his name.*
recorde *m. record (sports, etc.)* Ⓑ.
Ele bateu o recorde. *He broke the record.*
reco-reco *m. Brazilian musical instrument of bamboo.*
recorrer *to go over, to look over; to appear to.*
Recorremos a todos os meios. *We tried everything. (We resorted to all means.")*
recortar *to cut, to trim, to clip, to shorten.*
recorte *m. clipping; outline.*

Eu lhe mandei um recorte do jornal. *I sent him a newspaper clipping.*

recostar *to lean against.*

recostar-se *to lean back, to recline, to lie down.*

recreação *f. recreation, diversion, amusement.*

recrear *to entertain, to amuse, to delight.*

recrear-se *to have a good time.*

recreìo *recreation, diversion, amusement.*

recruta *m. recruit, new member.*

recrutar *to recruit.*

recuar *to recede, to back away.*

recuperar *to recuperate, to recover.*

Recuperar as forças. *To recover one's strength.*

Temos que recuperar o tempo perdido. *We have to make up for lost time.*

recurso *m. recourse; appeal; resource; pl. resources, means.*

Sem recursos. *Without means.*

recusar *to refuse, to deny; to reject; to prohibit.*

Recusamos o projeto (projecto). *We turned down the plan.*

redação *f. editing; editorial office.*

redator (redactor) *m. editor.*

rede *f. net; network; trap.*

Rede ferroviária. *Railroad system.*

O animal caiu na rede. *The animal was trapped. The animal fell into the trap.*

rédea *f. reins; control.*

À rédea solta. *At full tilt, at full speed; unrestrained.*

redenção *f. redemption.*

redigir *to write, to compose.*

REDONDO *adj. round; chubby.*

A mesa é redonda. *The table is round.*

Em números redondos. *In round numbers.*

redor *m. circle, circuit; environs.*

Em redor. *Around. All around.*

Ao redor. *Around. All around.*

redução *f. reduction.*

redundância *f. redundance.*

redundante *adj. redundant.*

redundar *to redound, to result.*

reduzir *to reduce, to cut down.*

De hoje em diante vou reduzir as minhas despesas. *From now on I'll cut down on my expenses.*

Reduzir a cinzas. *To reduce to ashes.*

reeleger *to reelect.*

reeleição *f. reelection.*

reembolsar *to reimburse.*

reembolso *m. reimbursement, refund.*

refazer *to make over, to redo.*

refeição *f. meal.*

Fazer uma refeição. *To have a meal.*

referência *f. reference.*

Com referência a. *With regard to.*

referente *adj. referring, relating.*

referir *to refer.*

refinado *adj. refined, polished.*

refinar *to refine, to improve.*

refinaria *f. refinery.*

refletir (reflectir) *to reflect.*

refletor (reflector) *adj. reflective; n. m. reflector.*

reflexão *(x = ks) f. reflection, thought.*

reflexionar *(x = ks) to think over, to reflect.*

reflexivo *(x = ks) adj. reflexive.*

reflexo *(x = ks) adj. reflected; n. m. reflex.*

Ação (Acção) reflexa. *Reflex action.*

reforçar *to reinforce, to strengthen.*

reforma *f. reform, reformation; alteration; remodeling.*

reformar *to reform; to correct; to alter; to remodel; to retire.*

reformar-se *to retire.*

Depois de quarenta anos de serviço militar, o general se reformou (reformou-se). *After forty years of military service, the general retired.*

reformatório *m. reformatory.*

refrão *m. refrain; chorus; saying, proverb.*

refrear *to curb, to restrain, to refrain.*

refrega *f. fight, skirmish, fray.*

refrescante *adj. cooling; refreshing.*

refrescar *to refresh; to cool.*

Refrescar a memória. *To refresh one's memory.*

refresco *m. refreshment; cold drink.*

refrigerador *adj. refrigerating, cooling; n. m. refrigerator, icebox.*

refrigerar *to refrigerate, to cool.*

refugiado *m. refugee.*

refugiar-se *to take refuge; to take shelter.*

refúgio *m. refuge, shelter, haven.*

regadeira *f. shower; gutter; irrigation ditch.*

regador *adj. irrigating; n. m. sprinkler, watering can.*

regalado *adj. regaled; pleased.*

Ele leva uma vida regalada. *He leads an easy life.*

regalar *to regale; to enjoy.*

regalo *m. regalement; pleasure; gift.*

regar *to water; to irrigate.*

regata *f. boat race, regatta.*

regatear *to bargain, to haggle; to stint.*

regateio *m. haggling.*

regeneração *f. regeneration.*

regenerar *to regenerate.*

regente *m. regent; leader; conductor.*

reger *to rule, to govern.*

região *f. region; district.*

Região campestre. *Country. Countryside.*

regime, regímen *m. regime; diet.*

Eu estou fazendo (a fazer) regime. *I'm on a diet.*

O país mudou de regime. *The country had a change of government.*

regimento *m. regiment.*

régio *adj. royal, regal.*

regional *adj. regional, local.*

registrar, registar *to register, to put on record.*

As compras se registram (registram-se) neste livro. *Purchases are entered in this book.*

Registrar uma carta. *To register a letter.*

registro, registo *m. registration; register; record.*

Registro de nomes. *Directory of names.*

REGRA *f. rule; ruler (for measuring).*

O passaporte está em regra? *Is the passport in order?*

Tudo está em regra. *Everything is in order.*

Estas são as regras do jogo. *These are the rules of the game.*

Não há regra sem exceção (excepção). *There is an exception to every rule.*

regressar *to return, to go back, to come back.*

Regressarei na sexta. *I'll be back Friday.*

regresso *m. return.*

regulamento *m. rule, regulation, law.*

REGULAR *to regulate; to adjust; adj. regular, ordinary; fair, moderate; fairly good.*

Regular o tráfico. *To regulate traffic.*

João recebe um salário regular. *John receives a moderate salary.*

rei *m. king.*

reimprimir *to reprint.*

reinado *m. reign.*

reinar *to reign; to predominate, to prevail.*

O rei reinou durante vinte anos. *The king reigned for twenty years.*

reino *m. kingdom, reign.*

reintegrar *to restore.*

réis *m. pl. former monetary unit of Brazil.*

reiterar *to reiterate.*

reitor *m. rector; dean.*

rejeitar *to reject.*

RELAÇÃO *f. relation, connection; report; pl. connections.*

Não há relação entre estas duas coisas. *There is no relation (connection) between these two things.*

Nós estamos em boas relações com eles. *We are on good terms with them.*

relacionado *adj. acquainted; related.*

relacionar *to relate; to connect.*

relâmpago *m. lightning.*

relampejar *to lighten (lightning).*

relatar *to relate, to tell.*

relativo *adj. relative.*

Relativo a. *With reference to.*

relato *m. account, statement; story.*

Ele fez um relato do que tinha acontecido. *He gave an account of what had happened.*

relatório *m. report; statement.*

reler *to reread.*

relevo *m. relief, projection.*

religião *f. religion.*

religioso *adj. religious.*

RELÓGIO *m. clock, watch.*

Relógio de bolso. *Pocket watch.*

Relógio-pulseira. *Wristwatch.*

Dar corda ao relógio. *To wind a watch.*

O relógio está adiantado. *The watch is fast.*

O relógio está atrasado. *The watch is slow.*

relojoaria *f. watchmaking; watchmaker's shop.*

relojoeiro *m. watchmaker.*

reluzir *to shine, to sparkle.*

Nem tudo que reluz é ouro. *All that glitters is not gold.*

remar *to row, to paddle.*

rematar *to complete; to put the finishing touches on.*

remate *m. end, conclusion, finish.*

remediar *to remedy; to make good; to help.*

Isso não se pode remediar. *That can't be helped.*

REMÉDIO *m. remedy; medicine.*

Isto não tem remédio. *There's no remedy for this. This can't be helped.*

Não há remédio. *It can't be helped.*

Sem remédio. *Irremediable.*

Remédio caseiro. *Household remedy.*

remendar *to mend, to patch.*

remessa *f. remittance; shipment.*

remetente *adj. sending; n. m. and f. sender.*

remeter *to remit, to send.*

Faça o favor de remeter (as) minhas cartas a este endereço. *Please forward my mail to this address.*

remir *to redeem.*

remitente *adj. remittent.*

remitir *to remit, to forgive; to abate.*

remo *m. oar, paddle.*

Remo de duas pás. *Double-bladed paddle*

remodelar *to remodel.*

remoinhar *to spin, to whirl.*

remontar *to remount, to repair; to go up; to go back.*

remorso *m. remorse.*

remover *to remove; to take away.*

remuneração *f. remuneration; reward.*

remunerar *to remunerate, to reward.*

renascença *f. renaissance, rebirth; Renaissance.*

renascer *to be reborn; to grow again.*

renascimento *m. rebirth.*

RENDA *f. income, revenue; rent; lace.*

Imposto de renda. *Income tax.*
Renda bruta. *Gross income.*
render *to subdue; to surrender; to produce, to yield; to tire out.*
Este negócio rende pouco. *This business is not very profitable.*
Render homenagem. *To pay homage.*
rendição *f. surrender.*
rendido *adj. split; submissive; overcome.*
rendimento *m. income, return; surrender.*
Rendimento bruto. *Gross income.*
renegado *m. renegade.*
renegar *to deny; to reject.*
renhido *adj. hard-fought; furious.*
renome *m. renown, fame.*
renomeado *adj. renowned, famous.*
renovação *f. renovation, renewal.*
renovar *to renovate, to renew; to reform.*
rente *adj. close; even with.*
Cortar bem rente. *To cut quite close.*
renúncia *f. renunciation; resignation.*
renunciar *to renounce; to reject, to resign.*
Eu renunciei o emprego. *I resigned the position.*
Renunciar um direito. *To give up a right.*
reorganização *f. reorganization.*
reorganizador *adj. reorganizing, reforming; n. m. reorganizer.*
reorganizar *to reorganize.*
reparação *f. reparation, repair; amends; satisfaction.*
reparador *adj. reparative; compensating; n. m. repairer.*
reparar *to repair; to notice.*
Reparei em que todos olhavam para ela. *I noticed that they were all looking at her.*
reparo *m. repair; notice; remark.*
repartição *f. partition; department.*
repartidor *adj. sharing; n. m. sharer.*
repartir *to distribute, to divide.*
Repartiram os lucros. *They divided the profits.*
repassar *to go over, to review; to soak.*
Vamos repassar a lição. *Let's review the lesson.*
repelir *to repel; to reject.*
repente *m. sudden act; outburst.*
De repente. *Suddenly. All of a sudden.*
repentino *adj. sudden.*
repercussão *f. repercussion; reaction.*
repercutir *to echo; to reverberate; to have a repercussion.*
repertório *m. repertory; repertoire; list, index.*
repetente *adj. repeating; n. m. and f. repeater (student).*
repetição *f. repetition.*
O relatório está cheio de repetições *The report is full of repetitions.*
REPETIR *to repeat.*

Faça o favor de repetir o que disse. *Please repeat what you said.*
Repito que eu não vou. *I repeat that I'm not going.*
repicar *to pierce; to ring, to peal, to toll; to mince, to chop.*
repleto *adj. full, replete.*
O ônibus (autocarro) está repleto. *The bus is full.*
réplica *f. reply, answer.*
Não gostamos (gostámos) de (da) sua réplica. *We didn't like your answer.*
replicar *to reply, to retort.*
Não me repliques! *Don't answer back! Don't talk back to me!*
repor *to replace; to restore.*
reportagem *f. reporting, report.*
reportor *to go back in time; to moderate.*
repórter *m. and f. reporter.*
repositório *m. repository.*
repreender *to reprimand, to reprehend.*
represa *f. dam.*
representação *f. representation; performance.*
representante *adj. representative; n. m. and f. representative, agent.*
representar *to represent; to act, perform.*
Que casa representa? *Which firm do you represent?*
Eu vi a peça; ela representou muito mal. *I saw the play; she performed very badly. I saw the play; her acting was very bad.*
repressão *f. repression.*
reprimir *to repress, to check, to hold in check.*
Não me pude reprimir por mais tempo. *I couldn't contain myself any longer.*
reprodução *f. reproduction.*
reproduzir *to reproduce.*
reprovar *to reprove; to fail.*
O aluno foi reprovado. *The student failed.*
reptil (réptil) *m. reptile.*
república *f. republic.*
republicano *adj. republican; n. m. republican.*
repudiar *to repudiate; to disavow.*
repugnância *f. repugnance; dislike.*
repugnante *adj. repugnant, distasteful.*
repugnar *to be distasteful, to be repugnant; to dislike, to detest; to reject; to oppose.*
Isso me repugna. *I detest it.*
repulsa *f. repulsion, aversion.*
repulsar *to repulse, to repeal.*
reputação *f. reputation, name.*
Ele tem uma boa reputação. *He has a good reputation.*
requerer *to require, to request.*
Isso requer muita atenção. *That requires a lot of attention.*
requisito *m. requisite, requirement.*
rés *adj. level; close.*

Rés-do-chão. *Ground floor.*

resenha *f. report; list; summary.*

resenhar *to report; to list.*

reserva *f. reserve; reservation; privacy.*
Reserva mental. *Mental reservation.*
Sem reserva. *Without reservation.*
Unreservedly.
De reserva. *Extra. Spare. In reserve.*
Fundo de reserva. *Reserve fund.*

reservado *adj. reserved; cautious; confidential.*

reservar *to reserve; to keep.*
Queremos que nos reserve um lugar. *We want you to reserve a place (to make a reservation) for us.*

resfriado *m. a cold.*
Apanhei um resfriado. *I caught a cold.*

resfriar *to cool.*

resgatar *to redeem; to release.*

resgate *m. redemption; release.*

resguardar *to protect, to guard.*

resguardo *m. protection; guard.*

residência *f. residence.*

residencial *adj. residential.*

residente *adj. residing, resident; n. m. and f. resident, inhabitant.*

residir *to reside, to live.*
Resido na Rua da Alfândega. *I live on Alfândega Street.*

resíduo *adj. residual; n. m. residue, remainder.*

resignação *f. resignation; patience.*

resignar *to resign.*

resignar-se *to resign oneself, to be resigned.*

resistência *f. resistance.*

resistente *adj. resistant; hardy.*

resistir *to resist, to endure.*
Resistir a tentação. *To resist temptation.*
Resistir à prova. *To stand the test.*

resmungar *to grumble, to mumble.*

resolução *f. resolution; determination; decision; solution.*
É preciso tomarmos uma resolução. *We must come to some decision.*

resoluto *adj. resolute.*

resolver *to resolve, to determine, to decide; to solve; to dissolve; to settle.*
Resolvi fazê-lo eu mesmo. *I was determined to do it myself.*
Este problema é difícil de resolver. *This problem is difficult to solve.*

respeitar *to respect, to honor.*

respeitável *adj. respectable.*

RESPEITO *m. relation; respect; reference; regard.*
Com respeito a. *With regard to. Concerning.*
A respeito de. *With regard to. Concerning.*
Falta de respeito. *Disrespect.*

respeitoso *adj. respectful, polite.*

respiração *f. respiration, breathing.*
Falta de respiração. *Shortness of breath.*

respirar *to breathe.*
Deixe-me *(x = sh)* respirar. *Give me a chance to catch my breath.*

respiro *m. breath, breathing; respite.*

resplandecer *to shine.*

RESPONDER *to answer, to respond; to be responsible for.*
Ele nem sequer me respondeu. *He didn't even answer me.*
Quem responde por ele? *Who answers for (is responsible for) him?*

responsabilidade *f. responsibility.*

responsável *adj. responsible, liable.*

RESPOSTA *f. answer, reply, retort, response.*
Resposta favorável. *Favorable reply.*
Resposta negativa. *Negative reply. Refusal.*

ressaltar *to rebound; to stand out; to stress.*

ressentir-se *to resent; to feel.*
Ela se ressentiu por nada. *She became offended over nothing.*

ressoar *to resound.*

ressonância *f. resonance.*

ressonar *to resound.*

ressurgimento *m. resurgence.*

ressurgir *to resurge; to reappear.*

ressuscitar *to resuscitate.*

restabelecer *to reestablish; to restore.*

restante *adj. remaining; n. m. remainder.*
Posta-restante. *General delivery.*

restar *to remain, to be left.*
Restam-me cinco dólares. *I have five dollars left.*

restauração *f. restoration.*

restaurante *m. restaurant.*

restaurar *to restore.*

restituição *f. restitution.*

restituir *to restore.*

RESTO *m. rest, remainder; pl. remains; leftovers.*
A cozinheira sabe aproveitar os restos. *The cook knows how to make good use of leftovers.*
De resto. *Besides.*

restrição *f. restriction.*

restringir *to restrain; to curtail; to restrict, to limit.*

RESULTADO *m. result.*
Qual foi o resultado? *What was the result?*

resultar *to result.*
Resultou-nos muito caro. *It was very costly for us.*

resumido *adj. condensed; abridged.*

resumir *to abridge, to cut short; to summarize.*
Resumir um discurso. *To cut a speech short.*

resumo *m. summary.*
retaguarda *f. rear guard.*
retalho *m. piece, scrap.*
  A retalho. *At retail.*
  Colcha de retalhos. *Patchwork quilt.*
retângulo (rectângulo) *m. rectangle.*
retardamento *m. delay.*
retardar *to retard, to delay.*
reter *to retain; to withhold; to keep; to
remember.*
  A polícia o reteve (reteve-o). *The police
detained him.*
  Não posso reter tanta informação. *I can't
retain so much information.*
reticência *f. reticence.*
retificar (rectificar) *to rectify, to correct.*
retina *f. retina.*
retirada *f. retreat, withdrawal.*
retirado *adj. withdrawn; retired.*
retirar *to withdraw; to retire; to take back.*
  O general retirou as tropas. *The general
withdrew his troops.*
retirar-se *to leave; to retire.*
  Ela se retirou (retirou-se) ao seu quarto.
She retired to her room.
retiro *m. retreat.*
reto (recto) *adj. straight; just, upright; erect.*
  Ele é um homem reto. *He is an
upright man.*
  Ângulo reto. *Right angle.*
  Linha reta. *Straight line.*
retocar *to retouch.*
retoque *m. retouch; finishing touch.*
retorcer *to twist.*
retornar *to return; to restore.*
retorno *m. return; exchange.*
retorsão *f. twisting.*
retraído *adj. withdrawn, reserved.*
  Ele é muito retraído. *He is quite
withdrawn.*
retraimento *m. reserve; retreat; seclusion.*
retrair *to retract, to hold back.*
retratar *to portray; to show.*
retrato *m. portrait; photograph; picture.*
  Tirar o retrato. *To take a picture.*
  Ele é o retrato fiel de seu pai. *He's the
living image of his father.*
retrete *f. toilet; lavatory.*
retribuição *f. reward.*
retribuir *to pay back; to reward.*
retrocedente *adj. retrocedent, retroceding.*
retroceder *to back up; to draw back; to fall
back; to grow worse.*
  Ele não pôde retroceder na sua decisão. *He
could not reverse his decision.*
retrospecção (retrospeção) *f. retrospection.*
retumbar *to resound.*
réu *m. male defendant; convict.*
reumatismo *m. rheumatism.*

reunião *f. reunion; meeting.*
  Haverá uma reunião às cinco. *There will be
a meeting at five o'clock.*
reunir *to gather; to collect; to bring together.*
  O professor reuniu os alunos numa festa.
*The teacher brought his students
together at a party.*
reunir-se *to get together; to meet; to join.*
  A que horas podíamos reunir-nos? *What
time could we get together?*
  Reunem-se de dois em dois anos. *They get
together every two years.*
revelação *f. revelation.*
revelar *to reveal, to show; to disclose; to
develop (photography).*
  Revelar um segredo. *To reveal a secret.*
  O autor revelou grande talento nesse livro.
*The author showed great talent in that
book.*
revendedor *m. dealer; retailer.*
revender *to resell; to retail.*
reverência *f. reverence; bow.*
  Fazer uma reverência. *To bow.*
reverso *adj. reverse, opposite; n. m. reverse.*
  O reverso da medalha. *The other side of
the coin. The other side of the question.*
revés *m. reverse; backhand; misfortune.*
  Ao revés. *Upside down. Inside out.*
revisão *f. revision; review.*
revisar *to look over; to revise; to review.*
  Revisar os livros. *To audit the books.*
revisor *m. conductor; reviewer; proofreader.*
REVISTA *f. review; magazine; musical
comedy.*
  Ainda não recebi esse número da revista. *I
haven't yet received that issue of the
magazine.*
reviver *to revive.*
revocação *f. revocation, repeal.*
revocar *to revoke, to repeal, to evoke.*
revolta *f. revolt.*
revoltoso *adj. rebellious.*
revolução *f. revolution.*
revolucionário *adj. n. m. revolutionary.*
revolver *to revolve; to turn; to stir.*
  Revolver céu e terra. *To move heaven and
earth.*
revólver *m. revolver.*
rezar *to pray; to read, to say.*
  Ela reza todos os dias. *She prays (says her
prayers) every day.*
  Reza aqui que . . . *It says here that . . .*
riacho *m. brook.*
ribeira *f. bank (river); shore.*
ribeiro *m. stream, brook.*
RICO *adj. rich, wealthy.*
  Se eu fosse rico não trabalharia tanto. *If I
were rich, I wouldn't work so much.*
ridicularizar *to ridicule.*

ridículo *adj. ridiculous, foolish; n. m.*
ridiculous thing; ridiculous person.
Fazer-se ridículo. *To make a fool of*
oneself.

rifa *f. raffle.*

rifar *to raffle.*

rifle *m. rifle.*

rigidez *f. rigidity; sternness.*

rígido *adj. rigid; severe; hard; stern.*

rigor *m. rigor.*

rigoroso *adj. rigorous, severe, strict.*

rijo *adj. rigid.*

rim *m. kidney.*

rima *f. rhyme.*

rinha Ⓑ *f. cockfight; fight.*

rinoceronte *m. rhinoceros.*

RIO *m. river.*
Rio abaixo *(x = sh). Down the river.*
Downstream.
O Rio de Janeiro. *Rio de Janeiro ("the*
river of January").

rio-grandense-do-norte *adj. and n. m. of the*
state of Rio Grande do Norte of Brazil.

rio-grandense-do sul *adj. and n. m. of the*
state of Rio Grande do Sul of Brazil.

riqueza *f. riches, wealth.*

RIR *to laugh.*
Rir às gargalhadas. *To laugh out loud. To*
laugh heartily.

RIR-SE *to laugh.*
Por que se ri dele? *Why do you laugh*
at him?

risada *f. laughter.*

risco *m. risk.*
Correr um risco. *To run a risk. To take a*
chance.

RISO *m. laughter, laugh.*
Um frouxo *(x = sh)* Ⓑ de riso. *A fit of*
laughter.
Isso não é motivo de riso. *That's no*
laughing matter.

risonho *adj. smiling, pleasing.*

ritmo *m. rhythm.*

rito *m. rite, ceremony.*

rival *adj., n. m. and f. rival.*

rivalidade *f. rivalry.*

rivalizar *to vie, to compete, to rival.*

robusto *adj. robust, strong.*
Ele é muito robusto. *He is very strong.*

roca *f. rock.*

roça *f. country, backwoods; plot of cleared*
land.

rocha *f. stone, boulder.*
Rocha calcária. *Limestone.*

rochoso *adj. rocky.*

rocio *m. dew.*
Rocio da manhã. *Morning dew.*

RODA *f. wheel, circle.*
Roda da sorte. *Wheel of fortune.*

Roda sobressalente. *Spare wheel.*

rodagem *f. set of wheels.*
Estrada de rodagem. *Highway.*

rodante *adj. rolling.*
Material rodante. *Rolling stock.*

rodapé *m. valance; baseboard; newspaper*
article at bottom of the page.

rodar *to roll; to revolve; to rake.*

rodeio *m. rodeo; evasion.*
Deixe *(x = sh)* de rodeios e responda
claramente. *Stop beating around the*
bush and give a straight answer.

rodovia *f. highway* Ⓑ.

rodoviário *adj. of or for a highway* Ⓑ.

roer *to gnaw; to nibble; to erode.*

rogar *to pray, to beg, to entreat, to request.*
Rogo-lhe que . . . *I beg you*
to . . . Please . . .

rogo *m. request, petition; plea.*

rol *m. roll, list.*

rolante *adj. rolling.*
Escada rolante. *Escalator.*

rolar *to roll, to revolve.*

rolha *f. cork, stopper.*
Saca-rolhas. *Corkscrew.*

rolo *m. roll; roller.*

romance *m. novel; romance.*

romanceiro *m. collection of songs, poems, etc.*

romano *adj., n. m. Roman.*

romanticismo *m. romanticism.*

romântico *adj., n. m. romantic.*

romantismo *m. romanticism.*

romaria *f. pilgrimage, excursion, tour.*

romeiro *m. pilgrim.*

ROMPER *to break; to smash; to tear; to rip;*
to fracture; to start, to begin.
De repente ela rompeu o silêncio.
Suddenly, she broke the silence.
Nós rompemos com eles. *We broke with*
them.
Romper em pranto. *To burst into tears.*
Ao romper do dia. *At daybreak.*

roncar *to snore; to roar.*

ronco *m. snore; roar.*

ronda *f. watch, patrol; rounds.*

rondar *to watch, to patrol.*

ronha *f. scabies; malice, ill will.*

roque *m. rock; rock music/song.*

roqueiro (-ra) *rock musician/fan.*

rosa *f. rose.*
Não há rosa sem espinhos. *No rose without*
a thorn.

rosal *m. rose garden.*

rosário *m. rosary.*

rosca *f. ring (bread or cake); thread (of a*
screw).

roseira *f. rosebush.*

ROSTO *m. face.*

rota *f. rout; route; course.*

roteiro *m. itinerary, schedule.*
rotina *f. routine; habit; rut.*
roubar *to rob, to steal.*
    Roubaram-me a carteira. *They stole my wallet.*
roubo *m. robbery, theft.*
ROUPA *f. wearing apparel, clothing, clothes.*
    Tenho que mudar de roupa. *I have to change my clothes.*
    Roupa feita. *Ready-made clothes.*
    Roupa de cama. *Bed linen.*
roupão *m. bathrobe; dressing gown.*
rouxinol *(x = sh) m. nightingale.*
roxo *(x = sh) adj. purple.*
RUA *f. street.*
    Rua de uma mão. *One-way street.*
    Rua principal. *Main street.*
rubi *m. ruby.*
rubo *m. brier, bramble.*
ruborizar *to redden, to blush.*
rude *adj. rude; rough; harsh.*
rudez, rudeza *f. rudeness; roughness, harshness.*
rugido *adj. roaring; n. m. roar.*
rugir *to roar; to bellow.*
ruído *m. noise.*
ruim *adj. bad; terrible; inferior.*
    Eu achei o filme muito ruim. *I thought the film was terrible.*
ruína *f. ruin; downfall; pl. ruins.*
ruinoso *adj. ruinous.*
rumar *to steer; to head (for).*
rumo *m. course; route, direction.*
    Vamos tomar outro rumo. *We'll take another course (road).*
    Sem rumo. *Adrift. Without direction.*
rumor *m. rumor; noise.*
ruptura *f. rupture; break.*
rural *adj. rural, rustic.*
russo *adj., n. m. Russian.*
rústico *adj. rustic, rural.*

SÁBADO *m. Saturday.*
SABÃO *m. soap.*
sabedoria *f. learning, knowledge, wisdom.*
SABER *to know; to know how; to be able to; to taste; to find out.*
    O senhor sabe a que horas abrem as lojas? *Do you know at what time the stores open?*
    O senhor sabe nadar? *Can you (do you know how to) swim?*
    Sei lá! *I don't know! How should I know?*
    Quem sabe! *Who knows!*

    Ela não sabe nada. *She doesn't know anything.*
    Como se sabe. *As is known.*
    Que eu saiba. *As far as I know.*
    Pelo que sei. *As far as I know.*
    Saber de cor. *To know by heart.*
sabiá *m. thrush, bird of Brazil.*
sábio *adj. wise, learned; n. m. scholar, sage.*
SABONETE *m. bath soap.*
sabor *m. taste, flavor.*
saborear *to flavor; to savor; to relish.*
saboroso *adj. delicious, tasty; pleasant.*
    O jantar foi muito saboroso. *The dinner was delicious.*
sabotagem *f. sabotage.*
sabotar *to sabotage.*
sabre *m. saber.*
saca *f. bag, sack.*
sacar *to draw out.*
saca-rolhas *m. corkscrew.*
saciar *to satiate.*
SACO *m. sack; bag; purse.*
    O que há neste saco de papel? *What's in this paper bag?*
sacramento *m. sacrament.*
sacrificar *to sacrifice.*
sacrifício *m. sacrifice.*
sacrilégio *m. sacrilege.*
sacristão *m. sexton.*
sacristia *f. sacristy, vestry.*
sacro *adj. sacred, holy.*
sacrossanto *adj. sacrosanct.*
sacudida *f. shock; shake, shaking, jolt.*
sacudidela *f. shock; shake, shaking, jolt.*
sacudidura *f. shaking.*
sacudir *to shake.*
    Sacudir a cabeça. *To shake the head.*
sadio *adj. sound, healthy.*
sagacidade *f. sagacity, shrewdness.*
sagaz *adj. sagacious; shrewd; clever.*
sagrado *adj. sacred.*
saia *f. skirt.*
SAÍDA *f. departure; exit; outlet; loophole.*
    Saída de emergência. *Emergency exit.*
    Um beco sem saída. *A blind alley.*
    Rua sem saída. *Dead-end street.*
sainete *m. short comedy or farce.*
SAIR *to go out; to leave; to depart; to appear; to come out.*
    Ela já saiu. *She's already left.*
    Ela sai à sua mãe. *She takes after her mother.*
    A família saiu de viagem. *The family left on a trip.*
    Vou sair ao ar livre. *I'm going out into the open air.*
    Tudo saiu bem. *It all came out fine.*
    Sair da linha. *To get out of line.*
    Sair caro. *To end up costing a lot.*

SAL *m. salt; wit.*
   Sal e pimenta. *Salt and pepper.*
SALA *f. room.*
   Quantos alunos há na sala de aula? *How many students are there in the classroom?*
   Sala de espera. *Waiting room.*
   Sala de jantar. *Dining room.*
salada *f. salad.*
salão *m. large room; hall; salon; parlor.*
   Salão de beleza. *Beauty parlor.*
   Salão de baile. *Dance hall. Ballroom.*
salário *m. salary, wages.*
saldar *to settle.*
saldo *m. balance, remainder.*
   Saldo negativo. *Debit balance.*
   Saldo positivo. *Credit balance.*
saleiro *m. salt shaker.*
salgado *adj. salty, salted; witty.*
salientar *to make clear, to point out.*
saliente *adj. salient, prominent.*
saliva *f. saliva.*
salmão *m. salmon.*
salmo *m. psalm.*
salpicar *to sprinkle (with).*
salpico *m. sprinkle; speck; a drop or dash of something.*
salsa *f. parsley; sauce.*
salsicha *f. sausage.*
SALTAR *to jump, to leap; to hop; to skip; to omit.*
   Você pode saltar a parede? *Can you jump over the wall?*
   Ela saltou várias palavras. *She skipped several words.*
   Saltar do ônibus (autocarro). *To get off the bus.*
   Saltar da cama. *To jump out of bed.*
saltear *to assault, to attack.*
SALTO *m. jump, leap; heel.*
   Dar saltos. *To jump. To leap.*
   Salto de borracha. *Rubber heel.*
salubre *adj. salutary, healthy.*
salva *f. salvo; volley; tray.*
   Uma salva de aplausos. *Thunderous applause.*
salvação *f. salvation.*
salvamento *m. salvage; rescue.*
salvar *to save (also on computer); to salvage; to jump over.*
   O médico perdeu a esperança de salvá-lo. *The doctor lost hope of saving him.*
salva-vidas *m. life preserver; lifeguard; lifeboat.*
salvo *adj. safe, saved; prep. besides, except.*
   São e salvo. *Safe and sound.*
   Em salvo. *Safe.*
   Todos vieram salvo ele. *Everyone came except him.*

salvo-conduto *m. safe-conduct, pass.*
samba *m. samba (Brazilian music and dance).*
sanar *to cure, to heal; to recover.*
sanatório *m. sanatorium, sanitarium.*
sanção *f. sanction.*
sancionar *to sanction; to confirm.*
sandália *f. sandal.*
sanduíche *m. sandwich.*
saneamento *m. sanitation.*
sanear *to make sanitary; to repair.*
sangrar *to bleed.*
sangrento *adj. bloody.*
SANGUE *m. blood.*
   A sangue e fogo. *Without mercy.*
   A sangue frio. *In cold blood.*
   Ter o sangue quente. *To be hot-blooded.*
sanha *f. anger, fury.*
sanitário *adj. sanitary, hygienic.*
SANTO *adj. saintly, holy; n. m. saint.*
   Semana Santa. *Holy Week (the week leading up to Easter).*
   Santo Antônio (António). *Saint Anthony.*
   Santa Bárbara. *Saint Barbara.*
   Despir um santo para vestir outro. *To rob Peter to pay Paul.*
SÃO *adj. sound, healthy; sane; safe; n. m. saint.*
   Regressou são e salvo. *He returned safe and sound.*
   São Pedro. *Saint Peter.*
sapataria *f. shoe store; shoe repair shop.*
sapateiro *m. shoemaker.*
SAPATO *m. shoe.*
   Um par de sapatos. *A pair of shoes.*
   Onde aperta o sapato? *Where does the shoe pinch?*
   Sapatos de tênis (ténis). *Tennis shoes. Sneakers.*
   Sapatos de salto alto. *High-heeled shoes.*
   Calçar os sapatos. *To put your shoes on.*
   Descalçar os sapatos. *To take your shoes off.*
sapo *m. toad.*
saque *m. bank draft; serve (tennis); sack, sacking, plunder.*
saquear *to sack, to loot, to pillage.*
sarampo *m. measles.*
sarar *to cure, to heal; to correct.*
sarcasmo *m. sarcasm.*
sardinha *f. sardine.*
sargento *m. sergeant.*
sarna *f. scabies, itch.*
satanás *m. Satan, devil.*
satélite *m. satellite.*
sátira *f. satire.*
satírico *adj. satiric.*
SATISFAÇÃO *f. satisfaction; pleasure; apology.*
   Eu tive a satisfação de conhecê-lo. *I had the pleasure of meeting him.*

Isso foi uma grande satisfação para mim. *That gave me great satisfaction.*

Dar satisfações. *To apologize.*

satisfatório *adj. satisfactory.*

SATISFAZER *to satisfy; to please; to pay (a debt).*

O trabalho dele não me satisfaz. *His work doesn't satisfy me.*

Satisfazer uma dívida. *To pay a debt.*

SATISFEITO *adj. satisfied, content; fulfilled.*

Queremos que todos estejam satisfeitos. *We want everyone to be satisfied.*

Estou satisfeito. *I'm satisfied.*

SAUDADE *f. longing, yearning, nostalgia, wistfulness; pl. regards, greetings; longing.*

Ter saudades de. *To miss. To long for.*

Tenho saudades de minha terra. *I'm homesick (for my country, district).*

saudar *to greet, to salute.*

Ela a saudou (saudou-a) muito afetuosamente (afectuosamente). *He greeted her affectionately.*

saudável *adj. healthful, good for the health; salutary; beneficial.*

SAÚDE *f. health.*

Ela está de boa saúde. *She is in good health.*

Ela está bem de saúde. *She is in good health.*

Ele está mal de saúde. *He is in bad health.*

Estamos gozando de boa saúde. *We are enjoying good health.*

À sua saúde! *To your health! (a toast).*

saudoso *adj. longing, yearning, homesick.*

sazão *f. season; time.*

Em sazão. *At the proper time. In season.*

sazonar *to season; to mature, to ripen.*

SE *(third person reflexive pronoun; also used as reciprocal pronoun and for the passive voice) himself, herself, themselves, etc.*

O menino não se lavou antes de sentar-se à mesa. *The boy did not wash before sitting at the table.*

Cale-se! *Be quiet! Be still!*

Diz-se que . . . *It's said that . . .*

Sabe-se que . . . *It's known that . . .*

Eles se conhecem (conhecem-se). *They know each other.*

Escrevem-se todos os dias. *They write to each other every day.*

Como se chama o senhor? *What is your name?*

Fala-se português. *Portuguese is spoken (here).*

SE *conj. if, whether.*

Se o senhor quiser. *If you wish.*

Se tivesse o dinheiro eu o compraria. *If I had the money, I would buy it.*

Se ela chegar antes das oito iremos ao cinema. *If she arrives before eight, we'll go to the movies.*

Se bem que . . . *Although . . .*

Se não. *If not.*

sé *f. see.*

A Santa Sé. *The Holy See.*

seca *f. drought, dry spell.*

secante *adj. drying, boring; n. m. drying agent; bore.*

secão (secção) *f. section; division; department; cutting, portion.*

Em que seção trabalha? *In what section do you work?*

SECAR *to dry.*

Ela pôs a roupa a secar ao sol. *She put the clothes out to dry in the sun.*

SECO *adj. dry, withered; lean; curt; rude.*

Tenho a garganta seca. *My throat is dry.*

Ele é um homem seco. *He is a very curt ("dry") person.*

Clima seco. *Dry climate.*

Vinho seco. *Dry wine.*

secretaria *f. secretariat; office.*

secretária *f. female secretary; desk.*

secretária electrônica *f. answering machine.*

secretário *m. male secretary.*

secreto *adj. secret; private.*

Serviço secreto. *Secret service.*

século *m. century; age; a long time.*

Estamos no século vinte. *We are in the twentieth century.*

Há um século que não o vejo. *I haven't seen you for ages.*

secundar *to second; to support; to aid.*

Ela o secunda em tudo. *She supports him in everything.*

secundário *adj. secondary.*

seda *f. silk.*

Bicho da seda. *Silkworm.*

Papel de seda. *Tissue paper.*

Gravata de seda. *Silk tie.*

sede *f. seat, headquarters.*

SEDE *f. thirst; desire, craving.*

Estou com sede. (Tenho sede.) *I'm thirsty.*

sedento *adj. thirsty.*

sedição *f. sedition; rebellion.*

sedimento *m. sediment.*

sedução *f. seduction, enticement.*

sedutor *adj. seductive, enticing; n. m. seducer.*

seduzir *to seduce; to tempt; to fascinate.*

segredo *m. secret; secrecy; mystery.*

Você pode guardar o segredo? *Can you keep the secret?*

segregacionismo *m. segregation.*

segregacionista *m. and f. segregationist.*

segregar *to segregate, to separate.*

seguido *adj. continued; following.*

Em seguida. *Right away. Immediately. Next.*

SEGUINTE *adj. following, next.*
No dia seguinte ele partiu. *The following day he left.*
Não gosto de todos; mande-me só os seguintes: *I don't like all of them; send me only the following:*

SEGUIR *to follow; to pursue; to continue, to go on, to keep on.*
Siga-me. *Follow me.*
Seguirei os seus conselhos. *I'll follow your advice.*
Siga bem em frente. *Continue straight ahead.*
Que segue depois? *What comes afterward?*
Como segue: *As follows:*
É preciso seguir as instruções. *You must follow the directions.*
Quem segue? *Who's next?*

SEGUNDA *f. Monday.*

SEGUNDA-FEIRA *f. Monday.*

SEGUNDO *adj. second; n. m. second; prep. according to.*
Ela mora no segundo andar. *She lives on the second floor.*
Desejo o segundo volume. *I want the second volume.*
Em segundo lugar. *In second place.*
Um bilhete de segunda. *A coach ticket. ("A second-class ticket.")*
De segunda mão. *Secondhand.*
Segundo o relatório. *According to the report.*

segurança *f. security; safety; certainty; protection.*
Com segurança. *Assuredly.*
Freio de segurança. *Emergency brake.*
Alfinete de segurança. *Safety pin.*

segurar *to secure; to assure; to insure.*

SEGURO *adj. secure, sure, safe, certain; insured; n. m. insurance; security.*
Você não está seguro? *Aren't you sure?*
Companhia de seguros. *Insurance company.*
Apólice de seguro. *Insurance policy.*
Seguro de vida. *Life insurance.*
Seguro contra acidentes. *Accident insurance.*

seio *m, breast, bosom.*

SEIS *six.*

seiscentos *six hundred.*

selar *to seal; to stamp; to saddle.*
Faça o favor de selar estas cartas. *Please put stamps on these letters.*

seleção (selecção) *f. selection, choice.*

selecionar (seleccionar) *to select, to choose.*

SELO *m. seal; stamp; postage stamp.*
Selo postal. *Postage stamp.*

selvagem *adj. savage, wild; n. m. and f. savage.*

SEM *without, besides.*
Iremos sem ele. *We'll go without him.*
Não posso ler sem os meus óculos. *I can't read without my glasses.*
Eu fiz sem pensar. *I did it without thinking.*
Sem falta. *Without fail.*
Sem dúvida. *Without a doubt. Undoubtedly.*
Sem fim. *Endless.*
Sem mais cerimônias. *Without further ado.*

SEMANA *f. week.*
Irei a semana que vem. *I'll go next week.*
Ela virá a próxima semana. *She'll come next week.*
A semana passada. *Last week.*
Numa semana mais ou menos. *In a week or so.*
Semana Santa. *Holy Week.*
Fim de semana. *Weekend.*

semanal *adj. weekly.*
Uma revista semanal. *A weekly magazine.*

semanário *adj. weekly; n. m. weekly (publication).*

semblante *m. countenance, face; look, aspect.*
Você tem bom semblante hoje. *You look well today.*

semear *to sow, to seed; to scatter, to spread.*

semelhança *f. similarity, resemblance, likeness.*

semelhar *to resemble, to be like.*

semente *f. seed.*

semestre *m. semester.*

seminarista *m. seminarian.*

semítico *adj. Semitic.*

sem-par *adj. unequaled, peerless.*

SEMPRE *always, ever.*
Ele sempre chega tarde. *He's always late.*
Como sempre. *As always. As usual.*
Para sempre. *Forever.*

senado *m. senate.*

senador *m. senator.*

senão *conj. if not, otherwise.*

senda *f. path.*

senha *f. signal; sign; password; readmission theatre ticket, pass.*

SENHOR *m. mister, sir; gentleman;* **o senhor** *you (masc.).*
Bom dia, senhor Silva. *Good morning, Mr. Silva.*
O senhor Silva não estará aqui hoje. *Mr. Silva won't be here today.*
Muito obrigado, senhor. *Thank you, sir.*
O senhor é americano? *Are you an American?*
Não conheço esse senhor. *I don't know that gentleman.*
Caro Senhor: *Dear Sir:*

Sim, senhor. *Yes, sir.*

SENHORA *f. Mrs., madam, lady; wife;* **a senhora** *you (fem.).*

A senhora Silva está em casa? *Is Mrs. Silva in?*

A senhora não está em casa. *The lady of the house is not at home.*

A senhora é americana? *Are you an American?*

Não conheço essa senhora. *I don't know that lady.*

Prezada Senhora: *Dear Madam:*

Sim, senhora. *Yes, ma'am.*

Minhas senhoras e meus senhores: *Ladies and gentlemen:*

senhoria *f. lordship, ladyship.*

Vossa Senhoria. *Your lordship. Your ladyship.*

SENHORINHA *f. miss, young lady* Ⓑ.

SENHORITA *f. miss; young lady.*

senil *adj. senile.*

sensação *f. sensation.*

sensacional *adj. sensational.*

sensatez *f. good sense, discretion.*

sensato *adj. sensible, discreet.*

sensibilidade *f. sensibility; sensitivity.*

sensível *adj. sensitive; appreciable.*

Os olhos são sensíveis à luz. *The eyes are sensitive to light.*

senso *m. sense.*

Senso comum. *Common sense.*

sensual *adj. sensual.*

sensualidade *f. sensuality.*

sentado *adj. seated.*

Ela estava sentada à minha esquerda. *She was seated on my left.*

sentar *to sit, to seat.*

SENTAR-SE *to sit (down).*

Os convidados se sentaram (sentaram-se) à mesa. *The guests sat at the table.*

Sentemo-nos. *Let's sit down.*

sentença *f. sentence; verdict; maxim.*

sentenciar *to sentence.*

SENTIDO *adj. felt; experienced; offended; sad; n. m. sense; meaning; direction.*

Ela ficou muito sentida. *She was very offended.*

sentimental *adj. sentimental, romantic.*

sentimentalismo *m. sentimentalism.*

sentimento *m. sentiment, feeling.*

Sentimentos nobres. *Noble sentiments.*

Sentimento de culpa. *Guilty feeling.*

SENTIR *to feel; to be sorry; to hear; to sense; to be (happy, cold, etc.); to appreciate; n. m. feeling; opinion.*

Sinto muito. *I'm very sorry.*

Sinto não poder ir. *I'm sorry I can't go.*

Agora sinto frio. *Now I'm cold.*

Sentimos falta dela. *We miss her.*

Sentimos que você não pudesse vir. *We are sorry you could not come.*

sentir-se *to feel.*

Ela se sente (sente-se) muito bem. *She feels very well.*

separação *f. separation.*

separar *to separate.*

Uma cortina separa as duas salas. *A curtain separates the two rooms.*

separar-se *to separate, to part company.*

Decidiram separar-se. *They decided to separate.*

septuagésimo *seventieth.*

sepulcro *m. sepulchre, grave, tomb.*

sepultar *to bury, to inter; to hide.*

sepultura *f. burial; grave, tomb.*

seqüência (sequência) *f. sequence; series; order.*

sequer *adv. at least, so much as, even.*

Nem sequer. *Not even.*

seqüestrar (sequestrar) *to kidnap; to confiscate.*

SER *to be.*

Quem é? *Who is it?*

É o João. *It's John.*

Quem será? *Who can it be?*

O senhor é o senhor Smith? *Are you Mr. Smith?*

Donde é o senhor? *Where are you from?*

Sou de Boston. *I'm from Boston.*

Somos brasileiros. *We are Brazilians.*

De quem é este lápis? *Whose pencil is this?*

É meu. *It's mine.*

É de João. *It's John's.*

Esta caixa (x = sh) é de madeira. *This box is made of wood.*

Ela é bonita. *She is pretty.*

Sou escritor. *I'm a writer.*

Que é isso? *What is that?*

Quanto é? *How much is it?*

Que horas são? *What time is it?*

É uma hora. *It's one o'clock.*

São duas (horas). *It's two o'clock.*

Ainda é cedo. *It's still early.*

É tarde. *It's late.*

Quando será a boda? *When will the wedding take place?*

Que dia é hoje? *What day is today?*

Hoje é segunda-feira. *Today is Monday.*

É fácil. *It's easy.*

É difícil. *It's difficult.*

É verdade? *Is it true?*

Não é verdade. *It's not true.*

Pode ser. *That may be.*

Farei quanto puder. *I'll do what I can.*

Fosse quem fosse. *Whoever it might be.*

Que é feito dele? *What has become of him?*

A carteira foi achada na rua. *The wallet was found in the street.*

Era uma vez. *Once upon a time.*
É isso mesmo! *That's it exactly!*
serenar *to calm down, to pacify.*
serenata *f. serenade.*
serenidade *f. serenity, coolness.*
sereno *adj. serene, calm; clear; n. m. dew;
open air.*
Foi uma noite serena. *It was a calm
evening.*
série *f. series.*
seriedade *f. seriousness, gravity.*
seringa *f. syringe.*
seringueira *f. rubber tree.*
seringueiro *m. rubber tapper.*
SÉRIO *adj. serious, earnest.*
Tomar a sério. *To take seriously.*
Você está sério? *Are you serious?*
sermão *m. sermon; lecture.*
serpente *f. serpent, snake.*
serpentina *f. paper streamer.*
serpentino *adj. serpentine.*
serra *f. saw; range of mountains, sierra.*
A serra não corta bem. *The saw doesn't cut
well.*
Serra de cadeia. *Chain saw.*
serrar *to saw.*
sertanejo *adj. of the **sertão,** of the
backwoods; m. backwoodsman.*
sertão *m. backwoods, interior.*
SERVIÇO *m. service, favor; set.*
Serviço de mesa. *Table service.*
Você me prestou (prestou-me) um grande
serviço. *You rendered me a great
service.*
O serviço neste hotel é muito ruim. *The
service in this hotel is terrible.*
Ele está de serviço. *He's on duty.*
Serviço militar. *Military service.*
Serviço de contestação. *Answering service.*
servidão *f. servitude.*
servidor *m. servant, server.*
Servidor público. *Public servant.*
SERVIR *to serve; to do a favor; to do, to be
useful; to serve at the table; to wait on a
table.*
Em que posso servi-lo? *What can I do
for you?*
Pode me servir (servir-me) um pouco de
vinho? *Can you serve me a little wine?*
Servir à mesa. *To wait on a table.*
Para que serve esta máquina? *What's this
machine for?*
Não serve. *It's no good.*
Não serve para nada. *It's no good. It's
good for nothing.*
Ela pode servir de intérprete. *She can act
as interpreter.*
servitude *f. servitude.*
sessão *f. session, meeting.*

Estar em sessão. *To be in session.*
SESSENTA *sixty.*
sesta *f. siesta, nap.*
seta *f. arrow.*
SETE *seven.*
Pintar o sete. *To have a wild time.*
Sete de setembro (Setembro). *September 7
(Brazilian Independence Day).*
setecentos *seven hundred.*
SETEMBRO *m. September.*
SETENTA *seventy.*
sententrional *adj. northern.*
sétimo *seventh.*
setuagenário *adj., n. m. septuagenarian.*
SEU *m. adj. and pron. your, his, her, its, their;
Mr. (a shortened form of **senhor**
corresponding to **dona** for females).*
João, onde deixou *(x = sh)* o seu livro?
John, where did you leave your book?
Os meus filhos estão com os seus avós. *My
children are with their grandparents.*
Este procedimento tem as suas vantagens e
desvantagens. *This procedure has its
advantages and its disadvantages.*
severidade *f. severity, strictness.*
severo *adj. severe, strict.*
sexagenário *(x = ks) adj., n. m. sexagenarian.*
sexagésimo *sixtieth.*
sexo *(x = ks) m. sex.*
SEXTA *(x = s) f. Friday.*
SEXTA-FEIRA *f. Friday.*
sexto *sixth.*
si *yourself, himself, herself, themselves, itself.*
Ela o quer para si mesma. *She wants it for
herself.*
sibilo *m. whistle; hiss.*
sicrano *m. Mr. so-and-so.*
Fulano, Beltrano e Sicrano. *Tom, Dick and
Harry.*
SIDA *f. AIDS.*
sidra *f. cider.*
significação *f. meaning, significance.*
significado *m. meaning, significance.*
significante *adj. significant.*
significar *to mean, to signify.*
Que significa isso? *What's the meaning of
that?*
significativo *adj. significant.*
signo *m. sign (zodiac).*
silaba *f. syllable.*
silêncio *m. silence.*
Silêncio! *Silence!*
Guardar silêncio. *To remain silent.*
Sofrer em silêncio. *To suffer in silence.*
O silêncio vale ouro. *Silence is golden.*
silencioso *adj. silent, noiseless; n. m. muffler
(auto).*
silvar *to whistle, to hiss (wind, etc.).*
silvestre *adj. wild, rustic.*

Plantas silvestres. *Wild plants.*
SIM *adv. yes; indeed; n. m. consent, assent.*
Sim senhor. *Yes, sir.*
Eu lhe disse que sim. *I told him yes.*
Acho que sim. *I think so.*
Um dia sim, um dia não. *Every other day.*
Pois sim! *Fine! All right! or Oh, yeah!*
   Come on now! (depends on inflection).
Dar o sim. *To say yes. To give consent.*
simbolizar *to symbolize.*
símbolo *m. symbol.*
simetria *f. symmetry.*
simétrico *adj. symmetrical.*
similar *adj. similar.*
similitude *f. similitude, similarity,*
   resemblance.
simpatia *f. sympathy.*
Ter simpatia por. *To sympathize with. To*
   have sympathy for.
simpático *adj. nice, pleasant, sympathetic.*
Ela é muito simpática. *She's very nice.*
simpatizar *to sympathize.*
SIMPLES *adj. simple; plain; n. m. and f.*
   simpleton.
É muito simples. *It's quite simple.*
Simplesmente. *Simply.*
Juros simples. *Simple interest.*
simplicidade *f. simplicity.*
simplificação *f. simplification.*
simplificar *to simplify.*
simulação *f. simulation; sham.*
simulacro *m. sham; imitation.*
simular *to simulate, to feign.*
simultâneo *adj. simultaneous.*
SINAL *m. sign; mark; signal; token; beauty*
   mark; deposit.
Ponha um sinal nessa página. *Put a mark*
   on that page.
Ela deu sinal de alarma. *She sounded the*
   alarm.
Sinal de perigo. *Danger signal.*
Sinal aberto. *Green light.*
Sinal fechado. *Red light.*
Ela fez o sinal da cruz. *She made the sign*
   of the cross.
sinalizar *to signal.*
sinceridade *f. sincerity.*
sincero *adj. sincere.*
Ele é um amigo sincero. *He's a true friend.*
síncope *f. fainting spell.*
sincronizar *to synchronize.*
sindical *adj. pertaining to a trade union;*
   syndical; union.
sindicato *m. labor union; trade union.*
sinfonia *f. symphony.*
sinfônico (sinfónico) *adj. symphonic.*
singelo *adj. simple; sincere; single.*
singular *adj. singular; unusual; individual;*
   odd.

"Lápis" é singular e plural: o lápis, os
   lápis. *"Lápis" is singular and plural:*
   the pencil, the pencils.
É um caso singular. *It's a strange case.*
singularidade *f. singularity; peculiarity.*
sinistra *f. left hand.*
sinistro *adj. left; sinister; unfortunate; n. m.*
   accident, loss.
Lado sinistro. *Left side.*
Tem um aspecto sinistro. *It looks*
   sinister.
Onde aconteceu o sinistro? *Where did the*
   accident occur?
sino *m. bell.*
sinônimo (sinónimo) *adj. synonymous; n. m.*
   synonym.
sinopse *f. synopsis, summary.*
sintaxe *(x = ks) f. syntax.*
síntese *f. synthesis.*
sintético *adj. synthetic.*
sintoma *m. symptom.*
sintonizar *to tune in (radio).*
O aparelho de rádio está mal sintonizado.
   The radio is not properly tuned.
sirena *f. siren, nymph.*
siri *m. crab.*
sisal *m. sisal.*
sistema *m. system.*
Sistema métrico. *Metric system.*
Sistema decimal. *Decimal system.*
sistemático *adj. systematic.*
sisudo *adj. pensive; prudent; calm.*
sitiar *to besiege.*
sítio *m. place, site, location; siege.*
SITUAÇÃO *f. situation; position;*
   circumstances; site, location.
Ele está em má situação. *He's in a bad*
   situation.
situar *to place, to locate, to situate.*
smoking *m. tuxedo, dinner jacket* Ⓑ.
SÓ *adj. alone; single; adv. only.*
O senhor está só? *Are you alone?*
Só para adultos. *Adults only.*
soalho *m. floor.*
SOAR *to sound; to ring.*
O sino soou. *The bell rang.*
sob *prep. under, below.*
Sob juramento. *Under oath.*
Sob medida. *Made to order.*
soberania *f. sovereignty.*
soberano *adj., n. m. sovereign.*
soberbo *adj. proud, haughty; magnificent.*
sobra *f. excess, surplus; pl. leftovers.*
Tenho tempo de sobra. *I have plenty of*
   time.
sobrado *adj. left over; plenty; n. m. wooden*
   floor; house of two or more stories Ⓑ;
   plantation owner's large home Ⓑ.
sobrancelha *f. eyebrow.*

Franzir as sobrancelhas. *To frown. To knit one's brows.*

sobrar *to be more than enough; to be left over.*

Sobrou muito alimento. *A great deal of food was left over.*

Parece-me que aqui sobro. *It seems to me that I'm not needed here.*

Sobram seis. *There are six too many.*

SOBRE *on; over; above; about.*

Ponha o copo sobre a mesa. *Put the glass on the table.*

Ele escreveu um livro sobre Portugal. *He wrote a book about Portugal.*

Sobre que falaram? *What did they talk about?*

sobrecarga *f. overload.*

sobrecarregar *to overload.*

sobremaneira *adv. excessively, greatly.*

SOBREMESA *f. dessert.*

sobrenatural *adj., n. m. supernatural.*

sobrenome *m. surname.*

sobrepor *to superimpose, to place over; to overlay; to overlap.*

sobressair *to stand out; to excel.*

sobressalente *adj. spare.*

Pneu sobressalente. *Spare tire.*

sobressaltar *to frighten; to startle; to surprise.*

sobressalto *m. fright; surprise; shock.*

sobretudo *adv. above all, especially; n. m. overcoat.*

sobreviver *to survive.*

sobriedade *f. sobriety, temperance, moderation.*

sobrinha *f. niece.*

sobrinho *m. nephew.*

sóbrio *adj. sober, temperate.*

socar *to strike, to hit, to beat, to punch, to pound.*

social *adj. social.*

Assistência social. *Social work.*

Ordem social. *Social order.*

socialismo *m. socialism.*

socialista *adj., n. m. and f. socialist.*

socializar *to socialize.*

sociável *adj. sociable.*

sociedade *f. society; community; company; corporation; partnership.*

A alta sociedade. *High society.*

Formaram uma sociedade. *They formed a partnership.*

Sociedade anônima (anónima). *Corporation.*

sócio *m. partner, associate; member.*

O senhor é sócio desse clube? *Are you a member of that club?*

Sócio principal. *Senior partner.*

sociologia *f. sociology.*

sociólogo *m. sociologist.*

soco *m. punch, sock.*

Dar um soco a alguém. *To punch someone.*

socorrer *to aid, to help, to assist; to rescue.*

Ninguém quer socorrê-lo. *Nobody wants to help him.*

socorro *m. aid, help, succor.*

soda *f. soda.*

sofá *m. sofa, couch.*

sofrer *to suffer, to stand.*

sofrido *adj. patient, long-suffering.*

sofrimento *m. suffering.*

software *m. software.*

soga *f. rope, lariat.*

sogra *f. mother-in-law.*

sogro *m. father-in-law.*

SOL *m. sun, sunshine.*

Tomar banho de sol. *To have a sunbath.*

Nascer do sol. *Sunrise.*

Pôr do sol. *Sunset.*

De sol a sol. *From sunrise to sunset.*

Queimadura de sol. *Sunburn.*

sola *f. sole (of the foot, of shoe).*

solar *to sole (shoe); to play a solo; adj. solar, manorial; n. m. mansion, manor house.*

Ano solar. *Solar year.*

Mancha solar. *Sunspot.*

soldado *m. soldier.*

Soldado raso. *Buck private.*

Soldado Desconhecido. *Unknown Soldier.*

soldar *to solder; to weld.*

solene *adj. solemn; serious, grave; religious.*

solenidade *f. solemnity.*

soletrar *to spell; to read slowly; to read badly.*

solicitação *f. solicitation, request.*

solicitador *adj. soliciting; n. m. solicitor.*

solicitar *to solicit; to ask; to apply for.*

Ele solicita um emprego. *He's applying for a position.*

solícito *adj. solicitious, concerned.*

solicitude *f. solicitude, concern.*

solidão *f. solitude.*

solidariedade *f. solidarity.*

solidário *adj. joint; mutual.*

solidez *f. solidity, firmness, soundness.*

sólido *adj. solid, sound; strong; firm; n. m. solid.*

Tem uma base muito sólida. *It has a very solid base.*

solitário *adj. solitary, lonely; n. m. hermit.*

solo *m. soil; ground; solo.*

soltar *to untie, to loosen; to set free; to let out; to let go.*

Soltaram o preso. *They set the prisoner free.*

Soltaram as amarras. *They loosened the cables.*

De repente ele soltou uma gargalhada. *Suddenly he burst into laughter.*

Soltar o cabelo. *To let one's hair down.*

soltar-se *to get loose.*

solteirão *m. confirmed bachelor.*

solteiro *adj. single, unmarried, bachelor; n. m. bachelor.*

O senhor é casado ou solteiro? *Are you married or single?*

Ainda sou solteiro. *I'm still a bachelor.*

solteirona *f. old maid, spinster.*

solto *adj. loose; free; licentious.*

Verso solto. *Blank verse.*

Ela tem a língua muito solta. *She has a very loose tongue.*

SOLUÇÃO *f. solution; answer; dénouement, outcome; payment.*

Isto não tem solução. *There's no solution to this.*

Essa é a melhor solução. *That's the best solution.*

soluço *m. sob.*

solúvel *adj. soluble; solvable.*

solvência *f. solvency.*

solvente *adj. solvent.*

solver *to solve; to resolve.*

SOM *m. sound; tone; noise; manner, way.*

Sem tom nem som. *Without rhyme or reason.*

À prova de som. *Soundproof.*

Em alto e bom som. *Loud and clear.*

soma *f. sum, amount, addition.*

Quanto é a soma total? *What's the total amount?*

somar *to add up, to sum up.*

SOMBRA *f. shadow; shade; darkness.*

Ela se sentou (sentou-se) à sombra duma árvore. *She sat down in the shade of a tree.*

Não há nem sombra de verdade no que ele diz. *There isn't a shadow of truth in what he says.*

sombrinha *f. parasol.*

sombrio *adj. shady; gloomy; somber.*

SOMENTE *solely, only.*

Aprendi somente um pouco de português. *I learned only a little Portuguese.*

sonâmbulo *m. sleepwalker.*

sonata *f. sonata.*

sondagem *f. sounding; survey, poll.*

sondar *to sound, to sound out.*

Estavam sondando (a sondar) a baía. *They were sounding the bay.*

soneca *f. nap (short sleep).*

Ele está tirando (a tirar) uma soneca. *He is taking a nap.*

soneto *m. sonnet.*

sonhador *m. dreamer.*

sonhar *to dream.*

Ela sonha com dias passados. *She dreams of days gone by.*

sonho *m. dream.*

Tudo parece um sonho. *It all seems like a dream.*

SONO *m. sleep.*

Você está com sono? (Você tem sono?) *Are you sleepy?*

Ele pegou no sono. *He fell asleep.*

sonoridade *f. sonority.*

sonoro *adj. sonorous.*

Um filme sonoro. *A talkie, a film with sound.*

SOPA *f. soup; easy, simple* Ⓑ.

Quer mais sopa? *Do you want more soup?*

Isto é sopa. *This is easy. There's nothing to this.*

sopapo *m. blow, slap.*

soprano *m. and f. soprano.*

soprar *to blow; to whisper.*

sopro *m. blowing; breath; puff.*

Instrumento de sopro. *Wind instrument.*

soro *m. serum; whey (milk).*

sorrir *to smile.*

Todos sorriram. *They all smiled.*

sorriso *m. smile.*

SORTE *f. chance, lot, fortune, luck; fate; manner; kind.*

Boa sorte! *Good luck!*

Ela tem muita sorte. *She is very lucky.*

Deitemos sortes. *Let's cast lots.*

Má sorte. *Bad luck.*

Quem tirou a sorte grande? *Who won the grand prize?*

sortear *to cast lots; to raffle.*

sorteio *m. raffle; drawing of lots.*

sortir *to supply; to mix.*

sorver *to sip; to absorb; to swallow.*

sorvete *m. ice cream; sherbet.*

soslaio *m. slant.*

De soslaio. *Askance.*

sossegado *adj. calm, quiet.*

sossegar *to calm, to quiet.*

Quando você sossegar, falaremos. *When you calm down we'll talk.*

sossego *m. peace, calm, quiet.*

Não tivemos um minuto de sossego. *We didn't have a moment's peace.*

sótão *m. attic.*

sotaque *m. accent, foreign accent.*

Ela fala português com um sotaque espanhol. *She speaks Portuguese with a Spanish accent.*

soviético *adj. Soviet.*

sozinho *adj. alone, all alone.*

SUA *f. adj. and pron. your, his, her, its, their, yours, hers, theirs.*

José, onde está (a) sua irmã? *Joseph, where is your sister?*

Ela está com (a) sua amiga Maria. *She is with her friend Mary.*

suar *to sweat, to perspire.*
suave *adj. soft; mild; gentle; mellow; sweet.*
Ele tem maneiras suaves. *He has gentle manners.*
suavidade *f. softness, gentleness.*
suavizar *to soften, to soothe.*
subalterno *adj., n. m. subaltern, subordinate.*
subarrendar *to sublet, to sublease.*
subconsciente *adj., n. m. subconscious.*
subdiretor (subdirector) *m. subdirector, assistant director.*
subdivisão *f. subdivision.*
SUBIR *to go up, to ascend, to rise; to climb; to mount; to raise.*
Subamos. *Let's go up.*
Suba ao quarto andar. *Go up to the fourth floor.*
Ela já subiu para o trem. *She has already boarded the train.*
Os preços vão subindo. *Prices keep going up.*
súbito *adj. sudden.*
De súbito. *Suddenly. All of a sudden.*
subjetividade (subjectividade) *f. subjectivity.*
subjetivo (subjectivo) *adj. subjective.*
subjugar *to subjugate, to overpower.*
subjuntivo *adj., n. m. subjunctive.*
sublevação *f. insurrection, uprising.*
sublevar *to stir up, to rebel.*
sublime *adj. sublime.*
sublinhar *to underline; to emphasize.*
submarino *adj., n. m. submarine.*
submeter *to submit; to subdue.*
Submeter à votação. *To put to a vote.*
subordinado *adj. subordinate.*
subordinar *to subordinate.*
subornar *to bribe.*
suborno *m. bribe, bribery.*
subscrever *to subscribe.*
O senhor quer subscrever a esta revista? *Would you like to subscribe to this magazine?*
subscrição *f. subscription.*
subscritor *m. subscriber.*
subsecretário *m. undersecretary.*
subseqüente (subsequente) *adj. subsequent.*
subsidiar *to subsidize, to aid.*
subsídio *m. subsidy, aid.*
subsistência *f. subsistence.*
subsistir *to subsist; to exist; to survive.*
substância *f. substance; essence.*
Em substância. *In substance. In short.*
substancial *adj. substantial.*
substanciar *to substantiate.*
substancioso *adj. substantial; nourishing.*
substantivo *adj. substantive; n. m. substantive, noun.*

substituição *f. substitution.*
substituir *to substitute.*
Ele substituiu o seu amigo. *He substituted for his friend.*
substituto *m. substitute.*
subterrâneo *adj. subterranean, underground.*
subtítulo *m. subtitle.*
subtração *f. subtraction.*
subúrbio *m. suburb.*
subvenção *f. subsidy, grant.*
subvencionar *to subsidize.*
subversão *f. subversion.*
suceder *to happen; to succeed.*
Que sucedeu depois? *What happened then (next)?*
Suceda o que suceda, eu estarei aqui. *No matter what happens, I'll be here.*
Crê-se que o filho dele lhe sucederá. *It is believed that his son will succeed him.*
sucessão *f. succession.*
sucessivo *adj. successive.*
sucesso *m. event, incident; result; success.*
A peça teve grande sucesso. *The play was a hit.*
sucessor *m. successor.*
suco *m. juice.*
Suco de laranja. *Orange juice.*
sucumbir *to succumb; to die; to yield.*
sucursal *adj., n. m. branch (post office, etc.).*
sudeste *adj., n. m. southeast.*
sudoeste *adj., n. m. southwest.*
sueco *adj. Swedish; n. m. Swede.*
suéter *m. sweater* Ⓑ.
suficiência *f. sufficiency, adequacy.*
suficiente *adj. sufficient, enough.*
Isso não é suficiente. *That's not enough.*
sufixo *(x ⟩ ks) m. suffix.*
sufocar *to suffocate; to strangle.*
sufrágio *m. suffrage, voting.*
sugerir *to suggest, to hint.*
Que me sugere o senhor? *What do you suggest (to me)?*
sugestão *f. suggestion; hint.*
Essa foi uma boa sugestão. *That was a good suggestion.*
sugestivo *adj. suggestive.*
suicida *m. f. suicide (person).*
suicidar-se *to commit suicide.*
suicídio *m. suicide (act).*
suíço *adj. Swiss; n. m. Swiss person.*
sujeitar *to subject; to subdue.*
SUJEITO *adj. subject; liable; n. m. subject; theme; fellow, guy.*
Estar sujeito a. *To be subject to.*
Quem é esse sujeito? *Who is that fellow?*
sujo *adj. dirty, soiled; foul.*
SUL *adj. south, southern; n. m. south.*

122

Cruzeiro do Sul. *Southern Cross.*
sulcar *to plow.*
súlfur *m. sulfur.*
sulista *adj. southern; n. m. southerner.*
sumário *m. summary.*
sumir, sumir-se *to disappear, to fade away.*
sumo *adj. great, high, supreme; n. m. juice; top.*
Ao sumo. *At most.*
suntuosidade *f. sumptuousness.*
suntuoso *adj. sumptuous, magnificent.*
suor *m. sweat, perspiration; hard work.*
superabundância *f. superabundance, oversupply.*
superabundante *adj. superabundant, very abundant.*
superar *to exceed, to excel, to surpass; to overcome.*
Esse trabalho supera todas as expectativas. *That work exceeds all expectations.*
superficial *adj. superficial.*
superficialidade *f. superficiality.*
superfície *f. surface, area.*
Superfície da terra. *Surface of the earth.*
supérfluo *adj. superfluous.*
superintendente *m. superintendent, supervisor.*
superior *adj. superior; higher; better; n. m. superior.*
Ele é um homem superior. *He's a great man.*
Este é um vinho superior. *This is an excellent wine.*
superioridade *f. superiority.*
superlativo *adj. superlative.*
supermercado *m. supermarket.*
supernumerário *adj. supernumerary.*
superprodução *f. overproduction.*
superstição *f. superstition.*
supersticioso *adj. superstitious.*
suplantar *to supplant, to displace.*
suplemento *m. supplement.*
suplente *adj., n. m. substitute, alternate.*
súplica *f. request, entreaty, petition.*
Ele não cedeu às súplicas dela. *He did not give in to her pleas.*
suplicar *to beg, to implore, to beseech, to entreat.*
Suplico-lhe que o perdoe. *I entreat (beg) you to forgive him.*
suplício *m. ordeal; torment; torture; execution.*
Ele passou pelo suplício de . . . *He went through the ordeal of . . .*
supor *to suppose, to imagine, to presume.*
Você bem pode supor o que aconteceu. *You can well imagine what happened.*
suportar *to support; to bear.*
suportável *adj. supportable, bearable.*

suposição *f. supposition, conjecture, assumption.*
suposto *adj. supposed, presumed.*
supremacia *f. supremacy.*
supremo *adj. supreme, highest.*
A Corte Suprema. *The Supreme Court.*
supressão *f. suppression.*
suprimir *to suppress; to eliminate; to omit.*
surdez *f. deafness.*
surdo *adj. deaf; muffled; n. m. deaf person.*
surgir *to arise, to emerge.*
surpreendente *adj. surprising.*
surpreender *to surprise.*
A chegada dele surpreendeu a todos. *His arrival surprised everybody.*
surpreendido *adj. surprised.*
surpresa *f. surprise.*
surpreso *adj. surprised.*
surrar *to beat, to thrash.*
surtir *to cause, to bring about.*
suscetibilidade (susceptibilidade) *f. susceptibility.*
suscetível (susceptível) *adj. susceptible, sensitive.*
suscitar *to stir up, to excite.*
suspeita *f. suspicion, doubt.*
suspeitar *to suspect, to distrust.*
Suspeito dele. *I'm suspicious of him. I suspect him.*
suspeito *adj. suspected; suspect; n. m. suspect.*
suspeitoso *adj. suspicious, doubtful.*
suspender *to suspend; to postpone; to put off; to discontinue; to stop; to adjourn.*
Suspendeu-se a publicação da revista. *The publication of the magazine was suspended.*
Suspender os pagamentos. *To stop payment.*
Suspender a sessão. *To adjourn the meeting.*
suspensão *f. suspension, cessation.*
suspenso *adj. suspended, hanging.*
Em suspenso. *In suspense. Pending.*
Deixar (x = sh) em suspenso. *To hold over. To hold in abeyance.*
suspirar *to sigh.*
Suspirar por. *To long for.*
suspiro *m. sigh.*
sussurrar *to whisper, to murmur.*
sussurro *m. whisper, murmur.*
sustância, substância *f. substance.*
sustentar *to support; to sustain; to assert.*
Devemos sustentar as artes. *We should support the arts.*
sustento *m. maintenance, support.*
suster *to support, to sustain.*
susto *m. fright.*
sutil (subtil) *adj. subtle.*
sutileza, subtileza *f. subtleness, subtlety.*

T

ta (*contr. of* **te** + **a**) *it to you (fam.); her to you.*
tabacaria *f. tobacco shop.*
tabaco *m. tobacco.*
  Tabaco em folha. *Leaf tobacco.*
taberna *f. tavern, inn, bar.*
taberneiro *m. tavern keeper, innkeeper.*
tabique *m. partition wall, partition.*
tablado *m. stage, platform; scaffold.*
tábua *f. table (of information); board, plank.*
  Tábua de multiplicação. *Multiplication table.*
  Tábua de mesa. *Leaf of a table.*
taça *f. cup (including measurement); trophy.*
tacanho *adj. stingy, miserly; narrow-minded; short.*
tacão *m. shoe heel.*
tacha *f. tack, nail; blemish, fault.*
tachar *to criticize; to stain.*
tácito *adj. tacit.*
taciturno *adj. taciturn.*
taco *m. golf club; billiard cue; hockey stick.*
tagarelar *to chatter, to gossip.*
TAL *adj. such, so, as.*
  Que tal? *What do you think about it?*
  Que tal uma cerveja? *How about a beer?*
  Não permitirei tal coisa. *I won't allow such a thing.*
  Um tal Smith o disse (disse-o). *A certain Smith said it.*
  Fulano de tal. *John Doe.*
  Tal pai, tal filho. *Like father, like son.*
talão *m. heel; check; stub; receipt.*
  Talão de bagagem. *Baggage check.*
talco *m. talcum, talc.*
talento *m. talent, ability.*
  Ele é um escritor de grande talento. *He's a very talented writer.*
talhar *to carve; to engrave; to cut.*
talhe *m. shape, figure.*
talher *m. table cutlery (set of knife, fork, and spoon).*
TALHO *m. butcher's shop, meat market* Ⓟ.
TALVEZ *perhaps, maybe.*
  Talvez aconteça como você disse. *Perhaps it will turn out as you said.*
tamanho *adj. such, so great, so big; n. m. size, dimensions.*
  Nunca vi tamanho medo. *I never saw such fear.*
  Qual é o tamanho? *What size is it?*
  De grande tamanho. *Very large.*
tâmara *f. date (fruit).*
TAMBÉM *also, too; as well; likewise.*
  Eu também. *Me too.*
  Ela também comprou dois romances. *She also bought two novels.*

tambor *m. drum; drummer; barrel.*
tampa *f. cover, lid; cap.*
tampão *m. cover; stopper, plug.*
tampar *to cover, to cap.*
tampouco *neither.*
  Ele não quer vê-la. Nem eu tampouco. *He doesn't want to see her. Neither do I.*
tanger *to play (musical instrument), to pluck (strings), to ring (a bell).*
tangerina *f. tangerine.*
tangível *adj. tangible.*
tango *m. tango.*
tanque *m. tank, vat.*
  Tanque de gasolina. *Gasoline tank.*
  Encher o tanque. *To fill the tank.*
TANTO *adj. so much, as much; pl. so many; adv. so, in such a manner, so much; n. m. some.*
  Não beba tanto. *Don't drink so much.*
  Por que tanta pressa? *Why the hurry?*
  Tanta gente. *So many people.*
  Ter tantos anos de idade. *To be so many years old.*
  Custou tanto? *Did it cost that much?*
  A tanto o metro. *So much a meter.*
  Algum tanto. *A little. Somewhat.*
  Outro tanto. *Just as much. As much more.*
  Outros tantos. *Just as many.*
  Tanto um como outro. *One as well as the other. Both of them.*
  Quanto mais lhe dou, tanto mais pede. *The more I give him, the more he asks for (wants).*
  Tanto melhor. *So much the better.*
  Tanto pior. *So much the worse.*
  Tantas vezes. *So often.*
  Estou um tanto cansado. *I'm somewhat tired.*
TÃO *adv. so, as, such.*
  Por que voltou tão cedo? *Why did you return so soon?*
  Ele é tão alto quanto o pai. *He's as tall as his father.*
  Tão bem. *So well. As well.*
  Tão mal. *So bad. As bad.*
tapar *to cover; to conceal, to hide.*
tapeçaria *f. tapestry; upholstery.*
tapete *m. carpet, rug, mat.*
tapioca *f. tapioca.*
taquígrafa *f. female stenographer.*
taquigrafia *f. shorthand.*
taquígrafo *m. male stenographer.*
tardança *f. delay, slowness.*
  Perdoe a minha tardança. *Pardon my delay.*
tardar *to delay; to be late.*
  Não tarde. *Don't be long. Don't take too long.*
  Não tardarei em voltar. *I'll be back before long.*

TARDE *adv. late; n. m. afternoon.*
   Boa tarde! *Good afternoon!*
   Hoje à tarde. *This afternoon.*
   Mais tarde. *Later.*
   Amanhã à tarde. *Tomorrow afternoon.*
   Ontem à tarde. *Yesterday afternoon.*
   É tarde. *It's late.*
   Fazer-se tarde. *To grow late.*
   Antes tarde do que nunca. *Better late than never.*
tardio *adj. tardy; slow; late.*
tarefa *f. job; task, chore.*
   A tarefa está concluida. *The job is finished.*
tarifa *f. tariff; table of rates.*
tartamudear *to stammer, to stutter.*
tartamudo *adj. stammering, stuttering; n. m. stammerer, stutterer.*
tartaruga *f. tortoise.*
tatear *to feel; to feel one's way; to probe.*
tática *f. tactics.*
tático (táctico) *adj. tactical; n. m. touch.*
tato (tacto) *m. sense of touch; tact.*
   Ele é um homem de muito tato. *He's a very tactful man.*
   É suave ao tato. *It feels soft. ("It's soft to the touch.")*
tatuagem *f. tattoo; tattooing.*
tatuar *to tattoo.*
taxa *(x = sh) f. tax, duty, toll; rate.*
   Taxa de exportação. *Export duty.*
   Taxa de juro. *Rate of interest.*
taxar *(x = sh) to tax; to price.*
TÁXI *(x = ks) m. taxi, taxicab.*
taxímetro *(x = ks) m. meter in a taxi.*
te *to, for you (fam.)*
teatral *adj. theatrical.*
TEATRO *m. theater.*
   Peça de teatro. *Play.*
teatrólogo *m. playwright.*
tecer *to spin, to weave; to intrigue.*
tecido *adj. woven; n. m. textile, fabric.*
   Tecido de algodão. *Cotton fabric.*
tecla *f. key (piano, computer, etc.).*
teclado *m. keyboard (piano, computer, etc.).*
técnica *f. technique.*
técnico *adj. technical; n. m. technician.*
tédio *m. boredom, tediousness.*
tedioso *adj. tiresome, tedious.*
teia *f. cloth, material; web.*
   Teia de aranha. *Cobweb. Spiderweb.*
teimar *to persist, to insist.*
teimoso *adj. stubborn; willful.*
tela *f. network, web; canvas (painting); screen (movie, computer, etc.).*
   Tela de cinema. *Movie screen.*
telão *drop curtain (theater).*
telecomando *m. remote control.*
telecomunicação *f. telecommunication.*
teleférico *m. cable lift.*

TELEFONAR *to telephone.*
   Telefone-me às cinco. *Call me at five.*
TELEFONE *m. telephone.*
   Telefone celular. *Cellular phone.*
   Telefone sem fio. *Cordless phone.*
telefonema *m. telephone call.*
telefônico (telefónico) *adj. telephonic, telephone.*
   Lista telefônica. *Telephone directory.*
   Cabine (or cabina) telefônica. *Telephone booth.*
telefonista *f. telephone operator.*
telegrafar *to telegraph, to wire.*
   Teremos que telegrafar-lhe. *We'll have to wire him.*
telegrafista *m. and f. telegraph operator.*
telégrafo *m. telegraph; telegraph office.*
   Onde é o telégrafo? *Where is the telegraph office?*
telegrama *m. telegram.*
   Quero passar um telegrama. *I want to send a telegram.*
teleguiado *adj. guided (missile).*
telenovela *f. TV soap opera.*
telepatia *f. telepathy.*
telescópio *m. telescope.*
telespectador(-a) *TV viewer.*
televisão *f. television.*
   Aparelho de televisão. *Television set.*
televisionar *to televise.*
televisor *m. television set.*
televisora *f. television station.*
telha *f. tile (roofing).*
telhado *m. roof.*
tema *m. theme, subject; written composition.*
TEMER *to fear, to dread, to be afraid.*
   Temo que seja muito tarde. *I'm afraid it's too late.*
temerário *adj. reckless, rash.*
temeroso *adj. afraid, fearful.*
temido *adj. fearsome, frightening.*
temível *adj. fearsome.*
temor *m. fear, dread.*
temperamento *m. temperament, nature.*
temperatura *f. temperature.*
   Ver a temperatura. *To take one's temperature.*
tempero *m. seasoning.*
tempestade *f. tempest, storm.*
TEMPO *m. time, tense; weather; tempo.*
   Por muito tempo. *For a long time.*
   Há muito tempo. *It's been a long time. A long time ago.*
   Há pouco tempo. *Lately. Not long ago.*
   Há quanto tempo você mora aqui? *How long have you been living here?*
   Quanto tempo? *How long?*
   Há tempo de sobra. *There's plenty of time.*
   Não tenho tempo. *I have no time.*

A tempo. *In time.*
Perder tempo. *To lose time. To waste time.*
Bom tempo. *Good weather.*
Mau tempo. *Bad weather.*
O tempo está péssimo. *The weather is terrible.*
Fora de tempo. *Out of season.*
O tempo é dinheiro. *Time is money.*
temporada *f. season, period.*
Esta peça é a melhor da temporada. *This play is the best of the season.*
tenacidade *f. tenacity.*
tenaz *adj. tenacious, stubborn; n. f. tongs.*
tencionar *to intend.*
Tencionamos visitá-lo mais tarde. *We intend to visit him later.*
tenda *f. tent; stall, booth.*
tendência *f. tendency, leaning, trend.*
tender *to spread out; to tend.*
tenebroso *adj. dark, gloomy.*
tenente *m. lieutenant.*
tênis (ténis) *m. tennis.*
Jogar tênis. *To play tennis.*
tenor *m. tenor.*
tenro *adj. soft, tender.*
tensão *f. tension, pressure.*
tenso *adj. tense, tight.*
tentação *f. temptation.*
Não nos deixeis cair em tentação. *Lead us not into temptation.*
tentar *to try, to attempt; to tempt.*
Vou tentá-lo hoje. *I'm going to try it today.*
tentativa *f. attempt.*
tentativo *adj. tentative.*
teor *m. meaning; content.*
Teor alcoólico. *Alcohol content.*
teoria *f. theory.*
teórico *adj. theoretical.*
TER *to have, to possess; to keep; to hold, to contain; to take; to be (hungry, tired, etc.).*
Que tem na mão? *What do you have in your hand?*
Você terá que partir hoje. *You will have to leave today.*
Não tenho muito tempo. *I haven't much time.*
Tenho muito que fazer antes de partir. *I have a lot to do before I leave.*
Não tenho troco. *I don't have any change.*
Não tenho mais. *I don't have any more.*
Que idade tem Maria? *How old is Mary?*
Quantos anos tem Maria? *How old is Mary?*
Maria tem dezoito anos. *Mary is eighteen years old.*
Aqui tem um livro interessante. *Here's an interesting book.*
Que é que você tem? *What's the matter with you?*

Não tenho nada. *There's nothing the matter with me.*
Tenho fome. *I'm hungry.*
Tenho sede. *I'm thirsty.*
Tenho vontade de almoçar agora. *I feel like having lunch now.*
Tenho muito frio. *I'm very cold.*
Tenho dor de cabeça. *I have a headache.*
Ela tem sono. *She is sleepy.*
Elas têm razão. *They are right.*
Elas não têm razão. *They are wrong.*
Tenha cuidado! *Be careful!*
Ter sorte. *To be lucky.*
Ter pressa. *To be in a hurry.*
Ter lugar. *To take place. To happen.*
Ter em conta. *To bear in mind.*
Ter em muito (em pouco). *To think much (little) of.*
Ter jeito. *To have a special skill or talent.*
Ter saudades de. *To miss. To long for.*
Ter notícias de. *To hear from.*
Tenha a bondade de repetir. *Please repeat.*
Não tem importância. *It doesn't matter.*
Quando eu cheguei, eles já tinham partido. *When I arrived, they had already left.*
TERÇA *f. Tuesday.*
TERÇA-FEIRA *f. Tuesday.*
TERCEIRO *adj. third; n. m. third person, mediator, intermediary.*
O terceiro capítulo. *The third chapter.*
A terceira lição. *The third lesson.*
Ele serviu de terceiro nas negociações. *He was an intermediary in the negotiations.*
TERÇO *m. third.*
terminação *f. termination, ending.*
terminal *adj. terminal.*
terminante *adj. terminating; decisive.*
TERMINAR *to end, to terminate, to finish.*
Quase terminei. *I'm almost finished.*
A reunião terminou às três. *The meeting ended at three o'clock.*
término *m. terminus, end; boundary, limit.*
terminologia *f. terminology.*
termo *m. Thermos; term; limit; span; end.*
Pôr termo a. *To put an end to.*
Termos técnicos. *Technical terms.*
termômetro (termómetro) *m. thermometer.*
termostato *m. thermostat.*
terno *adj. tender, affectionate; n. m. trio, group of three; man's suit* Ⓑ.
ternura *f. tenderness, fondness.*
TERRA *f. earth; soil; ground; land, country.*
Viajar por terra. *To travel by land.*
Terra natal. *Fatherland. Native land.*
Terra Santa. *Holy Land.*
Descer à terra. *To land. To go ashore.*
Minha terra. *My land. My country.*
terraço *m. terrace.*

terremoto *m. earthquake.*

terreno *m. land, soil, piece of ground; field.*
    Partiram o terreno em vários lotes. *They divided the land into several lots.*
    Sondar o terreno. *To sound out the situation.*
    Perder terreno. *To lose ground.*

terrestre *adj. ground, terrestrial.*

território *m. territory.*

TERRÍVEL *adj. terrible, dreadful.*

terror *m. terror.*

tertúlia *f. social gathering.*

tese *f. thesis.*

teso *adj. taut, stiff.*

tesoura *f. scissors, shears.*

tesouraria *f. treasury, bursar's office.*

tesoureiro *m. treasurer, bursar.*

tesouro *m. treasury.*

testa *f. forehead, brow; front.*
    Pôr-se à testa de. *To put oneself at the head of.*
    Testa de ferro. *Figurehead. Straw man.*

testar *to will; to bequeath; to testify.*

teste *m. test, examination; trial.*

testemunha *f. witness.*

testemunhar *to testify; to witness.*

testemunho *m. testimony; proof.*

testificar *to testify, to declare.*

teto (tecto) *m. ceiling; roof.*
    Preço teto. *Ceiling price.*

teu *m. adj. and pron. your, yours (fam.).*

têxtil *(x = sh) adj. textile.*

texto *(x = sh) m. text.*

tez *f. complexion; skin.*
    Ela tem uma tez muito suave. *Her skin is very smooth.*

ti *you (fam.) (used after a preposition).*

tíbia *f. tibia, shinbone.*

tíbio *adj. lukewarm, indifferent.*

tico *m. a bit.*

tifo *m. typhoid fever.*

tifóide *adj. typhoid.*
    Febre tifóide. *Typhoid fever.*

tigela *f. bowl, dish; cup.*

tigre *m. tiger.*

tijolo *m. brick.*

til *m. tilde (wavy line over a nasal vowel; ~).*

timbre *m. stamp; seal; timbre, tone.*

time *m. team* Ⓑ.

timidez *f. timidity, shyness.*

tímido *adj. timid, shy.*
    Maria é muito tímida. *Mary is very shy.*

timoneiro *m. helmsman.*

tina *f. vat, tub.*

tingir *to dye, to tinge.*

tino *m. judgment, prudence, discretion.*

tinta *f. ink; paint.*
    Não há tinta no tinteiro. *There's no ink in the inkwell.*
    Tinta fresca! *Wet paint!*

tinteiro *m. inkwell.*

tinto *adj. dyed, colored.*
    Vinho tinto. *Red wine.*

tintura *f. dye, dyeing.*

tinturaria *f. cleaner's, dry cleaning shop.*

tintureiro *m. (dry) cleaner; dyer.*

TIO *m. uncle.*
    Os meus tios. *My uncle and aunt.*
    O tio Sam. *Uncle Sam.*
    Ela foi ao cinema com a tia. *She went to the movies with her aunt.*

típico *adj. typical, characteristic.*

tipo *m. type, class; fellow, guy.*
    Tipo negrito. *Boldface type.*
    Tipo grifo. *Italic type.*
    Ele é um tipo esquisito. *He's a weird guy.*

tipografia *f. printing; printing shop.*

tipógrafo *m. printer, typographer, typesetter.*

tique-taque *m. tick-tock.*

tira *f. band, strip.*

tirada *f. drawing; tirade.*

tiragem *f. printing, circulation; drawing, draft.*

tirania *f. tyranny.*

tirano *m. tyrant.*

tirante *adj. pulling, drawing.*

TIRAR *to take, to take out, to withdraw; to deduct; to remove; to drag; to win; to draw out; to pull; to throw.*
    Ela tirou um lápis da gaveta. *She took a pencil out of the drawer.*
    O professor tirou a sorte grande. *The teacher won the grand prize.*
    A mãe retirou o filho da escola. *The mother withdrew her son from school.*
    Ao entrar na igreja ele tirou o chapéu. *On entering the church, he took off his hat.*
    Tirámos proveito do negócio. *We benefited from the business.*
    Tirar a prova. *To check (a computation).*
    Tirar uma fotografia. *To take a photograph.*

tiritar *to shiver.*

tiro *m. shot; shooting; drawing, hauling.*
    O tiro errou. *The shot missed.*
    Ao sairmos de casa depois de jantar, ouvimos um tiro. *On leaving home after dinner, we heard a shot.*
    Tiro ao alvo. *Target practice.*

tirotear *to fire, to volley.*

tiroteio *m. firing, volley.*

tísica *f. tuberculosis.*

tísico *adj. tubercular; n. m. consumptive, person with tuberculosis.*

tisnar *to blacken.*

titã *m. titan.*

títere *m. puppet, marionette.*

titubear *to hesitate; to stagger.*

A testemunha respondia sem titubear. *The witness answered without hesitation.*

titular *to title, to entitle; adj. titular; n. m. and f. person holding a title; head.*

título *m. title; degree; inscription; bond.*

Qual é o título do livro? *What is the title of the book?*

Título honorífico. *Honorary title.*

to *(contr. of* **te** + **o**) *it (m) to you, him to you (fam.).*

toada *f. tune, melody.*

TOALHA *f. towel; cloth.*

Toalha de rosto. *Face towel.*

Toalha de banho. *Bath towel.*

Toalha de mesa. *Tablecloth.*

toar *to sound; to be in tune with.*

toca-discos *m. record player.*

tocador *m. player (music).*

tocante *adj. touching, affecting, regarding.*

No tocante a. *Concerning. Regarding.*

TOCAR *to touch; to play (music); to concern, to interest; to ring (bells); to be one's turn; to be one's share; to call (at a port).*

Não toque! *Don't touch! Hands off!*

Tocar o violão. *To play the guitar.*

Tocar bem. *To play well.*

Tocar mal. *To play badly.*

A orquestra está tocando (a tocar) um samba. *The orchestra is playing a samba.*

A quem lhe toca agora? *Whose turn is it now?*

Agora toca a ele. *It's his turn now.*

O navio tocou em Lisboa. *The ship called (stopped) at Lisbon.*

Pelo que me toca. *As far as I'm concerned.*

Tocar de ouvido. *To play by ear.*

Tocar o piano. *To play the piano.*

tocha *f. torch, large candle.*

todavia *adv. however, yet.*

TODO *adj. each, every; all; n. m. all, whole; pl. all, everyone.*

Ele perdeu todo o seu dinheiro. *He lost all his money.*

Ela estudou toda a manhã. *She studied all morning.*

Todos dizem o mesmo. *They all say the same thing.*

Todo o dia. *All day.*

O dia todo. *All day long.*

Todos os dias. *Every day.*

Toda a família. *The whole family.*

Todo o mundo. *Everybody.*

Todos de uma vez. *All at once. All at the same time.*

Todos nós. *All of us.*

Em todo caso. *In any case.*

Todo homem. *Every man.*

A cidade toda. *The entire city.*

toldo *m. awning.*

tolerância *f. tolerance.*

tolerante *adj. tolerant.*

tolerar *to tolerate.*

Não podemos tolerar tal barulho. *We can't tolerate such noise.*

Não posso tolerá-lo. *I can't stand him.*

tolerável *adj. tolerable.*

tolice *f. foolishness, nonsense.*

Que tolice! *What nonsense!*

Não diga tolices. *Don't speak foolishness.*

tolo *adj. foolish; crazy; n. m. fool.*

Não seja tolo. *Don't be a fool.*

tom *m. tone; sound; color.*

Sem tom nem som. *Without rhyme or reason.*

TOMAR *to take; to get; to seize; to have (drink, food).*

Que quer tomar? *What will you have (to eat/drink)?*

Nunca tomo vinho. *I never drink wine.*

Tome o remédio às horas indicadas. *Take the medicine at the times indicated.*

Tomemos um táxi $(x = ks)$. *Let's take a taxi.*

Aconselho-lhe a tomar o trem (comboio) das oito. *I advise you to take the eight o'clock train.*

Tomar nota de. *To take note of.*

Tomaram as medidas necessárias. *They took the necessary measures.*

Tomar emprestado. *To borrow.*

Não quer tomar uma bebida? *Don't you want a drink?*

É preciso tomar uma decisão. *You have to make a decision.*

Tomar a palavra. *To take the floor.*

Tomar em conta. *To take into account.*

Tomar banho. *To take a bath.*

Não o tome a mal. *Don't take it wrong. Don't take it the wrong way.*

Tomar a peito. *To take to heart.*

Tomar o pulso. *To take the pulse.*

Tomar posse de. *To take possession of.*

Eu o tomei (tomei-o) por outro. *I took (mistook) you for somebody else.*

tomara *I hope. Would that* Ⓑ.

Tomara! *I hope so!*

Tomara que não! *I hope not!*

tomate *m. tomato.*

tombar *to fell, to bring down; to fall.*

tomo *m. volume (book).*

É uma obra em três tomos. *It's a three-volume work.*

tonelada *f. ton.*

tônico (tónico) *adj. stressed (syllable); tonic; n. m. tonic.*

tonsilite *f. tonsillitis.*

tontear *to act foolishly, to talk nonsense; to feel dizzy.*

tonto *adj. silly, foolish; dizzy; n. m. fool.*

topar *to meet by chance, to "run into."*
Topei com ele no cinema. *I ran into him (came across him) at the movies.*

topázio *m. topaz.*

tope *m. top, summit; clash, collision.*

topete *m. forelock; audacity, "nerve."*

tópico *adj. topical.*

topografia *f. topography.*

topógrafo *m. topographer.*

toque *m. touch; bugle call.*
Toque de alvorada. *Reveille.*
Toque de silêncio. *Taps.*

tora *f. portion; nap* Ⓑ.
Tirar uma tora. *To take a nap (slang)* Ⓑ.

tórax *(x = ks) m. thorax.*

torcedura *f. twisting; sprain.*

torcer *to twist; to sprain; to distort.*
Torcer o nariz. *To turn up one's nose.*
João torceu o tornozelo. *John sprained his ankle.*

torcida *f. group of rooters, cheering section.*

torcido *adj. twisted, crooked.*

tormenta *f. storm, tempest.*

tormento *m. torment, distress.*

tormentoso *adj. stormy.*

tornar *to come back; to change;* **tornar a** *to do again.*
Ela tornou a cantar. *She sang again.*

tornar-se *to become.*
José se tornou (tornou-se) chefe do grupo. *Joseph became leader of the group.*

torneio *m. tournament.*

torneira *f. faucet, spigot.*
Abrir a torneira. *To turn the faucet on.*
Fechar a torneira. *To turn the faucet off.*

torno *m. lathe; vise; faucet.*

tornozelo *m. ankle.*

toronja *f. grapefruit.*

torpe *adj. base, lowly.*

torpedeiro *m. torpedo boat.*

torpedo *m. torpedo.*

torrada *f. toast (bread).*

torrado *adj. toasted, roasted.*

torre *f. tower; turret; belfry; rook (chess).*
Torre de igreja. *Steeple.*

torrente *f. torrent.*

tórrido *adj. torrid.*

torta *f. pie, tart, cake.*
Torta de maçã. *Apple pie.*

torto *adj. twisted, crooked.*
A torto e a direito. *By hook or by crook.*

tortura *f. torture.*

torturar *to torture.*

torvar *to disturb, to upset.*

torvelinho, torvelino *m. whirlwind, eddy.*

tosar *to shear.*

tosco *adj. rough, clumsy, coarse.*

tosquiar *to shear.*
Ir buscar lã e vir tosquiado. *To go for wool and return shorn.*

tosse *f. cough.*

tossir *to cough.*

tostão *m. former Portuguese coin; Brazilian coin.*
Não vale um tostão. *It isn't worth peanuts. It's worthless.*

tostar *to toast, to brown, to tan.*

total *adj., n. m. total, whole.*
Quantos há no total? *How many are there in all?*

totalidade *f. totality, all.*

touca *f. bonnet, cap, coif.*

toucador *m. vanity, dressing table; dressing room.*

toucinho, toicinho *m. bacon, fatback, salt pork.*

tourada *f. bullfight.*
As touradas em Madrid. *The bullfights in Madrid.*

tourear *to fight bulls.*

toureiro *m. bullfighter.*

touro *m. bull.*

tóxico *(x = ks) adj. toxic, poisonous; n. m. poison.*

trabalhador *adj. hard-working, industrious; n. m. worker, laborer.*
O filho dele é muito trabalhador. *His son is very industrious.*

TRABALHAR *to work, to labor.*
Alberto trabalha como um mouro. *Albert works like a horse.*
Acho que ele não trabalha muito. *I don't think he works too hard.*

TRABALHO *m. work, labor; job; product, result.*
Garantimos o trabalho. *We guarantee the work.*
Tudo isto é trabalho perdido. *All this is wasted effort.*
Sem trabalho. *Unemployed. Out of work.*
Trabalho de noite. *Night work.*
Trabalhos forçados. *Hard labor.*

trabalhoso *adj. laborious, arduous.*

traçar *to draw, to sketch; to outline; to plan.*
Traçar uma linha. *To draw a line.*
Os engenheiros traçaram os planos para uma nova ponte. *The engineers drew up the plans for a new bridge.*

tracejar *to trace, to outline.*

tradição *f. tradition.*

tradicional *adj. traditional.*

tradução *f. translation.*
Tradução literal. *Literal translation.*
Tradução livre. *Free translation.*

tradutor *m. translator.*

traduzir *to translate.*
> Traduza esta carta para o inglês. *Translate this letter into English.*
> Não há maneira de traduzi-lo. *There's no way to translate it.*

tráfego *m. traffic; trading, trade.*
> Sinal de tráfego. *Traffic light.*

traficante *adj. dishonest; n. m. swindler.*

traficar *to traffic, to trade; to swindle.*

tráfico *m. traffic, trafficking, trade.*

tragar *to swallow; to devour.*

tragédia *f. tragedy.*

trágico *adj. tragic.*

trago *m. swallow, swig, drink.*
> Vamos tomar um trago. *Let's have a drink.*

traição *f. treason, treachery.*

traidor *adj. treacherous; n. m. traitor.*

trair *to betray; to divulge.*

traje, trajo *m. clothing, suit, dress.*
> Traje de banho (fato de banho). *Bathing suit.*

trama *f. weft (weaving); n. m. and f. web; plot, conspiracy.*

tramar *to weave; to plot, to scheme.*

tranca *f. crossbar, bar; obstacle.*

tranqüilidade (tranquilidade) *f. tranquility, peace.*

tranqüilo (tranquilo) *adj. tranquil, quiet, calm.*
> Este lugar é muito tranqüilo. *This place is very quiet.*

transação (transacção) *f. transaction.*

transatlântico *adj. transatlantic; n. m. ocean liner.*

transbordar *to overflow.*

transcendental *adj. transcendental.*

transcendente *adj. transcendent.*

transcender *to transcend.*

transcorrer *to pass, to elapse (time).*

transcrever *to transcribe.*

transcurso *m. course, lapse (time).*

transeunte *n. m. and f. pedestrian, passerby.*

transferência *f. transference, transfer.*

transferir *to transfer; to defer.*

transformação *f. transformation.*

transformador *adj. transforming; n. m. transformer.*

transformar *to transform.*
> A cidra se transformou (transformou-se) em vinagre. *The cider turned into vinegar.*

transfusão *f. transfusion.*

transgredir *to transgress.*

transição *f. transition, passage.*

transigir *to compromise, to agree.*

transístor *m. transistor.*

trânsito *m. passage, transit, transition; traffic.*
> Trânsito impedido. *No thoroughfare.*

transitório *adj. transitory.*

transmissão *f. transmission, broadcast.*

transmissor *adj. transmitting; n. m. transmitter.*

transmissora *f. transmitter.*

transmitir *to transmit, to send, to convey.*

transparente *adj. transparent; clear.*

transpiração *f. transpiration; perspiration.*

transpirar *to transpire; to perspire; to become known.*

transpor *to transpose, to cross over.*

transportar *to transport, to convey; to transpose.*
> Não sei se podem transportar tanta bagagem. *I don't know whether they can carry so much baggage.*

transporte *m. transport, transportation.*
> Transporte pago. *Carriage paid.*

transtornar *to overturn; to upset, to disturb.*

trapalhada *f. predicament, mess.*
> Que trapalhada! *What a mess!*

trapo *m. rag; pl. old clothes.*
> Boneca de trapos. *Rag doll.*

TRÁS *after, behind.*
> Ir para trás. *To go back, backward.*
> Um trás outro. *One after the other.*

traseiro *adj. back, rear.*
> A porta traseira dá para o jardim. *The back door opens out into the garden.*

trasladar *to transport, to move, to transfer; to postpone; to transcribe, to translate.*

traslado *m. transfer; transcript; translation; copy.*

traspassar *to cross; to transfer; to trespass.*
> Traspassar de um lado a outro. *To cross from one side to the other.*
> Traspassar um negócio. *To transfer a business.*

traste *m. household item of little value.*

tratado *m. treaty.*

tratamento *m. treatment; form of address.*

TRATAR *to treat, to deal with; to discuss.*
> De que se trata? *What's it about?*
> Trata-se dum assunto importante. *The matter in question is important.*
> De que trata este artigo? *What's this article about?*
> Este livro trata da vida de Camões. *This book is about the life of Camões.*
> Prefiro tratar com pessoas sérias. *I prefer to deal with serious people.*
> Você tem de tratar com esses problemas. *You must deal with those problems.*
> Tratam mal (os) seus empregados. *They don't treat their employees well.*

trato *m. treatment; form of address; contract, agreement.*
> Tenho tido pouco trato com eles. *I haven't had much to do with them.*
> Façamos um trato. *Let's make a deal.*

trator (tractor) *m. tractor.*

travar *to join, to unite, to bind, to link.*
Travar conversa. *To strike up a conversation.*
Travar amizade. *To make friends.*
Travar conhecimento. *To make someone's acquaintance. To strike up an acquaintance.*

través *m. bias, slant.*
Olhar de través. *To look sideways. To look out the corner of one's eyes.*

travessa *f. crosspiece, crossbeam; alley.*

travessão *crossbar, crossbeam; dash (punctuation).*

travesseiro *m. pillow.*

travessia *ocean crossing, sea voyage, crossing, passage.*

travessura *f. mischief, prank, trick.*

TRAZER *to bring, to carry; to wear.*
Traga-me uma cerveja. *Bring me a beer.*
Trouxeram *(x = s)* tudo o que lhes pedi. *They brought everything I asked for.*
Você trouxe *(x = s)* consigo *(or com você)? Did you bring it with you?*
Ela traz um chapéu novo. *She is wearing a new hat.*

trecho *m. distance, interval.*
A trechos. *At intervals.*

trégua *f. truce, respite.*

treinador *m. trainer, coach.*

treinamento *m. training, coaching.*

treinar *to train, to coach.*

TREM *m. train* Ⓑ; *pl. gear, belongings, "stuff."*
A que horas sai o trem (comboio) para São Paulo? *At what time does the train for São Paulo leave?*
Este trem pára em todas as estações? *Does this train stop at all stations?*
Vamos tomar o trem das oito. *Let's take the eight o'clock train.*
Os meus trens estão na malo. *My stuff is in the trunk.*

tremendo *adj. tremendous, dreadful, awful.*

tremer *to tremble, to shake.*

trenó *m. sled, sleigh.*

trepar *to climb.*

TRÊS *three.*
Ás duas por três. *Two out of three times.*
Dois é bom, três é demais. *Two's company; three's a crowd.*

trevas *f. pl. darkness.*

trevo *m. clover.*
Trevo de quatro folhas. *Four-leaf clover.*

treze *thirteen.*

trezentos *three hundred.*

triângulo *m. triangle.*

tribo *f. tribe.*

tribuna *f. tribune, platform.*

tribunal *m. tribunal (of justice).*

tributar *to pay taxes; to pay tribute; to tax, to assess.*

tributo *m. tribute, tax.*

tricotar *to knit.*

trigésimo *adj., n. m. thirtieth.*

trigo *m. wheat.*
Farinha de trigo. *Wheat flour.*

trigonometria *f. trigonometry.*

trilhar *to thresh; to tread.*

trilho *m. trail, way; track, rail* Ⓑ.

trimestre *m. trimester; quarter (of a year).*

trinar *to warble.*

trincar *to bite, to crunch; to grit (teeth).*

trinchar *to carve (meat).*

trincheira *f. trench, ditch.*

trindade *f. trinity, Trinity.*

TRINTA *thirty.*

trio *m. trio.*

tripa *f. tripe, intestines.*

triplicar *to triple.*

triplo *adj., n. m. triple.*

tripulação *f. crew.*

tripulante *m. and f. member of a crew.*

TRISTE *adj. sad, gloomy.*
Ele faz um papel triste. *He cuts a sorry figure.*
Isto é muito triste. *That's (this is) very sad.*
Ao ouvir a notícia ela ficou muito triste. *She became very sad when she heard the news.*

tristeza *f. sadness, grief, gloom.*
Tristeza não tem fim. *There's no end to sadness.*

triunfante *adj. triumphant.*

triunfar *to triumph, to succeed.*

triunfo *m. triumph.*

trivial *adj. trivial.*

troar *to thunder; to rumble.*

troça *f. mockery, derision; joke.*
Fazer troça de. *To make fun of.*

trocadilho *m. pun, play on words.*

trocar *to change, to exchange, to barter.*
Trocar dinheiro. *To change money.*
Trocar uma coisa por outra. *To exchange one thing for another.*
Trocar roupa. *To change clothes.*

troçar *to joke; to ridicule.*

trocista *m. and f. joker; mocker.*

troco *m. change (money); exchange.*
Fique com o troco. *Keep the change.*

trombada *f. crash, collision.*

trombeta *f. trumpet, horn.*

trombone *m. trombone.*

trompa *f. horn; tube.*

tronar *to thunder; to roar.*

tronco *m. trunk (wood, body); stem.*

trono *m. throne.*

tropa *f. troop.*

tropeçar *to stumble, to trip; to make a mistake.*

tropeço *m. stumbling, tripping; obstacle.*

tropical *adj. tropical.*

trópico *m. tropic.*

Trópico de Câncer. *Tropic of Cancer.*

trotar *to trot.*

trote *m. trot.*

trovão *m. thunder.*

trovoada *f. thunderstorm.*

trovoar *to thunder.*

truta *f. trout.*

tu *you (fam.).*

tua *f. adj. and pron. your (fam.).*

tuberculose *f. tuberculosis.*

tuberculoso *adj. tubercular; n. m. person with tuberculosis.*

tubo *m. tube, pipe.*

TUDO *all, everything.*

Ou tudo ou nada. *All or nothing.*

Ele sabe um pouco de tudo. *He knows a little about everything.*

Tudo está pronto. *Everything is ready.*

Antes de tudo. *First of all.*

Tudo quanto lhe digo é verdade. *Everything I'm telling you is the truth.*

Apesar de tudo. *Nevertheless.*

tule *m. tulle, silk net.*

tulipa (túlipa) *f. tulip.*

tumba *f. tomb, grave.*

tumor *m. tumor.*

túmulo *m. tomb, grave, vault.*

túnel *m. tunnel.*

tupi *adj., n. m. Tupi, Indian tribes of Brazil.*

tupi-guarani *adj., n. m. the Tupi-Guarani tribes.*

turba *f. mob, rabble, crowd.*

turbação *f. disturbance.*

turbante *m. turban.*

turbar *to disturb, to upset; to darken, to muddy.*

turbina *f. turbine.*

turbulência *f. turbulence, disturbance.*

turbulento *turbulent.*

turco *adj. Turkish; n. m. Turk.*

turismo *m. touring, tourism.*

Agência de turismo. *Travel agency.*

turista *m. and f. tourist.*

No ano passado houve muitos turistas em Portugal. *Last year there were many tourists in Portugal.*

turma *f. group, gang; class (school).*

turno *m. turn; shift; school period.*

Por turnos. *By turns.*

Turno de noite. *Night shift.*

turquesa *f. turquoise.*

turrão *adj. stubborn.*

turvar *to confuse, to upset; to darken, to muddy.*

tutear *to address someone in the familiar form, to use the "tu" form.*

tutela *f. guardianship, tutelage.*

tutor *m. tutor, guardian.*

U

ufa! *whew!*

ufanar-se *to be proud, to boast.*

ufano *adj. proud, haughty.*

ui! *oh! ouch! ow! ugh!*

uísque *m. whiskey* Ⓑ.

uivar *to howl.*

uivo *m. howl.*

úlcera *f. ulcer.*

ulterior *adj. ulterior.*

ultimato *m. ultimatum.*

ÚLTIMO *adj. last, latest; final, ultimate.*

José foi último a chegar. *Joseph was the last one to arrive.*

Por último. *Finally. At last.*

No último momento. *At the last moment.*

Ultimamente. *Recently.*

ultramar *m. overseas lands or areas.*

ultramarino *adj. overseas.*

ulular *to wail.*

UM, UMA *one; (ind. article) a, an.*

Um homem. *A man.*

Uma mulher. *A woman.*

Um pouco. *A little.*

Uma vez. *Once.*

Vou comprar somente um livro. *I'm going to buy only one book.*

Um dia sim, um dia não. *Every other day.*

umbral *m. threshold, doorway.*

umedecer *to moisten, to dampen.*

umidade *f. humidity, dampness, moisture.*

úmido *adj. humid, moist, damp.*

unânime *adj. unanimous.*

unanimidade *f. unanimity.*

undécimo *adj., n. m. eleventh.*

ungüento (unguento) *m. unguent, ointment.*

UNHA *f. fingernail, toenail; claw; hoof.*

Fazer as unhas. *To trim the nails.*

união *f. union, unity; coupling.*

A união faz a força. *there is strength in unity.*

Traço de união. *Hyphen.*

único *adj. only, only one, unique, singular.*

Essa foi a única vez que ele me falou. *That was the only time he spoke to me.*

unidade *f. unity; unit.*

Unidade de disco. *Disk drive.*

unido *adj. united, joined.*

unificar *to unify.*

uniforme *adj., n. m. uniform.*

uniformidade *f. uniformity.*

unir *to unite, to join together, to put together.*
Vamos fazer tudo possível para uni-los. *We're going to do everything possible to unite them.*

unir-se *to come together, to unite, to join.*
As duas firmas se uniram (uniram-se). *The two firms merged.*

universal *adj. universal.*

universidade *f. university.*

universitário *adj. of a university, academic; n. m. university faculty member or student.*

universo *m. universe.*

uno *adj. one, only one.*

untar *to grease, to anoint.*

urânio *m. uranium.*

urbanidade *f. urbanity, good manners, politeness.*

urbano *adj. urban; urbane, refined, polite.*

urdir *to warp; to scheme, to hatch a plot.*

urgência *f. urgency, pressure.*
Com urgência. *Urgently.*
A urgência dos negócios. *The pressure of business.*

urgente *adj. urgent.*
Entrega urgente. *Special delivery (mail).*
É urgente que você venha amanhã às oito horas. *It's urgent that you come tomorrow at eight o'clock.*

urgir *to urge, to press, to be urgent, to be pressing.*

urna *f. urn; ballot box.*

urrar *to roar, to yell.*

urro *m. roar, yell.*

urso *m. bear; rude individual.*
Urso-branco. *Polar bear.*
Amigo urso. *False friend.*
Ursa Maior. *Great Bear (constellation).*

urubu *m. black vulture.*

uruguaio *adj., n. m. Uruguayan.*

usança *f. usage, custom.*

USAR *to use; to be accustomed to; to wear.*
Usar o telefone. *To use the telephone.*
Sempre uso óculos para ler. *I always wear (use) glasses to read.*
No verão uso camisa de manga curta. *In the summer, I wear short-sleeved shirts.*

usina *f. factory, mill.*
Usina de aço. *Steel mill.*
Usina de açúcar. *Sugar mill.*
Usina hidrelétrica (hidroeléctrica). *Hydroelectric power station.*

USO *m. use; usage; custom; wear.*
Para uso externo. *For external use.*
Em uso. *In use.*
Fora de uso. *Out of use.*

USUAL *adj. usual, customary.*
Isso é muito usual. *That's very common.*
O usual. *The usual.*

usura *f. usury.*

usurário *m. usurer.*

usurpação *f. usurpation.*

usurpador *m. usurper.*

usurpar *to usurp.*

utensílio *m. utensil.*
Utensílios de cozinha. *Kitchen utensils.*

ÚTIL *adj. useful, profitable.*
Você o encontrará útil. *You'll find it very useful.*
Dias úteis. *Workdays. Weekdays.*

utilidade *f. utility, usefulness.*

utilizar *to utilize.*

Utopia *f. Utopia.*

uva *f. grape.*

V

VACA *f. cow.*
Carne de vaca. *Beef.*

vacante *adj. vacant; in abeyance.*

vacar *to vacate; to be vacant; to be free.*

vacilação *f. vacillation, hesitation.*

vacilante *adj. vacillating, wavering, uncertain, hesitating.*

vacilar *to vacillate, to waver, to hesitate.*
Eles não vacilaram em fazê-lo. *They did not hesitate to do it.*

vacina *f. vaccination; vaccine.*

vacinar *to vaccinate.*

vadear *to ford; to wade.*

vadiar *to waste time, to loaf.*

vadio *adj. lazy, idle; n. m. idler, loafer.*

vaga *f. vacancy.*

vagabundo *adj. vagabond, vagrant; cheap, shoddy; n. m. idler, vagabond, tramp.*

vagão *m. coach, car; wagon; freight car.*
Vagão restaurante. *Dining car.*

vagar *to rove, to roam; to vacate, to be vacant; to idle.*

vagem *f. string bean, green bean.*

vago *adj. vague, indefinite; vacant; vagrant.*
Horas vagas. *Spare time.*

vaia *f. boo, jeer.*

vaiar *to boo, to jeer at.*

vaidade *f. vanity.*
Ela o faz (fá-lo) por vaidade. *She does it out of vanity.*

vaidoso *adj. vain, conceited.*

vaivém *m. coming and going; vicissitude.*
Os vaivéns da sorte. *The ups and downs of life (of fortune).*

vale *m. IOU, voucher; valley.*
Vale postal. *Postal money order.*
O jogador assinou o vale. *The gambler signed the IOU.*

valente *adj. brave, valiant.*

valentia *f. valor, courage, bravery.*
VALER *to be worth, to amount to; to cost; to merit; to assist; to be of use.*
Quanto vale? *How much is it worth?*
Não vale nada. *It's worthless. It isn't worth anything.*
Acho que este vale mais (do) que esse. *I believe this one is better than that one.*
Mais vale tarde do que nunca. *Better late than never.*
Valer a pena. *To be worthwhile.*
Valha-me Deus! *God help me!*
validar *to validate.*
validez *f. validity.*
válido *adj. valid; sound.*
O passaporte é válido por um ano. *The passport is valid (good) for a year.*
valioso *adj. valuable, worthy.*
valise *f. valise, grip, traveling bag.*
VALOR *m. value; price; worth; valor, courage; pl. securities.*
De pouco valor. *Of little value.*
Sem valor. *Of no value. Worthless.*
Dar valor a. *To value.*
Valor nominal. *Face value. Par value.*
Bolsa de valores. *Stock exchange.*
valorizar *to value, to appraise; to increase in value.*
valsa *f. waltz.*
válvula *f. valve.*
Válvula de segurança. *Safety valve.*
VAMOS! *Come! Come on! Let's go! Hurry up!*
vanguarda *f. vanguard.*
vantagem *f. advantage; profit; odds (games); handicap (sports).*
Este procedimento tem as suas vantagens e desvantagens. *This procedure has its advantages and disadvantages.*
Levar vantagem. *To have the advantage. To gain the upper hand.*
vão *adj. (vã fem.) vain; futile; n. m. space, opening.*
Toda tentativa foi em vão. *Every attempt was in vain.*
vapor *m. vapor, steam; steamship.*
A todo vapor. *At full steam.*
Cavalo-vapor. *Horsepower.*
vaqueiro *m. cowboy.*
vara *f. rod, pole, stick, wand; judgeship; jurisdiction; measurement of 43.3 inches.*
varanda *f. veranda, balcony.*
varão *adj. male; n. m. man, male.*
varar *to pierce, to stick; to beat with a stick; to ford (a stream); to beach (a boat).*
varejo *m. retail Ⓑ; search, raid.*
Vender a varejo. *To sell at retail.*
variação *f. variation, change.*
Sem variação. *Unchanged.*
variado *adj. varied.*

variante *adj. varying, variant; f. variant, variation.*
variar *to vary, to change.*
Não varia nada. *It doesn't change (vary) a bit.*
variável *adj. variable, changeable.*
varicela *f. chicken pox.*
variedade *f. variety.*
VARIO *adj. different, changeable; pl. several, some.*
Hoje comprei vários livros sobre Portugal e o Brasil. *Today I bought several (some) books about Portugal and Brazil.*
varíola *f. smallpox.*
varonil *adj. manly, virile.*
varredor *adj. sweeping; n. m. sweeper.*
varrer *to sweep.*
várzea *f. meadow, field.*
vaselina *f. Vaseline.*
vasilha *f. vessel (for liquids).*
vaso *m. vase, bowl, vessel.*
Vaso de flores. *Flowerpot. Vase for flowers.*
vassoura *f. broom.*
vastidão *f. vastness.*
vasto *adj. vast.*
vatapá *m. a seasoned Brazilian meat dish Ⓑ.*
vaticano *adj., n. m. Vatican.*
vau *m. river crossing, ford; opportunity.*
vazar *to empty; to flow out; to drain.*
vazio *adj. empty, vacant; n. m. void, vacuum.*
veado *m. deer.*
vedar *to prohibit, to stop.*
vedeta *f. advanced guard, sentry; star (movies, theater).*
vegetação *f. vegetation.*
vegetal *adj., n. m. vegetable.*
veia *f. vein.*
Veia artéria. *Pulmonary artery.*
Continuamos na mesma veia. *Let's keep going in the same vein.*
veículo *m. vehicle.*
veio *m. grain (wood), streak, vein.*
vela *f. candle; sail.*
Apagar as velas. *To blow out the candles.*
Vela de cera. *Wax candle.*
Vela de ignição. *Spark plug.*
Barco à vela. *Sailboat.*
velar *to watch; to keep vigil; to veil.*
veleiro *m. sailboat.*
velhaco *adj., crooked; n. m. crook, lowlife.*
velhice *f. old age; old people.*
VELHO *adj. old; ancient; worn-out; old man.*
Somos velhos amigos. *We're old friends.*

A mãe dela é muito velha. *Her mother is very old.*

Esse velho é rico. *That old man is rich.*

Mais velho. *Older. Senior.*

Meu velho. *Old fellow. My friend* Ⓑ.

velocidade *f. velocity, speed; gear.*

Primeira, segunda, e terceira velocidade. *First, second, and third gear.*

Passaram a toda velocidade. *They went by at full speed.*

veloz *adj. swift, fast.*

veludo *adj. velvety; n. m. velvet; velour.*

vencer *to conquer, to vanquish, to win.*

vencido *adj. defeated; due, outstanding.*

Dar-se por vencido. *To give up.*

venda *f. sale; store; blindfold.*

vendar *to blindfold.*

vendedor *m. seller, trader, dealer.*

VENDER *to sell; to trade; to betray.*

Não vendemos a varejo; só por atacado. *We don't sell retail; only wholesale.*

Também não vendemos a crédito (or fiado); só a dinheiro. *We also don't sell on credit; only cash.*

veneno *m. venom, poison.*

venenoso *adj. poisonous.*

veneração *f. veneration.*

venerar *to venerate.*

venezuelano *adj., n. m. Venezuelan.*

venta *f. nostril.*

ventilação *f. ventilation.*

ventilador *m. ventilator, electric fan.*

ventilar *to ventilate, to air.*

VENTO *m. wind; breeze, air.*

Ir de vento em popa. *To get along very well. To be progressing. ("To go with the wind at your stern.")*

ventre *m. stomach, belly, paunch.*

ventura *f. happiness; fortune, chance; venture; risk.*

Por ventura. *By chance. Perchance.*

venturoso *adj. lucky, fortunate, happy.*

VER *to see; to visit; to meet; n. m. sense of sight; opinion.*

Deixe-me (x = sh) ver. *Let me see.*

Vamos ver. *Let's see.*

Que quadros deseja ver? *What paintings do you wish to see?*

Veja esta carta. *Look at this letter.*

Não ter nada que ver com. *To have nothing to do with.*

A meu ver. *In my view. As I see it.*

Tenha a bondade de ver quem é. *Please see who it is.*

Já se vê. *It is clear. It is evident.*

Agora estou vendo. *I see now. I understand.*

Vamos vê-los no sábado. *We're going to see them on Saturday.*

Veja só! *Just imagine!*

Quatro olhos vêem melhor que dois. *Two heads are better than one.*

Ver para crer. *Seeing is believing.*

VERÃO *m. summer.*

veras *f. pl. truth, reality.*

Com todas as veras. *Truthfully. In all truth.*

verba *f. item; entry; appropriation.*

verbal *adj. verbal, oral.*

verbete *m. entry; note.*

verbo *m. verb.*

VERDADE *f. truth.*

Diga a verdade. *Tell the truth.*

Quero saber se é verdade. *I want to know if it is true.*

Você chegou tarde, não é verdade? *You arrived late, didn't you?*

É verdade. *That's right. That's true.*

De verdade? *Really?*

Para dizer a verdade. *To tell the truth.*

verdadeiro *adj. true; real; sincere.*

VERDE *adj. green; not ripe; immature; n. m. green.*

verdugo *m. executioner, hangman; jerk (nasty person).*

verdura *f. greeness; pl. vegetables, greens.*

vereador *m. alderman, councilman.*

vereda *f. path, footpath, trail.*

veredicto *m. verdict.*

verga *f. stick, switch.*

vergar *to bend, to curve; to stoop.*

vergonha *f. shame, disgrace; timidity, embarrassment.*

Não tem vergonha? *Aren't you ashamed?*

Que vergonha! *What a shame!*

Sem vergonha. *Shameless.*

É uma vergonha. *It's a shame.*

vergonhoso *adj. shameful, disgraceful.*

verídico *adj. truthful, veracious.*

verificação *f. verification.*

verificar *to check, to verify.*

Verifique tudo. *Check everything.*

verificar-se *to take place.*

verme *m. worm, vermin, larva.*

VERMELHO *adj., n. m. red.*

A Cruz Vermelha. *The Red Cross.*

verminose *f. verminosis, disease caused by worms.*

verniz *m. varnish.*

verossímil (verosímil) *adj. verisimilar.*

verossimilhança (verosimilhança) *f. verisimilitude.*

versão *f. version, rendition.*

Cada um deles deu a sua versão. *Each one of them gave his own version.*

versar *to deal with; to be about; to examine; to put into verse.*

versátil *adj. versatile, fickle.*

ver-se *to see oneself, to find oneself, to be.*

verso *m. verse; back side.*

   Verso branco. *Blank verse.*

vértebra *f. vertebra.*

vertedor *m. water pitcher, jug.*

verter *to pour; to spill; to translate.*

   Verter lágrimas. *To weep. To shed tears.*

vertical *adj. vertical.*

vértice *m. vertex, apex, top.*

vertigem *f. dizziness; fainting.*

vesgo *adj. cross-eyed; n. m. cross-eyed person.*

vesguear *to squint.*

vespa *f. wasp, hornet.*

véspera *f. eve.*

   Véspera de Natal. *Christmas Eve.*

vespertino *m. evening newspaper.*

vestiário *m. checkroom, cloakroom.*

vestíbulo *m. vestibule, lobby, hall, foyer.*

   Encontrámo-nos no vestíbulo do teatro às oito. *We met in the lobby of the theater at eight.*

VESTIDO *adj. dressed; n. m. dress; garment; clothing.*

   Ela estava bem vestida. *She was well dressed.*

   Vestido de baile. *Evening dress.*

vestígio *m. vestige, trace.*

VESTIR *to dress, to put on.*

   Ele veste bem. *He dresses well.*

   A mãe está vestindo (a vestir) os filhos. *The mother is dressing her children.*

VESTIR-SE *to dress oneself, to get dressed.*

   Os meninos ainda não se vestiram. *The children haven't dressed yet.*

vestuário *m. wardrobe; clothing, apparel.*

veterano *adj., n. m. veteran.*

veterinário *m. veterinarian.*

veto *m. veto.*

vetusto *adj. old, ancient.*

vexar *(x = sh) to vex, to annoy.*

VEZ *f. time, turn.*

   Uma vez. *Once.*

   Duas vezes. *Twice.*

   Outra vez. *Again.*

   Repetidas vezes. *Again and again.*

   De uma vez para sempre. *Once (and) for all.*

   Raras vezes. *Seldom.*

   Muitas vezes. *Often.*

   Cada vez. *Each time. Every time.*

   Cada vez mais. *More and more.*

   De vez em quando. *Now and then.*

   Algumas vezes. *Sometimes.*

   Fazer as vezes de. *To take the place of.*

   Duas vezes três são seis. *Two times three are six.*

   É minha vez. *It's my turn.*

   Um de cada vez. *One at a time.*

via *f. road, way; manner; prep. via.*

   Por via de regra. *As a general rule.*

   Via férrea. *Railroad. Railway.*

   Via aérea. *By airmail.*

   Via pública. *Public road. Thoroughfare.*

   Via expressa. *Express highway.*

viação *f. traffic; transit system.*

viaduto *m. viaduct.*

viageiro *adj. traveling; n. m. traveler, passenger, voyager.*

VIAGEM *f. trip, voyage, journey, travel.*

   Boa viagem! *Pleasant journey! Bon voyage!*

   Estar de viagem. *To be on a trip.*

   Viagem de ida e volta. *Round trip.*

viajante *adj. traveling; n. m. and f. traveler.*

   Caixeiro-viajante. *Traveling salesman.*

VIAJAR *to travel.*

   Viajar de trem (comboio). *To go by train.*

   Eu viajei por Portugal. *I traveled through Portugal.*

viatura *f. vehicle.*

víbora *f. viper.*

vibração *f. vibration.*

vibrar *to vibrate, to throb; to brandish; to touch, to sound (stringed instrument).*

vice-almirante *m. vice admiral.*

vice-cônsul *m. vice-consul.*

vice-presidente *m. vice-president.*

vice-versa *adj. vice versa.*

viciado *adj. addicted; n. m. addict.*

   Viciado em. *Addicted to.*

viciar *to addict; to falsify.*

vício *m. vice; bad habit; failing; addiction.*

vicissitude *f. vicissitude, fluctuation.*

VIDA *f. life, living.*

   Ganhar a vida. *To earn a living.*

   Assim é a vida. *That's life. Such is life.*

   Seguro de vida. *Life insurance.*

   Custo de vida. *Cost of living.*

vidente *m. and f. seer.*

vídeo *m. video.*

videocassette *m. videocassette; VCR.*

videoclube *m. video rental club.*

videodisco *m. videodisk.*

videojogo *m. videogame.*

videoteipe *m. videotape.*

vidraça *f. windowpane.*

vidro *m. glass; bottle.*

   Vidro de aumento. *Magnifying glass.*

   Fábrica de vidro. *Glassworks.*

vienense *adj., n. m. and f. Viennese.*

viga *f. beam, girder.*

vigário *m. vicar.*

   Conto do vigário. *Swindle, fraud.*

vigésimo *adj. twentieth; n. m. twentieth.*

vigiar *to watch; to stand guard.*

vigilância *f. vigilance.*

vigília *f. vigil.*
vigor *m. vigor, strength.*
   Em vigor. *In force.*
vigoroso *adj. vigorous, strong.*
vil *adj. mean, low, vile, despicable.*
vila *f. village; villa.*
vilão *adj. villainous; rustic; n. m. villain,*
   scoundrel; peasant.
vime *m. wicker.*
   Cadeira de vime. *Wicker chair.*
vinagre *m. vinegar.*
vinda *f. arrival.*
   Eu lhe dou as boas vindas. *I welcome you.*
vindicar *to vindicate.*
vingador *adj. avenging, vindictive; n. m.*
   avenger.
vingança *f. vengeance, revenge.*
vingar *to avenge, to take vengeance.*
vingativo *adj. vindictive.*
vinha *f. vineyard, vine.*
vinho *m. wine.*
   Vinho branco. *White wine.*
   Vinho tinto. *Red wine.*
   Vinho do Porto. *Port.*
VINTE *twenty.*
vintém *m. former coin of Portugal and*
   Brazil.
   Eu estou sem um vintém. *I don't have two*
     cents to rub together.
viola *f. viola.*
violação *f. violation, breach.*
violão *m. guitar.*
violar *to violate; to offend.*
violência *f. violence.*
violento *adj. violent.*
violeta *adj. violet; n. m. violet (color); n. f.*
   violet (flower).
violinista *m. violinist, fiddler.*
violino *m. violin, fiddle.*
violoncelo *m. cello.*
VIR *to come, to approach.*
   Venha cá! *Come here!*
   O mês que vem. *Next month.*
   Venha o que vier. *Come what may.*
   Vem a ser a mesma coisa. *It's all the*
     same.
   Eles vieram do sul do país. *They came*
     from the southern part of the country.
virar *to turn; to upset.*
   Vire à esquerda. *Turn to the left.*
   Virar as costas. *To turn one's back on.*
viravolta *f. turnabout, sudden change.*
vírgula *f. comma.*
viril *adj. virile, manly.*
virilidade *f. virility.*
virtude *f. virtue.*
   Em virtude de. *By virtue of.*
virtuoso *adj. virtuous.*
virulência *f. virulence.*

virulento *adj. virulent.*
visar *to endorse; to visa; to aim at.*
viscosidade *f. viscosity.*
viscoso *adj. viscous, sticky.*
visibilidade *f. visibility.*
VISITA *f. visit, call; visitor.*
   Temos visitas. *We have company.*
   Fazer uma visita. *To call on.*
   Cartão de visita. *Calling card.*
VISITAR *to visit, to call on.*
   Eu os visito (visito-os) de vez em quando.
     I visit them from time to time.
VISTA *f. sight, view; glance, look; scenery.*
   Conheço-o de vista. *I know him by*
     sight.
   Não o perca de vista. *Don't lose sight*
     of him.
   À primeira vista. *At first sight.*
   Em vista de. *In view of. Considering.*
   Ponto de vista. *Point of view.*
   Vista curta. *Nearsightedness.*
   Até a vista. *So long. See you soon.*
visto *adj. seen; visaed; n. m. visa.*
   Está visto. *It's obvious. It's evident.*
   Visto que. *Considering that.*
vistoso *adj. showy, colorful, attractive.*
visual *adj. visual.*
vital *adj. vital.*
vitalício *adj. lifelong.*
vitalidade *f. vitality.*
vitalizar *to vitalize.*
vitamina *f. vitamin.*
vitela *f. female calf; veal.*
vitelo *m. male calf.*
vítima *f. victim.*
vitória *f. victory.*
   Vitória moral. *Moral victory.*
vitorioso *adj. victorious.*
vitrina *f. show window.*
viuva *f. widow.*
viuvez *f. widowhood.*
viúvo *m. widower.*
   Ele é viúvo e tem três filhos. *He's a*
     widower and has three children.
viva! *Hooray for! Long live!*
   Viva o Brasil! *Long live Brazil!*
vivacidade *f. vivacity.*
vivaz *adj. lively, spirited; perennial.*
viveiro *m. plant nursery; hatchery;*
   aquarium.
VIVER *to live, to exist; n. m. life, living.*
   Ele vive só. *He lives alone.*
   Eles vivem bem. *They live well. They lead*
     a good life.
   Comer para viver e não viver para comer.
     To eat to live and not live to eat.
víveres *m. pl. provisions, victuals.*
viveza *f. liveliness, vivacity.*
vivificar *to vivify, to animate.*

VIVO *adj. living, alive; lively; smart, bright.*
  Ele está vivo. *He's alive.*
  De viva voz. *By word of mouth.*
  Cor viva. *Bright color.*
  Os vivos e os mortos. *The quick and the dead.*
vizinhança *f. vicinity, neighborhood.*
vizinho *adj. neighboring, next; n. m. neighbor.*
  Um bom vizinho. *A good neighbor.*
VOAR *to fly; to flee; to blow up.*
  As horas voaram. *The hours flew (by).*
vocabulário *m. vocabulary.*
vocábulo *m. word, term.*
vocação *f. vocation.*
vocal *adj. vocal, oral.*
VOCÊ *you; pl. vocês.*
  Você tem razão. *You are right.*
vociferar *to vociferate, to shout, to cry out.*
vodu *m. voodoo.*
volante *adj. flying, mobile; n. m. steering wheel; balance wheel (watch); shuttlecock.*
volátil *adj. volatile, changeable.*
vo-lo *(contr. of vos + o, direct object) it to you, her to you.*
VOLTA *f. turn, turning; return; curve; change; walk.*
  Estar de volta. *To be back.*
  Dar uma volta. *To take a walk. To go for a stroll.*
  Passagem de ida e volta. *Round-trip ticket.*
  Meia volta, volver! *About, face!*
VOLTAR *to turn; to return; to change.*
  Volte amanhã. *Come back tomorrow.*
  Ela ainda não voltou. *She hasn't returned yet.*
  Voltar as costas. *To turn one's back.*
volume *m. volume; bulk; tome; piece of luggage; package.*
volumoso *adj. voluminous, bulky.*
voluntário *adj. voluntary, willing; volunteer.*
voluptuoso *adj. voluptuous, sensual.*
volver *to turn, to revolve.*
  À direita, volver! *Right face!*
  Volver a si. *To regain consciousness.*
vomitar *to vomit.*
vômito *m. vomiting.*
VONTADE *f. will; desire; intention.*
  Esteja à vontade. *Make yourself at home. Make yourself comfortable.*
  Estou com vontade de ir ao cinema. *I feel like going to the movies.*
  Ela o fará de boa vontade. *She will do it willingly.*
vôo *m. flight, flying.*
  Levantar vôo. *To take off. To take flight.*
voracidade *f. voracity, greediness.*

voragem *f. whirlpool, maelstrom.*
vórtice *m. vortex.*
vos *direct and indirect object, fam. pl. you, to you.*
vós *fam. pl. you.*
vosso *fam. pl. your.*
  Vossa Excelência. *Your Excellency.*
  Vossa Senhoria. *Informal correspondence or announcements this phrase is often used to translate "you."*
votação *f. ballot, voting.*
  Votação secreta. *Secret ballot. Secret vote.*
votante *m. and f. voter, elector.*
votar *to vote; to vow.*
  Eu não votarei nele. *I won't vote for him.*
voto *m. vote; ballot; vow; wish.*
  Voto de confiança. *Vote of confidence.*
VOZ *f. voice; outcry; word; rumor.*
  À meia voz. *In an undertone. In a whisper.*
  Em voz alta. *Aloud.*
  Em voz baixa (x = sh). *In a low voice.*
  Levantar a voz. *To raise one's voice.*
  A voz do povo. *Public opinion.*
vulcanizar *to vulcanize.*
vulgar *adj. vulgar, common, ordinary.*
vulgo *m. the masses, the common people.*
vulnerável *adj. vulnerable.*
vulto *m. form, figure; bulk; important person.*

xadrez *(x = sh) m. chess.*
xale *(x = sh) m. shawl.*
xampu *(x = sh) m. shampoo.*
xaropada *(x = sh) f. cough syrup; boring talk, blather.*
xarope *(x = sh) m. syrup, remedy.*
xavante *(x = sh) adj., n. m. and f. Chavante (Indian tribe of Brazil).*
XÍCARA *(x = sh) f. cup.*
  Uma xícara de chá. *A cup of tea.*
xingar *(x = sh) to call names, to abuse.*

zagal *m. shepherd.*
zangado *adj. angry.*
zangar *to anger, to annoy.*
zangar-se *to get angry.*
  Zangaram-se quando ouviram as palavras do rapaz. *They got mad when they heard the young man's words.*

zarpar *to weigh anchor, to set sail.*
zebra *f. zebra.*
zéfiro *m. zephyr.*
zelador *m. caretaker.*
zelar *to watch over, to take care of.*
zelo *m. zeal, devotion.*
zeloso *adj. zealous, dedicated.*
zênite (zénite) m. zenith.
ZERO *m. zero, nothing.*
　　Acima de zero. *Above zero.*

ziguezague *m. zigzag.*
ziguezaguear *to zigzag.*
zinco *m. zinc.*
zoar *to hum, to buzz.*
zona *f. zone, area, region.*
　　Zona temperada. *Temperate zone.*
　　Zona de silêncio. *Quiet zone.*
zorro *m. fox.*
zumbido *m. buzzing, hum.*
zumbir *to buzz, to hum.*

GLOSSARY OF PROPER NAMES

Adolfo Adolph
Afonso Alphonse
Alberto Albert
Alexandre Alexander
Alfredo Alfred
Alice Alice
Ana Ann, Anne, Anna
André Andrew
Antônio (António) Anthony
Artur Arthur
Augusto Augustus
Aurélio Aurelius

Bárbara Barbara
Beatriz Beatrice
Bernardo Bernard

Camilo Camillus
Carlos Charles
Carlota Charlotte
Carolina Caroline
Cecília Cecilia
Cláudio Claude, Claudius

Diogo James
Dorotéia (Doroteia) Dorothy

Edmundo Edmund
Eduardo Edward
Emília Emily
Ernesto Ernest
Ester Esther
Eugênio (Eugénio) Eugene
Eva Eve

Fernando Ferdinand
Filipe Philip
Francisco Francis
Frederico Frederick

Gertrudes Gertrude
Gil Giles
Glória Gloria
Guilherme William

Gustavo Gustave

Heitor Hector
Henrique Henry

Inácio Ignatius
Inês Agnes, Inez
Isabel Elizabeth

Jesus Jesus
João John
Joaquim Joachim
Jorge George
José Joseph
Josefa Josephine
Josefina Josephine
Júlio Julius

Leonardo Leonard
Leonor Eleanor
Lúcia Lucy
Luís Louis
Luísa Louise

Manuel Emanuel, Manuel
Margarida Margaret
Maria Mary
Mário Mario, Marius
Marta Martha
Maurício Maurice, Morris
Miguel Michael

Paulo Paul
Pedro Peter

Raimundo Raymond
Raquel Rachel
Ricardo Richard
Roberto Robert
Rodolfo Rudolph, Ralph
Rodrigo Roderic
Rosa Rose

Sebastião Sebastian

Teresa Theresa
Tomás Thomas

Vicente Vincent

GLOSSARY OF GEOGRAPHICAL NAMES

Açores Azores
África Africa
Alemanha Germany
Alpes Alps
América America
América do Norte North America
América do Sul South America
América Espanhola Spanish
    America
Andes Andes
Angola Angola
Argentina Argentina
Ásia Asia
Atenas Athens
Atlântico Atlantic
Austrália Australia

Barcelona Barcelona
Belém Belem; Bethlehem
Bélgica Belgium
Bolívia Bolivia
Brasil Brazil
Brasília Brasilia
Bruxelas (x = sh) Brussels
Buenos Aires Buenos Aires

Chile Chile
China China
Coimbra Coimbra
Colômbia Colombia
Costa Rica Costa Rica
Cuba Cuba

Dinamarca Denmark

Egito, Egipto Egypt
El Salvador El Salvador
Equador Ecuador
Escandinávia Scandinavia
Escócia Scotland
Eslovaquia Slovakia
Espanha Spain.
Estados Unidos da América (E.U.A.)
    United States of America
Estônia Estonia
Europa Europe

Filipinas Philippines
Finlândia Finland
França France

Galícia Galicia
Genebra Geneva

Grã-Bretanha Great Britain
Grécia Greece
Guatemala Guatemala

Haiti Haiti
Havaí Hawaii
Havana Havana
Hispano-América Spanish America
Holanda Holland
Honduras Honduras
Hungria Hungary

Inglaterra England
Irlanda Ireland
Israel Israel
Itália Italy

Japão Japan

Letônia Latvia
Lisboa Lisbon
Londres London

Macau Macao
Madeira Madeira
Madrid Madrid
Mediterrâneo Mediterranean
México (x = sh) Mexico
Moçambique Mozambique
Moscou, Moscóvia, Moscovo
    Moscow.

Nicarágua Nicaragua
Noruega Norway
Nova Iorque New York
Nova Zelândia New Zealand

Oceânia Oceania

Pacífico Pacific
Países Baixos (x = sh) Low Countries,
    Netherlands
Paraguai Paraguay
Paris Paris
Peru Peru
Pireneus, Pirenéus Pyrenees
Polônia, Polónia Poland
Porto Oporto
Porto Rico Puerto Rico
Portugal Portugal

República Checa Czech Republic
República Dominicana Dominican
    Republic
Rio de Janeiro Rio de Janeiro
Roma Rome

Romênia (Roménia)
  Romania
Rússia Russia

São Paulo São Paulo
Sicília Sicily
Suécia Sweden
Suíça Switzerland

Timor Timor
Turquia Turkey

Ucrânia Ukraine
Uruguai Uruguay

Vaticano Vatican
Viena Vienna

English-Portuguese

English Romances

A

a, an um, uma.

ability capacidade, habilidade; aptidão, talento.

able capaz.

   to be able to poder *(to have the capability of);* saber *(to know how).*

abnormal anormal.

aboard a bordo.

abolish abolir, suprimir.

abortion aborto.

about cerca de, quase, mais ou menos; sobre; em volta de.

   to be about (book, movie, etc.) tratar de.

   How about a beer? Que tal uma cerveja?

above sobre, acima de; acima.

abroad no estrangeiro, para o exterior, fora de casa.

absence ausência.

absent ausente.

absent-minded distraído.

absolute absoluto.

absorb (to) absorver, incorporar.

absurd absurdo, ridículo.

abundant abundante.

abuse abuso.

abuse (to) abusar, maltratar.

academic acadêmico (académico).

academy academia, colégio.

accent acento *(mark on letter),* sotaque *(regional pronunciation).*

accent (to) acentuar.

accept (to) aceitar, receber; reconhecer.

acceptance aceitação.

accident acidente.

accommodate (to) acomodar.

accommodations acomodações, alojamento.

accompany (to) acompanhar.

accomplish (to) efetuar (efectuar), realizar.

according to segundo, conforme.

account conta; relato, narrativa.

accuracy exatidão (exactidão) (x = z), precisão.

accusative acusativo.

accuse (to) acusar, denunciar.

accustomed acostumado.

   to get accustomed to acostumar-se a.

ache dor.

achieve (to) conseguir, realizar, ganhar.

acid ácido *(n. and adj.).*

acknowledge (to) reconhecer, admitir; acusar recebimento de.

acknowledgment reconhecimento; confirmação.

acquaintance conhecimento; conhecido (person).

acre acre.

across através; através de; no outro lado de.

act ato (acto); ação (acção).

act (to) agir, atuar (actuar) *(to do);* portar-se, comportar-se, conduzir-se *(to behave);* representar (theater).

action ação (acção).

active ativo (activo).

activity actividade (actividade).

actor ator (actor).

actual real, verdadeiro.

add (to) adicionar, aumentar.

addict *n.* viciado.

addicted viciado.

   to get addicted viciar-se.

addiction vício.

address endereço *(on letter),* discurso *(speech).*

address (to) endereçar, dirigir-se a.

adequate adequado.

adjective adjetivo (adjectivo).

adjoining contíguo, adjacente, vizinho.

administrative administrativo.

admiral almirante.

admiration admiração.

admire (to) admirar.

admirer admirador.

admission admissão, entrada.

   Free admission. Entrada gratuita.

admit (to) admitir, conceder; reconhecer.

admittance admissão, entrada.

   No admittance. Entrada proibida.

admonish (to) advertir, prevenir; repreender.

adopt (to) adotar (adoptar).

adoption adoção (adopção); aceitação.

adult adulto.

advance adiantamento, antecipação; avanço.

advance (to) avançar, adiantar.

advantage vantagem, benefício, proveito.

advantageous vantajoso, proveitoso.

adventure aventura.

adverb advérbio.

adversity adversidade.

advertise (to) anunciar, publicar, fazer propaganda.

advertisement anúncio, aviso.

advice conselho.

advise (to) aconselhar, recomendar.

affair assunto; negócio.

affected afetado (afectado), comovido.

affection afeição; amor.

affectionate afetuoso (afectuoso), carinhoso.

   Affectionately yours. Afetuosamente.

affirm (to) afirmar, confirmar.

affirmative afirmativo.

after depois de, após; atrás de; depois que.

afternoon tarde.

   Good afternoon! Boa tarde!

afterward depois, mais tarde.

again outra vez, de novo.

against contra.
age idade *(of person)*, época *(time period)*.
age (to) envelhecer.
agency agência.
aggravate (to) agravar, piorar; irritar.
aggressive agressivo.
ago há.
    a long time ago há muito tempo.
    How long ago? Quanto tempo há? Há
      quanto tempo?
agony angústia, agonia.
agree (to) concordar, estar de acordo.
agreeable agradável; satisfatório.
agreed combinado; de acordo.
agreement convênio (convénio), acordo.
agricultural agrícola.
agriculture agricultura, lavoura.
ahead avante, adiante.
    straight ahead bem em frente.
aid auxílio (x = s).
aid (to) auxiliar (x = s).
AIDS SIDA.
aim objetivo, meta.
air ar.
    open air ar livre.
    air conditioning condicionamento de ar.
airmail correio aéreo.
airplane avião.
airport aeroporto.
aisle passagem, corredor.
alarm alarme.
alarm (to) alarmar.
alarm clock despertador.
album álbum.
alcohol álcool.
alike parecido, semelhante.
alive vivo.
all todo; tudo.
    all day o dia todo.
    after all afinal de contas.
    not at all de modo algum.
allied aliado.
allow (to) permitir, deixar (x = sh).
    Allow me. Permita-me.
allowed permitido.
ally aliado.
almond amêndoa.
almost quase.
alone só, sozinho.
along ao longo de, ao lado de.
    along with junto com, com.
    all along sempre, continuamente.
    to get along with entender-se com.
    to go along with acompanhar.
alright bem.
    It's alright. Está bem.
also também, além disso.
alternate (to) alternar.
alternately alternativamente.

although embora, ainda que, posto que.
always sempre.
ambassador embaixador (x = sh).
amber âmbar.
ambition ambição.
ambitious ambicioso.
amen amém.
amend (to) emendar.
America América.
    North America América do Norte.
American americano, norte-americano.
among entre.
amount quantia, quantidade, soma.
ample amplo.
amuse (to) divertir.
amusement divertimento.
amusing divertido; engraçado.
analyze (to) analisar.
anchor âncora.
ancient antigo.
and e.
anecdote anedota.
angel anjo.
anger raiva, ira.
anger (to) irritar.
angry zangado, irado.
    to get angry zangar-se.
animal animal.
animate (to) animar.
ankle tornozelo.
annex anexo (x = ks).
annex (to) anexar (x = ks).
anniversary aniversário.
announce (to) anunciar.
annoy (to) aborrecer, irritar.
annual anual.
anonymous anônimo (anónimo).
another outro.
answer resposta, contestação.
answer (to) responder.
    answering machine máquina de
      contestação.
    answering service serviço de
      contestação.
ant formiga.
anxious ansioso.
any qualquer, algum, alguma.
anybody qualquer pessoa, alguém.
anyhow de qualquer maneira, de qualquer
    forma.
anyone qualquer pessoa, alguém.
anything qualquer coisa, alguma coisa.
anyway de qualquer maneria, em qualquer
    caso.
anywhere em qualquer parte, em qualquer
    lugar.
apart à parte; separado.
apartment apartamento.
apiece cada um.

apologize (to) desculpar-se, apresentar desculpas, pedir desculpas.
apology desculpa.
apparatus aparelho.
appeal apelação *(law);* súplica, apelo *(request);* atração (atracção), simpatia *(attraction).*
appear (to) aparecer, comparecer; parecer *(seem).*
appetite apetite.
applaud (to) aplaudir, aclamar, bater palmas.
applause aplauso.
apple maçã.
applicable aplicável.
applicant pretendente, requerente, candidato.
application aplicação; requerimento, solicitação, petição *(application for something).*
apply (to) aplicar.
   to apply for solicitar, pedir.
appointment hora marcada *(with doctor, etc.);* compromisso *(to meet someone).*
appreciate (to) apreciar, prezar.
appreciation apreciação, gratidão, reconhecimento.
approach acesso (access); enfoque *(manner of doing something).*
approach (to) aproximar-se (x = s) de *(to come near);* abordar (a subject).
approval aprovação, autorização.
approve (to) aprovar, autorizar.
April abril (Abril).
apron avental.
arbitrary arbitrário.
architect arquiteto (arquitecto).
architecture arquitetura (arquitectura).
area área, superfície, região.
Argentinean, Argentine argentino.
argument argumento; discussão.
arid árido, seco.
arm braço *(part of body).*
armed forces forças armadas.
arms armas *(weapons).*
army exército (x = z) força.
around em torno de, em redor de, em volta de
   Is there any coffee around? Há café por aí?
arrange (to) arranjar, preparar.
arrangement arranjo.
arrival chegada.
arrive (to) chegar.
article artigo.
artificial artificial.
artist artista.
artistic artístico.
as como.
   as ... as ... tão ... como ...
   as it were por assim dizer.
   as much tanto.

   as much as tanto quanto, tanto como.
   as many as tantos quanto.
ascertain (to) averiguar, indagar, verificar.
ashamed envergonhado.
aside à parte, de lado.
ask (to) perguntar *(question);* pedir *(request).*
asleep adormecido.
   He's asleep. Ele está dormindo (a dormir).
   to fall asleep adormecer, pegar no sono.
aspire (to) aspirar, ansiar.
aspirin aspirina.
assemble (to) reunir *(to gather);* montar, armar *(a machine);* ajuntar, acumular *(to collect).*
assembly assembléia (assembleia), reunião.
assets ativo (activo); bens.
assign (to) designar, nomear.
assimilate (to) assimilar.
assist (to) auxiliar (x = s).
assistance auxílio (x = s).
associate sócio, associado.
associate (to) associar, associar-se a.
assume (to) assumir, supor.
assumption suposição.
assurance segurança, certeza.
assure (to) assegurar, convencer, garantir.
astonish (to) assombrar, espantar.
astounded pasmado, assombrado.
astounding assombroso, pasmante.
at a, em.
   at first a princípio, no início.
   at last finalmente.
   at least pelo menos.
   at once imediatamente.
   at the same time ao mesmo tempo, à vez.
   at two o'clock às duas (horas).
   at that time naquele tempo.
   We were at John's. Estávamos na casa de João.
athlete atleta.
athletic atlético.
athletics atletismo.
atmosphere atmosfera; ambiente *(fig.).*
atom átomo.
attach (to) afixar (x = ks), unir, juntar.
attack ataque.
attack (to) atacar.
attempt tentativa, ensaio.
attempt (to) tentar, procurar; experimentar.
attend (to) assistir, estar presente *(be present);* tomar conta de *(take care of);* prestar atenção *(pay attention).*
attention atenção.
attentive atento, atencioso.
attic sótão.
attitude atitude.
attorney advogado.
attract (to) atrair.
attraction atração (atracção).

attractive atrativo (atractivo), atraente.
audience audiência; platéia (plateia) *(in theater);* público.
August agosto (Agosto).
aunt tia.
author autor.
authority autoridade.
authorize (to) autorizar.
automobile automóvel.
autumn outono (Outono).
available disponível, acessível.
avenue avenida.
average média.
avoid (to) evitar.
await (to) aguardar.
awake acordado.
awake (to) acordar.
aware ciente.
away ausente, fora, longe.
　　to go away ir-se embora.
　　ten miles away a dez milhas de distância.
awful terrível; horrível.
awkward desajeitado *(clumsy);* embaraçoso, difícil *(embarassing, difficult).*
ax, axe machado.

B

babble (to) balbuciar, palrar.
baby bebê (bebé) *(infant);* nenê (nené) *(term of endearment).*
bachelor solteiro.
back costas *(of the body);* posterior; atrás, para trás; reverso, verso; espaldar, encosto *(of a chair).*
　　behind one's back nas costas.
　　back door porta dos fundos.
　　to go back voltar.
　　to be back estar de volta.
　　to call back telefonar de volta.
background fundo *(scenery, painting, etc.);* educação *(education);* experiência.
backward atrasado, retrógrado; acanhado.
　　to go backwards ir para trás, ir de costas.
backwoods sertão ; interior .
bacon toicinho, toucinho.
bad *adv.* mal; *adj.* mau.
　　Too bad! Que pena!
badge emblema, crachá.
bag saco, saca; bolsa.
baggage bagagem.
bait isca.
baker padeiro.
bakery padaria.
balance balança; equilíbrio; saldo *(account).*
bald calvo, careca.

ball bola.
balloon balão; globo.
banana banana.
band banda.
bandage bandagem, atadura.
banister corrimão.
bank banco; margem *(of river).*
bankruptcy bancarrota.
baptize batizar (baptizar).
bar bar *(where liquor is served);* barra *(of metal, etc.);* tribunal; sabonete *(of soap).*
barber barbeiro.
barbershop barbearia.
bare nu, despido.
barefoot descalço.
bargain contrato, negócio *(business deal);* pechincha *(good buy).*
barge barcaça.
bark cortiça, casca *(of a tree);* latido *(of a dog).*
barley cevada.
barn celeiro; estábulo.
barrel barril.
barren estéril.
base base.
baseball basebol.
basic básico.
basin bacia.
basis base.
basket cesto, cesta.
bath banho.
bathe (to) banhar; banhar-se; tomar banho.
bathing suit roupa de banho.
battery bateria *(car),* pilha.
battle batalha, luta.
be (to) ser; estar; ficar.
　　to be hungry estar com fome, ter fome.
　　to be right ter razão.
　　to be sleepy estar com sono, ter sono.
　　to be slow ser lento; estar atrasado (of a watch).
　　to be sorry sentir.
　　to be thirsty estar com sede, ter sede.
　　to be used to estar acostumado a.
　　to be wrong estar errado.
beach praia.
beam viga *(of wood, etc.);* raio *(of light).*
beaming radiante, brilhante.
bean feijão.
bear urso.
bear (to) agüentar (aguentar), suportar, sofrer *(to endure, to suffer);* carregar, levar *(to carry);* parir, dar à luz *(children, etc.);* produzir *(fruit, etc.).*
　　to bear a grudge ter ressentimento.
　　to bear in mind guardar na memória, ter em mente.
beard barba.
bearer portador.

beat (to) palpitar *(heart);* bater, espancar *(strike);* tocar *(a drum);* bater *(eggs, etc.);* vencer, derrotar *(in a game).*

beating surra, açoitamento *(whipping);* palpitação, pulsação *(heart).*

beautiful belo, formoso.

beauty beleza.

because porque.

    because of devido a, por causa de.

become tornar-se, vir a ser, fazer-se.

bed cama.

bed linens roupa de cama.

bedroom quarto de dormir.

bee abelha.

beech faia.

beef carne de vaca.

beehive colméia.

beeper bip.

beer cerveja.

beet beterraba.

before antes; antes que *(time);* diante de; na frente de *(position).*

beforehand de antemão, anteriormente.

beg (to) mendigar *(for money);* suplicar *(for a favor).*

beggar mendigo.

begin (to) principiar, começar, iniciar.

beginning princípio, começo, início.

    in the beginning no início.

behind atrás, detrás.

Belgian belga.

belief crença, opinião.

believe (to) crer, acreditar, pensar, achar.

bell campainha, sino.

belong (to) pertencer, ser de.

below abaixo (x = sh), debaixo (x = sh).

belt cinto.

bench banco *(seat);* tribunal *(court).*

bend (to) dobrar, curvar, dobrar-se, inclinar-se.

beneath debaixo (x = sh), abaixo (x = sh).

benefit benefício.

benefit (to) beneficiar.

beside ao lado de.

besides além disso, também; além de.

best melhor.

bet aposta.

bet (to) apostar.

better melhor.

between entre, no meio de.

beyond mais longe, além; além de.

Bible Bíblia.

bicycle bicicleta.

big grande.

bill conta, nota *(check, account);* fatura (factura) *(invoice).*

billiards bilhar.

billion bilhão.

bind (to) atar, unir; encadernar *(book).*

binding encadernação *(book).*

birch vidoeiro.

bird pássaro.

birth nascimento.

    to give birth dar à luz.

birthday aniversário; data de nascimento *(date of birth).*

    My birthday is on November 21. Faço anos no vinte e um de Novembro.

biscuit biscoito.

bishop bispo.

bit bocado, pouquinho *(small amount).*

bite mordedura.

bite (to) morder.

bitter amargo.

bitterness amargor, amargura.

black preto, negro.

blackbird melro.

blackboard quadro-negro, lousa.

blacken (to) enegrecer; escurecer.

blade lâmina.

blame culpa.

blame (to) culpar, acusar.

blank *adj.* em branco; *n.* espaço em branco.

blanket cobertor.

bleed (to) sangrar.

bless (to) benzer, abençoar.

blessing bênção.

blind *adj.* cego.

blind (to) cegar.

blindness cegueira.

blister empola, bolha.

block (city) quadra, quarteirão.

block (to) obstruir, tapar.

blood sangue.

blouse blusa.

blow golpe, pancada.

blow (to) soprar.

blue azul.

blush rubor.

blush (to) ruborizar-se.

board tábua *(wood);* junta, conselho *(of directors, etc.);* tabuleiro *(for games).*

    on board a bordo.

boarder pensionista.

boardinghouse pensão.

boast jactância.

boast (to) jactar-se, vangloriar-se.

boat bote *(small),* barco *(medium),* navio *(large; ship).*

body corpo.

boil furúnculo.

boil (to) ferver.

boiler caldeira.

boiling fervendo, fervente.

bold corajoso, valente.

Bolivian boliviano.

bomb bomba.

bond união, laço, ligação; título *(stocks).*

bone osso.

book livro.
bookseller livreiro.
bookstore livraria.
boom! pum!
boot bota.
border fronteira, limite *(boundary);* beira, margem.
bore (to) aborrecer, amolar; furar, perfurar *(to make holes).*
boring aborrecido, tedioso.
born nascido.
   to be born nascer.
borrow (to) pedir emprestado, tomar emprestado.
boss chefe, patrão.
both ambos, os dois.
bother amolação, incômodo (incómodo).
bother (to) aborrecer, amolar.
bottle garrafa.
bottom fundo.
bound for com destino a, rumo a.
bound up atado, amarrado.
boundless ilimitado.
bow saudação, reverência *(greeting);* arco *(weapon, bow of a violin);* proa *(ship).*
bow (to) saudar, fazer uma reverência *(to bow in reverence);* ceder, submeter-se *(to submit or yield).*
bowl tijela, bacia.
bow tie gravata borboleta.
box caixa (x = sh).
box office bilheteria (bilheteira).
boy menino, garoto, moço, jovem.
bracelet bracelete, pulseira.
braid trança.
brain cérebro.
brake freio.
bran farelo.
branch ramo, galho *(of tree);* ramal *(railroad, etc.);* filial, sucursal *(local office, etc.)*
brand marca *(of goods).*
brave bravo, corajoso, valente.
Brazilian brasileiro.
bread pão.
break ruptura, quebra.
break (to) romper, quebrar.
breakfast café da manhã (pequeno almoço, primeiro almoço).
   to have breakfast tomar o café da manhã (tomar o pequeno almoço, tomar o primeiro almoço).
breath respiração, fôlego.
breathe respirar.
breeze brisa.
bribe suborno.
bribe (to) subornar.
bride noiva.
bridge ponte.
brief breve, curto.

briefcase pasta.
briefly brevemente.
bright claro *(opposite of dark);* radiante *(radiant);* inteligente; vivo *(color).*
brighten clarear, tornar claro *(to make clearer);* alegrar, animar *(to make cheerful).*
brilliant brilhante, luminoso.
brim aba *(hat).*
bring (to) trazer.
   to bring together juntar, unir, reunir.
   to bring toward aproximar (x = s), trazer.
   to bring up educar, criar *(to rear);* introduzir *(a matter, etc.).*
British britânico.
broad largo.
broadcast radiodifusão, emissão.
broil (to) grelhar *(meat).*
brook riacho.
broom vassoura.
brother irmão.
brother-in-law cunhado.
brotherly fraternal.
brown castanho.
bruise contusão, hematoma.
bruise (to) machucar.
brush escova; mato *(thicket, small shrubs).*
   clothes brush escova de roupa.
   toothbrush escova de dentes.
brute bruto.
bubble bolha.
bucket balde.
buckle fivela.
bud botão; broto Ⓑ.
budget orçamento.
buffet bufê Ⓑ.
bug inseto (insecto), bicho.
build (to) construir.
building edifício.
bull touro.
bulletin boletim.
bullfighter toureiro.
bundle pacote, embrulho.
burden carga, peso.
bureau cômoda (cómoda) *(in a bedroom);* escritório, departamento, agência *(office).*
burglar ladrão.
burial enterro.
burn queimadura.
burn (to) queimar.
   to burn up queimar-se, consumir-se.
burst estouro, explosão.
burst (to) estourar, explodir, rebentar.
   to burst out laughing cair na gargalhada.
   to burst into tears desatar a chorar.
bury (to) enterrar.
bus ônibus (ónibus, autocarro).
bush arbusto.
bushel alqueire.

business trabalho, ocupação; negócio.
businessman negociante, comerciante, homem de negócios.
businesswoman mulher de negócios.
busy ocupado.
but mas.
butcher açougueiro.
butcher shop açougue (talho).
butter manteiga.
button botão.
buy (to) comprar.
buyer comprador.
by por, a, em, de, para; junto a, perto de *(near)*.
    by and by daqui a pouco, logo.
    by and large de modo geral.
    by hand à mão.
    by reason of por causa de.
    by the way a propósito.
    by virtue of em virtude de.
    Finish it by Sunday. Termine-o antes do domingo.
    Send it by airmail. Envie-o por correio aéreo.

C

cab táxi (x = ks).
cabbage repolho, couve.
cabin cabana; cabine, camarote *(ship)*.
cabinet gabinete *(political);* armário *(furniture)*.
cable cabo.
cable car teleférico.
cadet cadete.
café café, restaurante; bar.
cage gaiola.
cake bolo; sabonete *(soap)*.
calendar calendário.
calf bezerro.
call chamada *(summons);* telefonema *(telephone);* visita *(visit)*.
call (to) chamar; convocar *(a meeting);* citar *(to summon to court)*.
    to call (someone) back telefonar de volta.
    to call on visitar.
    to call out gritar, bradar.
calling card cartão telefônico.
calm *adj.* calmo, quieto, tranqüilo (tranquilo); *n.* calma, silêncio.
camera câmara; máquina fotográfica.
camp acampamento.
camp (to) acampar.
campaign campanha.
can lata.
can poder *(to be able);* saber *(to know how);* enlatar *(to put in a can)*.

canal canal.
candidate candidato.
candle vela.
candy bala, doce, bombom.
can opener abridor de latas.
cap boné, gorro *(hat);* tampa *(on bottle)*.
capable capaz.
capital capital.
    capital letter letra maiúscula.
capitalism capitalismo.
captain capitão; comandante *(skipper of ship);* capitão de mar-e-guerra *(navy captain)*.
capture (to) capturar.
car carro; automóvel; vagão *(train)*.
card cartão; carta *(playing card)*.
cardboard cartão, papelão.
care cuidado.
    to take care ter cuidado, tomar cuidado.
    to take care of cuidar de, tomar conta de.
    in care of (c/o) ao cuidado de (a/c).
care (to) interessar-se, importar-se.
    I don't care to go. Não me interessa ir.
    He doesn't care at all. Não lhe importa nada.
    I don't care. Não me importa.
career carreira.
careful cuidadoso.
    Be careful! Cuidado!
careless descuidado.
carnival carnaval.
carpenter carpinteiro.
carpet tapete.
carry (to) levar, conduzir, carregar.
    to carry out levar a cabo *(finish)*.
    to carry on continuar *(continue)*.
cart carreta, carroça.
carve (to) trinchar, cortar *(meat);* esculpir, entalhar *(marble, wood, etc.)*.
case caso *(a particular instance; grammar, etc.);* estojo *(carrying box);* caixa (x = sh) *(case of beer, etc.)*.
    in case of em caso de.
    in case you want to . . . caso que quer . . .
cash dinheiro disponível, dinheiro em caixa (x = sh).
    cash on hand dinheiro em caixa.
    cash payment pagamento à vista.
cash (to) cobrar *(a check)*.
cashier o caixa (x = sh).
castle castelo.
casual casual.
casually casualmente.
cat gato.
catch (to) apanhar, agarrar.
    to catch cold pegar um resfriado.
    to catch on compreender, dar-se conta.
    to catch (on) fire pegar fogo.
    to catch up to alcançar.
Catholic católico.

cattle gado.
cause causa, motivo, razão.
cause (to) causar.
caution cautela.
cavalry cavalaria.
CD disco compacto, disco laser.
ceiling teto.
celebrate (to) celebrar.
celebration celebração, comemoração.
celery aipo.
cellar adega; porão Ⓑ.
cellular phone telefone celular.
cement cimento.
cemetery cemitério.
cent centavo Ⓑ; cêntimo Ⓟ.
center centro.
century século.
ceremony cerimônia (cerimónia).
certain seguro, certo; claro, evidente.
certainly certamente, sem dúvida,
  seguramente.
certificate certidão, certificado, atestado.
chain cadeia.
chain (to) encadear.
chair cadeira.
chairman presidente *(of a meeting)*.
chalk giz.
chance acaso, casualidade *(random
  probability, chance);* oportunidade
  (opportunity); probabilidade *(probability);*
  risco *(risk).*
  by chance por casualidade, por acaso.
  to take a chance arriscar-se.
chance (to) aventurar, arriscar.
change troco *(money);* mudança *(alteration).*
change (to) mudar, trocar; cambiar *(money).*
  to change your mind mudar de ideia.
  to change clothes trocar de roupa.
channel canal.
chapel capela.
chapter capítulo.
character caráter (carácter).
characteristic *adj.* característico, típico; *n.*
  característica.
charge carga *(load; quantity of powder,
  electricity, etc.);* ordem, comando *(order);*
  custo, preço *(price);* acusação
  (accusation); carga, ataque *(attack).*
  in charge of encarregado de.
charge (to) carregar *(a battery, etc.; to load);*
  cobrar *(a price);* acusar *(to accuse).*
  How much do you charge for this?
    Quanto cobra por isto?
charges despesas *(expenses);* instruções *(to a
  jury, etc.).*
charitable caridoso, caritativo, generoso.
charity caridade.
charm encanto.
charming encantador.

chart carta *(for the use of navigators);* mapa
  (outline, map); quadro, gráfico *(graph).*
chase (to) perseguir.
chat (to) conversar; bater papo Ⓑ.
cheap barato.
check cheque *(banking);* talão *(claim check);*
  conta, nota *(in a restaurant);* xeque (x =
  sh) *(chess);* controle Ⓑ, supervisão
  (control); restrição *(restraint);* obstáculo,
  empecilho *(hindrance);* verificação
  (verification).
check (to) investigar *(to investigate);* verificar
  (to verify); frear, reprimir *(to restrain);*
  depositar, enviar *(baggage);* dar xeque, pôr
  em xeque (x = sh) *(chess).*
cheek bochecha.
cheer *n.* alegria, bom humor; *pl.* vivas,
  aplausos *(applause).*
  Cheers! Saúde!
cheerful alegre, animado.
cheese queijo.
chemical químico.
chemist químico.
cherish (to) apreciar, estimar *(to hold dear).*
cherished estimado *(dear);* caro *(dear).*
cherry cereja.
chest peito (body); arca, caixa (x = sh) *(f.);*
  caixão (x = sh) *(m.).*
chestnut castanha.
chew (to) mastigar, mascar.
chicken galinha, frango.
chief *adj.* principal; *n.* chefe.
child criança; menino *(m.);* menina *(f.).*
childhood infância, meninice.
Chilean chileno.
chimney chaminé.
chin queixo (x = sh).
china louça, porcelana.
chocolate chocolate.
choice *adj.* seleto (selecto), escolhido; *n.*
  escolha, seleção (selecção).
choir coro.
choke (to) sufocar, afogar.
choose (to) escolher, eleger.
chop costeleta *(cut of meat).*
chop (to) cortar *(wood, etc.);* picar *(meat).*
chore tarefa.
Christian cristão.
Christmas Natal.
church igreja.
cider sidra.
cigar charuto.
cigarette cigarro.
cigarette lighter isqueiro.
cinnamon canela.
circle círculo.
circulation circulação.
citizen cidadão.
city cidade.

city hall prefeitura (câmara municipal).
civil civil.
    civil rights direitos civis.
civilization civilização.
civilize (to) civilizar.
claim pretensão, reclamação, título, direito.
claim (to) reclamar, pretender *(rights, etc.);* affirmar, a legar *(to assert).*
clam marisco.
clamor clamor, gritaria, tumulto.
clap (to) aplaudir, bater palmas.
class classe *(school).*
classify (to) classificar.
clause cláusula.
claw garra *(talon);* unha *(cats, etc.).*
clay argila.
clean limpo.
clean (to) limpar.
cleanliness asseio, limpeza.
clear claro.
clear (to) aclarar *(to clarify);* absolver *(of blame, guilt);* liqüidar (liquidar), pagar *(debts, accounts, etc.).*
    The weather is clearing up. O tempo está a melhorar.
    to clear the table tirar (levantar) a mesa.
clearly claramente.
clerk caixeiro (x = sh); escrivão.
clever destro, hábil; inteligente.
climate clima.
climb (to) subir.
cloak capa, manto.
clock relógio.
close (near) perto; próximo.
    close by muito perto.
close (to) fechar *(to shut, to shut down);* terminar *(to end);* encerrar *(a meeting);* fechar *(a deal).*
closed fechado.
closet armário *(piece of furniture);* guarda-roupa *(walk-in.).*
cloth tecido, fazenda, pano.
clothe (to) vestir.
clothes roupa.
    clothes brush escova de roupa.
    clothes dryer secador de roupa.
clothing roupa.
cloud nuvem.
cloudy nublado *(sky);* turvo *(liquids).*
clover trevo.
club clube, *(social group, nightspot);* sociedade, associação; *(association);* cacete, porrete *(stick).*
coach treinador *(sports, etc.).*
coach (to) treinar.
coal carvão.
coast costa.
coat paletó, casaco *(jacket);* sobretudo *(overcoat);* camada *(paint, etc.).*

cocktail coquetel.
coconut coco.
code código.
coffee café.
coffin caixão (x = sh).
coin moeda.
coincidence coincidência.
    by coincidence por casualidade.
cold frio.
cold cuts frios.
coldness frialdade.
collaborate colaborar.
collar colarinho.
collect (to) colecionar (coleccionar); cobrar *(money due).*
collection coleção (colecção).
collective coletivo (colectivo).
college escola de estudos universitários; colégio *(of cardinals, etc.).*
Colombian colombiano.
colonial colonial.
colony colônia (colónia).
color cor.
color (to) colorir, dar cor a.
colored de cor.
colt potro.
column coluna.
comb pente.
combination combinação.
combine (to) combinar.
come (to) vir.
    to come back voltar.
    to come forward adiantar; apresentar-se.
    to come across dar com, encontrar-se com.
    to come for vir por.
    to come in entrar.
    to come down descer, baixar (x = sh).
    to come up subir.
    Come on! Vamos!
    to come out well sair bem.
comedy comédia.
comet cometa.
comfort conforto, comodidade; consolo *(consolation).*
comfort (to) confortar, consolar.
comfortable comodo, confortável.
comma vírgula.
command ordem *(order);* mandado, comando *(authority to command).*
command (to) mandar, comandar.
commence (to) começar, iniciar.
commercial comercial.
commission comissão.
commit (to) cometer.
committee comissão, comitê Ⓑ.
common comum.
    common sense senso comum.
communicate (to) comunicar.
communism comunismo.

communist comunista.
community comunidade.
compact disc disco compacto.
companion companheiro.
company companhia *(firm);* hóspedes
 (guests); visitas *(visitors).*
compare (to) comparar.
comparison comparação.
 by comparison em comparação.
compete (to) competir.
competition concurso; concorrência,
 competição.
complain (to) queixar-se (x = sh), lamentar-se.
complaint queixa (x = sh).
complete completo.
complete (to) completar, acabar.
complex complexo (x = ks).
complexion cútis, tez *(skin);* aspecto
 (appearance).
complicate (to) complicar.
complicated complicado.
complication complicação.
compliment cumprimento.
compliment (to) cumprimentar.
compose (to) compor.
composition composição.
comprise (to) compreender, abranger.
compromise compromisso, acordo.
compromise (to) transigir, fazer concessão *(to
 settle by mutual concessions);* resolver,
 ajustar *(a difference between parties);*
 comprometer *(to endanger).*
compute (to) computar, calcular.
computer computador.
 laptop computer computador portátil.
 computer science informática.
computerize (to) computadorizar.
comrade camarada.
conceit presunção, vaidade.
conceive (to) conceber.
concentrate (to) concentrar.
concentration concentração.
concern assunto, negócio *(subject, business,
 affair);* interesse; firma, empresa comercial
 (a business organization); ansiedade,
 inquietação *(worry).*
concern (to) concernir; interessar, preocupar.
concert concerto.
conclusion conclusão.
concrete concreto.
condemn (to) condenar.
condense (to) condensar.
condition condição.
conduct conduta, comportamento
 (behavior).
conduct (to) conduzir, guiar *(to lead);*
 comportar-se *(to conduct oneself).*
conductor condutor.
cone cone.

confer (to) conferir *(to grant);* conferenciar
 (to hold a conference); consultar *(to
 consult, to compare views).*
confidence confiança.
confident seguro, confiado.
confidential confidencial, de confiança,
 secreto.
confirm (to) confirmar, verificar.
confirmation confirmação.
conflict conflito.
confusion confusão.
congratulate (to) felicitar, congratular.
congratulations felicitações, parabéns.
 Congratulations! Parabéns!
congress congresso.
congressman congressista; deputado; senador.
conjunction conjunção.
connect (to) ligar, juntar.
connection ligação, união, conexão (x = ks).
conquer (to) conquistar, vencer.
conquest conquista.
conscience consciência.
conscientious consciencioso, escrupuloso.
conscious consciente.
consent consentimento, permissão.
consent (to) consentir.
consequence conseqüência (consequência).
consequently por conseguinte, portanto.
conservative conservador.
consider (to) considerar.
considerable considerável.
consideration consideração.
consist (to) consistir, constar.
consistent constante *(in ideas, etc.);*
 congruente *(congruous).*
consonant consoante.
constable guarda, policial.
constant constante.
constitution constituição.
constitutional constitucional.
construct (to) construir.
consul cônsul.
consume (to) consumir.
consumer consumidor.
consumption consumo *(use of goods);*
 consumpção, consunção (consumpão)
 (tuberculosis).
contagion contágio.
contagious contagioso.
contain (to) conter.
container recipiente.
contemplation contemplação.
contemporary contemporâneo.
contend (to) sustentar, afirmar *(to assert, to
 maintain);* contender, disputar, competir
 (to strive, to compete).
content contente.
contents conteúdo.
continent continente.

continuation continuação.
continue (to) continuar.
contract contrato.
contract (to) contratar.
contractor contratante.
contradict (to) contradizer.
contradiction contradição.
contradictory contraditório.
contrary contrário.
   on the contrary ao contrário, pelo
     contrário.
contrast contraste.
contrast (to) contrastar, comparar.
contribute (to) contribuir.
contribution contribuição.
control controle Ⓑ; domínio, direção
   (direcção).
   out of control fora do controle.
control (to) controlar Ⓑ; dominar, dirigir.
convenience conveniência.
   at your convenience quando lhe convier.
convenient conveniente.
   if it's convenient for you ... se for
     conveniente para você ...
convent convento.
convention convenção, assembléia
   (assembleia).
conversation conversação, conversa.
converse (to) conversar.
convert (to) converter.
conviction convicção.
convince (to) convencer.
cook cozinheiro.
cook (to) cozinhar.
cool fresco *(temperature);* legal *("neat").*
cooperation cooperação.
cooperative cooperativo.
copier copidora.
   color copier copiadora de cor.
copy cópia; exemplar (x = z) *(of a*
   publication).
copy (to) copiar.
cordial cordial.
cordless sem fio.
cork cortiça *(in sheets);* rolha *(stopper for*
   wine bottle).
corn milho.
corner esquina *(street);* canto *(nook, corner of*
   a room).
corporation corporação, sociedade anônima
   (anónima).
correct correto.
correct (to) corrigir.
correction correção (correcção).
correspond (to) corresponder.
correspondence correspondência.
correspondent correspondente.
corresponding correspondente.
corrupt corrupto.

corrupt (to) corromper.
cost custo, preço.
   cost of living custo de vida.
cost (to) custar.
Costa Rican costarriquense, costarriquenho.
costume traje, costume *(suit of clothes);*
   fantasia *(for carnaval, Halloween, etc.).*
cottage casa pequena, casa de campo.
cotton algodão.
couch sofá, divã.
cough tosse.
   cough drop pastilha para a tosse.
cough (to) tossir.
council junta, concelho.
counsel conselho.
count conde *(title);* conta *(number of).*
count (to) contar.
counter balcão *(in a store).*
countess condessa.
countless incontável, sem conta, sem número.
country país *(nation);* região rural, campo
   (opposed to city); pátria *(fatherland).*
countryman compatriota; camponês.
couple casal *(romantic);* par *(two of*
   something).
courage coragem, valentia.
course curso; pista *(racing);* prato *(of a meal);*
   rumo *(route).*
   of course claro que.
court tribunal *(law).*
courteous cortês.
courtesy cortesia.
courtyard pátio, quintal.
cousin primo.
cover cobertura *(covering);* tampa *(lid).*
cover (to) cobrir; tampar *(to place a lid on);*
   percorrer *(a distance);* incluir,
   compreender *(to include).*
cow vaca.
cowboy vaqueiro.
crab caranguejo.
crack quebra, fenda *(split).*
crack (to) fender, rachar, quebrar, estalar.
cradle berço.
cramp cãibra (cãimbra).
crash estrépito, estrondo *(noise);* quebra, ruína
   (business); colisão *(collision).*
crash (to) estalar; colidir; espatifar-se *(a*
   plane, etc.).
crazy louco, demente, doido.
cream creme, nata.
create (to) criar; causar.
creation criação.
credit crédito.
creditor credor.
cricket grilo (insect).
crime crime, delito.
crisis crise.
critic crítico.

criticism criticismo, crítica.
criticize (to) criticar, censurar.
crook ladrão *(thief),* vigarista *(criminal).*
crooked torcido *(bent).*
crop colheita *(harvest).*
cross cruz *(symbol).*
cross (to) cruzar, atravessar *(a street);* riscar, cancelar *(to cross out).*
   to make the sign of the cross fazer o sinal da cruz, persignar-se.
   to cross one's mind ocorrer-lhe.
   to cross over atravessar.
   cross-examination interrogatório.
   cross-eyed vesgo, estrábico.
crouch (to) agachar-se.
crow corvo.
crowd multidão.
crowded apinhado, cheio.
crown coroa.
crown (to) coroar.
cruel cruel.
cruelty crueldade.
cruise cruzeiro, viagem.
crumb migalha.
cry grito; choro *(weeping).*
cry (to) gritar *(shout);* chorar *(weep).*
crystal cristal.
Cuban cubano.
cube cubo.
cucumber pepino.
cuff punho.
culture cultura.
cup xícara (x = sh), chávena.
cure cura.
cure (to) curar.
curiosity curiosidade.
curious curioso.
curl caracol *(hair).*
curl (to) enrolar, encaracolar.
current corrente.
curtain cortina; pano *(theater).*
curve curva.
cushion almofada.
custom costume.
customer freguês.
customhouse alfândega.
customs direitos aduaneiros *(duties).*
customs officer oficial alfandegário.
cut corte.
cut (to) cortar.
   Cut it out! Corte essa!

D

dad papai, papá Ⓟ.
dagger punhal, adaga.
daily diário, cotidiano.

daily newspaper jornal diário, diário.
dainty delicado.
dairy leitaria.
dam açude, represa (dique).
damage dano, prejuízo.
damp úmido.
dampness umidade.
dance baile.
dance (to) dançar.
dancer dançarino *(professional);* bailarino.
dandruff caspa.
danger perigo.
dangerous perigoso.
Danish dinamarquês.
dare (to) atrever-se, ousar *(venture);* desafiar *(challenge).*
dark escuro.
darkness escuridão.
darling querido, amado; caro.
darn (to) cerzir.
data dados.
date encontro *(romantic);* data *(of month);* datil, tâmara (fruit).
date (to) datar *(memo, etc.);* namorar *(romantic).*
daughter filha.
daughter-in-law nora.
dawn alvorada, madrugada.
   at dawn ao amanhecer, de madrugada.
day dia.
   the day after tomorrow depois de amanhã.
   the day before véspera.
   the day before yesterday anteontem.
   every day todos os dias.
daze ofuscação, confusão, entorpecimento.
   in a daze aturdido.
dead morto; falecido *(deceased).*
deadly mortal, fatal.
deaf surdo.
deal negócio, negociação, acordo.
   to deal with tratar com.
dealer negociante, mercador *(merchandise);* traficante *(drugs).*
dear querido, amado; caro, prezado.
death morte.
debatable contestável, discutível.
debate debate, discussão.
debate (to) discutir, disputar.
debt dívida.
debtor devedor.
decade década.
decadence decadência.
decay decadência *(decadence);* declínio *(decrease);* podridão *(rot).*
decay (to) decair, declinar *(decline);* deteriorar *(deteriorate);* apodrecer *(fruit);* cariar *(teeth).*
deceit engano.

deceive (to) enganar.
December dezembro (Dezembro).
decency decência.
decent decente, decoroso.
decide (to) decidir tomor uma decisão; resolver, solucionar *(a dispute)*.
decidedly decididamente.
decision decisão.
decisive decisivo.
deck convés *(of ship)*, baralho *(of cards)*.
declaration declaração.
declare (to) declarar, afirmar.
decrease diminuição, redução.
decrease (to) diminuir, minguar.
decree decreto.
dedicate (to) dedicar.
deduct (to) deduzir, diminuir.
deduction dedução, redução, desconto.
deep fundo, profundo.
deeply profundamente.
defeat derrota.
defeat (to) derrotar, vencer.
defect defeito.
defective defectivo, defeituoso.
defend (to) defender, proteger.
defender defensor.
defense defesa.
defer (to) diferir *(to put off)*.
defiance desafio.
definite definido, definitivo, preciso.
definition definição.
defy (to) desafiar.
degenerate (to) degenerar.
degree grau.
delay demora, atraso, tardança.
delay (to) demorar, atrasar, tardar.
delegate delegado.
delegate (to) delegar.
delegation delegação.
deliberate circunspeto (circunspecto). acautelado *(careful);* deliberado, considerado *(carefully thought out)* intencional *(intentional).*
deliberate (to) deliberar.
delicacy delicadeza *(finesse);* iguaria, guloseima *(food).*
delicate delicado.
delicious delicioso, saboroso.
delight delícia, encanto, alegria, prazer.
delight (to) encantar, deleitar.
delinquency delinqüência (delinquência).
deliver (to) entregar *(hand over);* livrar de *(deliver from);* pronunciar, proferir *(a speech).*
delivery entrega *(of goods);* distribuição *(mail).*
deluxe de luxo (x = sh).
demand demanda.
demand (to) demandar, exigir.

democracy democracia.
democrat democrata.
democratic democrático.
demon demônio.
demonstrate (to) demonstrar.
demonstration demonstração, exibição (x = z).
denial negativa, denegação.
denounce (to) denunciar.
dense denso.
density densidade.
dentist dentista.
deny (to) negar; recusar *(to refuse to grant).*
depart (to) partir.
department departamento.
depend (to) depender.
dependable de confiança, seguro.
dependence dependência.
dependent *adj.* dependente, pendente, sujeito; *n.* dependente.
deplore (to) deplorar, lamentar.
deposit depósito.
deposit (to) depositar.
depth profundidade.
descend (to) descer, baixar (x = sh).
descendant descendente.
descent descida.
describe (to) descrever.
description descrição.
desegregate (to) dessegregar.
desegregation dessegregação.
desert deserto.
desert (to) desertar, abandonar.
deserve (to) merecer.
desirable desejável.
desire desejo.
desire (to) desejar.
desirous desejoso, ansioso.
desk escrivaninha, secretária.
desolation desolação.
despair desespero.
despair (to) desesperar.
desperate desesperado.
despite apesar de, a despeito de.
dessert sobremesa.
destiny destino, fado.
destroy (to) destruir.
destruction destruição.
detach (to) separar, despegar *(to separate);* destacar *(soldiers).*
detail detalhe, pormenor.
detain (to) deter.
determination determinação.
determine (to) determinar.
detour desvio.
develop (to) desenvolver; revelar *(photography).*
development desenvolvimento; revelação *(photography).*
devil diabo.

devote (to) dedicar.
devotion devoção.
devour (to) devorar, engolir.
dew orvalho, rocio.
diabolical diabólico.
dial mostrador *(watch);* disco.
dial (to) discar.
dialogue diálogo.
diameter diâmetro.
diamond diamante; ouros *(cards).*
dictate (to) ditar.
dictator ditador.
dictionary dicionário.
die (to) morrer, falecer.
diet regime, dieta.
differ (to) diferençar *(to stand apart);* dissentir, não estar de acordo *(to disagree).*
difference diferença.
different diferente, distinto.
difficult difícil.
difficulty dificuldade.
diffuse (to) difundir.
dig (to) cavar, escavar.
digest (to) digerir.
digestion digestão.
dignity dignidade.
dim escuro, pouco claro.
dimple covinha.
dine (to) jantar.
dinner jantar.
diplomacy diplomacia.
diplomat diplomata.
diplomatic diplomático.
direct direito, em linha reta (recta).
   direct current corrente contínua.
direct (to) dirigir.
direction direção (direcção).
directly diretamente (directamente).
director diretor (director).
directory lista, catálogo.
   telephone directory lista telefônica (telefónica).
dirt sujeira, imundície (filth); solo *(soil).*
dirty sujo.
disadvantage desvantagem.
disagree (to) discordar, não concordar.
disagreeable desagradável.
disappear (to) desaparecer.
disappearance desaparição.
disappoint (to) desapontar.
disappointment desapontamento, decepção.
disapprove (to) desaprovar.
disarm (to) desarmar.
disaster desastre.
disastrous desastroso.
discipline disciplina.
discontent descontente.
discord discórdia, desacordo.

discourage (to) desanimar, dissuadir.
discouragement desânimo.
discover (to) descobrir.
discoverer descobridor.
discovery descoberta, descobrimento.
discreet discreto.
discretion discrição, prudência.
discuss (to) discutir, tratar de.
discussion discussão.
disease doença.
disgrace desonra, vergonha, desgraça.
disgust repugnância, asco.
disgust (to) repugnar, desagradar, enojar.
disgusting repugnante, nojento.
dish prato.
dishonest desonesto.
disk disco.
   floppy disk disquete.
   hard disk disco rígido.
   disk drive unidade de disco.
dismal lúgubre, triste, funesto *(morose);* sombre *(weather).*
dismiss (to) despedir.
disobey (to) desobedecer.
disorder desordem.
dispatch despacho, mensagem.
dispatch (to) despachar, enviar.
display exibição (x = z) *(show);* ostentação *(ostentation).*
display (to) exibir (x = z), mostrar *(to show);* ostentar *(to flaunt).*
displease (to) desagradar.
dispute disputa.
dispute (to) disputar, discutir.
dissolve (to) dissolver.
distance distância.
distinct distinto, claro.
distinction distinção.
distinguish (to) distinguir.
distinguished distinguido.
distort (to) falsear, corromper, torcer.
distract (to) distrair.
distraction distração (distracção).
distribute (to) distribuir, repartir.
distribution distribuição.
district distrito, bairro.
disturb (to) perturbar, incomodar.
disturbance perturbação, desordem.
dive mergulho *(into water);* picada *(a plane).*
dive (to) mergulhar *(into water);* dar picada, descer a pique *(aviation).*
divide (to) dividir.
dividend dividendo.
divine divino.
diving board trampolim.
division divisão.
divorce divórcio, separação.
divorce (to) divorciar, separar-se de.
dizzy tonto, aturdido.

do (to) fazer *(perform action);* praticar *(crafts, hobbies, etc.)*
   How do you do? Como vai? Como está?
   to do one's best fazer o possível.
   to do without passar sem.
   to have to do with ter que ver com.
   That will do. Chega. Basta. Isto serve.
   Do you believe it? Você crê? Você acredita? Você acha?
   to do your hair arrumar o cabelo.

dock doca, cais.
dock (to) atracar *(ship).*
doctor doutor, médico.
doctrine doutrina.
document documento.
dog cão, cachorro.
dogma dogma.
doll boneca.
dollar dólar.
dome cúpula.
domestic doméstico *(pertaining to the household);* do país, nacional *(trade, etc.).*
Dominican dominicano.
don dom.
door porta.
doorman portéiro.
double duplo.
doubt dúvida.
doubt (to) duvidar.
doubtful duvidoso.
doubtless sem dúvida, certo.
dough massa de farinha, pasta.
down abaixo (x = sh), para baixo (x = sh).
   to go down baixar (x = sh), descer.
   to come down baixar (x = sh), descer.
   down there lá em baixo.
downstairs em baixo (x = sh), para baixo (x = sh), no andar-térreo.
downtown na cidade, para a cidade, o centro.
dozen dúzia.
drain cäno de esgoto.
   His business went down the drain. A sua empresa foi pelo cano abaixo.
draft corrente de ar *(air);* saque, letra de câmbio *(bank);* sorteio *(military);* desenho, esboço rascunho *(sketch, outline).*
draft (to) rascunhar, esboçar *(to outline).*
drag (to) arrastar.
drama drama.
dramatist dramaturgo.
draw (to) debuxar (x = sh), desenhar *(to sketch);* tirar *(money, liquids, etc.);* correr *(curtains);* sacar *(bank draft);* ganhar, receber *(a salary);* formular, escrever *(to draw up).*
drawer gaveta.
drawing desenho.
dread (to) temer.
dreaded temido.

dreadful terrível, horrível.
dream sonho.
dreamer sonhador.
dress vestido, traje, roupa.
dress (to) vestir-se *(to get dressed);* limpar, medicar *(a wound).*
dresser cómoda (cômoda) *(furniture).*
drink bebida.
drink (to) beber, tomar.
drip (to) pingar, gotejar.
drive volta, passeio *(a ride in a car, etc.);* passeio, estrada *(a road);* campanha *(to raise money, etc.).*
drive (to) conduzir, dirigir *(a car, etc.);* cravar *(a nail)*
   to drive away expulsar, expelir.
driver motorista, chofer Ⓑ.
   driver's license carteira de chofer Ⓑ, carteira de motorista.
drop gota *(liquid);* queda, caída *(fall).*
   cough drops pastilhas para tosse.
drop (to) soltar, deixar (x = sh) cair *(to release, to let fall);* pingar, gotejar *(fall in drops);* abandonar, renunciar, desistir de, deixar *(to let go).*
   to drop in visitar, dar pula na cosa de.
   to drop a subject mudar de assunto.
drown (to) afogar, afogar-se.
drug droga (also **drugs**).
drugstore farmácia, drogaria.
drum tambor.
drunk bêbado, ébrio.
drunkard bêbado, ébrio.
drunkenness embriaguez, ebriedade.
dry seco.
dry (to) secar.
dry cleaning lavagem a seco.
dryness seca, secura, aridez.
duchess duquesa.
duck pato.
due devido; pagável *(payable);* suficiente, bastante *(enough).*
   due to circumstances . . . devido às circunstâncias . . .
duke duque.
dull opaco; apagada *(color);* pesado, aborrecido, grosseiro *(slow, boring).*
dumb estúpido *(stupid).*
durable durável.
during durante.
dusk crepúsculo, escuridão.
dust pó, poeira.
dust (to) tirar o pó, limpar do pó.
dusty poeirento, empoeirado, coberto de pó.
Dutch holandés.
duty dever.
dwelling morada, habitação, residência.
dye tintura, tinta.
dye (to) tingir, corar.

each cada.
  each one cada um.
  each other mutamente, um ao outro, uns aos outros.
eager ansioso.
eagle águia.
ear ouvido *(the organ of hearing, the internal ear);* orelha *(the external ear);* espiga *(of corn).*
early cedo.
earn (to) ganhar.
earnest sério *(serious);* ansioso *(eager).*
  in earnest a sério, de boa fé.
earth terra.
earthquake terremoto.
ease tranqüilidade (tranquilidade), alívio *(rest);* facilidade *(facility).*
  at ease a vontade.
ease (to) aliviar, mitigar.
easily facilmente.
east leste, este, oriente.
Easter Páscoa.
eastern oriental.
easy fácil.
eat (to) comer.
economic econômico (económico).
economics economia.
economy economia.
Ecuadorian equatoriano.
edge beira, margem *(of a stream, of collapse, etc.);* canto *(of a table);* gume, fio *(of a blade).*
edit (to) red; gir *(writing);* editar *(tape).*
edition edição.
editor redator (redactor), director (director).
educate (to) educar, ensinar.
education educação.
eel enguia.
effect efeito.
effect (to) efectuar (efectuar).
efficiency eficiência, eficácia.
effort esforço.
egg ovo.
eggplant berinjela.
eggshell casca de ovo.
egoism egoísmo.
eight oito.
eighteen dezoito.
eighteenth décimo oitavo.
eighth oitavo.
eightieth octagésimo.
eighty oitenta.
either ou; qualquer.
  one or the other um ou o outro.
  either of the two qualquer dos dois.
elastic elástico.

elbow cotovelo.
elderly idoso.
elect (to) eleger.
elected eleito.
election eleição.
elector eleitor.
electric elétrico (eléctrico).
electricity eletricidade (electricidade).
electronics eletrônica (electrónica).
elegance elegância.
elegant elegante.
element elemento.
elementary elementar.
elephant elefante.
elevation elevação, altura.
elevator elevador, ascensor.
eleven onze.
eleventh décimo-primeiro.
eligible elegível.
eliminate (to) eliminar.
eloquence eloqüência (eloquência).
eloquent eloqüente (eloquente).
else outro, mais, além disso.
  nothing else nada mais.
  something else outra coisa.
  or else senão, ou então.
  nobody else ninguém mais.
elsewhere em qualquer outra parte, noutra parte.
elude (to) eludir, evitar.
e-mail correio eletrônico.
e-mail (to) enviar por correio eletrônico.
embark (to) embarcar.
embarrass (to) embaraçar.
embarrassing embaraçante, embaraçoso.
embassy embaixada (x = sh).
embody (to) encarnar, incorporar.
embrace abraço.
embrace (to) abraçar.
embroidery bordado.
emerge (to) emergir, surgir.
emergency emergência, urgência.
emigrant emigrante.
emigrate (to) emigrar.
emigration emigração.
eminent eminente.
eminently eminentemente.
emotion emoção.
emphasis ênfase.
emphasize (to) enfatizar, acentuar.
emphatic enfático.
empire império.
employ (to) empregar.
employee empregado.
employer empregador.
employment emprego.
empty vazio.
empty (to) esvaziar, evacuar.
enclose (to) cercar *(ground, etc.);* incluir.

enclosed anexo (x = ks), incluso.
encourage (to) animar, estimular.
encouragement encorajamento, estímulo.
end fim; conclusão.
end (to) acabar, terminar.
endeavor esforço.
endeavor (to) esforçar-se.
endorse (to) endossar.
endow (to) dotar.
endure (to) suportar, resistir, agüentar (aguentar).
enemy inimigo.
energetic enérgico.
energy energia.
enforce (to) fazer cumprir, executar (x = z) *(a law);* forçar, compelir *(to compel).*
engage (to) empregar, contratar *(services).*
engagement compromisso, encontro *(appointment, date);* noivado *(for marriage);* contrato *(for employment).*
engine motor, máquina.
engineer engenheiro.
English inglês.
engrave (to) gravar.
enjoy (to) gozar, gostar de.
    to enjoy oneself divertir-se.
enjoyment gozo.
enlarge (to) aumentar, ampliar.
enlargement ampliação, aumento.
enlist (to) alistar, alistar-se.
enlistment alistamento.
enough bastante, suficiente.
enrich (to) enriquecer.
enroll (to) matricular, registrar *(school).*
entangle (to) enredar, complicar.
enter (to) entrar *(a house, etc.);* anotar, registrar *(in a register, etc.);* ingressar, matricular-se *(a school).*
entertain (to) divertir, entreter; considerar *(ideas).*
entertainment entretenimento, diversão.
enthusiasm entusiasmo.
enthusiastic entusiástico.
entire inteiro, todo.
entirely completamente, totalmente.
entrance entrada.
entrust (to) confiar.
entry entrada *(entrance);* registro, entrada *(books, records);* verbete *(dictionary).*
enumerate (to) enumerar.
envelope envelope.
enviable invejável.
envious invejoso.
environment ambiente.
envy inveja.
episode episódio.
epoch época, era.
equal igual.
equal (to) igualar.

equality igualdade.
equator equador.
equilibrium equilíbrio.
equip (to) equipar, guarnecer.
equipment equipamento.
equity eqüidade *(equidade).*
era era, época.
erase (to) apagar, riscar, extinguir.
eraser apagador, borracha.
err (to) errar, enganar-se.
errand recado, mandado, mensagem.
error erro.
escape fuga, escape.
escape (to) escapar, fugir.
escort escolta *(a body of soldiers, etc.);* acompanhante *(an individual).*
escort (to) escoltar, acompanhar.
especially especialmente, particularmente.
essay ensaio, composição.
essence essência.
essential essencial, indispensável.
establish (to) estabelecer.
establishment estabelecimento.
estate herança *(inheritance);* bens, propriedade *(properties, possessions);* fazenda *(a country estate).*
esteem estima, apreço.
esteem (to) estimar.
estimable estimável.
estimate cálculo; avaliação.
estimate (to) calcular, avaliar.
eternal eterno.
eternity eternidade.
euro euro.
European europeu.
evacuate (to) evacuar.
eve véspera.
even *adj.* par *(numbers);* plano, liso *(level); adv.* ainda, até, mesmo.
    to be even with estar quite com.
    even if mesmo que.
    even though embora.
    even so mesmo assim.
    even that até isso.
    not even nem sequer.
evening tarde, noite.
    Good evening! Boa tarde! Boa noite!
    yesterday evening ontem à noite.
event acontecimento.
    in the event that no caso de, caso que.
ever sempre.
    as ever como sempre.
    ever since desde então.
    not . . . ever nunca.
    nor . . . ever nem nunca.
every cada.
    every bit inteiramente.
    every day todos os dias.
    every other day um dia sim, um dia não.

every one cada um, todos eles.
every once in a while de vez em quando.
everybody todos, todo o mundo.
everyone todos, todo o mundo.
everything tudo.
everywhere em toda parte.
evidence evidência, testemunho *(court);* prova *(proof).*
evident evidente, claro.
evil *adj.* mau; *n.* mal.
evoke (to) evocar.
exact exato (exacto) (x = z), preciso.
exaggerate (to) exagerar (x = z).
exaggeration exageração (x = z), exagero (x = z).
exalt (to) exaltar (x = z).
examination exame (x = z).
examine (to) examinar (x = z).
example exemplo (x = z).
exasperate (to) exasperar (x = z), irritar.
excavate (to) escavar, cavar.
exceed (to) exceder (x = s), superar.
excel (to) sobressair, distinguir-se.
excellence excelência (x = s).
excellent excelente (x = s).
except exceto (excepto) (x = s), menos, a menos que, a não ser que.
except (to) excetuar (exceptuar) (x = s), excluir (x = sh).
exception exceção (excepção) (x = s).
exceptional excepcional (x = s).
exceptionally excepcionalmente (x = s).
excess excesso (x = s).
excessive excessivo (x = s).
exchange troca, câmbio.
   in exchange for em troca de.
exchange (to) trocar, cambiar.
excite (to) excitar (x = s).
excitement excitação (x = s), agitação.
exclaim (to) exclamar (x = sh).
exclamation exclamação (x = sh).
exclude (to) excluir (x = sh), eliminar.
exclusive exclusivo (x = sh).
excursion excursão (x = sh).
excuse escusa.
excuse (to) escusar, dispensar, desculpar.
execute executar (x = z).
executive executivo (x = z).
exempt (to) isentar, eximir (x = z).
exercise exercício (x = z).
exercise (to) exercer (x = z) *(power, etc.).* fazer exercícios (x = z), *(work out).*
exhaust (to) esgotar.
exhausted esgotado, exausto (x = z).
exhausting exaustivo (x = z).
exhibition exibição (x = z).
exile exílio (x = z), desterro, degredo.
exile (to) exilar (x = z), desterrar.
exist (to) existir (x = z).

existence existência (x = z).
existentialism existencialismo (x = z).
exit saída.
expand (to) expandir (x = sh), espalhar, desenvolver.
expansion expansão (x = sh).
expansive expansivo (x = sh).
expect (to) esperar, aguardar.
expectation expectativa (x = sh) Ⓑ, expectação, esperança.
expel (to) expelir (x = sh), expulsar (x = sh).
expense despesa.
   at one's expense à custa de.
expensive caro.
experience experiência (x = sh).
experience (to) experimentar (x = sh).
experiment experimento (x = sh).
experiment (to) experimentar (x = sh).
experimental experimental (x = sh).
expert perito.
expire (to) expirar (x = sh).
explain (to) explicar (x = sh).
explanation explicação (x = sh).
explanatory explicativo (x = sh).
explode (to) explodir (x = sh), estourar.
exploit façanha.
exploit (to) explorar (x = sh), utilizar.
exploration exploração (x = sh).
explore (to) explorar (x = sh).
explorer explorador (x = sh).
explosion explosão (x = sh), estouro (estoiro).
export exportação (x = sh).
export (to) exportar (x = sh).
expose (to) expor (x = sh).
express *adj.* expresso (x = sh); *n.* rapido.
express (to) expressar (x = sh), exprimir.
expression expressão (x = sh).
expulsion expulsão (x = sh).
extend (to) estender.
extension extensão (x = sh).
extensive extensivo (x = sh).
extent extensão (x = sh).
   to a certain extent até certo ponto.
exterior exterior (x = sh).
exterminate exterminar (x = sh).
external externo (x = sh).
extinguish (to) extinguir (x = sh).
extra extra (x = sh).
extract extrato (extracto) (x = sh).
extract (to) extrair (x = sh).
extraordinary extraordinário (x = sh).
extravagance extravagância (x = sh).
extravagant extravagante (x = sh).
extreme extremo (x = sh).
extremely extremamente (x = sh), sumamente.
extremity extremidade (x = sh).
eye olho.

eyebrow sobrancelha.
eyeglasses óculos.
eyelash pestana.
eyelid pálpebra.

F

fable fábula.
fabulous fabuloso.
face face, rosto, cara.
facsimile fac-símile, fax.
fact fato (facto).
   in fact de fato.
factory fábrica.
faculty faculdade *(ability);* corpo docente
   (teaching staff).
fade (to) murchar, enfraquecer.
fail (to) fracassar (in an undertaking); ser
   reprovado (in an examination); faltar (to
   fail to do something); malograr *(plans,*
   etc.).
   Don't fail to do it. Não deixe de fazê-lo.
failure fracasso; falha, falta (fault, defect);
   quebra (bankruptcy); avaria (motor).
faint (to) desmaiar, desfalecer.
fair *adj.* louro (loiro) *(hair);* branco
   (complexion); claro *(clear);* justo *(just);*
   regular *(moderate);* bom *(weather); n.*
   feira.
fairness justiça, eqüidade (equidade).
fairy tale conto de fadas.
faith fé.
faithful fiel, leal
fall queda, caída; outono (Outono)
   (autumn).
fall (to) cair.
false falso *(statement);* postiço *(teeth, etc.).*
fame fama.
familiar familiar.
familiarity familiaridade, confiança.
family família.
famine fome.
famous famoso, célebre.
fan leque *(hand);* ventilador *(electric);* fã,
   aficionado *(of sports, etc.).*
fantastic fantástico.
far longe.
   How far? A que distância?
   far away muito longe.
   so far até agora.
   As far as I'm concerned. Quanto a mim.
fare preço *(trains, buses, etc.);* torifa *(taxis).*
farewell despedida.
farmer fazendeiro, agricultor (lavrador).
farming lavoura, agricultura.
farther mais longe, mais distante.
fashion moda, uso.

fashionable à moda, da moda.
fast depressa, rapidamente.
fasten (to) prender, fixar (x = ks), segurar.
fat *adj.* gordo; *n.* gordura.
fate fado, destino.
father pai; padre *(priest).*
fatherhood paternidade.
father-in-law sogro.
fatherland pátria.
faucet torneira.
fault falta.
favor favor, serviço.
   in favor of a favor de.
favor (to) favorecer.
favorable favorável.
favorite favorito.
fax fax.
   to send a fax enviar un fax.
   to receive a fax receber um fax.
   fax machine máquina de fax.
fear medo, temor, receio.
fear (to) temer, recear.
fearless intrépido.
feast festa.
feather pena, pluma.
feature traço, característica.
February fevereiro (Fevereiro).
federal federal.
fee taxa, remuneração, honorários.
feeble débil, fraco; delicado.
feed (to) alimentar, dar de comer a.
feeding alimentação.
feel (to) sentir; tocar *(touch).*
feeling tato (tacto) *(tact);* sentimento
   (sentiment); sensibilidade *(sensitivity).*
fellow sujeito; companheiro.
   fellow student colega.
   fellow traveler companheiro de viagem.
female fêmea.
feminine feminino.
fence cerca.
ferment (to) fermentar.
fermentation fermentação.
ferry barco de passagem, barca.
fertile fértil, fecundo.
fertilize (to) fertilizar, fecundar.
fertilizer fertilizante, adubo.
fervent fervente.
fervor fervor.
festival festa, festival.
fever febre.
feverish febril, febricitante.
few poucos.
   a few alguns, algumas.
   quite a few muitos.
fewer menos.
fiber fibra.
fiberglass fibra de vidro.
fiction ficção.

field campo; campanha, campo de batalha *(military);* especialidade, ramo Ⓑ *(career, etc.).*
fierce feroz.
fiery veemente, impetuoso.
fifteen quinze.
fifteenth décimo quinto.
fifth quinto.
fiftieth qüinquagésimo.
fifty cinqüenta (cinquenta).
fig figo, figueira.
fight luta, batalha, peleja, briga.
fight (to) lutar, batalhar, pelejar, brigar.
　　to put up a fight dar luta.
figure figura.
file lima *(for nails, etc.,);* arquivo, fichário *(for papers, etc.).*
file (to) limar *(with an instrument);* arquivar *(papers, etc.);* arquivo *(computer).*
　　filing cabinet arquivo, fichário.
　　file card ficha.
Filipino filipino.
fill (to) encher.
　　to fill out a form preencher um formulário.
film filme *(residue);* fita *(recording medium);* película *(movie).*
filthy imundo sujo.
final final.
finally finalmente.
finance finança, finanças.
financial financeiro, financial.
find (to) achar, encontrar.
　　to find out saber.
fine *adj.* fino, bom, magnífico, excelente; *n.* multa, penalidade, pena.
finger dedo.
finish (to) terminar, acabar.
fire fogo; incêndio.
fire (to) disparar *(a gun);* demitir, despedir *(an employee).*
　　to set a fire incendiar.
firm *adj.* firme; *n.* firma, empresa *(business).*
firmness firmeza.
first *adj.* primeiro; *adv.* primeiramente.
　　first of all antes de tudo, antes de mais nada.
　　the first time a primeira vez.
　　in the first place em primeiro lugar.
　　first floor primeiro andar.
fish peixe (x = sh) *(in water);* pescado *(when caught).*
fish (to) pescar.
fisherman pescador.
fishing pesca.
fist punho.
fit *adj.* conveniente, apropriado, justo, digno.
　　to see fit achar conveniente.

fit (to) servir *(clothes);* caber *(object into a space).*
　　to fit something into a space encaixar (x = sh).
　　It fits you well. Une serve muito bem.
　　It fits badly. Lhe serve mal.
fitness saúde, boa forma.
fitting (be) ser apropriado.
five cinco.
five hundred quinhentos.
fix (to) fixar (x = ks) *(secure);* consertar *(repair).*
flag bandeira.
flagrant flagrante.
flame chama.
flannel flanela.
flash jato (jacto) de luz; relâmpago, clarão *(lightning).*
flashlight lanterna elétrica (eléctrica).
flat plano, liso; chato, insípido *(taste, etc.)*
flatten (to) nivelar, alisar *(smooth out);* achatar *(smash).*
flatter (to) lisonjear, adular.
flattery lisonja, adulação.
flavor sabor, gosto.
flavor (to) condimentar, sazonar.
flax linho.
flea pulga.
fleet frota, armada.
flesh carne; polpa *(fruit).*
flexibility flexibilidade (x = ks).
flexible flexível (x = ks).
flight vôo *(in the air);* fuga *(escape).*
flint pederneira; pedra *(of lighter).*
float (to) flutuar.
flood enchente, inundação, cheia.
flood (to) inundar.
floor chão, soalho *(of room);* andar *(of building).*
　　ground floor andar térreo, res-do-chão.
flour farinha.
flow (to) fluir, correr.
flower flor.
flowery florido.
fluid fluido.
fly mosca.
fly (to) voar.
foam espuma.
foam (to) espumar.
focus foco.
fog nevoeiro, névoa, cerração.
fold prega, dobra.
fold (to) preguear, dobrar.
foliage folhagem.
folks pais *(parents);* gente *(people).*
follow (to) seguir.
following seguinte.
food alimento, comida.
fool tolo.

fool (to) enganar.
foolish tolo, ridículo.
foolishness tolice.
foot pé.
   on foot a pé.
football futebol.
for para, por.
   This is for her. Isto é para ela.
   for example por exemplo (x = z).
   for the first time pela primeira vez.
   for the present por agora.
forbid (to) proibir.
forbidden proibido.
force força.
force (to) forçar, obrigar.
forced forçado, obrigado.
ford vau.
forecast prognóstico, previsão.
forecast (to) prognosticar, prever.
forehead fronte, testa.
foreign estrangeiro, alheio, estranho.
foreigner estrangeiro, forasteiro.
foresee prever.
forest floresta, selva.
forever para sempre.
forget (to) esquecer, esquecer-se.
forgetfulness esquecimento, olvido.
forgive (to) perdoar.
forgiveness perdão.
fork garfo.
form forma *(shape);* formulário *(paper).*
form (to) formar.
formal formal, cerimonioso, solene.
formality formalidade, cerimônia (cerimónia).
formation formação.
former anterior.
former (the) aquele, aquela, aqueles *(vs. latter);* antigo *(previous).*
formerly antigamente, em tempos passados.
formula fórmula.
forsake (to) deixar (x = sh), abandonar.
fortieth quadragésimo.
fortunate afortunado.
fortunately afortunadamente.
fortune fortuna, sorte.
fortune-teller adivinho; cartomante *(card reader),* quiromante *(palm reader).*
fortune-telling adivinhação, cartomancia, quiromancia.
forty quarenta.
forward adiante, avante.
forward (to) expedir, enviar, transmitir.
found (to) fundar.
foundation fundação.
founder fundador.
fountain fonte.
four quatro.
four hundred quatrocentos.
fourteen catorze.

fourteenth décimo quarto.
fourth quarto.
fowl ave, ave doméstica.
fragment fragmento.
fragrance fragrância, aroma.
fragrant fragrante, aromático.
frail débil, delicado, frágil.
frame quadro, moldura *(of a picture, etc.);* armação, estrutura *(structure).*
   frame of mind estado de espírito.
frame (to) enquadrar, emoldurar *(a picture, etc.)*
frank franco, sincero.
frankly francamente.
frankness franqueza.
free livre *(at liberty);* gratuito, grátis *(at no cost).*
free (to) livrar, libertar.
freedom liberdade.
freeze (to) gelar, congelar.
freight carga, frete.
French francês.
frequent freqüente (frequente).
frequent (to) freqüentar (frequentar).
frequently freqüentemente (frequentemente).
fresh fresco.
Friday sexta-feira, sexta.
friend amigo.
friendly amigável, amistoso, cordial.
friendship amizade.
frighten (to) assustar.
frightening assustador, alarmante.
frivolity frivolidade.
frivolous frívolo.
frog rã.
from de, desde.
   from a distance de longe.
   from memory de memória.
   from page one to page four desde a página um até a página quatro.
front adj. anterior, dianteiro, da frente; n. frente.
   in front of à frente de.
frown olhar carrancudo.
frown (to) franzir as sobrancelhas.
fruit fruta.
fry (to) fritar.
frying pan frigideira.
fuel combustível.
fugitive fugitivo.
fulfill (to) cumprir.
full cheio; lotado.
fully completamente.
fun divertimento, diversão.
   to have fun divertir-se.
   to make fun of fazer troça de, zombar de.
function função.
function (to) funcionar.
fundamental fundamental.

funds fundos.
funeral funeral, enterro.
funny engraçado, divertido, cômico (cómico).
fur pele.
furious furioso.
furnace fornalha, forno.
furnish (to) mobiliar (mobilar) *(a room, house, etc.);* fornecer *(supply, provide).*
furniture mobília, móveis.
furrow sulco.
further mais longe, mais distante; além, ademais.
furthermore além disso.
fury fúria.
future futuro.
   in the future no futuro.

G

gain ganho.
gain (to) ganhar.
   to gain weight engordar.
Galician galego.
gallant galante.
gamble (to) jogar.
game jogo; partida *(match);* caça *(hunting).*
   a game of chess uma partida de xadrez (x = sh).
garage garagem, garage Ⓑ.
garbage lixo (x = sh).
garden jardim.
gardener jardineiro.
gargle (to) gargarejar, fazer gargarejo.
garlic alho.
garment peça de roupa.
garter liga.
gas gás *(oxyen, natural gas, etc.);* gasolina *(gasoline).*
   gas station posto de gasolina.
   gas tank tanque de gasolina.
   gas pump bomba de gasolina.
gate portão, porta.
gather (to) reunir, juntar, recolher.
gay homossexual, gay.
gear engrenagem *(mechanics);* marcha *(car).*
gem gema.
gender gênero (género).
general *adj.* geral; *n.* general.
   in general em geral.
generality generalidade.
generalize (to) generalizar.
generally geralmente.
generation geração.
generosity generosidade.
generous generoso.
genius gênio (génio).
gentle suave; brando, meigo *(of a person).*

gentleman cavalheiro.
   gentlemen senhores; prezados senhores *(in a letter).*
gentleness brandura, meiguice; suavidade.
gently suavemente, meigamente.
genuine genuíno, autêntico.
geographic geográfico.
geography geografia.
geometric geométrico.
geometry geometria.
germ germe, micróbio.
German alemão.
gesture n. gesto.
get (to) conseguir, obter, adquirir, receber.
   to get ahead adiantar.
   to get away partir, ir-se embora, fugir.
   to get back voltar, regressar.
   to get home chegar em casa.
   to get old envelhecer.
   to get dark escurecer.
   to get better melhorar.
   to get worse piorar.
   to get in entrar.
   to get married casar-se.
   to get off descer, saltar, desmontar.
   to get on subir, montar.
   to get out sair; descer *(car).*
   to get up levantar-se; subir.
   Get over here! Chega aqui!
   Get out of here! Vá lá!
giant gigante.
gift presente, dá diva.
gifted talentoso, dotado.
gin gim Ⓑ, genebra.
ginger gengibre.
girl menina *(child),* moça *(preteen, teen).*
girlfriend noiva *(of man);* amiga *(of woman).*
girl scout escoteira.
give (to) dar.
   to give in ceder.
   to give up desistir.
   to give a gift presentear.
   He doesn't give a darn. Não lhe importa nado.
giver doador.
glad contente, alegre.
gladness alegria.
glance relance. olhadela.
glance (to) olhar de relance.
glass vidro; copo *(for drinking).*
   glasses óculos *(for eyes).*
glimpse n. olhadela.
glitter (to) brilhar, resplandecer.
globe globo.
gloomy sombrio; melancólico, triste *(sad).*
glorious glorioso.
glory glória.
glove luva.
glue cola, grude.

go (to) ir; percorrer *(to cover a distance)*.
   to go away ir-se embora, partir.
   to go back regressar, voltar.
   to go down descer, baixar.
   to go forward ir adiante, avançar.
   to go out sair; apagar-se *(a light, fire, etc.)*.
   to go up subir.
   to go with acompanhar.
   to go without passar sem.
goal meta, objetivo (objectivo), firm; gol *(sports)*.
   to reach one's goal conseguir o objetivo (objectivo).
God Deus.
godchild afilhado.
godfather padrinho.
godmother madrinha.
godparents padrinhos.
gold ouro.
golf golfe.
golf club taco de golfe.
good bom.
   good morning bom dia.
   good afternoon boa tarde.
   good night boa noite.
good-bye adeus.
goodness bondade.
   Goodness! Goodness gracious! Meu Deus!
   Goodness knows! Quem sabe!
goods mercadorias.
goodwill boa vontade.
goose ganso.
Gosh! Puxa! (x = sh)
gossip fofocas, mexerico (x = sh).
gossip (to) fofocar, mexericar (x = sh).
govern (to) governar.
government governo.
governor governador.
gown vestido, beca.
grab (to) agarrar, pegar em.
grace graça.
graceful gracioso.
gracious cortês, afável.
grade grau.
gradual gradual.
gradually gradualmente.
graduate diplomado, graduado.
graduate (to) formar-se, graduar-se.
grain grão.
grammar gramática.
grammatical gramatical.
grand grande, grandioso, magnífico.
grandchildren netos.
granddaughter neta.
grandfather avô.
grandmother avó.
grandparents avós.
grandson neto.

grant subvenção, subsídio.
grant (to) conceder, outorgar.
   to take for granted tomar por certo, achar natural.
   granting (granted) that admitido que.
grape uva.
grapefruit toronja.
grasp (to) agarrar, segurar; compreender, entender.
grass relva, grama.
grasshopper gafanhoto.
grateful agradecido.
gratefully agradecidamente.
gratitude gratidão, agradecimento.
grave *adj.* grave, sério; *n.* túmulo, sepultura.
gravity gravidade.
gravy molho.
gray cinza Ⓑ, cinzento.
grease graxa (x = sh).
great grande; *informal* ótimo, bacana.
   a great man um grande homem.
   a great many muitos.
   a great deal muito.
   Great! Estupendo! Magnífico! Ótimo!
greatness grandeza.
greedy avarento, ganancioso.
green verde.
greet (to) cumprimentar.
greeting cumprimento.
grief pesar, dor.
grieve (to) afligir-se, sofrer.
grill (to) grelhar.
grin sorriso largo.
grin (to) sorrir abertamente.
grind (to) moer.
groan gemido.
groan (to) gemer.
grocer merceeiro.
groceries comestíveis.
grocery store mercearia, armazém.
groom noivo.
groove ranhura.
grope (to) tatear (tactear).
ground *n.* terra, terreno; chão.
group grupo.
group (to) agrupar.
grow (to) crescer.
growth crescimento.
grudge rancor, ressentimento.
gruff brusco, áspero.
grumble (to) grunhir *(make a grumbling sound)*; resmungar *(complain)*.
guarantee garantia.
guarantee (to) garantir.
guard guarda.
guard (to) guardar, vigiar.
   to guard against guardar-se de.
Guatemalan guatemalteco.
guess conjetura (conjectura), suposição.

guess (to) adivinhar, conjeturar (conjecturar); supor *(suppose)*.
   to guess right acertar.
guest hóspede *(at an inn, etc.); convidado* (at a party); visita *(visitor)*.
guide guia.
guide (to) guiar, conduzir.
guidebook guia de viagem.
guilt culpa.
guilty culpado.
guitar violão.
gulf golfo.
gum chiclete *(for chewing); pl.* gengivas *(teeth)*.
gun arma de fogo, revólver, pistola, fuzil *(rifle)*.
guy tipo.
gymnasium ginásio.
gypsy cigano.

H

habit costume, hábito.
   to be in the habit of costumar, ter o hábito de.
habitual habitual, costumeiro.
habitually habitualmente.
hail granizo *(during storm);* viva, salve *(cheering, greeting)*.
hail (to) granizar *(in a thunderstorm);* saudar *(to greet)*.
hair cabelo.
   hairbrush escova para cabelo.
   haircut corte de cabelo.
   hair dye tintura para o cabelo.
   hairpin grampo para o cabelo.
   to do your hair arrumar cabelo.
hairdo penteado.
half meio; metade.
   half and half meio a meio; metades iguais.
   half past two duas (horas) e meia.
   half-hour meia hora.
half brother meio-irmão.
half sister meia-irmã.
halfway a meio caminho.
hall vestíbulo *(entrance, foyer);* salão *(assembly room);* corredor.
halt alto, parado (paragem).
halt (to) parar, deter, deter-se.
   Halt! Alto!
ham presunto.
hammer martelo.
hammer (to) martelar.
hand mão; ponteiro *(of a watch)*.
   by hand à mão, manual.
   in hand em mão.

   on hand à mão; em estoque *(in stock)*.
   on the one hand por um lado.
   on the other hand por outro lado.
hand (to) passar *(pass)*.
   to hand over entregar.
handbag bolsa.
handbook manual.
handful punhado.
handkerchief lenço.
handle asa *(of cup, etc.);* cabo *(of knife, etc.);* monivela *(of car door)*.
handmade feito à mão.
handshake aperto de mãos.
hang (to) pendurar.
hanger cabide *(clothes)*.
happen (to) acontecer.
happening acontecimento.
happiness felicidade.
happy feliz, contente.
harbor porto.
hard duro, difícil.
   hard luck má sorte.
   hard work trabalho difícil.
   to rain hard chover a cântaros.
harden (to) endurecer.
hardly apenas, mal, quase.
hardness dureza.
hardware ferragens *(tools);* hardware *(computer)*.
hardware store loja de ferragens.
hardy forte, robusto.
hare lebre.
harm mal, prejuízo, dano.
harmful prejudicial, nocivo, daninho.
harmless inofensivo.
harmonious harmonioso.
harmonize (to) harmonizar.
harmony harmonia.
harness arreios.
harsh severo, áspero.
harshness aspereza.
harvest colheita.
haste pressa.
   in haste à pressa, às pressas.
hasten (to) apressar-se, acelerar.
hastily apressadamente.
hasty apressado.
hat chapéu.
hatch (to) incubar, chocar.
hate ódio.
hate (to) odiar, detestar.
hateful odioso.
hatred ódio.
haughty soberbo, arrogante.
Havana Havana.
have (to) ter, possuir *(to possess);* ter, haver *(auxiliary)*.
   to have in mind ter em mente.
   to have to ter que, ter de.

to have a mind to estar disposto a.
hay feno.
he ele.
head cabeça; chefe *(chief)*.
head (to) encabeçar.
    to head for dirigir-se a.
    heading for rumo a.
headache dor de cabeça.
headline título, cabeçalho, manchete Ⓑ.
headquarters sede *(business)*; quartel-general *(military)*.
heal (to) curar; recobrar a saúde.
health saúde.
    to be in good health estar bem de saúde.
healthful saudável.
healthy são (sã *f.*), sadio *(in good health)*; saudável *(healthful)*.
heap montão, pilha.
heap (to) acumular, amontoar.
hear (to) ouvir.
    to hear from ter notícias de.
heart coração.
    by heart de cor.
    at heart no fundo.
    to take to heart tomar a sério.
heart attack ataque cardíaco.
hearth lareira, lar.
hearty cordial *(warm)*, entusiástico.
heat calor.
heat (to) aquecer.
heater aquecedor.
heating aquecimento.
heaven céu.
    Heavens! Céus!
heavy pesado.
hedge cerca viva, sebe.
heel calcanhar *(of foot)*; salto *(of shoe)*.
height altura.
heir herdeiro.
helicopter helicóptero.
hell inferno.
Hello! Alô! Olá!
help ajuda, auxílio (x = s).
help (to) ajudar.
    to help oneself to servir-se.
helper ajudante.
helpful útil, proveitoso *(thing)*; prestativo *(person)*.
hemisphere hemisfério.
hen galinha.
her a ela, seu, sua, lhe.
herb erva.
here aqui; cá.
    Here it is. Aqui está.
    Come here. Venha cá.
    around here por aqui.
    Here I go! Aí vou eu!
    near here perto daqui.
hereafter daqui em diante.

herein incluso, anexo (x = ks).
hero herói.
heroic heróico.
heroine heroína.
heroism heroísmo.
herring arenque.
hers seu, sua, dela; o seu, a sua, os seus, as suas.
herself ela mesma, si mesma; se, si.
    by herself sozinha.
    she herself ela mesma.
hesitant hesitante, indeciso.
hesitate (to) hesitar, vacilar.
hesitation hesitação, indecisão.
Hi! Oi!
    to say hi to cumprimentar.
hidden escondido, oculto.
hide (to) esconder, esconder-se, ocultar.
hideous horrível, horrendo.
high alto, elevado; caro *(price)*.
    It is two meters high. Tem dois metros de altura.
higher mais alto; superior.
highway rodovia, estrada.
hill colina, morro; ladeira *(slope)*.
him o, ele, lhe.
himself ele mesmo; si mesmo; se, si.
hinder (to) impedir, estorvar.
hindrance impedimento, estorvo, obstáculo.
hinge dobradiça, gonzo.
hint insinuação, alusão, sugestão.
hint (to) insinuar.
    Give me a hint. Me dá uma pista.
    to take the hint compreender.
hip quadril, anca.
hire (to) contratar.
his seu, sua, seus, suas, o seu, a sua, os seus, as suas, dele.
Hispanic hispânico.
hiss (to) silvar *(wind, etc.)*; chiar *(steam)*.
historian historiador.
historic histórico.
history história.
hit golpe, pancada *(blow)*; êxito *(song, etc.)*.
hit (to) bater em.
hive colméia.
hoarse rouco.
hoe enxada (x = sh).
hog porco.
hold (to) ter *(in one's hands, arms, etc.)*; agarrar, segurar *(to grasp, hold on to)*; caber, conter *(to contain)*; ter, ocupar *(a job, etc.)*.
    to hold a meeting realizar uma reunião.
    to hold one's own manter-se.
    to be on hold ficar pendurado.
    to hold hands dar mãos.
hole buraco.
holiday feriado.

holy santo.
   Holy cow! Credo!
homage homenagem.
home casa, lar, residência.
   at home em casa.
homely feio.
homemade caseiro, feito em casa.
homosexual homossexual; bicha *(colloquial)*.
Honduran hondurenho.
honest honesto; sincero, franco.
honesty honestidade.
honey mel.
honeymoon lua-de-mel.
honk (to) buzinar *(car horn)*.
honor honra.
honor (to) honrar.
honorable honroso, honrado.
hoof casco, pata.
hook gancho; anzol *(for fishing)*.
hope esperança.
hope (to) esperar.
hopeful esperançoso.
hopeless desesperado *(depressed);* incorrigível *(irremediable)*.
horizon horizonte.
horizontal horizontal.
horn chifre *(of animals);* buzina *(of car);* corneta, trompa *(music)*.
horrible horrível.
horror horror.
horse cavalo.
   on horseback a cavalo.
hosiery meias.
hospitable hospitaleiro.
hospital hospital.
hospitality hospitalidade.
host hospedeiro *(in hotel, etc.)* anfitrião *(of party)*.
hostess hospedeira; anfitriã.
hot quente.
hot dog cachorro-quente.
hotel hotel.
hour hora.
house casa.
household família, casa.
housekeeper governanta.
housemaid empregada.
housewife dona de casa.
how como; que; quanto.
   How are you? Como vai? Como está?
   How many? Quantos?
   How much? Quanto?
   How far? A que distância?
   How long? Quanto tempo?
   How pretty! Que linda!
   How old is she? Quantos anos ela tem?
   How about a beer? Que tal uma cerveja?
however porém, todavia.
hug abraço.

huge imenso, enorme.
human humano.
   human race raça humana.
humane humano, humano, humanitário.
humanity humanidade.
humble humilde.
humiliate (to) humilhar.
humiliation humilhação.
humility humildade.
humor humor.
humorous cômico (cómico), engraçado.
hundred cem.
   two hundred duzentos.
hundredth centésimo.
hunger fome.
hungry (be) estar com fome, ter fome.
hunt (to) caçar.
hunter caçador.
hunting caça.
hurry pressa.
   to be in a hurry estar com pressa, ter pressa.
hurt (to) machucar, ferir *(physically);* ofender *(one's feelings)*.
husband marido, esposo.
hydrant hidrante.
hygiene higiene.
hymn hino.
hyperbole hipérbole.
hypertension hipertensão.
hyphen hífen.
hypnotism hipnotismo.
hypnotize (to) hipnotizar.
hypocrisy hipocrisia.
hypocrite hipócrita.
hysteria histeria.
hysterical histérico.

I

I eu.
   I'm the one eu é.
Iberian ibero, ibérico.
ice gelo.
ice cream sorvete.
ice skate (to) patinar (no gelo).
idea idéia (ideia).
ideal ideal.
idealism idealismo.
identical idêntico.
identification identificação.
identify (to) identificar.
identity identidade.
idiocy idiotismo.
idiot idiota, imbecil.
idle ocioso.
idleness ociosidade, ócio.

if se.
  if not senão.
  even if ainda que, mesmo que.
  If I may. Com licença.
ignorance ignorância.
ignorant ignorante.
ignore (to) não saber; não fazer caso de;
  ignorar.
ill doente *(sick);* mau *(bad);* mal *(badly).*
  ill will má vontade.
illegal ilegal.
illegible ilegível.
illiteracy analfabetismo.
illiterate analfabeto.
illness doença.
illogical ilógico, absurdo.
illuminate (to) iluminar, alumiar.
illumination iluminação.
illusion ilusão.
illustrate (to) ilustrar.
illustration ilustração, gravura.
image imagem.
imagery imaginação, fantasia.
imaginary imaginário.
imagination imaginação.
imaginative imaginativo.
imagine (to) imaginar, supor.
  Just imagine! Imagine!
imitate (to) imitar.
imitation imitação.
immediate imediato.
immediately imediatamente.
immense imenso.
immigrant imigrante.
immigrate (to) imigrar.
immigration imigração.
imminent iminente.
immoderate imoderado, excessivo.
immoral imoral.
immorality imortalidade.
immortal imortal.
immortality imoralidade.
impartial imparcial.
impatience impaciência.
impatient impaciente.
imperative imperativo.
imperceptible imperceptível.
imperfect imperfeito.
impersonal impessoal.
impertinence impertinência.
impertinent impertinente.
impetuous impetuoso, impulsivo.
implement instrumento, utensílio, ferramenta.
implied implícito.
imply (to) implicar, significar.
impolite descortês.
import (to) importar.
importance importância.
important importante.

importation importação.
importer importador.
impose (to) impor *(rules, etc.).* abusar de
  (impose on).
imposing imponente.
impossibility impossibilidade.
impossible impossível.
impress (to) impressionar.
impression impressão.
  to have the impression ter a impressão.
impressive impressionante.
imprison (to) encarcerar.
improbable improvável.
improper impróprio.
improve (to) melhorar; progredir *(pupils, etc.).*
  melhorar-se, restabelecer-se *(health).*
improvement melhora, melhoria, progresso.
improvise (to) improvisar.
imprudence imprudência.
imprudent imprudente.
impure impuro.
in em.
  in fact de fato (de facto).
  in the afternoon de tarde, pela tarde.
  in a week daqui a uma semana, daqui a
    oito dias.
  to be in (the office) estar em casa, estar no
    escritório.
  in general em geral.
  in part em parte.
  in reality na verdade.
  in spite of apesar de.
  in vain em vão.
  in writing por escrito.
inability inabilidade, inaptidão, incapacidade.
inaccessible inacessível.
inaccuracy inexatidão (inexactidão) (x = z).
inaccurate inexato (inexacto) (x = z),
  incorreto (incorrecto).
inactive inativo (inactivo).
inadequate inadequado.
inaugurate (to) inaugurar.
incapability incapacidade.
incapable incapaz.
incapacity incapacidade.
inch polegada.
incident incidente.
inclination inclinação.
include (to) incluir, abranger, compreender.
inclusive inclusivo.
incoherent incoerente.
income renda.
  income tax imposto de renda.
incomparable incomparável.
incompatible incompatível.
incomprehensible incompreensível.
inconsistent inconsistente.
inconvenience inconveniência.
inconvenience (to) incomodar.

inconvenient inconveniente.
incorrect incorreto (incorrecto).
increase aumento.
increase (to) aumentar.
incredible incrível.
incurable incurável.
indebted em dívida; reconhecido, obrigado
   (for kindness shown).
indecent indecente, imoral.
indeed realmente, na verdade, de fato (facto),
   certamente, naturalmente.
indefinite indefinido.
independence independência.
independent independente; auto-suficiente.
indescribable indescritível.
index índice, índex.
index finger dedo indicador, índice, índex.
indicate (to) indicar.
indifference indiferença.
indifferent indiferente.
indigestion indigestão.
indignant indignado, furioso.
indignation indignação, raiva.
indirect indireto (indirecto).
indiscreet indiscreto, imprudente.
indispensable indispensável.
indisputable indisputável.
indistinct indistinto.
individual *adj.* individual, particular; *n.*
   indivíduo.
individuality individualidade.
individually individualmente.
indivisible indivisível.
indolence indolência, preguiça.
indolent indolente, preguiçoso.
indoors dentro de casa, em casa.
indulge (to) comprazer *(a person);* entregar-se
   a *(to indulge in).*
indulgence indulgência, tolerância.
indulgent indulgente.
industrial industrial.
industrious industrioso, trabalhador, diligente.
industry indústria.
inequality desigualdade.
inevitable inevitável.
inexcusable indesculpável, imperdoável.
inexhaustible inesgotável.
inexpensive barato.
inexperience inexperiência.
inexperienced inexperiente, sem experiência.
infallible infalível.
infant bebê (bebé).
infantry infantaria.
infection infecção.
infectious infeccioso, contagioso.
infer (to) inferir, deduzir, concluir.
inference inferência, dedução.
inferior inferior.
inferiority inferioridade.

infinite infinito.
infinitive infinitivo.
infinity infinidade, infinito.
influence influência.
influence (to) influenciar, influir.
influential influente.
influenza gripe, influenza.
information informação.
   information desk guichê (guichet) de
     informações.
infrequent infreqüente (infrequente), raro.
infrequently infreqüentemente
   (infrequentemente), raramente.
ingenious engenhoso.
ingenuity engenho.
ingratitude ingratidão.
inhabit (to) habitar, ocupar, morar.
inhabitant habitante.
inherit (to) herdar.
inheritance herança.
initial inicial.
initiative iniciativa.
injure (to) ferir, machucar *(physically);*
   prejudicar *(reputation, etc.).*
injurious prejudicial.
injury ferimento *(physical);* dano *(damage).*
injustice injustiça.
ink tinta.
inkwell tinteiro.
inland interior.
inn hospedaria, estalagem, pousada.
innate inato.
inner interno, interior.
innkeeper hospedeiro, estalajadeiro.
innocence inocência.
innocent inocente.
insane insano, demente.
insanity insanidade; demência.
inscribe (to) inscrever.
inscription inscrição, dedicatória.
insect inseto (insecto).
insecticide inseticida (insecticida).
insecure inseguro.
insecurity insegurança.
insensible insensível.
inseparable inseparável.
insert (to) inserir, introduzir.
insertion inserção.
inside dentro; interior.
   on the inside por dentro.
   toward the inside para dentro.
   inside out às avessas.
insignificance insignificância.
insignificant insignificante, sem importância.
insincere insincero, não sincero.
insincerity insinceridade, falta de sinceridade.
insist (to) insistir.
insistence insistência.
insolence insolência.

insolent insolente.
inspect (to) inspecionar (inspeccionar), examinar (x = z).
inspection inspeção (inspecção).
inspector inspetor (inspector).
inspiration inspiração.
install (to) instalar.
installation instalação.
instance instância; exemplo (x = z); caso.
    for instance por exemplo.
    in this instance neste caso.
instead of em lugar de, em vez de.
instinct instinto.
institute instituto.
institute (to) instituir, estabelecer.
institution instituição.
instruct (to) instruir, ensinar.
instruction instrução, ensino.
instructive instrutivo.
instructor instrutor.
instrument instrumento.
insufficiency insuficiência, deficiência.
insufficient insuficiente, deficiente.
insult insulto.
insult (to) insultar, ofender.
insulting insultante, ofensivo.
insuperable insuperável.
insurance seguro.
intact intato (intacto).
integral integral.
intellectual inteletual (intelectual).
intelligence inteligência.
intelligent inteligente.
intend (to) intentar, tencionar.
    to be intended for ter por finalidade.
intense intenso.
intensity intensidade.
intention intenção, propósito.
intentional intencional.
intentionally intencionalmente, de propósito.
interest interesse; juros *(bank)*.
interest (to) interessar.
interesting interessante.
interior interior, interno.
intermission intervalo.
internal interno.
international internacional.
interpose (to) interpor.
interpret (to) interpretar.
interpretation interpretação.
interpreter intérprete.
interrupt (to) interromper.
interruption interrupção.
intersection cruzamento *(roads);* intersecção *(lines, etc.).*
interval intervalo.
intervention intervenção.
interview entrevista.
interview (to) entrevistar.

intestine intestino.
intimacy intimidade.
intimate íntimo.
intimidate (to) intimidar.
into em, dentro, para dentro.
intonation entonação.
intoxicate (to) embriagar.
intoxicating inebriante.
intoxication embriaguez.
intricate intricado, complicado, complexo (x = ks).
intrigue intriga, trama.
intrinsic intrínseco.
introduce (to) introduzir *(a subject, etc.);* apresentar *(a person).*
introduction introdução; apresentação *(people).*
intruder intruso.
intuition intuição.
invade (to) invadir.
invalid *adj.* inválido *(person);* inválido, nulo *(void); n.* inválido.
invasion invasão.
invent (to) inventar.
invention invenção.
inventor inventor.
invert (to) inverter *(upside down, backwards);* virar *(inside out).*
invest (to) investir.
investigate (to) investigar.
investigation investigação; inquérito *(inquest).*
investment investimento.
investor investidor.
invisible invisível.
invitation convite.
invite (to) convidar.
invoice fatura (factura).
involuntary involuntário.
involve (to) implicar, comprometer, envolver.
iodine iodo.
iris íris.
iron ferro *(metal, and for ironing).*
iron (to) passar a ferro *(clothes).*
ironic irônico (irónico).
ironing roupa a ser passada.
irony ironia.
irregular irregular.
irresolute irresoluto, indeciso.
irresponsible irresponsável.
irrigate (to) irrigar.
irrigation irrigação.
irritable irritável.
irritate (to) irritar.
irritation irritação.
island ilha.
isolation isolamento.
issue questão, assunto, tema *(subject);* número *(magazine).*

issue (to) publicar, lançar *(report, etc.);* distribuir *(equipment).*

it ele, ela, o, a, lhe; isto, este, esta. ["It" is not translated in phrases like "it's raining" (chove), "it's late" (é tarde), "it's two o'clock" (são duas horas), etc.].

   I have it. Tenho. Tenho-o *(m.).*

   I have it. Tenho. Tenho-a *(f.).*

   I said it. Eu o disse. Disse-o.

   Isn't it? Não é verdade? Não é?

   That's it. Isso é. E desta *(It's over). (indicating an object).*

Italian italiano.

itinerary itinerário.

its seu, sua, seus, suas, dele, dela, deles, delas.

itself si mesmo, si, si próprio, se.

   by itself por si, por si mesmo.

   in itself em si.

ivory marfim.

ivy hera.

J

jack macaco *(tool);* valete *(cards).*

jacket paletó, jaqueta; sobrecapa, capa (book).

jail cadeia, cárcere; xadrez (x = sh) ⑧.

jam geléia (geleia); aperto (a fix); engarrafamento *(traffic).*

janitor zelador, porteiro.

January janeiro (Janeiro).

Japanese japonês.

jar jarro *(large);* pote *(small).*

jaw mandíbula.

jazz jazz.

jealous ciumento.

jealousy ciúme.

jelly geléia (geleia); gelatina.

jerk (to) arrancar, sacudir.

Jesuit jesuíta.

jet jato (jacto).

   jet plane avião a jato.

Jew judeu *(male);* judia *(female).*

jewel jóia.

jewelry jóias.

jewelry store joalheria.

Jewish judeu, judaico.

job emprego *(position);* trabalho *(duties at work);* tarefa *(task).*

John Doe Fulano de Tal.

join (to) unir, juntar *(to put together);* unir-se, associar-se *(to unite);* affiliar-se a, incorporar-se a *(an organization).*

joint encaixe (x = sh) *(woodworking);* articulacão *(body).*

joke piada, pilhéria, brincadeira.

   to play a joke on pregar peça em.

   to crack jokes lançar graças.

joke (to) gracejar, brincar.

jolly *adj.* alegre, jovial, convival.

jostle (to) acotovelar, empurrar.

journal diário *(diary);* jornal.

journalist jornalista.

journalistic jornalístico.

journey viagem.

jovial jovial.

joy alegria.

joyful alegre.

judge juiz.

judge (to) julgar.

judgment julgamento.

judicial judicial, judiciário.

juice suco, sumo.

juicy suculento; picante *(gossip, etc.).*

July julho (Julho).

jump salto, pulo.

jump (to) saltar, pular.

   Go jump in a lake! Vai ver se chove!

June junho (Junho).

junior *adj.* júnior, mais jovem, mais novo, mais moço; subordinado.

   junior partner sócio mais novo.

   Paul Fountain Jr. Paulo Fontes Júnior.

juror jurado.

jury júri.

just *adj.* justo; *adv.* justamente, exatamente (exactamente) (x = z), somente.

   just as I came in no momento em que eu entrava.

   just a moment um momento.

   just now agora mesmo.

   I just wanted to eu somente queria.

   to have just acabar de.

   I have just come. Acabo de chegar.

   Just as you please. Como você quiser.

   He's just a loser. Ele é apenas um falhado.

justice justiça.

justifiable justificável.

justification justificação.

justify (to) justificar.

juvenile *adj.* juvenil, menor de idade.

K

keep (to) guardar, manter, reter.

   to keep away manter afastado.

   to keep for oneself reter, deter.

   to keep from impedir *(hinder);* abster-se *(refrain).*

   to keep quiet calar-se, ficar quieto.

   to keep in mind ter em mente.

   to keep one's word cumprir (a) sua promessa.

   to keep a secret guardar um segredo.

   to keep in touch manter-se em contacto.

keep to the right conserve (à) sua direita.
kernel semente, grão.
kerosene querosene.
kettle bule *(for tea);* caldeirão, chaleira *(cauldron).*
key chave *(for doors, etc.);* tecla *(piano, computer, etc.).*
keyboard teclado.
kick pontapé, chute.
kick (to) dar pontapé, chutar.
kidney rim.
kill (to) matar.
kilo quilo *(kilogram).*
kilogram quilograma.
kilometer quilômetro (quilómetro).
kin família, parentes.
kind *adj.* bom, amável, bondoso; *n.* classe, espécie, gênero (género).
kindergarten jardim de infância.
kind-hearted bondoso, de bom coração.
kindly amavelmente, cordialmente.
   Kindly do it. Tenha a bondade de fazê-lo.
kindness bondade, amabilidade.
king rei.
kiss beijo.
kiss (to) beijar.
kitchen cozinha.
kite papagaio, pipa.
kitten gatinho.
knee joelho.
kneel (to) ajoelhar(-se).
knife faca.
knit (to) tricotar.
knock golpe, pancada; batida *(on door).*
knock (to) dar pancadas, bater *(on door).*
knot nó.
know (to) saber; conhecer *(be acquainted with).*
knowledge conhecimento.
knuckle nó dos dedos.

L

label rótulo, etiqueta.
labor trabalho, labor.
laboratory laboratório.
laborer trabalhador, operário.
lace *n.* renda.
lack falta, carência, deficiência.
lack (to) carecer de, faltar.
ladder escada de mão.
lady senhora.
   Ladies and gentlemen. Senhoras e senhores. Meus senhores e minhas senhoras.
lake lago.
lamb cordeiro.

lame coxo (x = sh), manco, aleijado.
lame (be) coxear (x = sh), manear.
lameness coxeadura (x = sh).
lament lamento, queixa.
lament (to) lamentar, lamentar, se de.
lamp lâmpada.
land terra *(ground);* terreno *(terrain);* país, terra *(country).*
land (to) desembarcar *(ship);* aterrar *(plane).*
landing desembarque *(from a ship);* aterrissagem *(of an airplane);* patamar *(a staircase).*
landlady proprietária.
landlord proprietário.
landscape paisagem.
language língua, idioma.
languid lânguido.
languish (to) languir.
languor langor, languidez.
lantern lanterna.
lap colo *(body);* volta *(around track).*
laptop computer computador portátil.
lard toucinho, banha.
large grande.
   at large em liberdade.
large-scale em grande escala.
lark cotovia.
larynx laringe.
laser printer impresora a laser.
last *adj.* último, derradeiro, passado; *adv.* por fim, finalmente, por último.
   at last finalmente.
   last night ontem à noite.
   last week a semana passada.
   last year o ano passado.
   the last time I saw her ... A última vez que a vi ...
last (to) durar.
lasting duradouro, durável.
latch trinco.
late *adj.* tarde.
   to be late chegar tarde.
   late in the year no fim do ano.
lately ultimamente, recentemente, há pouco tempo.
lateness atraso, demora.
later mais tarde.
latest último.
   the latest style a última moda.
   at the latest no mais tardar.
lather espuma.
Latin *adj.* latino; *n.* latim.
Latin American latino-americano.
laudable louvável.
laugh riso, risada; gargalhada *(guffaw).*
laugh (to) rir, rir-se.
   to make someone laugh fazer rir.
   to laugh at rir de.
laughable risível, ridículo.

laughter riso, risada.
launder (to) lavar e passar.
laundry lavanderia *(laundry shop)*; roupa para lavar *(clothes to be washed)*; roupa lavada *(laundered clothes)*.
lavish pródigo, generoso *(spending)*; luxuoso *(party, etc.)*.
law lei; jurisprudência *(legal science)*; direito *(body of laws)*; regra *(rule)*.
　　law school faculdade de direito.
　　international law direito internacional.
lawful legal, lícito.
lawn gramado.
lawyer avogado.
laxative laxativo (x = ch).
lay (to) pôr.
　　to lay aside pôr de lado.
　　to lay hold of agarrar.
　　to lay off despedir.
laziness preguiça.
lazy preguiçoso.
lead *(metal)* chumbo.
lead (to) conduzir, guiar.
　　to lead to levar a.
　　to lead the way mostrar o caminho.
leader líder Ⓑ, condutor, chefe; guia *(guide)*; diretor *(director)*.
leadership liderança, direção (direcção), chefia, comando.
leading principal, primeiro.
　　leading article artigo de fundo.
　　leading man galã, ator principal.
leaf folha.
lean (to) inclinar-se.
　　to lean back encostar-se.
　　to lean out or over debruçar-se.
leaning inclinação, propensão, tendência.
leap salto, pulo.
leap (to) saltar, pular.
　　by leaps and bounds em flecha.
learn (to) aprender *(to acquire knowledge, skill)*; tomar conhecimento de, saber de *(to find out about)*.
learned erudito, douto.
learning erudição, saber.
lease arrendamento.
lease (to) arrendar, alugar.
least mínimo, o mínimo, menor, menos.
　　at least pelo menos, ao menos.
　　not in the least de maneira alguma, de modo algum.
　　the least possible o menos possível.
leather couro.
leave (to) deixar.
　　to leave a message deixar um recado.
lecture *n.* conferência, discurso, palestra *(a speech)*; repreensão *(reprimand)*.
lecturer conferencista.
left *adj.* esquerdo; *n.* esquerda.

left hand mão esquerda.
　　to the left à esquerda.
left-handed canhoto.
　　There are two left. Ficam (restam) dois.
leg perna *(person)*; pata *(table)*.
legal legal, lícito.
legend lenda *(story)*; legenda *(caption)*.
legible legível.
legislation legislação.
legislator legislador.
legislature legislatura.
leisure lazer, folga, ócio.
lemon limão.
lemonade limonada.
lend (to) emprestar, dar emprestado.
　　to lend an ear prestar atenção.
　　to lend a hand ajudar.
length comprimento.
　　at length finalmente; detalhadamente *(extensively)*.
less menos.
　　more or less mais ou menos.
　　less and less cada vez menos.
lessen (to) reduzir, diminuir.
lesson lição.
let (to) deixar (x = sh), permitir.
　　Let's go. Vamos.
　　Let's see. Vejamos. Vamos ver.
　　Let them go. Que se vão.
　　to let someone alone deixar alguém em paz.
　　to let go soltar.
　　to let in deixar entrar.
　　to let know avisar.
letter carta; letra *(of the alphabet)*.
lettuce alface.
level *adj.* plano, raso, nivelado; *n.* nível.
level off (to) nivelar.
liable sujeito, exposto *(exposed to)*; responsável por *(accountable)*; capaz de *(likely)*.
liar mentiroso.
liberal liberal.
liberty liberdade.
library biblioteca.
license licença, autorização.
lick (to) lamber.
lid tampa.
lie mentira.
lie (to) mentir *(tell a falsehood)*; deitar-se *(to lie down)*; jazer *(dead, in grave)*.
lieutenant tenente.
life vida.
　　life preserver salva-vidas.
　　lifeboat barco salva-vidas.
　　life insurance seguro de vida.
lifetime tempo de vida.
lift (to) levantar, alçar.
light *n.* luz, lume, claridade, iluminação; *adj.* leve, ligeiro *(in weight)*; claro *(color)*.

light-hearted despreocupado, alegre.
light (to) acender *(a cigarette);* iluminar *(to illuminate).*
lightbulb lâmpada, lâmpada elétrica (eléctrica).
lighten (to) aliviar, mitigar.
lighthouse farol.
lighting iluminação.
lightness leveza.
lightning relâmpago, raio.
like parecido, semelhante *(similar).*
  to be like ser semelhante.
  I've never seen anything like this. Nunca vi coisa destas.
like (to) querer, gostar de.
  I like him very much. Gosto muito dele.
  As you like. Como você quiser.
  Do you like it? Você gosta?
  I like it. Gosto.
  I don't like it. Não gosto.
  She looks like her mother. Ela se parece com a mãe.
likely provável.
likeness semelhança.
likewise igualmente, do mesmo modo.
liking afeição, simpatia, gosto.
limb membro.
lime cal.
limit limite.
limit (to) limitar.
limp (to) coxear (x = sh), mancar.
line linha.
line (to) forrar *(coat, etc.);* linear *(streets).*
to line up (to) alinhar, alinhar-se.
linen linho.
lining forro.
link elo.
link (to) unir, ligar.
lip lábio.
lipstick batom.
liquid líquido.
liquor bebida alcoólica, licor.
lisp cicio.
list lista.
listen (to) escutar.
literal literal, ao pé da letra.
literally literalmente, ao pé da letra.
literary literário.
literature literature.
little pequeno *(size);* pouco *(amount).*
  a little um pouco.
  very little muito pouco.
  the little ones os pequenos, as crianças.
  little by little pouco a pouco.
live *adj.* vivo; ao vivo *(broadcast).*
live (to) viver; morar *(to reside).*
lively vivo, animado.
liver fígado.
living *adj.* vivo.

to make a living ganhar a vida.
living room sala de estar.
load carga.
load (to) carregar.
loaf pão.
loan empréstimo.
loan (to) emprestar.
lobby vestíbulo.
lobster lagosta.
local local.
locate (to) localizar, situar *(find);* colocar *(situate).*
location local, sítio *(place, locality);* posição *(position).*
lock fechadura.
lock (to) fechar à chave, trancar.
locomotive locomotiva.
locust gafanhoto.
lodging alojamento.
lodging house hospedaria, pensão.
log tora, tronco, lenho.
logbook diário de bordo *(ship).*
logic lógica.
logical lógico.
lonely solitário, só.
long *adj.* comprido, longo; *adv.* muito tempo, muito.
  It's five meters long. Tem cinco metros de comprimento.
  a long time ago há muito tempo.
  long-distance call telefonema interurbano.
  long ago há muito tempo.
  all day long o dia todo.
  not long ago não há muito tempo.
  How long ago? Quanto tempo há?
  How long? Quanto tempo?
longer *adj.* mais comprido; *adv.* mais tempo.
  How much longer? Quanto tempo mais?
  no longer não mais; já não.
  to long for ter saudades de, anelar por.
longing desejo, ânsia, saudade.
look olhar, olhada.
look (to) ver, olhar.
  Look! Olhe!
  to look for procurar, buscar.
  to look after cuidar de.
  to look like parecer-se com.
  to look forward to esperar.
  to look into examinar (x = z).
  to look as though it's going to rain parecer que vai chover.
  to look out ter cuidado (be careful).
  Look out! Cuidado!
  to look over (review) repassar.
  That dress looks good on you. Esse vestido lhe cai bem.
loose solto *(free);* frouxo (x = sh) *(not tight).*
loosen (to) desatar, soltar.
Lord Senhor, Deus.

lose (to) perder.
  to lose weight emagrecer.
loss perda.
  at a loss perplexo (x = ks), confuso.
lot (a) muito.
  a lot of money muito dinheiro.
loud alto.
love amor.
  to fall in love apaixonar-se (x = sh).
  to be in love estar apaixonado (x = sh).
love (to) amar, querer.
lovely encantador, lindo.
low baixo (x = sh).
lower mais baixo (x = sh), inferior.
  lower case letters letras minúsculas.
lower (to) baixar (x = sh), abaixar (x = sh), reduzir; arriar *(sails)*.
lowlife velhaco.
loyal leal, fiel.
loyalty lealdade.
luck sorte, fortuna.
  good luck boa sorte.
  bad luck azar.
  to have luck estar com sorte, ter sorte.
luckily felizmente, afortunadamente.
lucky afortunado.
luggage bagagem.
lukewarm morno, tépido *(water);* indiferente *(reaction).*
lumber madeira.
luminous luminoso.
lunch almoço.
  to have lunch almoçar.
lung pulmão.
luxurious luxuoso (x = sh).
luxury luxo (x = sh).
  deluxe de luxo (x = sh).

M

machine máquina.
  answering machine máquina de contestação.
machinery maquinaria.
mad zangado *(angry).*
  to get mad zangar-se.
made feito, fabricado.
madness loucura.
magazine revista.
magic *adj.* mágico; *n.* magia.
magistrate magistrado.
magnanimous magnânimo, generoso.
magnet ímã.
magnetic magnético.
magnificent magnífico.
magnify (to) aumentar, exagerar (x = z).
magnifying glass lente de aumento.

maid empregada, criada.
mail correio.
  e-mail correio eletrónico.
mailbox caixa (x = sh) de correio.
mailman carteiro.
main principal.
  main street rua principal.
  main reason motivo principal, razão principal.
mainly principalmente.
maintain (to) manter, conservar, sustentar *(insist).*
maintenance manutenção, conservação.
majestic majestoso.
majesty majestade.
major *adj.* maior, principal; *n.* major (military).
majority maioria.
make (to) fazer, fabricar, produzir.
  to make sad entristecer, tornar triste.
  to make happy alegrar, tornar alegre.
  to make a living ganhar a vida.
  to make possible fazer possível.
  to make room for dar lugar para.
  to make known dar a conhecer.
  to make a mistake errar, enganar-se.
  to make a stop parar, fazer uma parada.
  to make friends fazer amizade com.
  to make fun of fazer troça de, zombar de.
  to make haste apressar-se.
  to make headway progredir, avançar.
  to make into converter.
  to make no difference não importar.
  to make out compreender, decifrar *(understand).*
  That makes me sick! Isso me enche o saco!
  to make the best of tirar o maior proveito de, tirar o melhor partido de.
  to make up one's mind decidir-se, resolver-se.
maker fabricante, criador.
malady doença.
male macho *(animal);* masculino *(person).*
malice malícia.
malicious malicioso, maligno.
man homem.
  young man jovem.
  Men *(as on a sign)* Senhores. Homens. Cavalheiros.
manage (to) administrar, governar, dirigir *(organization);* conseguir *(to succeed).*
management administração, direção.
manager administrador, diretor (director); gerente *(sports).*
manifest (to) manifestar.
mankind humanidade, raça humano.
manly másculo, viril, varonil.
manner maneira, modo.
manners maneiras, educação.

mansion mansão.
manual manual.
manufacture (to) manufaturar (manufacturar), fabricar.
manufacturer fabricante.
manuscript manuscrito.
many muitos.
   many times muitas vezes.
   as many as tantos quanto, tantos como.
   How many? Quantos?
map mapa.
maple bordo.
marble mármore; bolinha de gude *(for children)*.
March março (Março).
march marcha.
march (to) marchar.
margin margem.
marijuana maconha.
marine marinho.
mark marca.
mark (to) marcar.
market mercado.
marketing marketing, mercadologia.
marriage matrimônio (matrimónio), casamento.
marry (to) casar-se com, casar.
   to get married casar-se.
marvel *n.* maravilha, prodígio.
marvel (to) maravilhar-se, admirar-se, estranhar.
marvelous maravilhoso.
marvelously maravilhosamente.
masculine masculino.
mask máscara.
mason pedreiro.
mass massa; missa *(religious)*.
massage massagem.
massage (to) fazer massagem, dar massagem.
massive maciço, sólido.
mast mastro.
master mestre; dono, senhor.
   master copy cópia mestre.
masterpiece obra prima.
mat esteira.
match fósforo *(to light with);* partida, jogo *(sports);* aliança, casamento *(marriage)*.
match (to) emparelhar, igualar; combinar *(colors)*.
material material; pano, lecido *(cloth)*.
maternal materno, maternal.
mathematical matemático.
mathematics matemática.
matinee matinê Ⓑ, vesperal.
matter matérial *(substance);* assunto, questão *(question)*.
   an important matter um assunto importante.
   What's the matter? O que é que há?

   no matter how bad it is ... tão mal que seja ...
   no matter what happens aconteça o que a conteçer.
matter (to) importar.
   It doesn't matter. Não importa.
mattress colchão.
mature *adj.* maduro.
mature (to) madurar, amadurecer.
maturity maturidade, madureza.
maximum máximo (x = s).
May maio (Maio).
may poder, ser possível.
   It may be. Pode ser. É possível.
   It may be true. Pode ser verdade.
   May I? Com licença. O senhor permite?
maybe talvez.
mayonnaise maionese.
mayor prefeito (administrador do concelho, presidente da câmara municipal).
maze labirinto.
me eu, me, mim.
   It's me! Sou eu!
meadow prado.
meal refeição.
mean *adj.* maldoso, cruel *(unkind)*.
mean (to) significar, querer dizer; tencionar *(intend)*.
   What do you mean? O que você quer dizer?
meaning propósito, intenção *(intent);* sentido, significado.
means meio, meios, recursos.
   by all means sem dúvida, certamente.
   by no means de nenhuma maneira.
meantime interim.
meanwhile entretanto, entrementes.
measure medida.
   in great measure em grande parte.
   to take measures tomar medidas.
measure (to) medir.
measurement medição, medida.
meat carne.
mechanic mecânico.
mechanical mecânico.
mechanically mecanicamente, maquinalmente.
mechanism mecanismo.
medal medalha.
meddle (to) intrometer-se, meter-se.
mediate (to) mediar.
medical médico.
   medical school faculdade de medicina.
medicine medicina *(in general)*, remédio, medicamento *(particular remedy)*.
medieval medieval.
meditate (to) meditar.
meditation meditação, contemplação.
Mediterranean Mediterrâneo.

medium *adj.* médio, mediano.
   medium-sized de tamanho médio.
meet (to) encontrar, encontrar-se, dar com *(to come across)*; conhecer *(for the first time)*; reunir-se *(to get together)*.
   Glad to meet you. (Tenho muito) prazer em conhecê-lo.
   I hope to meet you again. Espero ter o prazer de vê-lo de novo (tornar a vê-lo).
   Till we meet again. Até a vista.
meeting *n.* reunião; sessão *(congress, etc.)*.
melancholy *adj.* melancólico.
melody melodia.
melon melão.
melt (to) derreter; fundir *(metals)*.
member membro, sócio.
memorable memorável.
memorandum memorando.
memory memória.
mend (to) emendar, consertar; corrigir-se *(mend one's ways)*.
mental mental.
mention menção, alusão.
mention (to) mencionar.
menu menu, cardápio (ementa).
merchandise mercadorias.
merchant comerciante, negociante.
merciful misericordioso, compassivo, piedoso.
merciless impiedoso, despiadoso.
mercury mercúrio.
mercy piedade, misericórdia.
merit mérito.
merry alegre.
mess desordem, bagunça.
   to mess up bobeiar *(make a mistake)*.
message mensagem, recado.
messenger mensageiro.
metal *adj.* metálico; *n.* metal.
metamorphosis metamorfose.
metaphor metáfora.
metaphysics metafísica.
meteor meteoro.
meter metro *(measurement)*; medidor *(for gas, etc.)*.
method método.
methodical metódico.
methodically metodicamente.
metric métrico.
   metric system sistema métrico.
metropolis metrópole.
metropolitan metropolitano.
Mexican mexicano (x = sh).
microbe micróbio.
microcosm microcosmo.
microfiche microficha.
microfilm microfilme.
microfilm (to) microfilmar.
microphone microfone.

microscope microscópio.
microscopic microscópico.
microwave microonda.
   microwave oven forno de microondas.
midday meio-dia.
middle *adj.* médio; *n.* meio, centro.
   Middle Ages Idade Média.
   middle-aged de meia idade.
   middle-class da classe média.
   in the middle no meio, no centro.
midnight meia-noite.
might poder, força.
mighty poderoso, forte.
mild suave, brando, meigo; moderado *(moderate)*.
mile milha.
military militar.
milk leite.
milkman leiteiro.
milk shake milk-shake, batido de leite.
mill moinho; fábrica, engenho *(factory)*; usina *(steel mill, etc.)*.
miller moleiro.
million milhão.
millionaire milionário.
mind mente; idéia.
   to have in mind ter em mente, pensar em.
   to change one's mind mudar de idéia.
   to my mind . . . na minha idéia . . .
mine *pron.* meu, minha, meus, minhas, o meu, a minha, os meus, as minhas; *n.* mina.
   a friend of mine um amigo meu.
   your friends and mine (os) seus amigos e os meus.
miner mineiro.
mineral mineral.
miniature miniatura.
minimum mínimo.
minister ministro *(government)*; pastor *(religion)*.
minor *adj.* menor, secundário; *n.* menor de idade.
minority minoria; menoridade *(age)*.
mint menta *(plant)*; casa da moeda *(money)*.
minus menos.
minute minuto *(time)*.
   minute hand ponteiro dos minutos.
   Just a minute, please. Um minuto, por favor. Um momento, por favor.
   any minute de minuto em minuto.
   Wait a minute! Aguarde um momento!
miracle milagre.
miraculous milagroso, milacroso.
mirror espelho.
misbehave (to) comportar-se mal.
misbehavior mau comportamento, má conduta.
mischief travessura, diabrura.
mischievous travesso.

miser avaro, sovina.
miserable miserável; tristonho *(unhappy).*
misfortune infortúnio, desventura.
Miss senhorita, senhorinha.
miss (to) ter saudades de *(someone or something);* perder *(bus, etc.);* errar, não acertar *(mark, etc.).*
    to miss the point não compreender o verdadeiro sentido.
mission missão.
missionary missionário.
mistake erro, engano, equívoco.
    by mistake por engano.
mistake (to) confundir com.
    to be mistaken enganar-se.
Mister senhor.
mistrust desconfiança.
mistrust (to) desconfiar de, suspeitar de.
misunderstand (to) entender mal, compreender mal.
misunderstanding malentendido, desentendimento.
mix (to) misturar, mesclar.
mixture mistura, mescla.
moan gemido.
moan (to) gemer.
mobilization mobilização.
mobilize (to) mobilizar.
mode modo.
model modelo.
modem modem.
moderate *adj.* moderado.
moderate (to) moderar.
moderately moderadamente.
moderation moderação.
modern moderno.
modest modesto.
modesty modéstia.
modify (to) modificar.
moist úmido.
moisten (to) umedecer.
moisture umidade.
moment momento.
    Just a moment! Um momento!
momentary momentâneo.
momentous importantíssimo.
monarch monaraca.
monarchy monarquia.
Monday segunda-feira, segunda.
money dinheiro.
monk monge.
monkey macaco.
monologue monólogo.
monopoly monopólio.
monosyllable monossílabo.
monotonous monótono.
monotony monotonia.
monster monstro.
monstrous monstruoso.

month mês.
monthly mensal.
monument monumento.
monumental monumental.
mood humor.
    to be in a good mood estar de bom humor.
moon lua.
moonlight luar.
moral *adj.* moral, ético.
morale moral, estado de espírito.
morbid mórbido.
more mais.
    more or less mais ou menos.
    one more outra vez, mais uma vez.
    no more não mais.
    the more . . . the better quanto mais . . . tanto melhor.
moreover além disso.
morning manhã.
    Good morning! Bom dia!
morsel bocado.
mortal mortal.
mortgage hipoteca.
mosquito mosquito.
moss musgo.
most o mais, os mais, o maior número, a maior parte, a maioria.
    at most quando muito.
    for the most part em geral, na maior parte.
    most of us a maior parte de nós.
moth traça.
mother mãe.
mother-in-law sogra.
motion movimento; moção, proposta *(at meeting).*
motive motivo.
motor *n.* motor.
mount (to) montar.
mounting base, montagem *(base);* suporte *(for instruments, etc.).*
mountain montanha.
mountainous montanhoso.
mourn (to) lamentar.
mournful triste, pesaroso.
mourning luto.
    in mourning de luto.
mouse camundongo; rato.
mouth boca.
mouthful bocado.
movable móvel, móbil.
move (to) mexer-se, mover-se *(change position);* mexer *(to cause to move),* mudar-se *(to another house),* afastar, deslocar *(to change places),* jogar, fazer uma jogada *(in a game).*
movement movimento.
movie filme.

movies cinema.
moving *adj.* comovente, tocante *(emotionally).*
Mr. senhor, Sr.
Mrs. senhora, Sra.
much muito.
  as much tanto.
  as much as tanto . . . quanto,
     tanto . . . como.
  How much? Quanto?
  too much demais, demasiado.
  much the same quase o mesmo, mais ou
     menos o mesmo.
  much money muito dinheiro.
  so much the better tanto melhor.
  so much the worse tanto pior.
mud lama, lodo, barro.
muddy turvo, barrento.
mule mulo *(male),* mula *(female).*
multiple múltiplo.
multiplication multiplicação.
multiply (to) multiplicar.
murder assassínio.
murder (to) assassinar.
murderer assassino.
murmur *n.* murmúrio.
muscle músculo.
museum museu.
music música.
musical musical, músico.
musician músico.
must ter que, ter de, dever.
  I must go. Tenho que ir.
  It must be. Deve ser.
mustache bigode.
mustard mostarda.
mute mudo.
mutton carne de carneiro.
mutual mútuo.
my meu, minha, meus, minhas, o meu, a
   minha, os meus, as minhas.
  Oh my God! Meu Deus!
myself eu mesmo, me, para mim.
mysterious misterioso.
mystery mistério.

N

nail unha *(of finger);* cravo *(for hammering).*
nail polish esmalte de unhas.
nail (to) cravar, pregar.
naive ingênuo (ingénuo).
naked nu, despido.
name nome.
  first name prenome.
  surname sobrenome; apelido.
  What is your name? Qual é o seu nome?
     Como se chama?

  My name is . . . Chamo-me . . .
namely isto é, a saber.
nap soneca, cochilo.
napkin guardanapo.
narration narração.
narrative narrativa.
narrow estreito.
nation nação.
national nacional.
nationality nacionalidade.
nationalization nacionalização.
nationalize (to) nacionalizar.
native *adj.* nativo, indígena; *n.* natural.
  native land terra natal, pátria.
natural natural.
naturalist naturalista.
naturally naturalmente, claro.
naturalness naturalidade.
nature natureza; caráter (carácter), índole.
  good nature boa índole.
naughty travesso, levado.
naval naval.
navigable navegável.
navigator navegador, navegante.
navy marinha, armada.
near perto, perto de.
nearby perto, à mão; ali perto.
nearly quase, por pouco.
nearsighted míope.
nearsightedness miopia.
neat asseado, esmerado; em ordem,
   arrumado.
neatness asseio, limpeza.
necessarily necessariamente.
necessary necessário.
  to be necessary ser necessário, ser
     preciso.
necessitate (to) exigir, tornar necessário.
necessity necessidade.
  of necessity necessariamente.
neck pescoço.
necklace colar.
necktie gravata.
need necessidade.
need (to) necessitar, precisar de; faltar.
  to be in need of ter necessidade de,
     precisar de.
  to be in need estar necessitado.
  I need to go. Preciso ir.
needle agulha.
negative negativo.
  a negative answer uma resposta negativa.
neglect descuido, negligência.
neglect (to) descuidar.
neighbor vizinho.
neighborhood vizinhança.
neither *conj.* nem; *adj.* nenhum, nenhum dos
   dois; *pron.* nenhum.
  neither . . . nor nem . . . nem.

neither one nor the other nem um nem outro.
nephew sobrinho.
nerve nervo; topete *(audacity)*.
nervous nervoso.
nest ninho.
net rede.
network interligar *(computer);* rede *(broadcasting).*
neuter neutro.
neutral neutro; ponto mortu *(car).*
never nunca, jamais.
    never again nunca mais.
nevertheless não obstante, todavia, contudo.
new novo.
    new moon lua nova.
    New Year ano novo.
news notícias, notícia *(piece of news).*
newspaper jornal, diário.
newsstand banca de jornais, quiosque.
New York Nova Iorque.
next seguinte, próximo (x = s).
    the next day no dia seguinte.
    (the) next week a semana que vem.
    (the) next time a próxima vez.
    next to ao lado de, junto a.
    Who's next? Quem segue?
nice agradável, simpático, amável; bonito, lindo; bom.
nickname apelido, alcunha.
niece sobrinha.
night noite.
    by night de noite.
    good night boa noite.
    last night ontem à noite.
nightclub boate, clube.
nightfall anoitecer.
nightmare pesadelo.
nighttime noite.
nine nove.
nine hundred novecentos.
nineteen dezenove (dezanove).
nineteenth décimo nono.
ninetieth nonagésimo.
ninety noventa.
ninth nono, nona parte.
no não; nenhum, nenhuma.
    no other nenhum outro.
    no one ninguém.
    no longer já não.
    no more não mais.
    no matter não importa.
    (in) no way de modo algum.
    No admittance. É proibida a entrada.
    No smoking. É proibido fumar.
    No it's not. Nãoé não.
nobility nobreza.
noble nobre.
nobody ninguém.

nobody else ninguém mais.
nod (to) inclinar a cabeça, acenar com a cabeça; cabecear *(become sleepy).*
noise barulho, ruído.
noisy barulhento, ruidoso.
nominative nominativo.
none ninguém, nenhum, nada.
    none of us nenhum de nós.
nonsense tolice, asneira.
noon meio-dia.
nor nem.
    neither . . . nor . . . nem . . . nem . . .
normal normal.
normally normalmente.
north norte.
    North America América do Norte.
    North American norte-americano.
northeast nordeste.
northern do norte, setentrional.
nose nariz.
nostril narina.
not não; nem.
    if not se não.
    not any nenhum.
    not one nem um.
    not a word nem uma palavra.
    not at all de modo algum.
    not yet ainda não.
    not even nem sequer.
notable notável.
note nota, bilhete; cédula (bank note).
note (to) anotar, notar; reparar em, observar.
notebook caderno.
nothing nada.
    nothing doing nada disso, não pode ser.
    It's nothing. Não é nada.
    nothing much pouca coisa.
    for nothing grátis; em vão (in vain).
notice aviso, anúncio.
notice (to) notar, observar, perceber; dar conta de.
notwithstanding não obstante, apesar de, embora, ainda que.
noun nome, substantivo.
nourish (to) alimentar, nutrir.
nourishment alimento, nutrição.
novel romance, novela.
novelist romancista, novelista.
novelty novidade, inovação.
November novembro (Novembro).
now agora, pois bem.
    for now para já.
    until now até agora.
    now and then de vez em quando.
    Is it ready now? Já está pronto?
nowadays hoje em dia.
nowhere em nenhuma parte, em lugar algum.
nuclear nuclear.
nucleus núcleo.

number número.
numerous numeroso.
nun freira, monja.
nurse *n.* enfermeira *(f.)*, enfermeiro *(m.)*.
nursery quarto de crianças.
nut noz; amêndoa; porca *(for a bolt)*.

O

oak carvalho.
oar remo.
oat aveia.
oath juramento.
oatmeal farinha de aveia.
obedience obediência.
obedient obediente.
obey (to) obedecer.
object objeto (objecto), objetivo (objectivo);
    complemento *(grammar)*.
object (to) opor-se, objetar (objectar).
objection objeção (objecção).
objective objetivo (objectivo), propósito.
obligation obrigação.
oblige (to) obrigar, forçar.
oblique oblíquo.
obscure obscuro, pouco conhecido.
observation observação.
observatory observatório.
observe (to) observar, notar, perceber.
observer observador.
observing observador, atento.
obstacle obstáculo.
obstinacy teimosia, obstinação.
obstinate teimoso, obstinado.
obstruct (to) obstruir.
obstruction obstrução, impedimento.
obtain (to) obter, conseguir.
obvious óbvio.
occasion ocasião, oportunidade.
occasional pouco freqüente (frequente).
occasionally de vez em quando.
occidental ocidental.
occupation ocupação; emprego, profissão
    (job).
occupy (to) ocupar.
occur (to) ocorrer, acontecer.
occurrence ocorrência, acontecimento.
ocean oceano.
    ocean liner vapor, transatlântico.
o'clock horas.
    at nine o'clock às nove (horas).
    It's ten o'clock. São dez (horas).
October outubro (Outubro).
odd ímpar *(number)*; raro, estranho *(strange)*.
    odds and ends miudezas.
of de, do, da.
    to think of pensar em.

of course claro que, naturalmente.
of himself por si mesmo.
It's twenty of two. Faltam vinte para as
    duas. É uma hora e quarenta minutos.
That's very kind of you. O senhor é
    muito amável.
off desligado *(TV, etc.);* apagado *(light);*
    fechado *(faucet)*.
    off and on de vez em quando.
    The meeting is off. Cancelaram a reunião.
    off the coast perto da costa.
    day off dia de folga.
    to take off tirar *(coat, etc.)*.
offend (to) ofender.
    to be offended ressentir-se.
offense ofensa, injúria.
offensive *adj.* ofensivo, desagradável; *n.*
    ofensiva, ataque.
offer oferta, oferecimento, proposta.
offer (to) oferecer, propor.
offering oferecimento; oferenda, oblação *(gift,
    oblation)*.
office escritório, repartição *(a building, a
    room, etc.);* cargo, posição, posto
    (position).
officer oficial.
official oficial.
often muitas vezes, freqüentemente
    (frequentemente).
oil óleo, petróleo; azeite *(olive or vegetable)*.
    oil painting pintura a óleo.
ointment ungüento (unguento).
old velho, antigo.
    to be twenty years old ter vinte anos.
    old man velho.
    old age velhice.
    old maid solteirona.
olive azeitona, oliva.
    olive oil azeite (de oliva).
    olive tree oliveira.
omelette omeleta.
omission omissão.
omit (to) omitir.
on sobre, em cima de, em; a, ao; com, por;
    ligado *(TV, etc.);* aceso *(light);* aberto
    (faucet).
    on the table sobre a mesa.
    on the train no trem (comboio).
    on that occasion naquela ocasião.
    on the left à esquerda.
    on board a bordo.
    on foot a pé.
    on credit a crédito.
    on time na hora.
    on my part de minha parte.
    on the average em média.
    on the contrary pelo contrário.
    on the whole geralmente, em geral.
    on Monday na segunda.

once uma vez.
    once and for all uma vez por todas.
    at once imediatamente.
    all at once de repente, subitamente.
one um, uma.
    one by one um por um.
    this one este.
    the blue one o azul.
one hundred cem.
oneself si, se, si mesmo.
one thousand mil.
one-way de mão única (de um sentido, sentido único) *(street)*.
onion cebola.
only *adj.* só, único; *adv.* só, somente, apenas.
opaque opaco.
open aberto.
    open air ar livre.
open (to) abrir.
opening abertura.
opera ópera.
operate (to) funcionar, fazer funcionar *(machine);* operar *(surgery)*.
operation operação *(surgery);* funcionamento *(machine)*.
opinion opinião.
    in my opinion a meu ver.
opponent oponente, antagonista.
opportune oportuno.
opportunity oportunidade.
oppose (to) opor-se, resistir.
opposite oposto, contrário.
opposition oposição.
oppress (to) oprimir.
oppression opressão.
optic(al) ótico (óptico).
optician ótico (óptico), oculista.
optimism otimismo (optimismo).
optimistic otimista (optimista).
or ou.
oracle oráculo.
oral oral, verbal.
orange laranja.
oratory oratória.
orchard pomar.
orchestra orquestra.
order ordem, pedido *(of goods)*.
    in order that a fim de que, para que.
order (to) mandar, comandar; pedir, encomendar *(goods)*.
ordinal ordinal.
    ordinal number número ordinal.
ordinarily geralmente, ordinariamente.
ordinary usual, ordinário.
organ órgão.
organic orgânico.
organism organismo.
organization organização.
organize (to) organizar.

organizer organizador.
orient oriente.
oriental oriental.
origin origem.
original original.
originality originalidade.
originate (to) originar; originar-se, surgir.
ornament ornamento, adorno.
orphan órfão.
ostentation ostentação.
other outro, outra, outros, outras.
    the other day o outro dia.
    the others os outros.
    Give me the other one. Dê-me o outro.
ouch! ui!
ought dever.
    You ought to do it. Você devia fazê-lo.
ounce onça.
our, ours nosso, nossa, nossos, nossas, o nosso, a nossa, os nossos, as nossas.
out fora.
    out of breath sem fôlego, esbaforido.
    out of date antiquado, fora de moda.
    out of doors ao ar livre.
    out of order avariado, enguiçado.
    out of place fora do seu lugar, deslocado.
    out of print esgotado.
    out of respect for por respeito a.
    out of style fora de moda.
    out of work sem trabalho, desempregado.
    out of control fora do controle.
outcome resultado.
outdoor(s) ao ar livre.
outline perfil, esboço, esquema, contorno, croqui Ⓑ.
outline (to) esboçar, delinear.
output produção, rendimento.
outrage ultraje.
outrageous ultrajante.
outside externo, exterior; fora, fora de.
outstanding saliente, eminente, extraordinário; pendente, a pagar *(to be paid)*.
outward externo, exterior; aparente.
    outward bound rumo ao exterior.
oven forno.
over sobre, por cima de; ao outro lado; mais de; por; em.
    overnight durante a noite.
    to stay over the weekend passar o fim de semana.
    to be over ter passado; acabar-se; terminar-se *(done)*.
    all over por toda parte.
    all over the world por todo o mundo.
    over again outra vez, mais uma vez.
    over and over repetidas vezes.
overcoat sobretudo.
overcome (to) vencer, superar, conquistar.

overflow (to) transbordar.
overseas ultramarino, de ultramar.
oversight inadvertência, descuido.
overtake (to) ultrapassar.
overwhelm (to) esmagar, sobrepujar.
overwhelming esmagador, irresistível.
overwork trabalho excessivo, trabalho em
  excesso.
overwork (to) trabalhar demais, fazer
  trabalhar demais.
owe (to) dever.
  owing to devido a.
owl coruja.
own próprio.
  This is your own. Isto é o seu.
  I'll do it on my own. Eu farei por minha
    própria conta.
  our own (o) nosso próprio.
  to be on your own estar por sua conta.
own (to) possuir, ter, ser dono de.
owner dono, proprietário.
ox boi.
oyster ostra.

pace passo.
pack (to) empacotar, carregar, fazer a mala.
package pacote, embrulho.
packaging embalagem.
paddle remo curto *(oar)*.
paddle (to) remar *(boat)*.
page página.
page (to) mandar chamar por bip.
pager bip.
pail balde.
pain dor.
  He is such a pain! Ele é um tão bicho!
painful doloroso, penoso.
paint pintura, tinta de pintar.
paint (to) pintar.
painter pintor.
painting pintura, quadro.
pair *n.* par *(shoes, etc.);* casal *(couple);* dupla
  (duo).
pajamas pijama.
palace palácio.
palate palato, paladar.
pale pálido.
  to turn pale empalidecer.
paleness palidez.
palm palma *(of the hand).*
palm tree palmeira.
pamphlet panfleto.
pan panela, caçarola.
pancake panqueca.
pane vidraça.

panel painel.
panic pânico.
pant (to) ofegar, arfar.
pantry despensa, copa.
pants calças.
papa papai, papá Ⓟ.
paper papel.
  writing paper papel de escrever.
  newspaper jornal, diário.
paperback brochura.
paperwork papelada.
parade parada, desfile.
paradise paraíso.
paragraph parágrafo.
parallel paralelo.
paralysis paralisia.
paralyze (to) paralisar.
parcel pacote, embrulho.
  parcel post encomenda postal.
pardon perdão.
  I beg your pardon. Perdoe(-me).
    Desculpe (-me).
pardon (to) perdoar, desculpar.
parentheses parêntese, parêntesis.
parents pais.
parish paróquia, freguesia.
park parque.
park (to) estacionar.
parking estacionamento.
  parking lot parque de estacionamento.
  parking space vaga.
parliament parlamento.
parliamentary parlamentar.
parlor sala, salão.
parrot papagaio.
parsley salsa.
part parte.
  a great part of, most of a maior parte de.
  for my part de minha parte.
  he did his part ele cumpriu com o seu
    dever.
  to play the part of desempenhar o
    papel de.
  to play a part in desempenhar um
    papel em.
partial parcial.
partiality parcialidade.
partially parcialmente.
participant participante.
participle particípio.
particular particular.
particularly particularmente.
partly em parte, parcialmente.
partner sócio, companheiro.
party partido *(political);* festa, recepção
  (social, entertainment).
pass passagem; passe *(permit).*
pass (to) passar; ser aprovado *(in an exam);*
  ultrapassar *(in car).*

passage passagem.
passenger passageiro, viajante.
passerby transeunte.
passion paixão (x = sh).
passive passivo.
passport passaporte.
past *prep.* além de, depois de; *adj.* passado; *n.* passado.
    the past year o ano passado.
    half past two as duas e meia.
paste pasta, massa; cola, grude *(for sticking)*.
paste (to) grudar.
pastime passatempo, diversão.
pastry massa, bolos.
past tense pretérito, pretérito perfeito.
patent patente.
paternal paternal, paterno.
path caminho, senda, trilha.
patience paciência.
patient *adj.* paciente; *n.* paciente, doente.
patriot patriota.
patriotic patriótico.
patriotism patriotismo.
pave (to) pavimentar.
    to pave the way abrir caminho.
pavement pavimento.
pavilion pavilhão.
paw pata.
pawn (to) penhorar, empenhar.
pawnshop casa de penhores.
pay pagamento, paga, ordenado, salário.
pay (to) pagar; prestar *(attention); fazer (a visit)*.
    to pay in installments pagar a prestações.
    to pay on account pagar por conta.
    to prepay pagar adiantado.
    to pay dearly pagar caro.
payment pagamento, paga.
pea ervilha.
peace paz.
peach pêssego, pessegueiro.
peanut amendoim.
pear pêra.
pear tree pereira.
pearl pérola.
peasant camponês.
peculiar peculiar.
peddler camelô, mascate Ⓑ.
pedestal pedestal, base.
pedestrian pedestre.
peel casca.
peel (to) descascar.
peg cavilha.
pen caneta.
penalty pena; multa *(fine)*.
pencil lápis.
penetrate (to) penetrar.
penetration penetração.
peninsula península.

pension pensão.
pensive pensativo.
people gente, povo; pessoal.
    many people muita gente.
    people say dizem, diz-se.
    Hey, people, let's go! Eh, pessoal, andamos!
pepper pimenta.
perceive (to) perceber.
percent por cento.
percentage percentagem, porcentagem.
perfect perfeito.
perfection perfeição.
perform (to) executar (x = z), realizar.
performance execução (x = z), cumprimento; representação *(theater)*.
perfume perfume.
perfume (to) perfumar.
perhaps talvez.
period período; ponto *(punctuation)*.
periodical periódico.
perish (to) perecer.
permanent permanente.
permanently permanentemente.
permission permissão, licença.
permit (to) permitir.
perpendicular perpendicular.
persecute (to) perseguir.
persecution perseguição.
persistent persistente.
person pessoa.
personal pessoal.
personality personalidade.
personally pessoalmente.
personnel pessoal.
persuade (to) persuadir.
persuasion persuasão.
persuasive persuasivo.
pertaining pertencente, relativo.
pessimist pessimista.
pessimistic pessimista.
petal pétala.
petition petição.
petroleum petróleo.
petty insignificante, trivial, pequeno.
    petty cash dinheiro para despesas menores.
pharmacist farmacêutico.
pharmacy farmácia.
phase fase.
phenomenon fenômeno (fenómeno).
philosopher filósofo.
philosophical filosófico.
philosophy filosofia.
phone telefone.
phone (to) telefonar.
phonograph fonógrafo.
photograph fotografia.
photograph (to) fotografar.

to take a photograph tirar uma
  fotografia.
physical físico.
physician médico.
physics física.
piano piano.
pick picareta *(tool);* escolha *(choice).*
pick (to) escolher *(choose).*
  to pick up pegar, apanhar; acelerar
    (speed); arrumar *(tidy up).*
  to have a bone to pick with ter conta a
    ajustar com.
  to pick on atormentar, perseguir.
pickle pepino em escabeche, picles *pl.* Ⓑ.
picnic piquenique.
picture quadro, foto, fotografia.
  to take a picture tirar uma fotografia.
picturesque pitoresco.
pie pastelão; torta *(tart).*
piece pedaço, parte.
pier cais, molhe.
pig porco.
pigeon pombo.
pill pílula.
pillow travesseiro (almofada).
pilot piloto.
pin alfinete.
pinch (to) beliscar.
pineapple abacaxi (ananás).
pink cor de rosa.
pipe cachimbo *(smoking);* tubo, cano
    (plumbing).
pistol pistola.
pitch arremesso, lance *(throw);* inclinação
    (slope).
pitcher jarro, cântaro *(for water, etc.);*
    lançador *(baseball).*
pitiful lastimável.
pity pena, piedade, compaixão (x = sh).
  It's a pity. É pena. É uma pena.
  What a pity! Que pena!
pity (to) ter pena de, compadecer-se de.
place lugar, posição.
  in the first place em primeiro lugar.
  in place no seu lugar.
  in place of em lugar de, em vez de.
  out of place fora do seu lugar.
  to take place realizar-se.
place (to) colocar, pôr.
plain plano, liso; simples; franco.
  the plain truth a pura verdade.
plan plano, projeto (projecto).
plan (to) planejar, projetar (projectar).
planet planeta.
plant planta.
plant (to) plantar.
plantation plantação.
plaster reboco *(for walls);* gesso *(of Paris).*
plastic plástico.

plate prato *(food);* chapa, lâmina *(metal in
    sheets);* chapa *(photography).*
  a bowl of soup um prato de sopa.
plateau planalto.
platform plataforma.
play jogo *(game);* peça *(theater).*
play (to) jogar *(sports);* tocar *(music);* brincar
    (games, recreation); representar *(theater).*
  to play a part representar, fazer um papel.
  to play a game jogar uma partida.
  to play a joke on pregar uma peça em.
player jogador.
playful brincalhão.
playground pátio de recreio.
plea rogo, apelo, argumento, pleito *(law).*
plead (to) rogar, suplicar; pleitear *(law).*
pleasant agradável, amável.
please (to) agradar, dar prazer a.
  I'm pleased. Estou satisfeito. Estou
    contente.
  It pleases me. Agrada-me.
  It doesn't please me. Não me agrada.
  He was quite pleased. Ele ficou contente.
  please faça o favor (de), tenha a bondade
    (de), queira, por favor.
  Please tell me. Faça o favor de me dizer
    (dizer-me).
  Pleased to meet you. Prazer em
    conhecê-lo.
pleasing agradável, amável.
pleasure prazer, gosto.
plenty abundância.
plot conspiração, intriga *(scheme);* lote Ⓑ,
    pedaço de terra *(land);* trama, enredo
    (novel, etc.).
plow arado.
plug tomada *(electric);* tampão *(stopper).*
plum ameixa (x = sh).
plumber bombeiro, encanador.
plumbing encanamento.
plump rechonchudo, roliço.
plural plural.
plus mais.
pocket bolso (algibeira).
poem poema.
poet poeta.
poetic poético.
poetry poesia.
point ponto; ponta *(of a pin, etc.)*
  point of view ponto de vista.
  cardinal points pontos cardeais.
  6.5 seis ponto cinco.
point (to) apontar, indicar.
pointed pontudo, aguçado.
poise porte, equilíbrio.
poison veneno.
poison (to) envenenar.
poisonous venenoso.
polar polar.

pole poste, vara; pólo *(of the earth)*.
police polícia.
policeman polícia, policial.
police station delegacia (esquadra).
policy política *(of a government);* costume, plano; apólice *(insurance)*.
polish polimento, requinte *(manners);* graxa (x = sh) *(for shoes);* esmalte *(for nails)*.
polish (to) polir, lustrar; engraxar (x = sh) *(shoes)*.
polite cortês.
political político.
politician político.
politics política.
pond lagoa.
pool piscina *(for swimming)*.
poor pobre.
   Poor me! Coitado de mim!
pope papa.
poppy papoula.
popular popular.
population população.
porch varanda, pórtico.
pork carne de porco.
   pork chop costeleta de porco.
port porto; vinho do Porto *(wine)*.
portable portátil.
porter carregador.
portion porção, parte.
portrait retrato.
Portuguese português.
position posição.
positive positivo.
positively certamente, positivamente.
possess (to) possuir.
possession possessão, posse.
   to take possession of tomar posse de.
possessor possessor.
possibility possibilidade.
possible possível.
   as soon as possible o mais cedo possível.
possibly possivelmente, talvez.
post poste; posto guarnição *(military)*.
   postcard cartão postal, bilhete postal.
   post office correio.
postage porte.
   postage stamp selo postal.
posterity posteridade.
postman carteiro.
postscript pós-escrito.
pot panela, caçarola *(cooking);* pote *(for plants)*.
potato batata.
   fried potatoes batatas fritas.
   mashed potatoes purê (puré) de batatas.
pound libra.
pour despejar; chover a cântaros *(rain)*.
poverty pobreza.

powder pó; pó de arroz *(for face);* pólvora *(gunpowder)*.
power poder, força, potência.
   electric power força elétrica (eléctrica).
   horsepower cavalo-vapor.
   the great powers as grandes potências.
   power of attorney procuração.
powerful poderoso.
practicable praticável.
practical prático.
practice prática; uso, costume *(usage);* desempenho *(of a profession);* ensaiao *(rehearsal)*.
practice (to) praticar; desempenhar *(a profession);* ensaiar *(to rehearse)*.
praise elogio, louvor.
praise (to) elogiar, louvar.
prank peça, brincadeira, travessura.
pray (to) rezar, orar; suplicar.
prayer oração; súplica.
precede (to) preceder.
precedent precedente.
preceding precedente.
precept preceito.
precious precioso, de grande valor.
precipice precipício.
precise preciso, exato (exacto) (x = z).
precisely precisamente, exatamente (exactamente) (x = z).
precision precisão.
precocious precoce.
predecessor antecessor.
predicament apuro.
predict (to) predizer, profetizar.
prediction predição, profecia.
predominant predominante.
preface prefácio.
prefer (to) preferir.
preferable preferível.
preferably preferivelmenta, de preferência.
preference preferência.
prejudice preconceito.
preliminary preliminar.
premature prematuro.
premonition pressentimento.
preparation preparação.
prepare (to) preparar.
preposition preposição.
prescribe (to) prescrever; receitar *(medicine)*.
prescription receita *(medicine)*.
presence presença.
present presente, oferta.
   at present atualmente (actualmente).
   for the present por agora.
   present participle particípio presente.
   present-day atual (actual).
   the present month o corrente.
   to give a present fazer presente, dar de presente.

to be present estar presente.
present (to) apresentar *(introduce);* dar de presente, ofertar.
presentation apresentação.
preservation preservação, conservação.
preserve (to) preservar, conservar.
preside (to) presidir.
president presidente.
press prensa; imprensa *(printing, "the press").*
press (to) apertar; passar a ferro *(clothes);* insistir, urgir *(to urge).*
pressing urgente.
pressure pressão.
prestige prestígio.
presumable presumível.
presume (to) presumir, supor.
pretend (to) fingir, pretender.
pretense pretensão, pretexto, simulação.
    under the pretense of sob o pretexto de.
    under false pretenses sob falsos pretextos.
pretension pretensão, pretexto.
preterit, preterite pretérito.
pretext pretexto.
pretty *adj.* belo, bonito, lindo; *adv.* um tanto, bastante, um pouco.
    pretty tired um tanto cansado.
    pretty good bastante bom.
    pretty much quase *(almost).*
    pretty much the same quase o mesmo.
prevail (to) prevalecer, predominar.
    to prevail over vencer, triunfar.
    to prevail upon persuadir, convencer.
prevent (to) prevenir, impedir.
prevention prevenção, impedimento.
previous prévio.
    previous to antes de.
previously previamente, antes.
price preço.
pride orgulho.
priest sacerdote, padre.
primarily principalmente.
primary primário, principal *(first in importance);* elementar *(elementary).*
    primary color cor primária.
    primary school escola primária.
prince príncipe.
principal principal.
principally principalmente.
principle princípio.
    in principle em princípio.
print (to) imprimir, publicar.
printed impresso, publicado.
    printed matter impressos.
printer impressora.
    laser printer impressora a laser.
    color printer impressora de cor.
prior anterior, precedente, prévio.
    prior to antes de.
prison prisão, cadeia, cárcere.

prisoner prisoneiro, preso.
private privado, particular, pessoal, confidencial, reservado, secreto.
    private office escritório particular.
    private secretary secretária particular.
    in private em particular.
privately em segredo, confidencialmente.
privilege privilégio.
prize prêmio (prémio).
pro pro *(advantage);* profissional *(sports).*
probability probabilidade.
probable provável.
probably provavelmente.
problem problema.
procedure procedimento.
proceed (to) seguir, prosseguir, continuar.
process processo, procedimento, método *(method);* curso, marcha *(of time);* citação *(law).*
    in the process of no decurso de.
procession procissão, cortejo.
proclaim (to) proclamar.
proclamation proclamação.
produce (to) produzir, fabricar, render.
product produto.
production produção.
productive produtivo.
profession profissão.
professional profissional.
professor professor.
proficient proficiente, competente.
profile perfil.
profit lucro, ganho.
profit (to) lucrar, tirar proveito.
profitable lucrativo, proveitoso.
program programa.
progress progresso.
progressive progressivo.
prohibit (to) proibir.
prohibition proibição.
project projeto (projecto), plano.
project (to) projetar (projectar); ressaltar *(to jut out).*
prolong (to) prolongar.
prominent proeminente, saliente.
promise promessa.
promise (to) prometer.
promote (to) promover *(advertise);* elevar *(in grade).*
promotion promoção, elevação.
prompt pronto, preparado; pontual.
promptly prontamente.
promptness prontidão, pontualidade.
pronoun pronome.
pronounce (to) pronunciar.
pronunciation pronúncia.
proof prova.
propaganda propaganda.
propeller hélice.

proper próprio, correto (correcto), apropriado.
properly propriamente, corretamente (correctamente).
property propriedade; bens.
prophecy profecia, predição.
prophesy (to) profetizar, predizer.
proportion proporção.
   in proportion em proporção.
   out of proportion fora de proporção, desproporcionado.
proposal proposta, oferta.
propose (to) propor, sugerir.
proprietor proprietário, dono.
prosaic prosaico.
prose prosa.
prosper (to) prosperar.
prosperity prosperidade.
prosperous próspero.
protect (to) proteger.
protection proteção (protecção).
protector protetor (protector).
protest protesto.
protest (to) protestar.
Protestant protestante.
proud orgulhoso *(pleased);* soberbo *(arrogant).*
prove (to) provar, demonstrar, comprovar; revelar-se, mostrar-se *(to turn out).*
proverb provérbio, rifão.
provide (to) prover, fornecer.
   to provide oneself with prover-se de.
   provided that sempre que, contanto que.
providence providência.
province província.
provincial provinciano.
provisions mantimentos, víveres *(supplies);* provisões *(plans).*
prudence prudência.
prudent prudente.
psalm salmo.
pseudonym pseudônimo.
pst! psiu!
psyche psique.
psychiatrist psiquiatra.
psychiatry psiquiatria.
psychic *n.* médium; *adj.* psíquico.
psychoanalysis psicanálise.
psychological psicológico.
psychology psicologia.
psychotic psicótico.
public público.
publication publicação.
publicity publicidade.
publish (to) publicar.
publisher editor.
publishing house casa editora.
pudding pudim.
pull (to) puxar (x = sh).

to pull in chegar, entrar *(train);* encostar *(to a parking space).*
to pull out sair, partir *(train);* arrancar *(of a parking space).*
to pull apart separar, romper.
to pull through sair bem.
pulpit púlpito.
pulse pulso.
pump bomba.
punch soco *(blow);* ponche *(drink).*
punch (to) socar.
punctual pontual.
punctuate (to) pontuar.
punctuation pontuação.
puncture puntura (punctura).
punish (to) punir, castigar.
punishment castigo, punição.
pupil aluno *(school);* pupila *(eye).*
purchase compra.
purchase (to) comprar.
purchaser comprador.
pure puro.
purely puramente, simplesmente.
purple púrpura.
purpose propósito, fim, finalidade, objetivo (objectivo), intenção.
   on purpose de propósito.
   to no purpose inutilmente, em vão.
   for the purpose of com o fim de.
   With what purpose? Com que finalidade?
purse bolsa.
pursue (to) perseguir *(chase);* prosseguir *(a matter, etc.).*
pursuit perseguição, procura.
push (to) empurrar.
put (to) pôr, colocar.
   to put away guardar, pôr de lado.
   to put in order pôr em ordem.
   to put off adiar.
   to put up for sale pôr à venda.
   to put up with suportar, agüentar (aguentar), aturar.
   to put on vestir, pôr.
   to put out publicar *(a book);* apagar *(a light).*
   to put to bed pôr na cama, fazer deitar.
   to put to sleep fazer dormir *(anesthetize).*
   to put together juntar.
   to put to a vote submeter a votação.
puzzle quebra-cabeça; enigma, problema.
   to be puzzled estar perplexo (x = ks).

quaint curioso, raro, singular.
qualify (to) qualificar.
quality qualidade.

quantity quantidade.
quarrel briga, disputa.
quart quarto.
quarter quarto, quarta parte.
    a quarter hour um quarto de hora.
quarters alojamento; quartel *(military)*.
queen rainha.
quell (to) esmagar, sufocar.
quench (to) matar *(thirst);* apagar.
question pergunta *(query);* questão *(matter).*
    to ask a question fazer uma pergunta.
    to be a question of tratar-se de, ser uma
      questão de.
    question mark ponto de interrogação.
    What's the question? De que se trata?
    without any question sem dúvida.
    to be out of the question ser impossível.
quick rápido.
quickly depressa, rapidamente.
quiet quieto, sossegado, tranqüilo (tranquilo).
quietly quietamente, tranqüilamente
    (tranquilamente).
quietness quietude.
quilt colcha, acolchoado.
quinine quinina.
quit deixar (x = sh), parar, cessar *(to stop);*
    desistir *(give up).*
    to quit smoking deixar de fumar.
quite completamente, muito, realmente, bem.
    quite good muito bom.
    quite soon bem cedo.
    quite difficult bem difícil.
    quite well done muito bem feito.
    She seems quite different. Ela parece
      outra.
quotation citação, cotação.
    quotation marks aspas.
quote (to) citar.

R

rabbit coelho.
race raça *(ethnic);* corrida, carreira.
racial racial.
radiance brilho, esplendor.
radiant radiante, brilhante.
radiator radiador.
radio rádio.
    radio set aparelho de rádio.
    radio station estação de rádio,
      radioemissora.
radish rabanete.
radium rádio.
rag trapo, farrapo.
rage raiva, ira.
ragged esfarrapado, andrajoso.
rail barreira, barra; trilho *(train).*

railroad estrada de ferro (caminho de ferro),
    ferrovia.
rain chuva.
rain (to) chover.
rainbow arco-íris.
raincoat impermeável.
rainfall chuva.
rainy chuvoso.
raise aumento.
    to get a raise conseguir um aumento.
raise (to) levantar, elevar; aumentar, subir
    (prices, salary); criar *(children);* cultivar
    (a crop).
    to raise an objection levantar uma
      objeção (objecção), objetar (objectar).
    to raise money angariar fundos.
raisin passa.
rake ancinho.
rake (to) usar ancinho.
ranch fazenda, estância.
range alcance *(reach);* extensão (x = sh)
    (voice); cadeia *(mountains).*
rank posto *(military, etc.);* fileira *(line of
    soldiers);* posição.
    rank and file gente comum.
rapid rápido.
rapidly rapidamente.
rare raro *(unusual);* mal passado *(meat).*
rarely raramente.
rash *adj.* precipitado, temerário; *n.* erupção
    (skin); vaga *(of deaths, etc.).*
rat rato.
rate preço, taxa (x = sh).
    at the rate of à razão de.
    rate of exchange taxa de câmbio.
    at any rate de qualquer maneira.
rather um pouco, antes, meio um tanto.
    rather expensive um tanto caro, meio
      caro.
    rather than em vez de.
ratio proporção.
ration ração.
rational racional.
raw cru *(food);* bruto *(materials).*
ray raio.
rayon raiom.
razor navalha *(straight);* gilete *(safety).*
    razor blade lâmina (de borbear).
reach alcance *(range).*
    out of reach fora do alcance.
    within reach ao alcance.
reach (to) alcançar, chegar a, chegar até.
    to reach the end terminar, chegar ao fim.
      conseguir o objetivo (objectivo).
    to reach out one's hand estender a mão.
    to reach someone chegar a alguem *(get
      through to their heart).*
react (to) reagir.
reaction reação (reacção).

reactionary reacionário (reaccionário).
read (to) ler.
reader leitor.
reading leitura.
reading room gabinete de leitura.
ready pronto, disposto.
   to get ready arrumar-se (bathe and dress).
ready-made feito, já feito.
   ready-made clothes roupa feita.
real real, verdadeiro.
   real estate bens imóveis.
realist realista.
reality realidade.
realization realização; compreensão.
realize (to) dar-se conta de, compreender;
   realizar, conseguir *(obtain, achieve),* levar
   a cabo *(bring to reality).*
   to realize a danger dar-se conta do perigo.
   to realize a project levar a cabo um
     projeto (projecto).
   to realize a profit tirar proveito, tirar
     lucro.
really de fato (facto), realmente *(in reality);*
   muito, bem *(very).*
reap (to) colher, segar.
rear *adj.* traseiro, posterior; *n.* parte traseira,
   fundo.
   to bring up the rear fechar a retaguardo.
reason razão, motivo, causa.
   by reason of por causa de.
   for this reason por isto.
   without reason sem razão.
reason (to) raciocinar, pensar.
reasonable razoável, módico.
reasonably razoavelmente, moderadamente.
reasoning raciocínio.
rebel rebelde.
rebel (to) rebelar-se, revoltar-se.
rebellion rebelião, revolta.
rebellious rebelde, revoltoso.
recall (to) lembrar, recordar.
receipt recibo *(document);* recebimento
   (action).
   to acknowledge receipt acusar o
     recebimento.
receive (to) receber.
receiver fone *(telephone);* recebedor,
   destinatário *(mail, etc.).*
recent recente.
recently recentemente.
reception recepção, recebimento, acolhida.
recipe receita.
recite (to) recitar.
reckless temerário, imprudente.
recklessly temerariamente, imprudentemente.
recline (to) reclinar-se, recostar-se.
recognition reconhecimento.
recognize (to) reconhecer.
recollect (to) recordar, lembrar *(to remember).*

recollection recordação, lembrança.
recommend (to) recomendar.
recommendation recomendação.
reconcile (to) reconciliar, harmonizar.
reconciliation reconciliação.
record registro; disco *(phonograph);* recorde
   Ⓑ *(sports);* evidência; *pl.* arquivo, anais.
   on record registrado.
recover (to) recuperar *(from illness);* recobrar
   (to get back).
recovery recuperação.
recreation recreio, divertimento, passatempo.
recuperate (to) recuperar-se, restabelecer-se.
red vermelho.
   Red Cross Cruz Vermelha.
reduce (to) reduzir, diminuir.
reduction redução, abatimento, desconto
   (prices).
refer (to) referir.
reference referência.
   reference book livro de consulta.
refine (to) refinar.
refinement refinamento, requinte.
reflect (to) refletir (reflectir), pensar.
reflection reflexão (x = ks), reflexo (x = ks).
reflexive reflexivo (x = ks).
reform reforma.
reform (to) reformar, corrigir.
refrain (to . . . from) abster-se de.
refresh (to) refrescar.
refreshment refresco.
refrigerator refrigerador, geladeira.
refuge refúgio, asilo, amparo.
refugee refugiado.
refusal recusa.
refuse (to) recusar, negar.
refute (to) refutar.
regard consideração, respeito, estima.
   in regard to com referência a.
   in this regard a esse respeito, neste
     respeito.
   with regard to com referência a.
   without any regard to sem nenhuma
     consideração para.
regard (to) considerar, estimar, julgar.
regarding com respeito a, quanto a.
regardless of não obstante, apesar de.
regards lembranças, cumprimentos.
   regards to lembranças a.
regime regime.
regiment regimento.
region região, área.
register registro.
register (to) inscrever, registrar.
   registered letter carta registrada.
regret pesar, remorso.
regret (to) sentir, deplorar, lamentar.
   I regret it very much. Sinto(-o) muito.
   I regret that . . . Sinto que . . .

regular regular.
regularity regularidade.
regularly regularmente.
regulation regulamento, regra, ordem.
rehearsal ensaio.
rehearse (to) ensaiar.
reign reinado.
reign (to) reinar.
reject (to) rejeitar.
rejection rejeição.
rejoice (to) alegrar, regozijar.
rejoicing alegria, júbilo, regozijo.
relate (to) relatar, narrar, contar *(story);* relacionar *(be connected).*
   everything relating to quanto se relaciona com.
relation relação; parente *(family member).*
relationship relação; parentesco *(family).*
relative *adj.* relativo, respectivo; *n.* parente *(family).*
relax descontrair-se.
release (to) soltar, libertar; permitir *(publication, etc.).*
reliability confiança.
reliable de confiança.
relief alívio *(from pain);* socorro, auxílio *(aid).*
religion religião.
religious religioso.
relish (to) saborear, gostar de.
reluctance relutância, resistência.
reluctant relutante, hesitante.
reluctantly relutantemente, de má vontade.
rely on (to) confiar em, contar com.
remain (to) ficar, permanecer, restar.
   to remain silent ficar quieto, calar.
   to remain to be done ficar por fazer.
remains restos.
remark observação, comentário.
   to make a remark fazer um comentário.
remark (to) observar, comentar, notar *(notice).*
remarkable notável, extraordinário.
remarkably notavelmente.
remedy remédio.
remedy (to) remediar, corrigir.
remember (to) lembrar, lembrar-se, recordar.
   I don't remember. Não me lembro.
   Remember me to him. Dê-lhe (as) minhas lembranças.
remembrance lembrança.
remind (to) lembrar.
reminder lembrete, aviso.
remit (to) remeter.
remorse remorso.
remote control (TV) controle remoto; telecomando Ⓟ.
removal remoção, demissão.
remove (to) tirar, retirar; demitir *(from a job).*
renew (to) renovar, recomeçar.

   to renew a subscription renovar uma assinatura.
rent aluguel, renda.
   for rent aluga-se.
rent (to) alugar.
repair conserto.
   in good repair em bom estado.
repair (to) consertar.
repeal (to) revogar, anular.
repeat (to) repetir.
repeatedly repetidamente.
repetition repetição.
reply resposta, réplica.
reply (to) responder, replicar.
report relatório, informação.
report (to) informar, comunicar, fazer relatório; denunciar *(to the police).*
   it is reported diz-se que, dizem que.
reporter repórter, jornalista.
represent (to) representar.
representation representação.
representative representante, agente; deputado *(political).*
reproach censura, repreensão.
reproach (to) censurar, repreender.
reproduce (to) reproduzir.
reproduction reprodução.
reptile réptil.
republic república.
republican republicano.
reputation reputação, renome, fama.
request pedido, petição.
request (to) pedir, rogar.
rescue salvamento.
rescue (to) salvar, socorrer.
resemblance semelhança.
resemble (to) parecer-se com.
   He resembles his father. Ele se parece com o pai.
resent (to) ressentir-se.
reservation reserva.
reserve reserva.
   without reserve sem reserva.
reserve (to) reservar.
reside (to) morar, residir.
residence residência, domicílio.
resident residente.
resign (to) demitir-se; resignar-se *(to resign oneself).*
resignation renúncia, demissão; resignação *(despair).*
resist (to) resistir, opor-se.
resistance resistência, oposição.
resolute resoluto, determinado.
resolution resolução, solução.
resolve (to) resolver, determinar, decidir.
resource recurso.
respect respeito.
   in this respect neste respeito.

with respect to com respeito a.
with all due respect com todo respeito.
in all respects em todo sentido, sob todos os pontos de vista.
in every respect em todo sentido.
respect (to) respeitar, estimar.
respectable respeitável.
respectful respeitoso.
respectfully yours atenciosamente.
respective respectivo.
response resposta, réplica.
responsibility responsabilidade.
responsible responsável.
rest resto *(remainder);* descanso, repouso *(when tired).*
rest (to) descansar, repousar.
restaurant restaurante.
restful sossegado, tranqüilo (tranquilo).
restless inquieto, impaciente.
restore (to) restaurar, restabelecer.
restrict (to) restringir, limitar, confinar.
result resultado, conseqüência (consequência).
result (to) resultar.
    to result in acabar em, terminar em, resultar em.
retail venda a varejo, venda a retalho ℗.
retail (to) vender a retalho, vender a varejo.
retire (to) reformar-se.
    She is retired now. Ela já é reformada.
return volta.
    in return for em troca de.
    by return mail à volta do correio.
    return trip viagem de volta.
return (to) voltar, regressar; devolver *(to return something).*
    to return a book devolver um livro.
    to return a favor retribuir um favor.
    to return home voltar para casa.
review revista *(summary);* revisão, repasso *(recheck);* exame (x = z).
review (to) rever, revisar, repassar; criticar *(movies, etc.).*
revise (to) revisar.
revision revisão.
revive (to) ressuscitar *(person);* restaurar *(custom).*
revolt revolta, rebelião.
revolt (to) revoltar(-se), rebelar(-se).
revolution revolução.
reward recompensa.
reward (to) recompensar.
rewind rebobinagem.
rhyme rima.
rhythm ritmo.
rib costela.
ribbon fita.
rice arroz.
rich rico; forte *(food).*
riches riquezas.

riddle adivinha, enigma.
ride passeio.
ride (to) montar a cavalo, andar a cavalo *(on horseback);* viajar.
ridiculous ridículo.
rifle rifle.
right *adj.* direito; justo *(just);* correto (correcto); *n.* direito; *adv.* bem; certo; certamente; justamente; perfeitamente; mesmo.
    the right man o homem certo.
    right hand mão direita.
    right-handed destro.
    the right time a hora certa.
    right or wrong com razão ou sem razão.
    right side lado direito.
    Is this right? Está certo?
    It's right. Está certo.
    to be right ter razão.
    to the right à direita.
    keep to the right conserve a sua direita.
    to have a right ter direito.
    by rights de direito.
    right here aqui mesmo.
    right away imediatemente, já.
    right now agora mesmo.
    all right está bem, bem.
    Everything is all right. Tudo vai bem.
ring anel *(for finger).*
ring (to) tocar, soar *(bells).*
riot motim, desordem.
riot (to) amotinar-se.
ripe maduro.
ripen (to) amadurecer.
rise aumento, subida.
    sunrise nascer do sol, levantar do sol.
rise (to) subir; levantar-se *(to get up);* sair *(sun);* revoltar-se *(revolt);* aumentar *(taxes).*
risk risco, perigo.
    to run a risk correr um perigo, arriscar.
risk (to) arriscar.
river rio.
road estrada, caminho.
    main road estrada principal, caminho principal.
roar rugido, berro.
roar (to) rugir, berrar.
roast assado.
    roast beef rosbife, carne assada.
roast (to) assar.
rob (to) roubar.
robber ladrão.
robbery roubo, furto.
rock rocha; rock *(music).*
rock (to) balançar, embalar *(to sleep).*
rocket foguete, projétil (projéctil).
rocking chair cadeira de balanço.
roll rolo; pãozinho *(bread);* lista *(list).*

roll (to) enrolar, rolar.
romance romance.
romantic romântico.
roof telhado *(house);* teto (tecto) *(car).*
room sala, quarto, peça (divisão).
    to make room dar lugar, fazer lugar.
    There's not enough room. Não há
      bastante espaço.
    There's no room for doubt. Não cabe
      dúvida.
    living room sala de estar.
    dining room sala de jantar.
rooster galo.
root raiz.
rooted enraizado, radicado.
rope corda.
    to be at the end of one's rope estar na
      última.
rose rosa.
rosebush roseira.
rotary giratório, rotativo.
    rotary press rotiva.
rough áspero.
    rough draft rascunho.
round *adj.* redondo; *n.* rodada *(drinks).*
    a round table uma mesa redonda.
    round number número redondo.
    round trip viagem de ida e volta.
    all year round o ano todo.
route rota, rumo, caminho, curso.
routine rotina.
row fila, fileira.
row (to) remar.
rub (to) esfregar, friccionar.
rubber borracha.
rude rude, grosso, descortês.
rudeness rudeza, grosseria.
rug tapete.
ruin ruína.
rule regra, norma; reinado, dominio *(reign).*
    as a rule em regra.
    to be the rule ser regra, ser uso.
rule (to) reger *(king);* governar *(government);*
    determinar *(court).*
    to rule out excluir, eliminar.
    to rule over governar.
ruler soberano *(monarch);* régua *(for drawing*
    lines).
rumor rumor.
run (to) correr; andar, funcionar *(a watch, a*
    machine, etc.).
    to run across someone encontrar, dar com.
    to run into someone encontrar-se com,
      topar com.
    to run away escapar, fugir.
    to run the risk of correr o risco de,
      arriscar.
    to run up and down correr de cá para lá
      (acolá).

    to run a business dirigir um negócio.
rural rural.
rush pressa *(haste).*
    to be in a rush estar com pressa.
rush (to) ir depressa, apressar-se.
    to rush in entrar correndo, entrar
      precipitadamente.
    to rush through fazer depressa.
Russian russo.
rusty enferrujado, ferrugento.
rye centeio.

S

Sabbath sábado.
saccharine sacarina.
sack saco, saca.
sacred sagrado, sacro.
sacrifice sacrifício.
sacrifice (to) sacrificar.
sad triste.
saddle sela.
sadly tristemente.
sadness tristeza.
safe *n.* cofre, caixa (x = sh) forte; *adj.* seguro;
    salvo, ileso *(unhurt);* sem perigo *(safe from*
    danger); sem risco *(safe from risk).*
    safe and sound são e salvo.
    Have a safe trip! Feliz viagem! Boa
      viagem!
safely a salvo.
safety segurança.
sail vela.
    sailboat barco a vela, veleiro.
sail (to) velejar, navegar; fazer à vela *(set sail).*
sailor marinheiro, marujo.
saint santo, são.
    Saint Paul São Paulo.
    Saint Barbara Santa Bárbara.
    Saint Andrew Santo André.
sake causa, motivo, amor, bem, consideração.
    for your sake para seu próprio bem.
    for the sake of por, por amor a, por
      causa de.
    for the sake of brevity por brevidade.
    for mercy's sake por misericórdia.
    for God's sake, for the love of God por
      Deus, pelo amor de Deus.
salad salada.
salary salário, ordenado.
sale venda.
    for sale à venda.
salesgirl caixeira, vendedora.
salesman caixeiro, vendedor.
    traveling salesman caixeiro viajante.
salmon salmão.
salt sal.

salt (to) salgar, pôr sal.
　salt shaker saleiro.
same mesmo, igual.
　the same o mesmo, os mesmos.
　It's all the same to me. Tanto faz. Para
　　mim é o mesmo.
　much the same quase o mesmo.
　the same as o mesmo que, os mesmos que.
sample amostra.
sand areia.
sandpaper lixa (x = sh).
sandwich sanduíche.
sandy arenoso.
sane são.
sanatorium, sanitarium sanatório.
sanitary sanitário.
sanitation saneamento.
sanity sanidade *(medical)*; juízo, razão
　(sensibility).
sap seiva.
sarcasm sarcasmo.
sarcastic sarcástico.
sardine sardinha.
Satan satanás, satã.
satisfaction satisfação.
satisfactorily satisfatoriamente.
satisfactory satisfatório.
satisfy (to) satisfazer.
Saturday sábado.
sauce molho.
saucer pires.
sausage salsicha, lingüiça (linguiça).
savage selvagem.
save *prep.* salvo, exceto (excepto), menos;
　conj. a não ser.
save (to) salvar, resgatar *(a person)*; poupar,
　economizar. *(money)*; salvar *(computer)*.
　to save face salvar as aparências.
savings poupanças, economias.
　savings bank caixa (x = sh) econômica
　　(económica).
saw serra; serrote *(hand saw)*.
say (to) dizer.
　that is to say quer dizer, isto é.
　it is said diz-se, dizem.
saying dito, provérbio, rifão.
　as the saying goes como diz o provérbio,
　　como se costuma dizer.
scale *n.* balança *(for weighing)*; escala
　(proportion); escama *(of fish, etc.)*.
scalp couro cabeludo.
scan (to) escandir.
scandal escândalo.
Scandinavian escandinavo.
scanner escáner.
scanty escasso, pouco, insuficiente.
scar cicatriz.
scarce escasso, raro.
scarcely apenas, mal, quase não.

scarcity escassez.
scarf cachecol *(long)*; lença *(square)*.
scarlet escarlate.
scene cena.
scenery cenário, decoração *(theater)*;
　paisagem, vista *(view)*.
scent cheiro, aroma, odor.
schedule horário *(timetable)*; programa lista
　(of events); *(list)*.
scheme plano, esquema; projeto (projecto).
scholarship bolsa de estudos.
school escola.
　schoolteacher professor.
　schoolbook livro escolar.
　schoolmate colega, condiscípulo.
　schoolroom sala de aula.
science ciência.
scientific científico.
scientist cientista.
scissors tesoura.
scold (to) ralhar, repreender.
score escore, contagem; partitura *(music)*.
score (to) fazer pontos, marcar os pontos;
　riscar *(for cutting, etc.)*.
scorn dezprezo, desdém.
scorn (to) desprezar, desdenhar.
scornful desdenhoso.
Scottish escocês.
scrape (to) raspar *(on a surface)*.
scratch arranhadura, arranhão *(on the hand,
　etc.)*; raspadura *(on a table, etc.)*.
scratch (to) arranhar *(with the nails)*; rasgar *(a
　table, etc.)*; cancelar, apagar *(eliminate)*.
scream (to) berrar, gritar.
screen biombo *(partition)*; tela *(windows,
　movie, computer)*; cortina, barreira.
screw parafuso.
screw (to) parafusar, atarraxar (x = sh).
scruple escrúpulo.
sculptor escultor.
sculpture escultura.
sea mar.
seal selo.
seal (to) selar; lacrar.
seam costura.
search busca, procura *(act of looking for)*;
　pesquisa, investigação *(research,
　investigation)*.
　in search of em procura de, em busca de.
search (to) procurar, buscar *(to search for)*;
　examinar *(to comb through)*; revistar *(a
　place)*; explorar *(to explore)*.
　to search after indagar, perguntar por.
　to search for procurar, buscar.
seasick enjoado.
season estação *(of the year)*; temporada
　(sports).
　in season na época.
　out of season fora da época.

season (to) sazonar, condimentar *(food)*.
seat *n.* assento; banco *(car);* sede
(government, etc.).
   to take a seat sentar-se, tomar assento.
   front seat assento dianteiro.
   back seat assento traseiro.
   seat belt cínto de seguiança.
second segundo; em segundo lugar.
   second-class de segunda classe.
   second year o segundo ano.
   Wait a second! Espere um momento!
   on second thought depois de pensá-lo bem.
   second to none sem par.
secondary secundário.
secondary school escola secundária.
secondhand de segunda mão, usado.
secrecy segredo, reserva, silêncio.
secret secreto.
   in secret em segredo, secretamente.
secretary secretário, secretária.
section seção (secção).
secure seguro, certo, firme.
secure (to) assegurar; garantir; conseguir
(obtain).
securely seguramente, certamente.
security segurança *(assurance; crime
prevention)*, garantia.
see (to) ver.
   See? Sabe? Compreende?
   I see. Já estou compreendendo. Já estou
   vendo.
   Let's see. Vamos ver.
   to see about averiguar, indagar.
   to see someone off despedir-se.
   See ya! Até logo!
   to see someone home acompanhar à
   casa.
   to see the point perceber, compreender.
   to see a thing through terminar, levar a
   cabo.
   to see fit achar conveniente.
   to see one's way clear ver o modo de
   fazer alguma coisa.
   to see to cuidar de, encarregar-se de.
   seeing that visto que, desde que.
seed semente.
seek (to) procurar, buscar.
seem (to) parecer.
   it seems to me parece-me.
   it seems parece.
seize (to) agarrar *(to grasp);* pegar, apanhar *(to
get hold of, to take);* apoderar-se de *(to
take possession of)*.
seldom raramente, poucas vezes.
select seleto (selecto), escolhido.
select (to) escolher, selecionar (seleccionar).
selection seleção (selecção).
self mesmo, por si mesmo; si, se.
   myself eu mesmo.

I said to myself. Disse para mim. Eu me
   disse.
   yourself você mesmo; o senhor mesmo.
   himself ele mesmo.
   He said to himself. Ele disse para si. Ele
   se disse.
   She said to herself. Ela disse para si. Ela
   se disse.
   ourselves nós mesmos.
   yourselves vocês mesmos; os senhores
   mesmos.
   themselves eles mesmos.
   Wash yourself. Lave-se. Lave-te *(fam.)*.
   by himself por si mesmo.
self-confidence autoconfiança.
self-defense autodefesa.
self-determination autodeterminação.
self-evident evidente, claro, patente.
selfish egoísta.
selfishness egoísmo.
self-taught autodidata (autodidacta).
sell (to) vender.
semester semestre.
senate senado.
senator senador.
send (to) enviar, mandar, expedir, transmitir.
   to send away despedir, mandar embora.
   to send word mandar recado, mandar
   dizer.
   to send back devolver.
   to send in mandar entrar.
   to send for mandar buscar.
senior mais velho, mais antigo, superior.
   John Williams, Sr. João Guimarães
   Senior.
sense sentido, senso.
   common sense senso comum.
   to be out of one's senses ter perdido o
   juízo.
   sense of humor senso de humor.
sensible sensato, razoável.
sensibly sensatamente.
sentence frase *(grammar);* sentença,
julgamento *(court)*.
sentence (to) sentenciar, condenar.
sentiment sentimento.
sentimental sentimental.
separate separado, distinto.
separate (to) separar, afastar.
separately separadamente.
separation separação.
September setembro (Setembro).
serene sereno.
sergeant sargento.
serial em série, serial.
series série.
serious sério.
seriously seriamente.
   to take seriously levar a sério.

seriousness seriedade, gravidade.
sermon sermão.
servant empregado, criado.
serve (to) servir.
  to serve the purpose servir.
  to serve notice notificar, fazer saber, avisar.
  to serve one right ser bem feito, ser merecido.
  to serve as servir de.
service serviço.
  at your service às suas ordens.
  to be of service ser útil, servir.
session sessão.
set *adj.* fixo (x = ks), estabelecido, determinado; *n.* jogo, aparelho.
  set price preço fixo.
  set of dishes jogo de copos.
  aparelho de TV TV set.
set (to) pôr.
  to set aside pôr de lado.
  to set back impedir; atrasar *(watch)*.
  to set free liberar.
  to set in order pôr em ordem.
  to set on fire incendiar.
  to set to work começar a trabalhar.
  to set up cadastrar.
settle (to) arranjar, arrumar *(arrange);* pagar, liquidar, saldar *(an account, a debt);* fixar residência, estabelecer-se *(to settle down);* pousar, assentar *(to go down, as liquids).*
  to settle an account saldar uma conta.
settlement acordo, entendimento *(adjustment, agreement);* colônia (colónia), povoção *(village);* colonização *(colonization).*
seven sete.
seven hundred setecentos.
seventeen dezessete (dezassete).
seventeenth décimo sétimo.
seventh sétimo.
seventieth septuagésimo.
seventy setenta.
several vários, alguns.
  several times várias vezes.
severe severo.
severity severidade, gravidade.
sew (to) coser, costurar.
sewing costura.
  sewing machine máquina de costura.
sex sexo (x = ks).
sexual sexual (x = ks).
shade sombra.
shade (to) sombrear.
shadow sombra.
shady sombreado; suspeito *(disreputable).*
shake sacudida, tremor; aperto de mãos *(handshake);* batida *(drink).*
shake (to) sacudir; estremecer *(to tremble);* apertar a mão *(shake hands).*

  to shake your head abanar a cabeça.
shame vergonha.
shame (to) envergonhar.
shameful vergonhoso, escandaloso.
shameless desavergonhado, sem vergonha.
shampoo xampu (x = sh), lavagem de cabeça.
shape forma, figura.
shape (to) formar, dar forma.
share porção, parte; ação (acção) *(stock).*
share (to) partilhar, repartir *(to apportion);* participar, tomar parte em *(to share in).*
shareholder acionista (accionista).
sharp agudo, afiado, pontiagudo *(sharp-pointed).*
  a sharp pain uma dor aguda.
  a sharp curve uma curva fechada.
  sharp-witted esperto, inteligente.
  at two o'clock sharp às duas horas em ponto.
sharpen (to) afiar, aguçar; apontar, fazer a ponta *(a pencil).*
shatter (to) despedaçar, estilhaçar, espatifar.
shave (to) barbear, fazer a barba.
  shaving brush pincel de barba.
  shaving cream creme de barbear.
shawl xale (x = sh).
she ela.
shears tesoura.
shed alpendre, galpão, barracão.
shed (to) perder *(fur, etc.),* derramar *(tears, etc.).*
sheep carneiro, ovelha.
sheet lençol *(bed);* folha *(paper).*
shelf estante, prateleira.
shell concha, carapaça; casca *(egg, nut);* granada, bomba *(military).*
shelter refúgio, abrigo.
  to take shelter abrigar-se.
  to give shelter abrigar, proteger.
shelter (to) abrigar, proteger, dar asilo.
shepherd pastor.
sheriff xerife (x = sh).
sherry xerez (x = sh).
Shh! Psiu!
shield escudo, defesa.
shield (to) proteger, defender, servir de escudo.
shift mudança *(change);* turno *(work).*
shift (to) mudar.
shine (to) brilhar, iluminar; polir, lustrar *(shoes, etc.).*
shining brilhante, reluzente, lustroso.
shiny lustroso, brilhante.
ship navio, vapor.
  merchant ship navio mercante.
ship (to) embarcar, despachar, enviar, mandar.
shipment embarque, despacho, carregamento.
shipwreck naufrágio.
shipyard estaleiro.

shirt camisa.
   sport shirt camisa-esporte.
shiver tremor, arrepio, calafrio.
shiver (to) tremer *(from cold)*, tiritar.
shock choque; descarga *(electrical)*.
shock (to) chocar, abalar.
shoe sapato.
   shoe store sapataria.
   shoelaces cordões de sapato.
   shoe polish graxa (x = sh) para sapato.
shoehorn calçadeira.
shoemaker sapateiro.
shoot (to) atirar, disparar; filmar *(to film)*.
shop loja.
   to go shopping ir às compras.
shore costa, praia *(sea);* margem *(lake)*.
short curto *(not long);* baixo (x = sh) *(not tall);* breve, conciso *(brief);* com falta de *(of goods)*.
   shortcut atalho.
   short circuit curto-circuito.
   short story conto.
   in short em resumo.
   in a short while dentro de pouco, em breve.
   a short time ago há pouco tempo.
shorten (to) encurtar, abreviar.
shorts calças curtas.
shot tiro, descarga.
should deve, deveria, devia.
   I should go eu devia ir.
   The window should be open. A janela devia estar aberta.
shoulder ombro.
   shoulder to shoulder ombro a ombro.
shout grito, berro.
shout (to) gritar, berrar.
shovel pá.
show exposição (x = sh) *(exhibition);* espetáculo (espectáculo) *(spectacle);* entretenimento *(entertainment)*.
   show window vitrina (montra).
show (to) mostrar, ensinar, provar, demonstrar.
   to show someone in mandar entrar.
   to show to the door acompanhar até a porta.
   to show off exibir-se.
   to show up apresentar-se, aparecer.
shower aguaceiro, chuveiro.
   shower bath (banho de) chuveiro.
shrewd astuto, sutil.
shrimp camarão.
shrink (to) encolher, contrair-se.
shrub arbusto.
shrug (to) encolher os ombros.
shut (to) fechar.
   to shut in encerrar, confinar.
   to shut out excluir.
   to shut up calar, fazer calar.

shutter veneziana; obturador *(photography)*.
shy tímido, acanhado.
sick doente.
   to feel sick sentir-se mal, sentir-se doente.
   I'm sick of this! Estou farto disto!
sickness doença.
side lado.
   side by side lado a lado.
   on this side deste lado.
   on that side desse lado.
   on the other side de outro lado.
   wrong side out ao revés.
   I'm on your side. Estou do seu lado.
sidewalk calçada.
sieve peneira.
sigh suspiro.
sigh (to) suspirar.
sight vista *(sense);* espetáculo *(spectacle)*.
   at first sight à primeira vista.
   to keep in sight não perder de vista.
sightseeing (to go) ver as coisas de interesse, visitar os lugares notáveis.
sign sinal *(mark);* letreiro, tabuleta *(as over a shop)*.
   sign of the cross sinal da cruz.
sign (to) assinar.
   to sign a check assinar um cheque.
   to sign up alistar-se.
signal sinal, aviso.
signal (to) fazer sinal, fazer sináis, comunicar por meio de sinais.
signature assinatura.
significance significado, importância.
significant significante, importante.
silence silêncio.
silence (to) silenciar, fazer calar.
silent silencioso; calado *(person)*.
silently silenciosamente.
silk seda.
silly tolo, bobo.
silver prata.
silverware prataria.
similar semelhante, similar.
similarity semelhança, similaridade.
simple simples.
simplicity simplicidade.
simplification simplificação.
simplify (to) simplificar.
simply simplesmente.
sin pecado.
sin (to) pecar.
since *adj.* desde então, depois; *conj.* já que, desde que, visto que *(because, seeing that); prep.* desde, depois de.
   since then desde então.
sincere sincero.
sincerely sinceramente.
   sincerely yours atenciosamente.
sincerity sinceridade.

sing (to) cantar.
singer cantor.
single só, único; solteiro *(unmarried).*
    not a single word nem uma só palavra.
    single room quarto de solteiro.
singly individualmente, separadamente.
singular singular.
sink pia, bacia.
sink (to) afundar, ir a pique.
sinner pecador.
sip sorvo, golinho.
sip (to) sorver, beber em golinhos.
sir senhor.
    Dear Sir: Prezado Senhor:
siren sirena *(alarm);* sereia *(mythology).*
sister irmã.
sister-in-law cunhada.
sit (to) sentar-se.
situated situado.
situation situação.
six seis.
six hundred seiscentos.
sixteen dezesseis (dezasseis).
sixteenth décimo sexto.
sixth sexto, sexta parte.
sixtieth sexagésimo.
sixty sessenta.
size tamanho, medida.
skate patim.
    ice skate patim para o gelo.
    roller skate patim de rodas.
skate (to) patinar.
skeleton esqueleto.
sketch esboço, desenho.
sketch (to) esboçar.
skill destreza, habilidade.
skillful destro, habilidoso.
skin pele.
skinny magro.
skirt saia.
skull crânio, caveira.
sky céu.
    sky blue azul-celeste.
slander calúnia.
slang gíria.
slap bofetada, palmada, tapa.
slap (to) dar tapa, dar bofetada, esbofetear.
slate ardósia.
slaughter matança.
slave escravo.
slavery escravidão.
slay (to) matar, assassinar.
sleep sono.
    to go to sleep deitar-se, adormecer.
sleepy sonolento.
    to be sleepy estar com sono, ter sono.
sleeve manga.
slender delgado, magro, esbelto.
slice fatia.

slice (to) cortar, cortar em fatias.
slide (to) escorregar, deslizar.
slight ligeiro, leve; insignificante.
slight (to) menosprezar.
slightly ligeiramente, levemente; um pouco.
slim delgado, magro, esbelto.
sling tipóia *(medical).*
slip escorregão *(slide);* combinação
    (underwear).
slip (to) escorregar, deslizar.
    to slip one's mind escapar à memória.
    to slip away fugir, escapulir(-se).
slippers chinelos.
slippery escorregadio, escorregadiço,
    resvaladiço.
slope inclinação, declive.
slow lento, devagar.
    to be slow *(as a watch)* atrasar-se.
    to slow down reduzir a velocidade.
slowly lentamente, devagar.
    Drive slowly. Dirija devagar.
    Go slowly. Vá devagar.
slowness lentidão.
slumber sono leve.
slumber (to) dormitar.
slums bairros pobres; favelas Ⓑ.
sly astuto.
small pequeno.
    small change troco.
smallness pequenez.
smart esperto.
smash (to) esmagar, escangalhar.
smell cheiro, odor.
smell (to) cheirar.
smile sorriso.
smile (to) sorrir.
smoke fumaça, fumo; cigarro *(a cigarette).*
smoke (to) fumar *(tobacco);* fumegar.
    No smoking. É proibido fumar.
smoker fumante (fumador).
smokestack chaminé.
smooth liso, macio, plano, suave.
snail caracol.
snake cobra, serpente.
snatch (to) agarrar. arrebatar.
sneeze espirro.
sneeze (to) espirrar.
snore (to) roncar (resonar).
snow neve.
snow (to) nevar.
snowflake floco de neve.
snowy nevoso *(weather);* coberto de neve
    (streets, etc.).
so assim, tal; de modo que, de maneira que.
    That is so. Assim é.
    so-and-so fulano de tal.
    so much tanto.
    at so much a meter a tanto o metro.
    so that para que, de modo que.

so-so regular; mais ou menos; assim, assim.
  So long! Até logo!
  Is that so? Realmente? É verdade?
  I think so. Acredito. Acho que sim.
soak (to) embeber, pôr de molho.
soap sabão, sabonete *(bar of soap)*.
  soap opera telenovela.
sob soluço.
sob (to) soluçar.
sober sóbrio *(not drunk);* sério, solene.
so-called chamado.
sociable sociável.
social social.
socialism socialismo.
society sociedade.
socket cavidade; tomada *(electric)*.
  eye socket órbita de olho.
socks meias.
soda soda; soda pop.
  soda water água gasosa, água com gás.
sofa sofá.
soft macio, suave, mole.
  soft-boiled eggs ovos quentes.
soften (to) amolecer, suavizar.
softness moleza, maciez, suavidade.
software software.
soil solo, terra.
soil (to) sujar, manchar.
soiled sujo.
solar solar.
sold vendido.
  sold out esgotado.
soldier soldado.
sole *adj.* só, único; *n.* sola *(shoe);* linguado *(fish)*.
solemn solene.
solemnity solenidade.
solid sólido *(object);* contínuo *(line)*.
solidity solidez.
solidly solidamente.
solitary solitário.
solitude solidão.
soluble solúvel.
solution solução.
solve (to) solver, resolver.
some um pouco; algum, alguns, alguma, algumas, uns, umas.
  Some people think so. Há quem pensa assim.
  at some time or other em qualquer ocasião.
  Bring me some cigars. Traga-me alguns charutos.
  There are some left. Ainda ficam alguns.
  some of his books alguns dos seus livros.
  some two hundred uns duzentos.
somebody alguém.
  somebody else alguém mais.

somehow de algum modo, de alguma maneira.
something alguma coisa, algo.
  Something else? Mais alguma coisa?
sometime algum dia, alguma vez.
sometimes algumas vezes, às vezes.
somewhat um tanto.
  somewhat busy um tanto ocupado.
somewhere em alguma parte, algures.
  somewhere else em outra parte.
son filho.
song canção, canto.
son-in-law genro.
soon logo, breve, cedo.
  as soon as logo que, assim que.
  as soon as possible o mais cedo possível.
  sooner or later mais cedo ou mais tarde.
  the sooner the better quanto antes melhor.
  How soon will you finish? Quanto tempo demorará para terminar?
soothe (to) aliviar, acalmar, suavizar.
sore *adj.* dolorido, doído; *n.* chaga *(on the body)*.
  sore throat dor de garganta.
sorrow dor, tristeza, pesar, mágoa.
sorry arrependido; lamentável *(pathetic)*.
  to be sorry sentir.
  Sorry. Desculpe.
  I'm very sorry. Sinto muito.
sort espécie, classe, maneira.
  all sorts of people toda classe de gente.
  a sort of uma espécie de.
  nothing of the sort nada disso.
soul alma.
sound *adj.* são, firme; *n.* som, ruido, barulho.
  safe and sound são e salvo.
  sound sleep sono profundo.
soup sopa.
  soup plate prato de sopa, prato fundo.
  vegetable soup sopa de legumes.
sour azedo, ácido.
source fonte.
south sul.
  South America América do Sul.
  South American sul-americano.
southern do sul, meridional, sulista.
souvenir lembrança.
soviet soviético.
sow (to) semear.
space espaço.
spaceship nave espacial.
spacious espaçoso, amplo, vasto.
spade pá.
Spaniard espanhol.
Spanish espanhol.
  Spanish America América Espanhola, Hispano-América.
  Spanish American hispano-americano.
spare de sobra; sobressalente, de reserva.

spare time horas vagas, tempo livre.
spare money dinheiro de reserva.
spare room quarto de hóspedes.
spare parts peças sobressalentes.
spare tire pneu sobressalente.
spare (to) poupar *(to save);* perdoar *(to forgive).*
sparingly frugalmente.
spark faísca.
spark (to) faiscar.
spark plug vela.
sparrow pardal.
speak (to) falar.
    to speak for falar em favor de, falar em nome de.
    to speak for itself ser evidente, ser claro.
    to speak one's mind dizer o que se pensa.
    to speak out falar claramente.
    to speak to falar a.
    to speak up falar, dizer.
speaker orador, locutor.
spear lança.
spearmint hortelã.
special especial.
    special delivery entrega urgente.
specialist especialista.
specialize (to) especializar.
specially especialmente.
specialty especialidade; ramo especializado *(medicine, etc.).*
specific específico.
specifically especificamente.
specify (to) especificar.
specimen espécime, amostra.
spectacle espetáculo (espectáculo).
spectacles óculos.
spectator espectador.
speculation especulação.
speech fala; discurso; língua.
    to make a speech fazer um discurso.
speechless estupefato.
speed velocidade.
    at full speed a toda velocidade.
    speed limit velocidade máxima (x = s).
    to speed up acelerar, apressar-se.
speed (to) ir em alta velocidade.
spell (to) soletrar.
spelling ortografia.
spend (to) gastar *(money);* passar *(time).*
    to spend time passar tempo.
    to spend the night passar a noite.
    I'll spend the winter in the south. Vou passar o inverno (Inverno) no sul.
spice especiaria, condimento.
spicy condimentado, picante.
spider aranha.
spin giro, volta; parafuso *(aviation).*
spin (to) fiar *(thread, etc.);* girar, virar, rodar.
spinach espinafre.

spine espinha *(thorn);* espinha dorsal *(backbone).*
spiral espiral.
spirit espírito.
spiritual espiritual.
spit espeto *(for roasting);* cuspe *(saliva).*
spit (to) cuspir.
spite rancor, despeito, ressentimento.
    in spite of apesar de.
spiteful rancoroso, vingativo.
splash (to) borrifar; salpicar *(splash with).*
splendid esplêndido, ótimo (óptimo), magnífico.
splendor esplendor.
split fendido, dividido, partido.
split (to) fender, dividir, partir, repartir.
    They split the difference. Repartiram a diferença.
    to split hairs perder-se em minúcias.
spoil (to) danificar, arruinar, estragar *(to ruin);* apodrecer *(to rot).*
spoke raio *(of a wheel).*
sponge esponja.
sponsor patrocinador *(TV, etc.),* padrinho.
spontaneity espontaneidade.
spontaneous espontâneo.
spool carretel, bobina.
spoon colher.
    teaspoon colher de chá.
    tablespoon colher de sopa.
spoonful colherada.
sport *adj.* esportivo, de esporte; *n.* esporte (desporto).
    sport shirt camisa-esporte.
sports esportes (desportos).
spot mancha *(stain);* borrão *(of ink, paint);* lugar, ponto *(place).*
    on the spot no lugar, no mesmo lugar; imediatamente; em apuros *(in trouble).*
sprain torcedura, distensão.
sprain (to) torcer.
spray (to) pulverizar, borrifar.
sprayer pulverizador.
spread difusão, extensão.
spread (to) espalhar; propagar, difundir *(news, etc.);* estender, distribuir.
spring primavera (Primavera) *(season);* fonte, manancial *(water);* salto, pulo *(jump);* mola *(of wire, etc.).*
    box spring colchão de molas.
spring (to) saltar, pular.
    to spring at lançar-se sobre.
sprinkle (to) regar *(lawn);* chuviscar *(rain);* salpicar *(in cooking).*
sprout (to) brotar, germinar.
spy espião.
spy (to) espiar, espionar.
squad pelotão, esquadra.
squadron esquadra, esquadrão, esquadrilha.

square quadrado; praça *(town).*
  two square meters dois metros quadrados.
squash abóbora.
squash (to) esmagar.
squeeze (to) espremer, comprimir, apertar.
squirrel esquilo.
stab punhalada.
stab (to) apunhalar.
staff pau *(pole);* bastão, bengala *(rod, stick);* pessoal *(personnel);* estado-maior *(military).*
  office staff pessoal de escritório.
  editorial staff redação.
  staff officer oficial de estado-maior.
stage palco, tablado *(theater);* etapa *(life, etc.).*
  by stages por etapas.
stage (to) representar, encenar *(theater).*
stain mancha; tinta, tintura *(coloring).*
stain (to) manchar.
stair degrau; *pl.* escada.
stake estaca, poste *(for driving into the ground).*
  at stake arriscado, em perigo.
stake (to) estacar, estaquear *(into the ground);* apostar, arriscar *(money).*
stammer (to) gaguejar, tartamudear.
stamp selo; timbre; carimbo *(rubber).*
  postage stamp selo de correio.
stand posto, banca (quiosque) *(stall);* tribuna, plataforma *(platform);* posição, opinião *(opinion);* resistência *(defense).*
  newsstand banca (quiosque) de jornais.
stand (to) colocar, pôr em pé *(to set upright);* levantar-se, pôr-se em pé, estar em pé *(to stand, be standing);* resistir, sustentar, agüentar (aguentar) *(put up with);* parar *(to stop moving).*
  Stand up! Levante-se!
  I'm up. I'm standing. Estou em pé.
  I can't stand him. Não o posso agüentar (aguentar).
  to stand a chance ter uma probabilidade.
  to stand by estar a postos, estar de prontidão.
  to stand for estar por, favorecer, aprovar; significar, querer dizer *(to mean);* agüentar (aguentar), tolerar, permitir *(to tolerate).*
  to stand in line fazer fila.
  to stand off manter-se à distância.
  to stand on one's own two feet ser independente.
  to stand one's ground resistir, manter-se firme.
  to stand out salientar-se, distinguir-se.
  to stand up levantar-se, pôr-se em pé.
standard norma, padrão, modelo; estandarte, bandeira *(flag).*
  standard of living padrão de vida.

  standard time hora oficial.
standpoint ponto de vista.
star estrela, astro.
starch amido *(food);* goma *(for clothes).*
start princípio, começo *(beginning);* partida, começo, saída *(starting point, departure);* arranque *(of car, engine).*
start (to) começar *(to begin);* principiar, partir, sair *(to start out);* arrancar *(an engine).*
starvation fome, morte de fome.
starve (to) morrer de fome.
state estado, condição, situação.
state (to) afirmar, declarar.
statement declaração, afirmação; relatório *(report);* extrato (extracto) de contas, conta *(of account, bill).*
stateroom camarote *(ship),* cabina.
statesman estadista.
station estação.
  broadcast station emissora.
  railroad station estação ferroviária.
  police station delegacia.
stationary estacionário, parado.
stationery artigos de papelaria, papel de carta.
stationery store papelaria.
statistical estatístico.
statistics estatística.
statue estátua.
stay estadia, permanência; suspensão *(legal).*
stay (to) ficar, permanecer, morar, residir, parar; suspender *(to put off).*
  to stay in ficar em casa.
  to stay in bed ficar na cama.
  to stay away estar ausente, não voltar.
steadily constantemente.
steady firme, fixo (x = ks), estável, constante.
steak bife.
steal (to) roubar, furtar.
steam vapor.
steamboat barco a vapor.
steam engine máquina a vapor.
steamer navio a vapor, vapor.
steamship navio a vapor.
  steamship line companhia de navegação.
steel aço.
steep íngreme, escarpado.
steer (to) guiar, dirigir, pilotar, conduzir.
steering wheel volante.
stem talo, tronco; raiz *(grammar).*
stenographer taquígrafo, estenógrafo.
stenography taquigrafia, estenografia.
step passo; degrau *(stair).*
  step by step passo a passo.
  in step em cadência.
  out of step fora de cadência.
  steps escada *(stairs).*
step (to) dar um passo, pisar, andar, caminhar.
  to step aside dar passagem.
  to step back retroceder.

to step down descer.
to step in entrar; intervir *(intervene)*.
to step on pisar.
to step out sair; descer *(down)*.
stepbrother meio-irmão.
stepchild enteado.
stepdaughter enteada.
stepfather padrasto.
stepmother madrasta.
stepsister meia-irmã.
stepson enteado.
stern *adj.* austero, severo; *n.* popa, ré.
stew cozido, guisado.
steward camareiro, aeromoço.
stewardess camareira, aeromoça.
stick pau, vara; bastão, bengala *(cane)*.
stick (to) apunhalar *(to stab)*; transpassar, perfurar *(to penetrate)*; colar, grudar *(to glue)*; fixar (x = ks).
    to stick by manter-se fiel a.
    to stick out pôr para fora; salientar.
    to stick it out agüentar (aguentar) firme.
    to stick up for defender, tomar a defesa de.
    to stick to perseverar, sustentar, manter, aderir a.
stiff rígido, duro, teso; afetado *(not natural in manners)*; cerimonioso *(formal)*; forte *(wind, drink)*; caro *(of prices)*.
    stiff collar colarinho engomado.
    stiff neck torcicolo.
stiffen (to) endurecer, fortalecer; obstinar-se.
stiffness rigidez, dureza.
still *adj.* quieto, imóvel, tranqüilo (tranquilo); *adv.* ainda, não obstante, entretanto.
    to stand still ficar quieto.
    still life natureza morta.
    Stay still! Não se mexa!
    She's still at home. Ela ainda está em casa.
stillness calma, quietude, silêncio.
sting picada.
sting (to) picar.
stir (to) mexer, agitar, misturar; mexer-se *(move)*.
    to stir the fire atiçar o fogo.
    to stir up comover, excitar.
stirrup estribo.
stock estoque (existência), mercadoria *(supply of goods)*; ações (acções) *(stocks, shares)*; gado *(animals)*; estirpe *(lineage, race)*.
    stock market Bolsa, mercado de valores.
    in stock em estoque (em existência).
    out of stock esgotado.
stockings meias.
stomach estômago.
stone pedra.
stool banquinho, banco, tamborete.
stop parada (paragem).

stop (to) parar, deter, deter-se; parar, ficar *(to stay)*.
    to stop raining deixar (x = sh) de chover.
    Stop! Alto!
    Stop that! Basta! *(That's enough!)*
    Stop a minute. Fique um momento.
store loja, armazém.
    department store magazine, grande armazém.
stork cegonha.
storm tempestade.
stormy tempestuoso.
story história, conto *(tale)*; andar *(building)*; mentira *(lie)*.
    short story conto.
    as the story goes conforme consta, segundo consta.
stout sólido, corpulento, gordo.
stove fogão *(for cooking)*; estufa *(for heating)*.
straight direito, reto *(recto)*.
    straight line linha reta.
    Go straight ahead. Siga bem em frente.
straighten (to) endireitar, pôr em ordem.
straightforward direito; reto *(recto)*; franco *(frank)*; honesto, honrado *(honest)*.
strain tensão *(tension)*; esforço *(force)*.
strain (to) coar *(through a strainer)*; cansar *(the eyes, etc.)*; esforçar-se *(to make an effort)*.
    to stand the strain agüentar (aguentar) o esforço.
strainer coador, peneira.
strange estranho, raro *(odd)*; desconhecido *(not known)*.
strangeness estranheza, singularidade.
stranger estrangeiro, estranho, desconhecido.
strap correia.
strategic estratégico.
strategy estratégia.
straw palha.
    straw hat chapéu de palha.
    to be on the last straw a última gota, o cúmulo.
strawberry morango.
stream corrente, riacho.
street rua.
streetcar bonde Ⓑ (carro eléctrico).
strength força.
strengthen (to) fortalecer(-se), reforçar(-se).
stress stress *(mental strain)*; força *(force)*; esforço *(effort)*; tensão *(strain)*; pressão *(pressure)*; acento *(accent)*; ênfase *(emphasis)*; importância *(importance)*.
stress (to) acentuar, dar ênfase a.
stretch (to) estirar, esticar.
stretcher maca, padiola.
strict estrito (estricto), rigoroso, severo.
strike greve *(of workers)*.

strike (to) bater, dar pancada, golpear; entrar em greve *(workers)*.
   to strike at atacar.
   to strike a match acender um fósforo.
   to strike against chocar-se contra, colidir com.
   to strike back revidar.
   to strike home acertar, acertar no alvo.
striking surpreendente, extraordinário.
string barbante, fio, cordel, corda.
strip faixa *(land);* tiro *(paper).*
stroll passeio, volta.
   to go for a stroll dar uma volta.
stroll (to) passear.
strong forte, poderoso.
stronghold fortaleza, baluarte.
structure estrutura, construção.
struggle luta.
struggle (to) lutar.
stubborn teimoso, obstinado, cabeçudo.
student estudante, aluno.
studious estudioso.
study estudo.
study (to) estudar.
stuff fazenda, pano *(cloth, material);* troços, trens *(belongings);* coisas, trastes, bugigangas *(miscellaneous things);* bobagem, tolice *(foolishness).*
stumble (to) tropeçar.
stump toco *(tree);* coto *(limb).*
stupid estúpido.
   to be stupid ser estúpido.
stupidity estupidez.
stupor estupor.
style estilo, maneira, modo; moda *(fashion).*
subdue (to) subjugar.
subject súdito *(of king);* matéria, assunto, tema *(subject matter).*
subject (to) submeter.
submarine submarino.
submission submissão.
submit (to) submeter, submeter-se.
subordinate subordinado.
subscribe (to) subscrever.
subscriber assinante, subscritor.
subscription subscrição; assinatura *(to magazine).*
subsequent subseqüente (subsequente), seguinte, ulterior.
substance substância.
substantial substancial.
substitute substituto.
substitute (to) substituir.
substitution substituição.
subtract (to) subtrair, deduzir.
suburb subúrbio.
subway metrô.
succeed (to) sair bem, suceder, ter sucesso, ter êxito (x = z); lograr.

success sucesso, êxito (x = z).
successful feliz, bem sucedido, próspero.
successive sucessivo, consecutivo.
successor sucessor.
such tal *(pl.* tais); semelhante.
   such as tal como.
   in such a way de tal modo, de tal maneira.
   such that de modo que, de forma que.
sudden repentino, súbito.
   all of a sudden de repente.
suddenly repentinamente, subitamente.
suffer (to) sofrer.
suffering sofrimento, padecimento.
suffice (to) ser suficiente, bastar.
sugar açúcar.
suggest (to) sugerir.
suggestion sugestão.
suicide suicídio.
   to commit suicide suicidar-se.
suit terno (fato), traje completo *(clothes);* processo *(court);* naipe *(cards).*
suit (to) acomodar, adaptar *(to make suitable);* satisfazer, agradar *(to please, to satisfy);* vestir *(to clothe).*
suitable adequado, apropriado.
suitably adequadamente, apropriadamente.
suitcase mala.
sulfur enxofre.
sum soma, total.
summary sumário.
summer verão (Verão).
   summer resort lugar de veraneio.
summit topo, cume; cúmulo.
summon (to) convocar, chamar.
summons citação *(to court).*
sun sol.
   sunbath banho de sol.
   to take a sunbath tomar banho de sol.
sunbeam raio de sol.
sunburn queimadura de sol.
sunburnt queimado pelo sol.
Sunday domingo.
sunlight luz do sol.
sunny de sol, ensolarado *(weather);* alegre, jovial *(disposition).*
sunrise nascer do sol, levantar do sol.
sunset pôr do sol.
sunshine luz solar.
superb esplêndido, soberbo, magnífico.
superfluous supérfluo.
superintendent superintendente.
superior superior.
superiority superioridade.
superstition superstição.
superstitious supersticioso.
supper jantar, ceia.
supplement suplemento.
supply abastecimento.
   supply and demand oferta e procura.

supply (to) abastecer, fornecer, prover.
support apoio, sustento; manutenção *(act of providing for)*.
support (to) apoiar, sustentar; manter *(to provide for)*.
suppose (to) supor.
supposition suposição, conjetura (conjectura).
suppress (to) suprimir.
suppression supressão.
supreme supremo.
  Supreme Court Corte Suprema.
sure certo, seguro.
  to be sure estar certo.
  be sure to não deixe (x = sh) de.
  for sure ao certo.
surely seguramente, certamente.
surface superfície.
surgeon cirurgião.
surgery cirurgia.
surname apelido, sobrenome.
surprise surpresa.
surprise (to) surpreender.
surprising surpreendente.
surprisingly surpreendentemente.
surrender rendição, entrega.
surrender (to) render(-se), entregar(-se).
surround (to) cercar, rodear.
surrounding circundante.
surroundings arredores, vizinhança; meio, ambiente *(atmosphere)*.
survey sondagem *(poll);* exame (x = z), estudo; inspeção (inspecção) *(inspection);* levantamento topográfico *(land)*.
survey (to) examinar (x = z), estudar; inspecionar (inspeccionar) *(to inspect);* levantar um plano *(land)*.
survival sobrevivência.
survivor sobrevivente.
susceptible suscetível (susceptível).
suspect suspeito.
suspect (to) suspeitar.
suspend (to) suspender.
suspenders suspensórios.
suspicion suspeição, suspeita.
suspicious suspeito *(suspect);* suspeitoso *(distrustful)*.
swallow andorinha (bird); bocado *(food);* trago *(drink)*.
swallow (to) engolir.
swamp pântano.
swan cisne.
swarm enxame (x = sh).
swarm (to) enxamear (x = sh).
swear (to) jurar, prestar juramento.
  to swear by jurar por.
sweat suor.
sweet doce.
  sweet potato batata doce.

  to have a sweet tooth ser guloso.
sweetheart noivo, noiva.
sweetness doçura.
swell (to) inchar *(medical),* engrossar.
swift rápido, veloz.
swiftly rapidamente, velozmente.
swim (to) nadar.
  My head's swimming. Estou com a cabeça zonza.
swimmer nadador.
swimming pool piscina.
swing balanço *(in playground);* balanceio, oscilação.
  in full swing em plena atividade (actividade).
swing (to) balançar, oscilar, fazer girar.
switch chave *(key);* interruptor, comutador *(electric switch);* agulha *(railroad)*.
switch (to) ligar, desligar *(to turn electric switch on or off);* desviar *(railroad);* trocar *(to change)*.
sword espada.
syllable sílaba.
symbol símbolo.
sympathetic simpático.
sympathize (to) compadecer-se, simpatizar.
sympathy compaixão, simpatia, pêsames *(condolences)*.
symphony sinfonia.
  symphony orchestra orquestra sinfônica (sinfónica).
symptom sintoma.
synthetic sintético.
syrup xarope (x = sh).
system sistema.
systematic sistemático, metódico.

T

table mesa; tabela *(of measures, etc.)*.
  to set the table pôr a mesa.
tablecloth toalha de mesa.
table lamp lâmpada de mesa.
tablespoon colher de sopa; colherada *(measurement)*.
tablet comprimido *(of aspirin, etc.);* bloco de papel *(for writing);* tábua, chapa, placa *(with an inscription)*.
tableware utensílios de mesa.
tact tato (tacto).
tactful com tato (tacto), diplomático.
tactical tático (táctico).
tactics tática (táctica).
tactless sem tato (tacto), indelicado.
tag etiqueta *(on clothing)*.
tail rabo; cauda *(of comet, etc.)*.
tailor alfaiate.

take (to) tomar; pegar em *(to grasp);* ganhar *(prize).*
>**to take a bath** tomar banho, banhar-se.
>**to take a picture** tirar uma fotografia, tirar uma foto.
>**to take a walk** dar um passeio, dar uma volta.
>**to take a nap** tirar uma soneca.
>**to take a trip** fazer uma viagem.
>**to take an oath** prestar juramento.
>**to take apart** desarmar *(a machine).*
>**to take a step** dar um passo.
>**to take away** levar.
>**to take back** levar de volta, receber de volta.
>**to take into account** levar em conta.
>**to take advantage of** aproveitar-se de.
>**to take advice** tomar conselho.
>**to take care of** ter cuidado de.
>**to take charge of** encarregar-se de.
>**to take into consideration** levar em consideração.
>**to take to heart** levar a sério.
>**to take it easy** ir com calma.
>**to take leave** despedir-se.
>**to take notes** tomar notas.
>**to take notice** observar, notar.
>**to take out** tirar; levar para fora.
>**to take after** parecer-se com *(resemble).*
>**to take off** decolar, levantar vôo *(plane);* tirar *(a piece of clothing).*
>**to take one's clothes off** despir-se, desnudar-se.
>**to take one's shoes off** descalçar-se.
>**to take part** tomar parte.
>**to take place** acontecer.
>**to take possession** tomar posse.
>**to take refuge** refugiar-se.
>**to take upon oneself** encarregar-se de.

talcum talco.
>**talcum powder** talco em pó.

tale conto, história, narrativa.

talent talento.

talk conversa, conversação *(conversation);* palestra, conferência, discurso *(speech);* rumor, boato *(rumor).*

talk (to) falar, conversar, dizer.
>**to talk back** retrucar.
>**to talk over** discutir.
>**to talk to** falar a.

talkative loquaz, tagarela.

tall alto.

tame domesticado, manso.

tame (to) domar, domesticar.

tan *n.* bronzeado *(from sun); adj.* bronzeado, marrom, moreno.

tan (to) bronzear-se, amorenar; curtir *(hides).*

tangled emaranhado.

tank tanque; aquário *(for fish).*

tape fita.
>**tape measure** fita métrica.
>**tape recorder** gravador.

tapestry tapeçaria, tapete.

tar breu, alcatrão.

target alvo, objetivo (objectivo).
>**to hit the target** dar no alvo.

task tarefa.

taste gosto, sabor.
>**in bad taste** de mau gosto.
>**in good taste** de bom gosto.
>**to have a taste for** ter gosto por.

taste (to) sentir o gosto, saborear; provar *(to try);* ter gosto de.
>**The soup tastes of onion.** A sopa tem gosto de cebola.

tavern taverna.

tax taxa (x = sh), imposto.
>**income tax** imposto de renda.

tax (to) tributar, taxar (x = sh); sobrecarregar *(to test).*

taxi táxi (x = ks).

tea chá.

teach (to) ensinar.

teacher professor.

teacup xícara de chá, chávena de chá.

teakettle chaleira.

team equipe, time Ⓑ; junta, parelha *(horses, etc.).*
>**teamwork** trabalho de equipe.

teapot bule.

tear lágrima *(from weeping);* vasgão *(rip).*
>**in tears** em pranto, chorando.

tear (to) rasgar.
>**to tear down** derrubar, demolir.
>**to tear to pieces** despedaçar, estraçalhar.
>**to tear one's hair out** arrancar-se os cabelos.

tease (to) implicar com, zombar de.

teaspoon colher de chá.

technical técnico.

technique técnica.

tedious tedioso, chato.

teeth dentes.
>**false teeth** dentes postiços, dentadura postiça.
>**set of teeth** dentadura.

telecommunications telecomunicções.

telegram telegrama.

telegraph telégrafo.

telegraph (to) telegrafar.

telepathy telepatia.

telephone telefone.
>**telephone book** lista telefônica.
>**telephone booth** cabina telefônica (telefónica).
>**telephone call** telefonema, chamada telefônica.
>**telephone exchange** estação telefônica.

telephone operator telefonista.
telephone directory lista telefônica.
telephone (to) telefonar.
telescope telescópio.
television televisão *(the technology);* televisor, aparelho de televisão *(set).*
    on television em televisão.
tell (to) dizer; contar, narrar.
    to tell a story contar uma história.
    Who told you so? Quem lhe disse isso?
    Tell him to stop. Manda-lhe parar.
temper temperamento, disposição, humor.
    bad temper mau humor.
    to lose one's temper perder a paciência.
temperament temperamento, disposição.
tempest tempestade, temporal.
temple templo; têmpora, fonte *(of the head).*
temporarily temporariamente.
temporary temporário, provisório.
tempt (to) tentar, provocar.
temptation tentação.
tempting tentado.
ten dez.
tenacious tenaz.
tenant inquilino, locatário.
tendency tendência.
tender tenro, macio; carinhoso,
    tender-hearted compassivo.
tennis tênis (ténis).
    tennis court quadra de tênis.
tense tenso.
tension tensão.
tent tenda, barraca.
tentative provisório, tentativo.
tenth décimo.
term termo, prazo; *pl.* condições; mandato *(office).*
    to be on good terms with ter boas relações com.
    to come to terms chegar a um acordo.
terminal *adj.* terminal, final, último; *n.* terminal, estação final.
terrace terraço.
terrible terrível.
terribly terrivelmente.
territory território.
terror terror, pavor.
terse conciso, breve, sucinto.
terseness concisão, brevidade.
test prova, ensaio *(trial);* exame (x = z), análise.
test (to) ensaiar, experimentar, examinar (x = z).
testify (to) testemunhar testificar.
text texto.
textbook livro escolar.
than que, do que.
    more than that mais (do) que isso.
    fewer than menos que, menos de.

He is richer than I am. Ele é mais rico (do) que eu.
thank (to) agradecer.
    Thank you. Obrigado.
    Thank God! Graças a Deus!
thankful agradecido, reconhecido.
thanks obrigado.
    thanks to graças a.
that *dem. adj. and pron.* esse, essa, isso, aquele, aquela, aquilo; *rel. pron.* que, quem, o qual, a qual; *adv.* tão; *conj.* que, para que.
    that man aquele homem, esse homem.
    that woman aquela mulher, essa mulher.
    That's it. Isso é. Isso mesmo.
    That is to say. Isto é.
    That may be. É possível. Talvez.
    That's all. É tudo.
    That way. Por ali.
    That's how it's done. Assim é como se faz.
    not that far não tão longe.
    so that de modo que, para que.
    in order that para que, de maneira que.
the o, a, os, as.
    the man o homem.
    the men os homens.
    the woman a mulher.
    the women as mulheres.
    the sooner the better quanto antes melhor.
theater teatro.
theatrical teatral.
their seu, sua, seus, suas, deles, delas.
them os, as, lhes, eles, elas.
theme tema.
themselves eles mesmos, elas mesmas, si mesmos, se.
then então, nesse tempo.
    now and then de vez em quando.
    and then e então.
    just then nesse mesmo momento.
    by then naquela altura.
    what then? e então?
theoretical teórico.
theory teoria.
there ali, aí *(near the person addressed),* lá, acolá *(more remote).*
    Put it there. Ponha-o aí.
    I was there. Eu estive ali.
    Go there. Vá lá.
    Over there. Por ali. Lá.
    there is há.
    there are há.
thereabouts por aí, por ali.
thereafter depois disso, daí em diante.
thereby assim, desse modo.
therefore portanto, por isso.
thermometer termômetro (termómetro).
these estes, estas.

thesis tese.
they eles, elas.
thick grosso, denso.
   three inches thick três polegadas de grossura.
   thick-headed estúpido.
thickness espessura, grossura.
thief ladrão.
thigh coxa (x = sh).
thimble dedal.
thin magro, delgado *(person)*; ralo *(liquid)*.
thing coisa, objeto (objecto).
   something alguma coisa.
   anything qualquer coisa.
think (to) pensar, crer, achar.
   to think of pensar em.
   to think well of pensar bem de.
   As you think fit. Como você quiser.
   to think it over pensá-lo.
   to think nothing of não ligar a mínima importância.
   to think twice pensar bem.
   I don't think so. Não acho. Acho que não.
   I think so. Acho que sim.
   Don't even think it! Nem pensar!
thinness magreza.
third terceiro, terceira parte.
   a third person um terceiro.
thirst sede.
   to be thirsty estar com sede, ter sede.
thirteen treze.
thirteenth décimo terceiro.
thirtieth trigésimo.
thirty trinta.
this este, esta.
   this man este homem.
   this woman esta mulher.
   this evening hoje à noite.
   this one and that one este e aquele.
   this and that isto e aquilo.
   like this assim.
thorn espinho.
thorough completo, minucioso, profundo.
thoroughfare via, passagem.
thoroughly completamente, minuciosamente.
those aqueles, aquelas.
though embora, ainda que.
   as though como se.
   even though mesmo que.
thought pensamento.
   to give thought to pensar em.
thoughtful pensativo, atento; atencioso, solícito.
thoughtfully atenciosamente, pensativamente.
thoughtfulness reflexão (x = ks), meditação, atenção.
thoughtless descuidado, imprudente.
thoughtlessly descuidadamente, sem reflexão (x = ks).

thousand mil; *pl.* milhares.
thousandth milésimo.
thread linha, fio; rosca *(of screw).*
thread (to) enfiar.
threat ameaça.
threaten (to) ameaçar.
three três.
three hundred trezentos.
threshold limiar, soleira.
thrift economia, frugalidade.
thrifty frugal, econômico (económico).
thrill emoção, sensação.
thrill (to) emocionar(-se), excitar.
throat garganta.
   sore throat dor de garganta.
throne trono.
through *adj.* direto (directo); *adv.* de uma parte a outra, de lado a lado, completamente, totalmente; *prep.* por, através de, por meio de, devido a, por causa de.
   through and through completamente.
   to be through ter terminado.
   to be through with cortar relações com, ter acabado com.
   a through train um trem direto (um comboio directo).
   through the door pela porta.
   through his influence devido a sua influência.
   through the years ao longo dos anos.
   health through honey saúde atraves do mel.
throughout *prep.* durante todo, por todo, em todo; *adv.* por toda parte, completamente.
throw (to) atirar, lançar.
   to throw out deitar fora, jogar fora.
   to throw light on esclarecer.
thumb polegar.
thumbnail unha do polegar.
thumbtack percevejo.
thunder trovão.
thunder (to) trovejar.
thunderbolt raio.
thunderstorm trovoada.
Thursday quinta-feira, quinta.
thus assim, deste modo, como segue.
   thus far até aqui, até este ponto.
ticket bilhete.
   round-trip ticket bilhete de ida e volta.
   ticket window guichê (guichet), bilheteria (bilheteira).
tickle (to) fazer cócegas.
tide maré.
   high tide maré alta.
   low tide maré baixa (x = sh).
tie gravata *(necktie);* vínculo, laço *(bond);* nó *(knot);* dormente *(of railroad);* empate *(score);* jogo empatado *(tie game).*

tie (to) atar, amarrar.
tiger tigre.
tight apertado, justo, firme; escasso *(money)*.
tighten (to) apertar.
tile telha *(for roof)*, azulejo.
till até, até que.
   till now até agora.
till (to) cultivar.
timber madeira.
time tempo; hora; vez; época.
   What time is it? Que horas são?
   the first time a primeira vez.
   What time is dinner? A que horas vamos jantar?
   on time a tempo, na hora.
   a long time ago há muito tempo.
   at the same time ao mesmo tempo.
   at no time nunca.
   one at a time um por vez.
   at this time agora *(now)*.
   at that time a estas horas *(time of day)*.
   at times às vezes.
   for the time being por agora.
   from time to time de vez em quando.
   in no time imediatamente, num instante.
   to be on time estar na hora.
   Have a good time! Divirta-se!
   spare time horas vagas.
timely *adj.* oportuno, conveniente.
timetable horário.
time zone fuso horário.
timid tímido.
timidity timidez.
tin estanho.
   tin can lata.
tincture tintura.
   tincture of iodine tintura de iodo.
tinfoil papel de estanho.
tint matiz.
tip ponta, extremidade *(point, end)*; gorjeta *(gratuity)*; palpite *(inside information)*; aviso dica *(suggestion)*.
tip (to) inclinar *(to slant)*; dar uma gorjeta *(to give a gratuity)*; avisar *(to tip off)*.
tire pneu.
   flat tire pneu vazio.
tire (to) cansar, fatigar; aborrecer *(to bore)*.
tireless incansável, infatigável.
tissue tecido *(skin, etc.)*; lenço de papel *(for blowing nose)*.
   tissue paper papel de seda.
title título.
   title page frontispício, página de rosto.
to a, para, de, por, até, que.
   to give to dar a.
   to go to ir a.
   ready to go pronto para ir-se embora.
   It's time to leave. Está na hora de sair.
   the time has come chegou a hora.

   from house to house de casa em casa.
   to be done por fazer.
   letters to be written cartas por escrever.
   to this day até agora.
   in order to para, a fim de.
   to and fro para cá e para lá.
   I have to go. Tenho que ir-me. Tenho de ir-me.
   I have something to do. Tenho alguma coisa para fazer.
   It's twenty (minutes) to three. Faltam vinte para as três. São duas horas e quarenta minutos.
toad sapo.
toast torradas *(bread)*; brinde *(drink)*.
toast (to) torrar; brindar.
toaster torradeira.
tobacco tabaco, fumo.
   tobacco shop tabacaria.
today hoje.
   a week from today daqui a oito dias.
toe dedo do pé.
together juntos; juntamente, ao mesmo tempo.
   Let's go together. Vamos juntos.
   together with junto com.
   to call together reunir.
toil labuta.
toilet banheiro *(bathroom)*.
   toilet soap sabonete.
   toilet paper papel higiênico (higiénico).
   toilet bowl vaso sanitário.
   toilet water água-de-colônia (colónia) *(cologne)*.
tolerance tolerância.
tolerant tolerante.
tolerate (to) tolerar.
tomato tomate.
   tomato juice suco de tomate.
tomb túmulo, sepultura.
tomorrow amanhã.
   the day after tomorrow depois de amanhã.
   tomorrow morning amanhã de manhã.
ton tonelada.
tone tom.
tongs tenaz.
tongue língua.
   to hold one's tongue calar-se.
tonic tônico (tónico).
tonight hoje à noite, esta noite.
tonsil amígdala.
tonsilitis amigdalite.
too demais *(too much)*, também *(also)*.
   too much demais, muito.
   too many demais, muitos.
   Too bad! Que pena!
   It's too early. É cedo demais.
   That's too much. That's the last straw. É o cúmulo.

me (I) too eu também.
one dollar too much um dólar demais.
That's too little. Isso é muito pouco.
tool ferramenta.
tooth dente.
    toothache dor de dente(s).
toothbrush escova de dentes.
toothpaste pasta de dentes.
toothpick palito.
top pico, cume; parte superior; superfície, topo; pião *(toy)*; top *(shirt)*.
    the top of the mountain o cume da montanha.
    at top speed a toda velocidade.
    from top to bottom de cima para baixo (x = sh).
    from top to toe da cabeça aos pés.
topcoat sobretudo.
torch tocha.
torment tormento.
torrent torrente, toró, borbotão.
torrid tórrido.
    torrid zone zona tórrida.
tortoise tartaruga.
torture tortura, tormento.
torture (to) torturar, atormentar.
total total.
touch toque, contato (contacto).
    to be in touch with estar em contato com.
touch (to) tocar.
touching comovedor, comovente, tocante.
tough duro, forte; difícil.
toughen (to) endurecer(-se).
tour viagem, viagem de turismo; turnê, digressão *(by musician)*.
    to go on tour fazer turnê.
tour (to) percorrer, viajar por.
touring turismo.
tourist turista.
    tourist agency agência de turismo.
    tourist guide guia de turismo.
tournament torneio.
toward para, para com, em direção a.
    to go toward a place ir para um lugar.
    his attitude toward me a atitude dele para mim.
towel toalha.
    face towel toalha de rosto.
    bath towel toalha de banho.
tower torre.
town cidade.
    town hall prefeitura (câmara municipal).
tow truck reboque.
toy brinquedo.
trace indício, rasto.
trace (to) seguir a pista de, investigar; traçar, esboçar *(to mark out)*.
track rasto, pista; trilho *(rail)*; pista *(race)*.
trade comércio, ofício *(skill, job)*.

trademark marca registrada, marca de fábrica, marca de comércio.
trade union sindicato.
trading comércio.
tradition tradição.
traditional tradicional.
traffic tráfego, trânsito; tráfico *(illegal)*.
tragedy tragédia.
tragic trágico.
train trem (comboio).
    train car vagão.
train (to) treinar, instruir; amestrar *(dogs)*.
training treinamento, treino.
traitor traidor.
tramp vagabundo.
tranquil tranqüilo (tranquilo).
transatlantic transatlântico.
transfer transferência; passagem, bilhete *(bus, etc.)*; transporte.
transfer (to) transferir, transportar.
translate (to) traduzir.
translation tradução.
translator tradutor.
transparent transparente.
transport transporte.
transport (to) transportar.
transportation transporte.
trap armadilha.
trap (to) apanhar, capturar.
trash lixo.
travel (to) viajar.
traveler viajante.
tray bandeja.
treacherous traiçoeiro; perigoso *(dangerous)*.
treachery traição.
tread passo, pisada.
tread (to) pisar.
treason traição.
treasure tesouro.
treasure (to) prezar, apreciar.
treasurer tesoureiro.
treasury tesouraria.
treat (to) tratar; convidar *(with food, etc.)*.
    to treat a patient tratar de um paciente.
    to treat well (badly) dar bom (mau) tratamento.
treatment tratamento.
treaty tratado.
tree árvore.
tremble (to) tremer, estremecer.
trembling *adj.* trêmulo (trémulo); *n.* tremor, estremecimento.
tremendous tremendo, enorme; sensacional *(wonderful)*.
trench trincheira.
trend tendência.
    to set the trend dar o tom.
trial prova, ensaio, tentativa; julgamento *(law)*.

triangle triângulo.
tribe tribo.
tribunal tribunal.
trick truque, trapaça, peça.
   to do the trick resolver o problema.
   to play a trick pregar uma peça.
trifle bagatela, insignificância.
trim (to) cortar, aparar *(hair)*; podar *(trees)*; adornar, decorar *(clothes)*.
trimming adorno, decoração.
trinket bugiganga, berloque.
trip viagem *(voyage)*; tropeço *(stumble)*.
   one-way trip viagem de ida.
   round trip viagem de ida e volta.
trip (to) tropeçar, fazer tropeçar.
triple triplo.
triumph triunfo.
triumph (to) triunfar.
triumphant triunfante.
trivial insignificante, trivial.
trolley bonde (carro eléctrico).
troops tropas.
trophy troféu.
tropic trópico.
tropical tropical.
trot (to) trotar.
trouble dificuldade *(difficulty)*; incômodo *(bother)*; desordem *(disorder)*; doença *(illness)*.
   to be in trouble estar em apuros.
   not to be worth the trouble não valer a pena.
   It's no trouble at all. Incômodo (incómodo) nenhum.
trouble (to) preocupar, perturbar; importunar *(ask)*.
troubled preocupado, perturbado.
troublesome importuno, difícil, desagradável.
trousers calças.
trout truta.
truck caminhão.
true certo, exato (exacto) (x = z), verdadeiro; fiel, leal *(faithful)*.
   It's true. É verdade.
trunk tronco *(tree)*; baú, mala *(for packing)*; mala *(of car)*.
trust confiança.
   in trust em fideicomisso.
trust (to) confiar em, ter confiança em.
   I trust her. Confio nela.
trustworthy digno de confiança.
truth verdade.
truthful verdadeiro, verídico.
truthfulness veracidade, autenticidade.
try (to) tentar; experimentar; provar *(test)*; procurar *(try and)*.
   to try on clothes provar roupa.
   Try to do it. Tente fazê-lo.

   Try the shrimp! Experimento os camarões!
tub tina.
   bathtub banheira.
tube tubo, cano.
Tuesday terça-feira, terça.
tuna atum.
tune toada, melodia.
   to be out of tune estar desafinado.
tune (to) afinar *(musical instrument)*; sintonizar *(radio)*.
tunnel túnel.
turkey peru.
turn turno, período, vez *(time, order)*; volta, giro *(motion)*; favor *(favor)*.
   by turns alternativamente.
   in turn por sua vez.
   to take turns cada uma ter a sua vez.
   It's my turn now. Agora é a minha vez.
turn (to) girar *(key in lock)*, rodar *(wheel)*; dobrar, virar *(to change direction)*; tornar-se *(to become)*.
   to turn around virar.
   to turn down recusar, rejeitar *(to refuse)*; abaixar (x = sh), diminuir *(lights, etc.)*.
   to turn into transformar, converter.
   to turn off fechar *(faucet)*; desligar *(radio, etc.)*; apagar *(light)*.
   to turn on ligar *(radio, etc.)*; abrir *(faucet)*; acender *(light)*.
   to turn back voltar atrás.
   to turn one's back on dar as costas a.
   to turn over transferir *(to transfer)* entregar, dar *(to hand over)*; ponderar, considerar *(to think about)*; fazer girar *(motor)*.
   to turn sour azedar.
   to turn up aparecer.
   in turn por sua vez.
turnip nabo.
turtle cágado.
tweezers pinças.
twelfth décimo segundo.
twelve doce.
twentieth vigésimo.
twenty vinte.
twice duas vezes.
twilight crepúsculo.
twin gêmeo.
   twin brother irmão gêmeo.
twist (to) torcer, retorcer.
two dois, *f.* duas.
two hundred duzentos.
type tipo.
type (to) escrever à máquina.
typewriter máquina de escrever.
   portable typewriter máquina de escrever portátil.

typewriter ribbon fita de máquina de escrever.
typical típico.
typist datilógrafo.
tyrannical tirânico.
tyranny tirania.
tyrant tirano.

U

ugly feio.
ulcer úlcera.
umbrella guarda-chuva.
umpire árbitro.
unable incapaz.
　I was unable to do it. Não pude fazê-lo. Foi-me impossível.
unanimous unânime.
unaware inconsciente.
unbearable insuportável.
unbutton (to) desabotoar.
uncertain incerto.
uncertainty incerteza.
unchangeable imutável, permanente.
uncle tio.
uncomfortable incômodo (incómodo) *(accommodations);* desagradável *(situation).*
unconquered invicto, indomado.
undecided indeciso.
under debaixo (x = sh), em; menos, sob.
　under the table debaixo da mesa.
　under consideration em consideração.
　under penalty of sob pena de.
　underage menor de idade.
　under contract conforme o contrato.
　under the circumstances em tais circunstâncias.
　under obligation dever favores.
　under one's nose nas barbas.
　in under an hour em menos de uma hora.
undergo (to) agüentar (aguentar), passar por, sofrer, submeter-se.
　to undergo an operation submeter-se a uma operação.
underground subterrâneo.
underline (to) sublinhar.
underneath embaixo (x = sh), debaixo (x = sh), sob.
understand (to) compreender, entender.
　Do you understand? Compreende?
understanding entendimento, acordo.
　to come to an understanding chegar a um acordo.
undertake (to) empreender, encarregar-se de.
undertaking empresa, compromisso, promessa *(promise).*

underwear ropa de baixo.
undo (to) desfazer, desatar; desprender *(belt, etc.).*
undress (to) despir-se.
uneasiness inquietude, desassossego.
uneasy inquieto, desassossegado.
unequal desigual.
uneven desigual; irregular *(surface).*
unexpected inesperado.
unfair injusto.
unfaithful infiel, desleal.
unfavorable desfavorável.
unfinished inacabado, incompleto.
unfit inadequado, impróprio.
unfold (to) desdobrar, estender; revelar, esclarecer *(plot, etc.).*
unforeseen imprevisto.
unforgettable inespecível.
unfortunate desventurado, infeliz.
unfortunately infelizmente.
unfurnished desmobiliado (desmobilado), sem móveis.
　unfurnished apartment apartamento sem móveis.
ungrateful ingrato.
unhappy infeliz, descontente com *(with something).*
unhealthy doentio *(person);* malsão.
unheard of inaudito *(extraordinary);* desconhecido *(unknown).*
unhurt ileso.
uniform uniforme.
union sindicato.
unit unidade; grupo *(team).*
unite (to) unir(-se).
united unido.
　United States Estados Unidos.
unity unidade.
universal universal.
universality universalidade.
universe universo.
university universidade.
unjust injusto.
unkind cruel.
unknown desconhecido.
unless a menos que, a não ser que, se não.
unlike ao contrário de.
unlikely improvável *(results, etc.);* inverossímil *(explanation).*
unload (to) descarregar.
unlucky desafortunado, infeliz.
unmarried solteiro.
　bachelor, unmarried man solteiro.
　unmarried woman solteira.
unmoved impassível, indiferente, frio.
unnecessary desnecessário.
unpaid a pagar, não pago *(bills);* não remunerado *(worker).*
unpleasant desagradável.

unquestionable indiscutível, indisputável.
unreasonable irracional, injusto.
unrest desassossego, inquietação; distúrbios *(political)*.
unruly ingovernável, rebelde.
unsatisfactory insatisfatório, inadequado.
unseen não visto, inobservado.
unselfish desinteressado.
unsettled inquieto; variável, inconstante *(not stable);* não pago, não saldado *(not paid).*
unsteady instável; inconstante, inseguro.
unsuccessful sem exito *(artist);* malogrado, frustrado *(plan).*
unsuitable impróprio, inadequado, inconveniente.
until até.
untiring incansável, infatigável.
unusual extraordinário, raro, incomum, insólito.
unwelcome mal acolhido *(feeling);* indesejável *(occurrence, etc.).*
unwilling relutante, sem vontade.
unwillingly de má vontade.
unwise imprudente.
unworthy indigno.
unwritten não escrito; tácito *(secret).*
up para cima; em pé, de pé.
   up and down para cima e para baixo (x = sh), de um lado para outro.
   to go up a mountain ir montanha acima.
   to go up subir.
   to go upstairs subir a escada.
   What's up? Que (se) passa? O que é que há?
   She's not up yet. Ela ainda não se levantou.
   up-to-date moderno, contemporaneo; atualizad *(updated).*
update (to) atualizar.
upon sobre, em cima de.
upper superior, de cima.
   upper floor andar superior.
   upper lip lábio superior.
upright vertical; direito, justo *(character).*
upset (to) transtornar *(disrupt);* perturbar *(make someone upset).*
upside down invertido; de cabeça para baixo (x = sh).
upstairs andar superior; em cima, para cima.
   to go upstairs subir.
upstart arrivista.
upward para cima, acima.
urgency urgência.
urgent urgente.
Uruguyan uruguaio.
use uso.
   to make use of utilizar, servir-se de.
   in use em uso.
   of no use inútil, não servir para nada.

It's no use. Não adianta. É inútil.
What's the use? Para quê? É inútil. Não adianta.
use (to) usar, servir-se de, utilizar, empregar.
   to use up gastar, esgotar, consumir.
   to get used to acostumar-se a.
   I'm used to it. Estou acostumado.
   I used to see her every day. Eu acostumava vê-la todos os dias. Eu a via (via-a) todos os dias.
used usado, de segunda mão.
useful útil.
useless inútil, vão.
usher indicador, lanterninha *(theater, etc.).*
usual usual, habitual, costumeiro.
   as usual como de costume.
usually normalmente, geralmente.
   I usually get up early. Geralmente eu me levanto (levanto-me) cedo.
utensil utensílio.
   kitchen utensils utensílios de cozinha.
utility utilidade.
utilize (to) utilizar, empregar.
utmost maior, máximo (x = s).
utterly inteiramente, totalmente, completamente.

V

vacancy vaga, vacância; quarto livre.
vacant vago *(post);* vazio *(house);* livre *(rental, seat).*
vacation férias.
   to go on vacation ir de férias.
vaccinate (to) vacinar.
vaccine vacina.
vacuum vácuo.
vacuum cleaner aspirador de pó.
vague vago.
vain vão.
   in vain em vão.
vainly inutilmente, futilmente.
valid válido.
valley vale.
valuable valioso, de valor.
value valor, valia; preço *(price);* apreço, estima *(regard).*
value (to) avaliar *(to estimate the value);* apreciar, estimar *(to think highly of).*
valve válvula.
vanilla baunilha.
vanish (to) desaparecer.
vanity vaidade.
variable variável.
variety variedade.
various vários, diversos.
varnish verniz.

vary (to) variar.
vaseline vaselina.
vast vasto, imenso, enorme.
VCR videocassete.
veal carne de vitela.
    veal cutlet costeleta de vitela.
vegetable legume, *pl.* verduras.
vegetation vegetação.
vehement veemente.
vehicle veículo.
veil véu.
vein veia *(body)*, veio, filão *(mineral).*
    Let's continue in the same vein.
        Continuamos no mesmo veio.
velvet veludo.
vendor vendedor; camelô *(street).*
Venezuelan venezuelano.
vengeance vingança.
    with a vengeance para valer.
ventilate (to) ventilar.
ventilation ventilação.
veranda varanda.
verb verbo.
verdict veredicto, decisão.
verse verso *(poetry);* estrote *(stanza);*
    versículo *(in scripture).*
vertical vertical.
very muito.
    very much muito, muitíssimo.
    very many muitíssimos, muitíssimas.
    very much money muito dinheiro.
    (Very) much obliged. Muito
        agradecido.
    Very well, thank you. Muito bem,
        obrigado.
    the very same man o mesmo homem.
    on the very same day precisamente no
        mesmo dia.
vessel vaso, vasilha *(for liquids);* navio *(ship);*
    vaso *(blood).*
vest colete.
veteran veterano.
veterinary veterinário.
vex (to) irritar, amolar.
vexation amolação, irritação.
vibration vibração.
vice vício.
vice-president vice-presidente.
vice versa vice versa.
vicinity vizinhança.
vicious vicioso, malvado, malévolo.
    vicious circle círculo vicioso.
victim vítima.
victor vencedor.
victorious vitorioso.
victory vitória.
video vídeo.
videocassette videocassete.
videodisk videodisco.

video game videogame, videojogo.
video recorder videocassete.
videotape videoteipe.
view vista, panorama, paisagem.
    in view of em vista de.
    point of view ponto de vista.
    What a view! Que vista! Que paisagem!
view (to) olhar, ver.
vigil vigília.
vigilant vigilante.
vigor vigor, força, vitalidade.
vigorous vigoroso.
vile vil, baixo (x = sh).
villa casa de campo.
village aldeia, povoado.
villager aldeão.
villain vilão.
vine vinha, videira.
vinegar vinagre.
vineyard vinha.
violate (to) violar.
violation violação.
violence violência.
violent violento.
violet violeta.
violin violino.
violinist violinista.
virgin virgem.
virtue virtude.
virtuous virtuoso.
visa visto.
visible visível.
vision visão.
visit visita.
    to pay a visit visitar, fazer uma visita.
visitor visitante, visita.
visual visual.
vital vital, essencial.
vitamin vitamina.
vivid vívido, vivo.
vocal vocal.
    vocal cords cordas vocais.
voice voz.
    voice mail correio de voz.
void *adj.* inválido, nulo; *n.* vazio.
volcano vulcão.
volt volt.
volume volume; tomo *(book).*
voluntary voluntário.
volunteer voluntário.
vomit vômito *(vómito).*
vomit (to) vomitar.
vote voto; votacão *(voting);* sufrágio *(right to*
    vote).
vote (to) votar.
voter votante, eleitor.
vow voto.
vow (to) fazer voto.
voyage viagem.

voyager viajante.
vulgar vulgar.
vulture abutre.

W

wade (to) vadear.
wage (to) empreender, fazer.
   to wage war fazer guerra.
wager aposta.
wager (to) fazer aposta.
wages salário, ordenado.
wagon carroça *(horse-drawn);* carro de mão
   (child's).
waist cintura.
wait (to) esperar; aguardar *(to await).*
   Wait for me. Espere-me.
   to keep waiting fazer esperar, deixar
     esperando.
   to wait on servir.
waiting room sala de espera.
waiter garçom (empregado).
waitress garçonete (empregada).
wake (to) acordar, despertar.
   to wake up acordar, despertar.
   I woke up at seven. Acordei às sete.
walk passeio.
   to take a walk dar um passeio.
walk (to) andar, caminhar.
   to walk away from afastar-se.
   to walk down descer.
   to walk up subir.
   to walk out sair.
   to walk out on abandonar, desertar.
   to go for a walk dar um passeio.
   walking cane bengala.
wall parede; muro *(exterior);* muralha
   (city, etc.).
   wallpaper papel de parede.
walnut noz; nogueira *(tree).*
waltz valsa.
waltz (to) valsar, dançar uma valsa.
wand vara, varinha.
wander (to) vagar; desviar-se *(to go astray).*
want necessidade, falta.
   to be in want estar necessitado.
   for want of por falta de.
want (to) querer, desejar *(to desire);* precisar
   de, necessitar *(to need).*
   What do you want? Que deseja o senhor?
   Don't you want to come? Não quer vir?
   Cook wanted. Precisa-se cozinheiro.
wanting falto, insuficiente.
   to be wanting faltar.
war guerra.
   War Department Ministério da Guerra.
   to wage war fazer guerra.

ward ala, divisão *(hospital);* bairro, distrito
   (city); pupilo, tutelado *(under a guardian).*
warden administrador, diretor *(prison).*
ward off (to) aparar, desviar, repelir.
wardrobe guarda-roupa.
warehouse armazém.
wares mercadorias.
warfare guerra, combate.
warlike bélico, belicoso.
warm quente; cordial *(welcome, etc.).*
   It's warm. Está quente.
   I am warm. Estou com calor. Tenho calor.
   warm water água quente.
warm (to) aquecer.
   to warm up aquecer *(leftovers, etc.);*
     esquentar *(athletic).*
warmly calorosamente, cordialmente.
warn (to) advertir, prevenir, avisar.
warning advertência, aviso.
   to give warning advertir.
warrant autorização; mandado *(legal).*
warrior guerreiro.
wash lavagem, roupa para lavar, roupa lavada.
   washbasin lavatório, bacia.
   washing machine máquina de lavar roupa.
wash (to) lavar(-se).
   to wash one's hands lavar as mãos.
waste desperdício; perda *(time).*
waste (to) desgastar, desperdiçar; perder
   (time).
wastebasket cesto para papéis.
watch relógio; guarda *(guard).*
   wristwatch relógio-pulseira.
   to wind a watch dar corda a.
watch (to) ver, olhar; guardar, vigiar *(to watch
   over).*
   to watch out ter cuidado.
   to watch TV ver televisão.
watchful alerta, vigilante, atento.
watchmaker relojoeiro.
watchman guarda, vigia.
watchword lema.
water água.
   fresh water água doce.
   hot water água quente.
   mineral water água mineral.
   running water água corrente.
   seltzer water água gasosa.
   water faucet torneira.
   water power força hidráulica.
   to make one's mouth water dar água na
     boca.
water (to) regar *(houseplants);* irrigar *(fields);*
   lacrimejar *(eyes).*
waterfall cachoeira, queda d'água.
watermelon melancia.
waterproof impermeável, à prova d'água.
wave onda, ondulação; vaga *(of people, etc.).*
   short wave onda curta.

long wave onda longa.
sound wave onda sonora.
wavelength comprimento de onda.
wave (to) ondular; fazer sinais *(to signal by waving)*; agitar *(an object)*.
    to wave one's hand fazer sinais com a mão.
    to wave to someone acenar.
waver (to) vacilar, hesitar.
wavering vacilante, hesitante.
wavy ondulado.
wax cera.
    wax candle vela de cera.
    wax paper papel encerado.
wax (to) encerar.
way caminho, via, rumo *(path, direction)*; modo, maneira *(manner)*.
    way in entrada.
    way out saída.
    by way of via.
    by the way a propósito.
    in such a way de tal maneira.
    in this way deste modo.
    any way de qualquer modo.
    in no way de nenhum modo, de maneira alguma.
    this way assim, desta maneira.
    Go this way. Vá por aqui.
    on the way to a caminho para, rumo de.
    out of the way fora do caminho; longe; raro.
    Which way? Por onde?
    Step this way. Venha por aqui. Venda cá.
    No way! De modo nenhum!
    in some way or other de um modo ou de outro.
    under way a caminho, em marcha.
    the other way around ao contrário.
    I'm on my way. Já vou.
    all the way todo o caminho.
    to give way ceder.
    to make way abrir caminho.
we nós.
    the five of us nós cinco.
weak débil, fraco.
weaken (to) debilitar(-se), enfraquecer(-se).
weakness debilidade, fraqueza.
wealth riqueza, abundância.
wealthy rico, abastado.
weapon arma.
wear (to) usar, vestir.
    to wear down desgastar.
    to wear off passar, diminuir.
    to wear out gastar-se, desgastar.
    to wear well durar (to last).
weariness cansaço, fadiga.
weary cansado, fatigado.
weary (to) cansar(-se), fatigar(-se).
weather tempo.

bad weather mau tempo.
nice weather bom tempo.
weave (to) tecer.
web teia; rede *(network)*.
    spider web teia de aranha.
wedding boda, casamento.
    wedding dress vestido de noiva.
    wedding ring aliança.
wedge cunha.
Wednesday quarta-feira, quarta.
weed erva daninha.
week semana.
    weekday dia útil.
    last week a semana passada.
    next week a semana que vem.
weekend fim de semana.
weekly *adj.* semanal; *adv.* semanalmente.
    weekly publication semanário.
weep (to) chorar.
    to weep for, to weep over chorar por.
weigh (to) pesar; levantar ferro *(to weigh anchor)*.
weight peso.
    gross weight peso bruto.
    net weight peso líquido.
    to gain weight engordecer.
    to lose weight cmagrecer.
    weights and measures pesos e medidas.
weighty pesado; importante.
weird esquisito, estranho.
welcome *adj.* bem-vindo; *n.* acolhimento, recepção.
    Welcome! Bem-vindo!
    You're welcome. De nada *(answer to "Thank you.")*.
welcome (to) dar as boas-vindas.
welfare assistência social *(public dole)*.
well poço.
well *adj.* bom; *adv.* bem.
    to be well sentir-se bem.
    very well muito bem.
    I don't feel well. Não me sinto bem.
    well-being bem-estar.
    well-bred bem educado.
    well-done bem feito; bem passado *(meat)*.
    well-to-do rico, abastado, próspero.
    well-known conhecido.
    well-timed oportuno.
    as well as assim como, tanto como, tanto quanto.
    Well then? E agora?
    Very well! Está bem!
    Well, I'm not sure. Bem, não tenho certo.
west oeste, ocidente.
western ocidental.
wet molhado, úmido.
    to get wet molhar-se.
wet (to) molhar.
wharf cais.

what que, o que.
    What's that? Que é isso?
    What's the matter? O que é que há?
    What else? Que mais?
    What for? Para quê?
whatever qualquer que, tudo quanto.
    whatever you like o que você quiser.
wheat trigo.
wheel roda.
    steering wheel volante.
    wheelchair cadeira de rodas.
wheelbarrow carrinho de mão.
when quando.
    Since when? Desde quando?
whenever quando, sempre que, quando quer
    que.
    whenever you like quando você quiser.
where onde.
    Where is Onde está; cadê *(colloquial).*
    Where are you from? Donde (de onde) é
    o senhor?
    Where are you going? Para onde vai?
whereby pelo qual, por meio de que, por meio
    do qual.
wherever onde quer que.
whether se, quer, ou.
    I doubt whether duvido que.
    whether he likes it or not quer queira
    quer não.
which qual, que, o qual, a qual.
    Which book? Que livro?
    Which way? Por onde? Por que caminho?
    Which of these? Qual destes?
    all of which todo o qual, todos dos quais.
whichever qualquer.
while *n.* momento, tempo; *conj.* enquanto;
    embora *(whereas).*
    in a little while daquia pouco.
    a little while ago há pouco tempo.
    for a while por algum tempo.
    once in a while de vez em quando.
    to be worthwhile valer a pena.
whim capricho.
whip açoite, chicote, látego.
whip (to) chicotear, açoitar; bater *(cream,*
    eggs, etc.).
    whipped cream nata batida.
whirl remoinho, rodopio.
whirl (to) girar, rodopiar, redemoinhar.
whirlpool remoinho.
whirlwind remoinho de vento, furacão.
whisper sussurro, cochicho, murmúrio.
whisper (to) sussurrar, cochichar, murmurar.
    in a whisper em voz baixa (x = sh).
whistle apito, assobio.
whistle (to) assobiar, apitar.
white branco.
    white of egg clara de ovo.
    white lie mentira inofensiva.

White House Casa Branca.
whiten (to) branquear.
who quem, que, qual, o qual, a qual, os quais,
    as quais, aquele, aquela.
    Who is it? Quem é?
whoever quem quer que, qualquer que.
    whoever it may be quem quer que for,
    seja quem for.
whole todo, inteiro, completo.
    the whole of Portugal todo Portugal.
    whole wheat bread pão integral.
    on the whole em geral.
    whole number número inteiro.
wholehearted sincero, dedicado.
wholesale por atacado.
wholesome salubre, sádio.
wholly totalmente, inteiramente.
whom quem, que.
whose de quem *(used as first word in*
    questions); cujo *(of whom, of which).*
why por que.
    Why not? Por que não?
wicked mau, malvado.
wickedness maldade.
wide largo, vasto, amplo, extenso.
    two inches wide duas polegadas de
    largura.
    wide open aberto de par em par.
    wide awake bem acordado, desperto, vivo.
widely muito, extensamente.
    widely different completamente diferente.
    widely used muito usado.
    widely known muito conhecido.
widen (to) alargar, ampliar.
widespread difundido, muito espalhado,
    comum.
widow viúva.
widower viúvo.
width largura.
wife mulher, esposa.
wig peruca.
wild selvagem *(savage);* silvestre *(plants);* não
    domesticado *(not tamed);* bárbaro;
    desenfreado *(unruly).*
wilderness ermo.
will vontade; testamento *(legal).*
    at will à vontade.
    against one's will contra a vontade.
will (to) querer, desejar; legar.
    Will you tell me the time? Quer ter a
    bondade de me dizer (dizer-me) que
    horas são?
    Will you do me a favor? Quer me fazer
    (fazer-me) um favor?
    I won't go. Não irei. Não quero ir.
    You won't do it, will you? Não o farei, tá?
    auxiliary the future tense of the indicative
    is formed by adding -ei, (-ás), -á,
    -emos, (-eis), -ão to the infinitive.

I will go irei.
you will go *(fam.)* irás.
he will go irá.
we will go iremos.
you will go ireis.
they will go irão.
willing disposto, pronto, inclinado.
   to be willing estar disposto, querer.
   God willing. Se Deus quiser.
willingly de boa vontade, de bom grado.
willingness boa vontade.
win (to) ganhar, vencer, triunfar.
   to win out sair bem, triunfar.
wind vento.
   wind instrument instrumento de sopro.
wind (to) enrolar *(roll up);* dar corda a *(a watch);* serpentear *(river, road).*
windmill moinho de vento.
window janela.
   windowpane vidro, vidraça.
windshield pára-brisa.
windy com muito vento.
   It's windy. Está ventando.
wine vinho.
   red wine vinho tinto.
   white wine vinho branco.
wing asa; ala *(of building).*
wink piscadela.
wink (to) piscar.
winner vencedor.
winter inverno (Inverno).
wintry invernal.
wipe (to) limpar.
   to wipe out eliminar, destruir.
   wiped out arrasado *(tired).*
wire arame *(metal);* telegrama *(telegram).*
   barbed wire arame farpado.
wire (to) telegrafar.
wisdom sabedoria, prudência, bom senso.
   wisdom tooth dente do siso.
wise sábio, prudente.
wish desejo.
wish (to) desejar, querer.
wit engenho *(humor);* agudeza *(mental sharpness).*
witch bruxa (x = sh).
with com, de, a, em, por meio de, contra.
   coffee with milk café com leite.
   to touch with the hand tocar com a mão.
   She came with a friend. Ela veio com um amigo.
   to identify oneself with identificar-se com.
   to struggle with lutar contra.
   with respect to com respeito a.
   the young girl with the red dress on a jovem de vestido vermelho.
   That always happens with friends. Isso sempre acontece entre amigos.

   with much study por meio de muito estudo.
withdraw (to) retrair, tirar, remover.
withdrawal retirada.
within dentro de, dentro, a pouco de.
   within a week dentro de uma semana.
   within a short distance a pouca distância.
without sem.
   coffee without sugar café sem açúcar.
   without fail sem falta.
   without a doubt sem dúvida.
   without thinking it over well sem pensar bem.
witness testemunha.
witness (to) presenciar, ver, testemunhar.
witty engenhoso, gracioso.
wolf lobo.
woman mulher.
   young woman mulher jovem.
wonder maravilha.
   no wonder não é de admirar.
wonder (to) admirar-se *(be amazed);* perguntar-se *(to be unsure).*
   I wonder whether it's true. Eu me pergunto (pergunto-me) se será verdade.
   to wonder at admirar-se de.
wonderful maravilhoso.
   wonderful city cidade maravilhosa.
wood madeira; floresta, lenha *(firewood); pl.* selva, mato.
woodwork madeiramento *(around windows, etc.);* carpintaria *(woodworking).*
wool lã.
woolen de lã.
word palavra.
   word for word palavra por palavra.
   in other words em outras palavras.
   by word of mouth oralmente, verbalmente.
   upon my word palavra de honra.
   to leave word deixar (x = sh) recado.
work trabalho; obra *(of art).*
   to be at work estar ocupado, estar trabalhando (a trabalhar).
   out of work desempregado.
workday dia útil, dia de trabalho.
work (to) trabalhar; funcionar, andar *(a machine);* cultivar.
   to work out resolver *(a problem).*
   the radio is not working o rádio não está funcionando (a funcionar).
worker trabalhador, operário, empregado.
workshop oficina.
world mundo.
   all over the world por todo o mundo.
   worldwide mundial.
   World War Guerra Mundial.
worm verme; minhoca, lombriga *(earthworm).*

worn-out gasto *(object)*; estragado, batido *(tired)*.

worry preocupação, ansiedade.
>**Don't worry.** Não se preocupe.
>**to be worried** estar preocupado.

worse pior.
>**to get worse** piorar.
>**so much the worse** tanto pior.
>**from bad to worse** de mal a pior.
>**to take a turn for the worse** piorar.

worship adoração.

worship (to) adorar, venerar *(God);* idolatrar *(money, etc.)*.

worst o pior.
>**the worst** o pior.
>**at worst** no pior dos casos.
>**if worst comes to worst** se acontecer o pior.

worth valor, mérito.
>**What's it worth?** Quanto vale?
>**It's not worth that much.** Não vale tanto.
>**to be worthwhile** valer a pena.

worthless inútil, sem valor.

worthwhile que vale a pena.

worthy digno, merecedor.

would The conditional tense is generally expressed by adding -ia, (-ias), -ia, íamos, (íeis), -iam to the infinitive of the verb. The imperfect indicative is also used in this sense, especially in conversation. The verbs of the second and third conjugations (infinitives ending in -er, -ir) add the above endings to the stem of the infinitive to make the imperfect indicative tense. Verbs of the first conjugation (infinitives ending in -ar) add -ava, (-avas), -ava, -ávamos, (-áveis), -avam to the stem of the infinitive.
>**I would go** eu iria, eu ia.
>**I would like to go.** Gostaria de ir. Gostava de ir.
>**I would go if I could.** Eu iria (ia) se pudesse.
>**She wouldn't come.** Ela não quis vir.
>**I wish she would come.** Oxalá (x = sh) que venha.
>**I would like to ask you a favor.** Gostaria de lhe pedir (pedir-lhe) um favor.

wound ferida, ferimento.

wound (to) ferir.

wounded ferido.

Wow! Ena! Opa!

wrap (to) envolver, embrulhar *(package);* enrolar *(to roll up)*.

wrapper envoltório, invólucro.

wrapping paper papel de embrulho.

wreath grinalda, coroa.

wreck destruição, ruína; naufrágio *(shipwreck)*.

wreck (to) arruinar, destruir; naufragar *(ship)*.

wrench chave inglesa *(tool)*.

wrench (to) torcer *(ankle, etc.);* arrancar.

wrestle (to) lutar.

wring (to) torcer, espremer.

wrinkle ruga *(skin);* prega.

wrinkle (to) enrugar(-se), franzir.
>**she wrinkled her brow** ela franziu a testa.

wrist pulso, munheca.
>**wristwatch** relógio-pulseira.

write (to) escrever.

writer escritor.

writing escrita, escrito, escritura; letra *(handwriting)*.
>**in writing** por escrito.
>**writing desk** escrivaninha, secretária.
>**writing paper** papel de escrever.

written escrito.

wrong *n.* mal; dano *(harm);* injúria, injustiça; erro; transgressão, infração (infracção); *adj.* mau, incorreto (incorrecto), falso, errado, injusto; *adv.* mal.
>**to do wrong** fazer mal.
>**You are wrong.** Você não tem razão. Você está errado.
>**to get up on the wrong side of the bed** levantar-se com o pé esquerdo.
>**That's wrong.** Está mal escrito *(written)*. Está mal feito *(done)*.
>**Something is wrong with the engine.** O motor não funciona bem.
>**wrong side out** do lado do avesso.
>**What's wrong with him?** O que há com ele?

X ray raio X *(ray);* radiografia *(x-ray picture)*.

yank (to) arrancar.

yard jarda *(measurement);* pátio, quintal *(of a house)*.

yawn bocejo.

yawn (to) bocejar.

year ano.
>**last year** o ano passado.
>**next year** o ano que vem.
>**many years ago** há muitos anos.
>**every year** todos os anos.
>**all year long** o ano todo.
>**I am 35 years old.** Tenho trinta e cinco anos.

yearbook anuário.

yearly *adj.* anual; *adv.* anualmente.

yeast levedura, fermento.
yell grito, berro.
yell (to) gritar, berrar.
yellow amarelo.
yes sim.
yesterday ontem.
    the day before yesterday anteontem.
yet *adv.* ainda; *conj.* porém, todavia, não
    obstante.
    not yet ainda não.
    as yet até agora.
    I don't know yet. Ainda não sei.
yield rendimento, renda, produção, produto.
yield (to) render, produzir; ceder *(to give in).*
yoke jugo.
yolk gema.
you tu *(fam.);* você *(friendly);* o senhor, os
    senhores, a senhora, as senhoras *(polite).*
young jovem.
    young man jovem, moço.
    young lady jovem, moça.
    young people jovens.
    younger sister irmã mais nova.
your, yours teu, tua, teus, tuas *(fam.);* seu, sua,
    seus, suas, de você, de vocês, do senhor,
    dos senhores, da senhora, das senhoras.

    This book is yours. Este livro é seu.
    Sincerely yours. atenciosamente.
yourself você mesmo, o senhor mesmo, a
    senhora mesma, se.
    Wash yourself. Lave-se.
yourselves vocês mesmos, os senhores
    mesmos, as senhoras mesmas.
youth juventude, mocidade; jovem *(person).*
youthful jovem, juvenil.

Z

zeal zelo, fervor, ardor.
zealous zeloso, ardoroso.
zero zero.
zest entusiasmo, gosto.
zigzag ziguezague.
zinc zinco.
zit borbulha.
zone zona.
    time zone fuso horário.
zoo jardim zoológico.
zoological zoológico.
zoology zoologia.

GLOSSARY OF
PROPER NAMES

Adolph Adolfo
Alexander Alexandre
Alfred Alfredo
Alice Alice
Alphonse Afonso
Andrew André
Ann, Anna, Anne Ana
Anthony Antônio
   (António)
Arthur Artur
Augustus Augusto

Barbara Bárbara
Beatrice Beatriz
Bernard Bernardo

Caroline Carolina
Cecilia Cecília
Charles Carlos
Charlotte Carlota

Dorothy Dorotéia
   (Doroteia)

Edward Eduardo
Eleanor Leonor
Elizabeth Isabel
Emily Emília
Ernest Ernesto
Esther Ester
Eugene Eugênio
   (Eugénio)

Francis Francisco
Frederick Frederico

George Jorge
Gertrude Gertrudes
Gloria Glória

Helen Helena
Henry Henrique

Inez Inês

John João
Joseph José
Josephine Josefa, Josefina
Julius Júlio

Leonard Leonardo
Louis Luís
Louise Luísa
Lucy Lúcia

Manuel Manuel
Margaret Margarida
Martha Marta
Mary Maria
Michael Miguel

Paul Paulo
Peter Pedro
Philip Filipe

Raymond Raimundo
Richard Ricardo
Robert Roberto
Rose Rosa

Theresa Teresa
Thomas Tomás

Vincent Vicente

William Guilherme

GLOSSARY OF
GEOGRAPHICAL NAMES

Africa África
Alps Alpes
America América
Andes Andes
Angola Angola
Argentina Argentina
Asia Ásia
Athens Atenas
Atlantic Ocean Oceano Atlântico
Australia Austrália
Azores Açores

Barcelona Barcelona
Belgium Bélgica
Bolivia Bolívia
Brasilia Brasília
Brazil Brasil
Brussels Bruxelas (x = sh)
Buenos Aires Buenos Aires

Canada Canadá
Chile Chile
China China
Coimbra Coimbra
Colombia Colômbia
Costa Rica Costa Rica
Cuba Cuba
Czech Republic Republica Checa

Denmark Dinamarca
Dominican Republic República
   Dominicana

Ecuador Equador
Egypt Egito (Egipto)
El Salvador El Salvador
England Inglaterra
Estonia Estônia
Europe Europa

Finland Finlândia
France França

Galicia Galícia
Geneva Genebra
Germany Alemanha
Great Britain Grã Bretanha
Greece Grécia
Guatemala Guatemala

Haiti Haiti
Havana Havana
Hawaii Havaí
Hispanic America Hispano-América
Holland Holanda

Honduras Honduras
Hungary Hungria

Ireland Irlanda
Israel Israel
Italy Itália

Japan Japão

Latvia Letônia
Lisbon Lisboa
London Londres
Low Countries Países Baixos (x = sh)

Macao Macau
Madeira Madeira
Madrid Madri (Madrid)
Mediterranean Sea Mar
   Mediterrâneo
Mexico México (x = sh)
Moscow Moscou
Mozambique Moçambique

Netherlands Países Baixos (x = sh),
   Holanda
New York Nova Iorque
New Zealand Nova Zelândia
Nicaragua Nicarágua
North America América do Norte
Norway Noruega

Oceania Oceania

Pacific Ocean Oceano Pacífico
Panama Panamá
Paraguay Paraguai
Paris Paris
Peru Peru
Philippines Filipinas
Poland Polônia (Polónia)
Portugal Portugal
Puerto Rico Porto Rico
Pyrenees Pireneus

Rio de Janeiro Rio de Janeiro
Romania Romênia (Roménia)
Rome Roma
Russia Rússia

São Paulo São Paulo
Scandinavia Escandinávia
Scotland Escócia
Sicily Sicília
Slovakia Eslováquia
South America América do Sul
Spain Espanha
Spanish America América Espanhola.
   Hispano-América
Sweden Suécia

224

Switzerland Suíça

Turkey Turquia

Ukraine Ucrânia
United States of America Estados Unidos
   da América

United Nations Organização
   das Nações Unidas, ONU
Uruguay Uruguai

The Vatican O Vaticano
Venezuela Venezuela
Vienna Viena

Also available from **LIVING LANGUAGE®**

The **best-selling** language course
Completely revised and updated!

Words, phrases, sentences, conversations: speak a new language with confidence right from the start with our simple four-step building block approach. Designed to be effective in a short period of time, these comprehensive courses have everything you need—pronunciation, vocabulary, grammar, culture, and practice.

Each course package includes:

- A coursebook with 40 step-by-step lessons
- 4 audio CDs with all the essential course content
- An extensive grammar reference section
- Supplemental sections on e-mail and internet resources
- A learner's dictionary or a reading and writing guide

Available In:

4 CDs/Coursebook/
Reading and Writing Guide
$29.95/$34.00 Can.

Arabic: 978-1-4000-2408-7

Reading and Writing Guide
$8.99/$9.99 Can.

Arabic Script: 978-1-4000-0924-4

---

4 CDs/Coursebook/Dictionary
$29.95/$34.00 Can.

Chinese:	978-1-4000-2426-1
[Mandarin]	
French:	978-1-4000-2410-0
German:	978-1-4000-2412-4
Inglés:	978-1-4000-2414-8
Italian:	978-1-4000-2416-2
Japanese:	978-1-4000-2418-6
Portuguese:	978-1-4000-2420-9
Russian:	978-1-4000-2422-3
Spanish:	978-1-4000-2424-7

Coursebook Only
$10.95/$12.50 Can.

Arabic:	978-1-4000-1992-2
Chinese:	978-1-4000-2525-4
[Mandarin]	
French:	978-1-4000-2409-4
German:	978-1-4000-2411-7
Inglés:	978-1-4000-2413-1
Italian:	978-1-4000-2415-5
Japanese:	978-1-4000-2417-9
Portuguese:	978-1-4000-2419-3
Russian:	978-1-4000-2421-6
Spanish:	978-1-4000-2423-0

Dictionary Only
$7.95/$9.95 Can.

Chinese:	978-1-4000-2452-0
[Mandarin]	
French:	978-1-4000-2444-5
German:	978-1-4000-2445-2
Inglés:	978-1-4000-2446-9
Italian:	978-1-4000-2447-6
Japanese:	978-1-4000-2448-3
Portuguese:	978-1-4000-2449-0
Russian:	978-1-4000-2450-6
Spanish:	978-1-4000-2451-3

AVAILABLE AT BOOKSTORES EVERYWHERE
www.livinglanguage.com

Also available from **LIVING LANGUAGE**

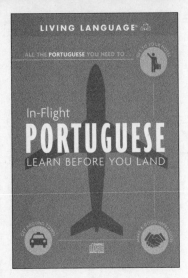

In-Flight Portuguese

Wondering how to make use of all that spare time on the plane? Between your in-flight meal and in-flight movie, brush up on your Portuguese! This 60-minute program covers just enough Portuguese to get by in every travel situation.

CD Program
978-0-609-81076-7 • $13.95/$21.00 Can.

Ultimate Portuguese Beginner-Intermediate

Our most comprehensive program for serious language learners, business-people, and anyone planning to spend time abroad. This package includes a coursebook and eight 60-minute CDs.

CD Program
978-1-4000-2115-4 • $79.95/$110.00 Can.

Coursebook Only
978-1-4000-2114-7 • $18.00/$26.00 Can.

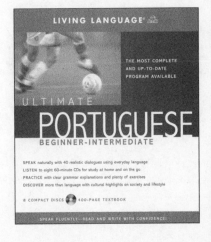

AVAILABLE AT BOOKSTORES EVERYWHERE
www.livinglanguage.com